DATE			
FEB 7 1981			
APR 3 1981			
APR 30 1981			
FEB. 22 1982			
FE 24 '86			
MR 19 '90			
SE 23 '92			
OC 8 '92			
MAR 08 '95			
3/24/97			

the Consumer's Guide to Wood Heat

FireFacts

the Consumer's Guide to Wood Heat

FireFacts

By Jerry Kipp

Drawings by John Robinson

The Countryman Press
Taftsville, VT 05073

Printed in the United States of America
First Printing February 1980

Library of Congress Cataloging in Publication Data

Kipp, Jerry, 1949–
FireFacts.

Includes index.
1. Wood as fuel. 2. Stoves, Wood. 3. Fireplaces.
I. Title.
TP324.K56 697'.1 80-11292
ISBN 0-914378-61-9
ISBN 0-914378-58-9 pbk.

Some of the material on pages 70, 71, and 72 was compiled with the help of the National Fire Protection Association, and was reprinted from *Using Coal and Wood Stoves Safely*, 1978 (NFPA Bulletin HS-10). Copyright © National Fire Protection Association, Boston, Massachusetts. Reprinted by permission. Material on chimney height on page 79 was adapted from the requirements of NFPA 211, *Standard on Chimneys, Fireplaces and Vents*.

FireFacts is distributed to the book trade by the Independent Publishers Group, and to the wood energy trade and special markets by The Countryman Press, Taftsville, VT. 05073.

CONTENTS

PUBLISHER'S FOREWORD

Growing up on a Vermont farm in the Depression meant that one of my childhood chores was to feed stove wood to the trusty old Glenwood kitchen range, coal to the furnace, and birch logs to the fireplaces. Now, we and thousands of other New Englanders are re-converting to wood heat: as independent cusses, we don't like being held hostage to the oil cartels, foreign and domestic, who would just as soon let us freeze in the dark unless we pay their ransom.

With the powers-that-be doing practically nothing to remedy the energy crisis except argue and fumble around in Washington and make more money in Houston, enlightened self-interest prompts sensible individuals to conserve fuel and to seek alternative sources whenever and wherever we can.

Travel on any road in Vermont these days and you will see stove wood everywhere—in neat piles, on porches, in sheds. And several new manufacturers of high-quality stoves have just opened up within a few miles of us. Being in the country, we have an advantage, of course, which our suburban friends lack: access to reasonably-priced wood. Some of it we can cut ourselves; some, to be sure, has to be bought. Deplorably, inflation (and a few fast-buck woodleggers) have driven up prices per cord in suburbia to intolerable levels, a factor prospective woodburners there must consider.

Aside from all the practical aspects, burning wood provides other gratifications: sensory pleasure and the satisfaction that, in a carelessly wasteful culture, we are for once consuming a *renewable* resource. But while we rhapsodize about relaxing in front of an open fire, let's not forget that plain old fireplaces lose ninety percent of their heat, which means that more efficient "places for fire" have to be used.

Because wood should be appreciated, we begin this book with its cultivation. We are aware that not all of our readers own woodlots; but who knows—maybe an upcountry friend or relative has a few forested acres tucked away that you can help farm according to *FireFacts'* tested management tips.

To echo a recent stove store magazine ad, "Don't Get Burned, Get Warm." This book can save your life, literally. In our eagerness to beat the system, far too many of us have ignored (in the absence of enforced building or fire codes) the basic rules of SAFETY when installing fireplace units and stoves, which is why we have emphasized them here. The same caution applies to the siren song of the chain saw. *FireFacts* also shows how to use chain saws and axes safely.

FireFacts' comprehensive buying guide can be used profitably by architects, builders, and interior designers, as well as consumers as a showcase and as a means of comparing models, prices, and effectiveness, and measuring quality against sometimes extravagant claims.

Of special interest, we think, are the newer hydronic units listed in this directory which can be linked to solar collectors, thus effecting further cost savings and assuring a back-up supply of hot water when the sun may be obscured for days or even weeks.

"Hard times comin'," an old-timer hereabouts says. Mindful of his warnings, The Countryman Press has tried to help advance the self-sufficiency movement with such books as *Backyard Livestock: How to Grow Meat for Your Family*, *Backyard Sugarin'*, and *Growing with Community Gardening*. When we read the handwriting on the fuel oil well, we looked for an equally helpful wood energy book. There are, of course, many other titles on the market. Like cookbooks, they multiply and subdivide. But we jumped at the chance to publish *FireFacts* because we wanted to bring out the most useful woodburning handbook available. Here it is—the distillation of Jerry Kipp's personal experience and two years of intensive research.

Let me add a word of gratitude to the people principally responsible for transforming Mr. Kipp's concept into print: our "angel," Katherine Wells; Christopher Lloyd, managing editor; Wayne Thompson, designer and art director; and John Robinson, the illustrator. It has been a truly cooperative, country-style enterprise. We hope *FireFacts* will help you live better and that it will become a standard resource for all woodburners.

Peter S. Jennison

Taftsville, Vermont

ACKNOWLEDGEMENTS

American Council of Independent Laboratories
Peter S. Albertsen
Alliance to Save Energy
American Forestry Association
American Tree Farm System (American Forest Institute)
Consumer Product Safety Commission
Corning Glass Works
Steve Donovan, Environmental and Technical Consulant
Fireplace Institute
Terrence A. Fuller, Attorney
Peter S. Jennison
Kipp Farms
Lightning Protection Institute
Dr. Timothy T. Maxwell
Auburn University Woodburning Laboratory
National Center for Appropriate Technology
National Fire Protection Association
National Wildlife Federation
Pine View Farms
Dr. Tom Reed, Solar Energy Research Institute, DOE
Lyle Taylor
Trumbower Farms
U.S. Department of Energy

All material in *FireFacts* is presented as a guide for consumers in the field of wood energy. Though it contains detailed information on chain saw safety and wood heat unit installation, all information should be used as a guide only. In addition to the suggestions for chain saw use and safety provided in this book, readers should pay strict attention to the operating and safety instructions provided by the manufacturer of the particular chain saw used. The information supplied in the wood heat unit installation and use section is based on the recommendations of the National Fire Protection Association. However, installation requirements vary from locality to locality. Therefore, the only *legal* installations are those approved by your local building code official.

All specifications and statistics provided in the *FireFacts* Buying Guide were compiled from information submitted to *FireFacts* by the individual manufacturers. *FireFacts* is not responsible for the accuracy of this information, or for any changes in this information subsequent to submission.

Part 1
From Woodlot to Wood Heat

PRIVATE AMERICAN WOODLANDS 1

Figure 1

Most of the privately owned woodlands in the United States are stagnant in growth, and energy and lumber production are at only one-half of their potential. The 500 million acres of woodlands in America are capable of providing 160 million cords of wood per year. That's enough renewable energy for 33 million homes, each winter, every year.[1] But only one-third of that woodland is easily accessible. If we were to manage that one-third, we could double the production of wood for fuel and lumber supply by simply gardening woodlots the way we grow vegetables. At present, the content of our woodlands lends itself to little more than abundant firewood, with an unfortunate lack of quality saw timber for lumber. Because of our continual interference with nature's balance of trade and natural selection (survival of the fittest), we have degraded our woodlands until they now depend on man for their care, health, and future. They are so degraded that one-quarter to often as much as one-half of them consists of overcrowded, bush-shaped wolf trees (fig. 1), which should be culled out for firewood. By doing that, we could bring about a forest ecology of straight, single-trunked, healthy trees (fig. 2) that produce energy and lumber from the same woodlot.

During the era of the American virgin forests, the average tree was three to six feet in diameter and 75 to 150 feet tall. They all were self-pruned and toothpick straight. The wolf tree was the exception in that forest, not the rule.

Figure 2

The little that remains of America's virgin forests is spectacular to see; but they are nothing more than sparsely scattered zoos that we call Wilderness Areas, or primitive areas. The virgin forests as the American Indians knew them are gone forever.

Many present-day landowners express an interest in allowing their woodlands to "return to virgin forest." That cannot happen in small-scale woodlots, or even in much larger tracts of land, because virgin forest is not just a matter of the size of the trees. It is an ecological system that takes eons to develop. Insects, tree disease, animals, forest fires, and most of all the wind, have to be overcome by a forest before it can exist 75 to 150 feet above the forest floor.

By contrast, our present-day forest canopies rise no more than fifty to seventy-five feet above the forest floor. Virgin-size trees cannot remain standing in a low canopy that gives them no protection from the force of the wind.

As we enter the 1980s, private individuals hold deed to sixty percent of the total of our nation's woodland. There is $110 billion worth of wood in the total of

1. Federal Energy Commission

America's woodland;[2] yet there are very few saleable "lumber trees" in private woodlots. The reason for this lack is that a suitable timber tree must have a trunk of a minimum diameter of at least eighteen to twenty-four inches, and have straight sections of that diameter for not less than twelve feet. Good, prime timber trees have bases of twenty to thirty inches in diameter, and have trunks that are straight from the ground to the top of the crown fifty to seventy-five feet high. Large, straight-trunked trees are becoming so scarce in our private American woodlands that small business timbermen all across the country are slowly but surely being driven out of business. This is a major reason why building lumber is becoming so expensive, and why, by the year 2000—just twenty years away—building lumber supply will not meet demand in America.[3] The problem is compounded by the fact that of the sixty percent of our nation's woodlands that are in private hands, the vast majority of American landowners are not planning for the future of their woodlots. Thus, in contrast to the virgin ecosystem, the predominant character in our private forests is the near-useless wolf tree, which cannot yield saw logs for lumber. Overall, the average acre of private forest is so overcrowded that conditions are counterproductive to producing tall, single-trunked, straight trees, capable of yielding lumber.

In the past, building lumber supply from our forest products industry has not been a problem. For example: one-third of the entire country's building lumber comes from a narrow strip of land on the Northwest Pacific Coast that is only 100 miles wide and extends from Northern California to Southern Alaska. This strip of land is one of the richest lumber producing centers in the world.[4]

But now, with the Environmental Protection Agency ban on the chemical dioxin (as was used in "Agent Orange"), the forestry herbicide 2,4,5-T is also outlawed because it contains dioxin. Without the herbicide "T", forest industry managed[5] lands cannot be economically sprayed to kill the hardwoods and "release" the evergreens. The release of evergreens is necessary for them to grow into saw timber for building lumber. And so the Northwest Pacific Coast land and thus the entire United States building lumber industry will not be able to economically produce and deliver enough building lumber to satisfy future American needs. The triumph for ecology, and for humanity itself, over the deadly chemical dioxin, is also a setback for our national economy.

The future of our private forests can either be a continuation of the stagnant growing conditions that exist, or we can turn our low-yield woodland into healthier, high-yield managed woodlots and effectively counter the national decline in building lumber supply while simultaneously producing wood for energy.

2. President Carter, 26 July 79 Address
3. Lester Brown, President, World Watch Institute, "Plowboy Interview," Mother Earth News, March/April '79.
4. American Forest Institute
5. *American Forests Magazine*, April, 1979.

Figure 3

The future of wood energy itself, from the point of view of fuel availability, is as bright as the sun. For since history repeats itself, we have been given a new balance of trade of forest life. We once reaped a great harvest of saw logs from our original virgin forests. Billions of boards were churned out of the water-driven lumber mills of 100 to 200 years ago (fig. 3). Now, nature is again providing us with a great harvest from those same forests. However, instead of the billions of trees being beyond the grasp of the average individual, they are small, abundant, and easy to cut into firewood-size pieces. That lesson from nature should tell us that we can harvest both lumber and wood fuel from managed woodlots.

In short, we need to bring our private woodlands up to the production standards of our "shrinking" forest industry lands, because while building lumber supply is beginning to decline, our demand is increasing at a pace equal to that of imported oil. Increased production of lumber can only come about through proper timberstand improvement.

Nationwide cutting of trees for firewood is beginning to take place. Some sixty-three million cords of fuelwood were harvested in the United States in 1977.[6] But without a conscious management plan in the minds of woodcutters before they take to the woods, their actions will benefit the moment only, and our woodlots will remain stagnant. Then, America will have little defense against a building lumber crisis within our lifetime.

6. *Wood Energy*, p. 2, by Richard G. Fitz.

Wood energy and woodcutters could be the most beneficial partner that the American forest products industry has had since the time of the virgin forests, if we simply educate ourselves in basic woodlot management.

When you follow the principles of woodlot management that are contained in *FireFacts*, you can be a contributing force in the efforts to double the yield from our nation's forests. And, by managing your woodlots, you can also provide yourself or your future family with homemade building lumber, building poles and fence posts, a recreational area, and even a wildlife sanctuary. The prolific solid solar energy from your woodlot that renews itself with the simplest of care can make your future and that of your children very warm and very independent.

THE WOODLOT CONCEPT 2

A woodlot is a parcel of land of ten to fifty acres in size. That is the size of a piece of land that the average individual can care for by himself. Ten acres is the average minimum size for a woodlot that can supply enough wood to heat a three-bedroom house year round. An acre of a well-watered, managed woodlot should produce one ton of wood (approximately one cord) per year.

That same acre is capable of producing up to ten tons of managed hybrid poplar trees per year, or nearly twice the amount of energy as that from even a well managed woodlot of common trees.[1]

A woodlot can be capable of yielding timber as a long term cash crop with wood fuel as a byproduct; or it can yield a primary wood energy crop with a side benefit of homemade rough cut lumber, made with a chain saw and a lumber cutting attachment.

Poles can be grown for fences and animal coops, especially if you plant fast-growing pines just for that purpose. And, a well managed woodlot can be a focal point for family outings. Your local game warden will gladly tell you how to erect bird nesting boxes and how to provide other animals in your woodlot with food and shelter.

1. Dr. Tom Reed, Solar Energy Research Institute, DOE.

Figure 4

Natural Woodlot Management

Survival of the fittest (and tallest) is nature's plan for healthy woodlot management. Wind and foul weather insure that this plan of action is carried out for the mutual benefit of all forest life. The heart of all forest life is the forest canopy, for within its shelter, birds and animals keep the forest manicured and healthy, and they form themselves and each individual tree into an interdependent ecosystem.

Since our present day forest canopies rise no more than fifty to seventy-five feet above the forest floor (which is about one-half the height of our ancient virgin forests), tall, springy evergreens are usually the only trees that can surpass that height. If a tree does grow, or is allowed to grow above the shelter of the rest of the canopy, it stands alone in the wind and it begins to succumb to nature's management plan (fig. 4). In just five to ten years the wind begins to take its toll. The higher the tree grows, the more wind it is exposed to. Each time a gust strikes the tree, the tree is shaken, and dead, useless branches are snapped off. That's called self-pruning. This action of nature is designed to prevent such branches from robbing sunlight from the live branches. But it is also the only defense the tree has against the wind: by streamlining itself it doesn't act like a giant sail and get blown over. However, the persistence of wind and foul weather eventually means that one-half of the extra tall tree tops will be broken off in summer thunderstorms or icy winter blizzards.

If an entire forest canopy is pushed down by mountains of cold heavy air, then the extra tall trees are bent farther than the others and they can snap in half. Or, their roots can let go and then the tall trees are ripped out of the ground. That's called a windfall.

All of these actions are designed to make way for new life in a forest ecosystem. The sweeping of the forest canopy and the downing of the old trees are designed to prevent shrouding of the ground and the repression of new seedlings. Thus it is the wind that is nature's primary woodlot manager.

If a tree does grow and exist above the canopy, nature goes to work with a phenomenon called "wind shock." Since the tree top is above the protective windbreak of the rest of the canopy and consequently the landscape itself, it is subjected to the full power of the wind. As wind gusts repeatedly strike a tree, the tree bends and twists, and small cracks develop inside its base. The inside of a tree is completely dead, and year after year this cracking increases. Eventually the tree's standing strength is weakened, because only the tree's outer cambium bark can renew itself. At this point, the tree may snap right off at its base. But more often than not, large black carpenter ants find their way into the soft wind-shocked heart wood, and the core of the tree is quickly devoured. Then it is just a matter of time before a severe wind storm blows the tree down in a fury of crashing branches. This phenomenon, wind-shock, will eventually bring down every over-mature, virgin-size tree that grows in a non-virgin ecosystem.

If an over-mature, wind-shocked tree does remain standing until cut for lumber, the soft, or ant-eaten heart wood renders the bottom half useless for saw logs. And so it is to your advantage to cut down and use all mature trees, or nature will lay them down, broken on the ground.

Wolf Tree Development

Figure 5 Figure 6

Figure 7

Have you ever wondered how wolf trees get to be so crippled looking? In many cases (primarily in the East) the timbering industry is in its third round of cutting, which results in many stump-sprouted wolf trees (figs. 5, 6, 7). That means that after the virgin forests were cut down, a second crop grew in their place. Because there was no large scale woodlot management, the forest that grew back was only a little better than what we have today. When a chain saw that one man could handle was developed, the 1930s and '40s saw a rebirth of the logging industry. The smaller supply of good saw timber prompted the timbermen to selectively cut only the "clean" trees that were self-pruned on the bottom half, and thus produced knot-free lumber (which always is the most valuable). During that time, large scale industrial forests began supplying most of the building lumber used in the United States; and so the private woodlots were forgotten as suppliers of lumber and fuel. So the prior selective cutting of only the clean

Figure 8

trees, which had been going on for one or even two centuries, "hygraded" our forests into a man-caused, degraded hybrid condition. The accompanying illustrations (figs. 8, 9, 10) show what happens after just one round of selectively cutting only the "clean" trees. Presently, our low-yield woodlands are the result of two or even three hygrade cuttings.

Simple Woodlot Management

Woodlot management is like vegetable gardening. No sensible person would buy ten different kinds of vegetable seeds, put them all into a bowl, mix them up, then go out to the garden plot, scatter them around and forget them. The plants that do come up will never be good producers because they'll choke each other. Growing trees is similar. You "garden" trees by doing the following:

1. Harvest the residue wood lying on the ground.

2. Cull out (weed) the four-D's: dead; dying; diseased; and disabled trees (figs. 11, 12, 13, 14).

3. Cull out even some healthy trees to give your crop trees some "elbow room."

Figure 9

Figure 10

Yield

Woodlots produce a yearly harvest of fuel just as vegetable gardens produce a yearly harvest of food. Uncared for, *woodland* yields about a half a cord of residue wood (4-D's) per acre per year. Properly cared for, a *woodlot* will yield upwards of one full cord per acre per year, depending on tree species and growing conditions, primarily water and sunlight. Most importantly, thinning and yield are directly proportionate. The taller and faster the trees grow, the greater the total yield will be.

Figure 11

ACCELERATED GROWTH YIELD

If you have a large woodlot of upwards of fifty acres, you will come out ahead if you do all your selective cutting at the same time. Extra cords can be sold. But even if you stack them for two to three years and some decay takes place, the accelerated growth of the thinned-out woodlot will be far above the growth realized from slow, selective cutting and thinning.

Figure 12

Figure 13

Figure 14

Girdling is an excellent way to manage without cutting down all of the trees at once. Simply mark your cull trees, using the TSI selective cutting plan in Chapter three. Cut a three-inch ring around each one, and the tree will die. This way, "tops" will break off and fall onto the ground, which helps replace the forest floor nutrients. The crop tree crowns will expand and grow much faster; and you'll still have firewood "on the stump" ready for cutting and seasoning whenever you want it.

Harvest Time—Fall

Fuel harvesting is best done in the fall, since that is the end of the current growing season and less sap is flowing. At this time, newly-fallen leaves help protect the forest floor from vehicle tires. Fall also gets rid of most ants and insects from the bark and allows injured young seedlings a fresh start when spring comes.

A harvesting technique that many foresters recommend is cutting down the selected trees and allowing them to lie on the ground for four weeks or so to air-dry. The leaves will draw a considerable amount of moisture out of the wood and can reduce drying time when the wood is split and stacked.

Caring for the Forest Floor

The young trees on the forest floor are vulnerable, so establish logging roads throughout your woodlot and *stick with them.* They usually provide grass for animals and insects for birds, so they are not a loss to the environment.

Follow the natural terrain when establishing roads. Windy logging roads add a nice touch to your woodlot. But most of all, they keep you on an established path, and prevent your truck, tractor, or car from running over seedlings. If you constantly drag whole trees out of your woodlot, your vehicle tires and the treetops being towed will kill new growth that must replenish the forest that you depend on for fuel.

Best solution: cut them up where they fall; and where possible, carry smaller pieces to the logging road and to your trailer or truck.

Figure 15

STUMPS

Stumps provide a mini-life cycle system unique to the forest floor. Insects thrive on them, and they, in turn, provide food for animals and birds. Stumps also return some vital nutrients back into the soil.

TREE TOPS

When you cut down a green tree, leave the fine top sections behind. They are a vital part of the natural system of replacing nutrients. But don't allow large areas to be littered with tops not cut up, as this could prove to be a fire hazard.

Buying a Woodlot

Remember that a woodlot should be a garden of trees. Look for land that is well-watered bottom land, with lots of sun. Here is a list of other possible qualities to look for:
—Old farm land
—South sloping
—Fairly level
—Already wooded (showing what grows there and how well)
—Soft rich top soil (black or dark and very moldy smelling)
—Look for moss on rocks, ground and tree roots above ground (this indicates water and good acid Ph for trees).
—Bordering swamp land
—Fairly rocky (rocks hold moisture underneath)
Also, ask your county agriculture agent to test the soil for hybrid tree growing suitability.

FAST GROWING HYBRIDS: *The New Breed*

Hybrid pines and poplars (similar to aspens) have been under development since the 1920s. In 1966 I saw hybrid poplars at the University of Maine's School of Forestry that grew thirty feet tall and ten inches in diameter in three years. These experimental trees, and many developed at other forestry schools and private nurseries, have made it possible for the landowner to *now buy* poplar seedlings that will grow twenty to thirty feet tall and twelve inches in diameter in five to eight years. They can produce up to sixty million BTU's of energy per acre per year compared to thirty-seven million BTU's per acre per year from oak.

Your county forester is the best source of free information on hybrid trees that are suited to your particular area.

Planning for the Future

If you have a woodlot of twenty-five to fifty acres, it is wiser in general to manage for timber (pine, spruce, fir, and hemlock are your most valuable crop trees), and to utilize the residue for fuelwood. The land itself is worth more on the real estate market if it has managed timber on it. Timber production can provide extra income to any landowner. Or you can utilize the timber yourself by rough cutting the lumber with a chain saw lumber cutting attachment.

Remember though that a woodlot managed for future timber is a long term plan, so take an afternoon to walk around your woodlot with your county forester or county extension agent. For a list of other agencies that can be of use, see the appendix in the back of this book.

Woodlot Wildlife

A managed woodlot is a beautiful sight. And any woodlot has the potential to draw birds and animals. The birds and animals that you will be able to *see* will

Figure 16

make picnics and outings a real treat. For wildlife, a managed woodlot is the best of both worlds, it's half meadow and half forest (fig. 16).

Your local game warden will be happy to give you pamphlets on building and erecting bird houses and squirrel nesting boxes. He'll also show you how to plant hedgerows for rabbits and ground nesting birds. And your local fish warden (sometimes the same person) will show you how to make improvements if you have a creek or stream running through your woodlot.

County foresters, game wardens, and fish wardens are trained to help you take care of your woodlot. USE THEIR SERVICES—they're free—because you and your woodlot are the reason that they are there.

State Foresters of the United States

ALABAMA
State Forester
Forestry Commission
513 Madison Avenue
Montgomery, Alabama 36104

ALASKA
State Forester
Division of Lands
Forestry Section
323 E. Fourth Avenue
Anchorage, Alaska 95501

ARIZONA
State Forester
1624 West Adams
Phoenix, Arizona 85007

ARKANSAS
State Forester
Arkansas Forestry Commiss
Box 4523 Asher Station
3821 Roosevelt Road
Little Rock, Arkansas 7220

CALIFORNIA
State Forester
Department of Forestry
1416 Ninth Street
Sacramento, California 95814

COLORADO
State Forester
State Forest Service
Colorado State University
Fort Collins, Colorado 80523

CONNECTICUT
State Forester
Department of Environmental Protection
Preservation & Conservation Div.
Forestry Unit
State Office Building
Hartford, Connecticut 06115

DELAWARE
State Forester
Dept. of Agriculture
Drawer D
Dover, Delaware 19901

FLORIDA
Director
Division of Forestry
Collins Building
Tallahassee, Florida 32304

GEORGIA
Director
Forestry Commission
Box 819
Macon, Georgia 31202

HAWAII
State Forester
Division of Forestry
1151 Punchbowl Street
Honolulu, Hawaii 96813

IDAHO
Commissioner
Department of Public Lands
State Capitol Building
Boise, Idaho 83720

ILLINOIS
State Forester
Illinois Division of Forestry
605 State Office Building
Springfield, Illinois 62706

INDIANA
State Forester
Department of Natural Resources
613 State Office Building
Indianapolis, Indiana 46204

IOWA
State Forester
State Conservation Commission
State Office Building
300 4th Street
Des Moines, Iowa 50319

KANSAS
State Forester
Kansas State University
Manhattan, Kansas 66502

KENTUCKY
Director
Division of Forestry
519 Capitol Plaza Tower
Frankfort, Kentucky 40601

LOUISIANA
State Forester
P.O. Box 1628
Broadview Station
Baton Rouge, Louisiana 70821

MAINE
Commissioner
Bureau of Forestry
State Office Building
Augusta, Maine 04333

MARYLAND
Director
Maryland Forest Service
Tawes State Office Building
Annapolis, Maryland 21401

MASSACHUSETTS
Director Forests & Parks
Dept. of Natural Resources
Saltonstall Office Building
100 Cambridge Street
Boston, Massachusetts 02202

MICHIGAN
Chief, Forestry Division
Department of Natural Resources
Mason Building
Lansing, Michigan 48926

MINNESOTA
Director
Division of Forestry
Centennial Building
658 Cedar Street
St. Paul, Minnesota 55155

MISSISSIPPI
State Forester
Mississippi Forestry Commission
908 Robert E. Lee Building
Jackson, Mississippi 39201

MISSOURI
State Forester
Department of Conservation
P.O. Box 180
Jefferson City, Missouri 65101

MONTANA
State Forester
Office of State Forester
2705 Spurgin Road
Missoula, Montana 59801

NEBRASKA
Extension Forester
College of Agriculture
University of Nebraska
Lincoln, Nebraska 68583

NEVADA
State Forester
201 South Fall Street
Carson City, Nevada 89701

NEW HAMPSHIRE	Director Division of Forests and Lands State House Annex Concord, New Hampshire 03301
NEW JERSEY	State Forester and Chief Bureau of Forestry Dept. of Environmental Protection P. O. Box 1390 Trenton, New Jersey 08625
NEW MEXICO	State Forester Department of State Forestry P. O. Box 2167 Santa Fe, New Mexico 87501
NEW YORK	Director Lands and Forests Division Department of Environmental Conservation 50 Wolf Road Albany, New York 12233
NORTH CAROLINA	State Forester Division of Forest Resources P. O. Box 27687 Raleigh, North Carolina 27611
NORTH DAKOTA	State Forester State Forest Service North Dakota State University Bottineau, North Dakota 58318
OHIO	Chief Division of Forestry Fountain Square Columbus, Ohio 43224
OKLAHOMA	Director Division of Forestry Capitol Building Oklahoma City, Oklahoma 73105
OREGON	State Forester State Forestry Department 2600 State Stret Salem, Oregon 97310
PENNSYLVANIA	State Forester Dept. of Environmental Resources Harrisburg, Pennsylvania 17120
RHODE ISLAND	Chief Division of Forest Environment 83 Park Street Providence, Rhode Island 02903
SOUTH CAROLINA	State Forester State Commission of Forestry Box 21707 Columbia, South Carolina 29221
SOUTH DAKOTA	State Forester Department of Game, Fish & Parks Sigurd Anderson Building Pierre, South Dakota 57501
TENNESSEE	Director Department of Conservation 2611 W. End Avenue Nashville, Tennessee 37203
TEXAS	Director Forest Service College Station, Texas 77843
UTAH	State Forester 1596 W. North Temple Salt Lake City, Utah 84116
VERMONT	Commissioner Department of Forests and Parks State Office Building Montpelier, Vermont 05602
VIRGINIA	State Forester Division of Forestry P. O. Box 3758 Charlottesville, Virginia 22903
WASHINGTON	Commissioner, Public Lands Dept. of Natural Resources Olympia, Washington 98504
WEST VIRGINIA	State Forester Department of Natural Resources 1800 Washington Street East Charleston, West Virginia 25305
WISCONSIN	Director Bureau of Forestry Department of Natural Resources Box 460 Madison, Wisconsin 53701
WYOMING	State Forester State Forestry Division Capitol Building Cheyenne, Wyoming 82002

SELECTIVE CUTTING 3

IDEAL TREE SHAPE

This shape of tree structure is usually called a "crop tree." It has self-pruned the lower half of its branches. It is tall and straight, and is prime saw timber quality (fig. 17).

Figure 17

Crown: A Key to Selective Cutting

It is generally acknowledged that a healthy tree should have fifty percent of its height in crown. But that rule is only a guide in initial selective cutting of a woodlot. Do not cut down a tall straight tree simply because it only has a small amount of crown. After proper woodlot thinning, the tree crowns will expand and fill in the newly cut-out openings in the canopy (fig. 18). Follow our guide to selective cutting, and keep in mind that an old, unmanaged woodlot will need a rather slow, deliberate management program to insure proper growth and production.

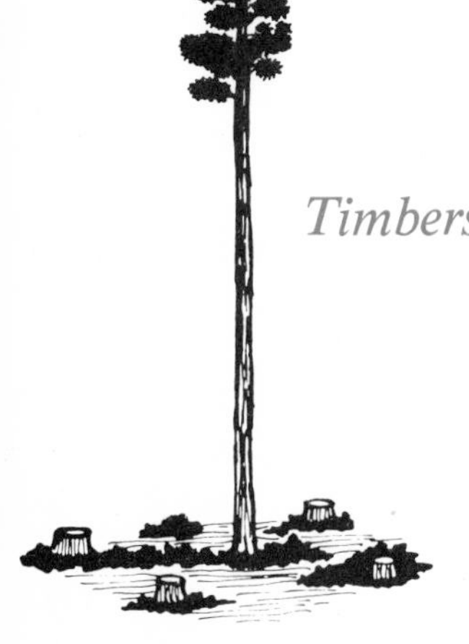

Figure 18

Timberstand Improvement Plan

FIRST: Survey Your Woodlot

Survey your woodlot spring or fall when the leaves are off and you can see well into it and understand its strengths and weaknesses. Study the species and sizes. Most county foresters will help select trees to be timbered off for lumber. But often it takes months for them to get to your particular woodlot. At the least, call them and ask them if they know of any rare trees in your area and ask for some tree species identification pamphlets.

Because windshock results in over-mature trees being blown down by windstorms, and because windshock itself can destroy the core of a tree for ten to twenty feet above the ground, which renders them useless for lumber, trees should be harvested as soon as they reach maturity. Maturity is, in simplest terms, the largest trees on your property. Any tree over eighteen to twenty-four inches in diameter is definitely mature. At this point it slows down in growth and more volume will be gained in the adjacent younger trees if the mature ones are cut down.

SECOND: Save the Rare Trees

Any rare or uncommon species of trees should be left alone no matter what their physical condition (exception being severe disease). These are called seed trees. Check your library for a tree guide.

A REVERENCE FOR HICKORY

The American hickory should be our national tree. Few trees on earth match this tree in the role it plays in nature. It provides unusually tasty food for animals and man. During severe winters, especially during years of acorn famine, the hickory is one of the only food that sustains squirrels and carries through till spring. It is so hardy that it easily resists disease, wind and foul weather. Yet it grows slowly, and so some woodsmen have the feeling that the tree should be spared.

THIRD: Sell the Timber

A professional timberman will cut the trees himself. Most timbermen will not buy trees unless they do the cutting themselves. If you intend to sell trees for saw logs (lumber) or pulpwood (for paper products), check the yellow pages for timbermen, sawmills, and pulp and paper companies. Get two or three estimates on price per ton. Walk around with the buyer and have him point out the trees to be cut. You likely won't get rich, but it may pay the taxes, and you'll be starting your woodlot towards efficiency. Novice landowners should be warned that there will be some unavoidable damage to the woodlot from timbering.

TIMBERING CONTRACTS

1. If it is your first timber sale, consult your county forester first for advice.
2. Physically count all trees over eighteen to twenty-four inches in diameter. Get a per acre estimate of tonnage from the timberman, and get an estimate from each man who looks it over. If you're selling several thousand dollars' worth of timber from a good fifty-acre stand, you should have several estimates as you could get cheated from the first buyer that comes along, and you'll never know it. A "prime" evergreen tree thirty inches in diameter and fifty to sixty feet tall will dress out to be approximately one to one and a half tons, and will sell for five to seven dollars per ton (in 1977).
3. A two-year contract is the maximum, and a one-year contract is better.
4. Read the contract over and understand it before you sign it. (Once you sign it, the trees legally belong to the timberman.)
5. Ask to see all weigh slips. It is a good idea to keep track of the number of loads that leave your property.

FOURTH: Cut the Four D's: (See figs. 11, 12, 13, 14)

FIFTH: Cut out the Wolf Trees

Wolf trees are prone to wind and bad weather damage, and thus disease; and also they shroud the forest floor, robbing seedlings of sunlight.

Figure 19

SIXTH: Cut the tall, crooked trees (fig. 19).

LAST: Thin the Trees (release cutting)

Even some tall, straight trees may need to be cut out. The American Forestry Association recommends that trees average twenty feet apart for maximum growth. Some may be only fifteen feet apart, while others will be twenty-five feet apart. Make a rope twenty feet long, and use it as a guide. Mark the cull trees with bright plastic ribbon. If the trees are approximately the diameter of your leg, tall, straight, and half way up to the forest canopy, then fifteen feet apart is sufficient. When they reach all the way up to the top of the forest canopy, then begin culling them out to twenty feet apart.

Note how each crown has its own air space.

If you have two trees of similar size, side by side, leave the one that is straighter, even though it may be the smaller of the two.

If you have two tall straight trees too close together, choose one of the following:

A. Cut the smaller one if you intend to sell timber someday.
B. Cut the larger one if you are managing your woodlot for firewood.

If you have over ten acres of dense wetland forest, then you probably have more wood growing than you can burn in one household per year. Cull out the smaller trees and grow yourself some timber.

If you want poles for pole buildings or fences around your farm, cut the bigger one and let the smaller one grow tall and straight. To get a healthy polestand of trees, the trees should be no more than ten feet apart to force them up tall and thin. Hybrid pines make excellent pole trees.

Canopy Openings

If you are thinning around an opening in the forest canopy, use the following method for selecting which trees to cut out: Toothpick straight trees get preference for staying. But if you have two similar trees very close together, *leave* the one that does *not* have branches already growing toward the opening (no matter which direction the sun comes from). This way, it will grow limbs out into the opening and double crown size, because the crown develops fastest if it grows *into* an opening. The tree which already has limbs in the opening cannot grow as large a crown away from the opening.

Crown Damage

If the top of the crown of a tree is damaged, the tree loses its ability to grow straight up. Pines, firs, spruce, and hemlocks suffer the most severely if their crowns are "topped" by wind, porcupines, or disease. Follow this rule when thinning: If a tree is only halfway up (or less) to the forest canopy when it loses its crown tip, you may as well cut it down because it will only become a wolf tree. If its crown is already near or in the canopy and the sunlight, consider leaving it for five more years, because though it cannot grow much taller, it can still enlarge its trunk diameter reasonably well.

Note: If you have two or three tree tops that suddenly "brown out" and die from disease, call your county forester! An uncontrolled blight could kill all of your trees of that species.

Woodlot Disease

Disease can cause a large number of one single species to die, year after year. Example: there is a white oak blight going on in the northeastern United States. If you were to cut down most other species and just leave the oaks, you would lose too many of them to disease year after year.

If you notice something peculiar about the color or health of your trees, call your county forester. Disease diagnosis is difficult for the uninitiated.

Hardwood versus Softwood

If it feels light, it's probably softwood. If it feels heavy, it's probably hardwood. When it comes to firewood, it is just about as simple as that, because *one pound* of softwood contains 8600 BTUs of heat, and *one pound* of hardwood contains 8600 BTUs of heat. Softwood burns at 1400° Fahrenheit; hardwood burns at 1400° Fahrenheit. They both contain the same amount of energy! And so, there is no advantage in cutting only hardwoods for fuel. In fact, that could prove to be a detriment to our forest ecology. We have to live in a balance with nature. Forest ecologists believe that the unbalanced use of fossil fuels is what prompted the rebirth of the wood energy industry, and that a balanced use of our forest energy should include using ALL non-rare species of trees, or we will leave our forests open to natural and man-made disaster. (Example: one-fifth of the world's deserts are man-made from erosion!)

ANNUAL TREE CARE 4

Natural Pruning

Have you ever wondered how trees get to be toothpick straight and seventy-five feet tall? Chances are that that tree has outlived and outgrown *hundreds* of competitors to get to be as tall and as straight as it is. It has managed to shoot up tall and straight because of a phenomenon of nature called self-pruning. As the forest canopy grows taller and more dense, the lower branches of the trees can't get enough sunlight to keep their leaves alive and growing—so the leaves, and consequently the branches, die. As discussed in Chapter One, wind storms break away the dead limbs, and the tree simply grows new cambium over the scar, which soon disappears. Thus a tree can care for itself through self-pruning.

Management Pruning

The simplest rule in management pruning is: cut the limb or "sucker" off as close to the trunk as you can without scarring the trunk bark. Excessive scarring of the bark with a chain saw invites insects and disease. The light green cambium bark underneath the outer protective bark is the living and growing part of the tree, and so it should not be disturbed, because it regenerates very slowly in that spot.

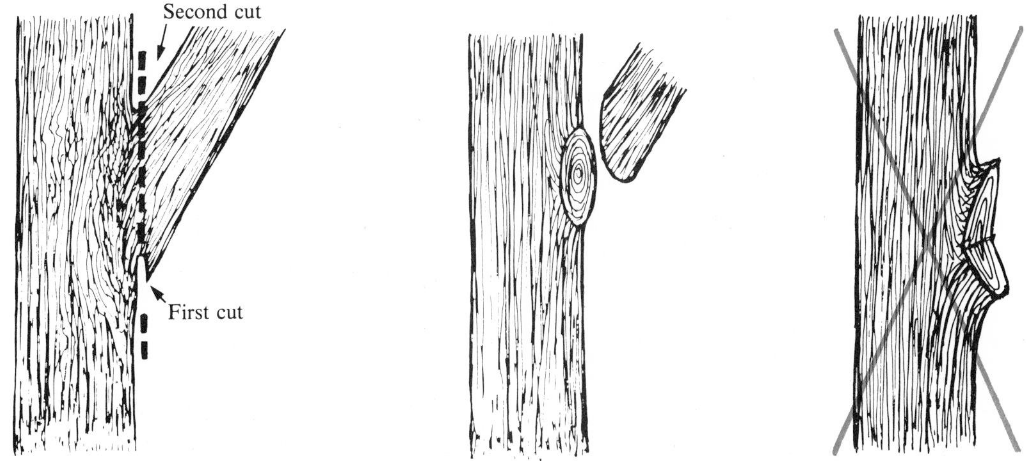

Cut ⅓ up first, or else the down cut (second cut) can tear the bark as the limb falls off.

It's always advisable to paint or spray the fresh cut with an anti-fungicide sold at your local hardware store. There are many simple aerosol or hand-pumped sprays available.

If you have a small woodlot of predominantly wolf trees, use the foregoing pruning method to remove unwanted limbs and tree parts. You can thereby harvest wood for fuel without cutting down all of your trees.

This "sucker" is like the tiny unwanted suckers on tomato plants. It robs the tree of necessary nutrients for growth, so prune it off.

Prune off

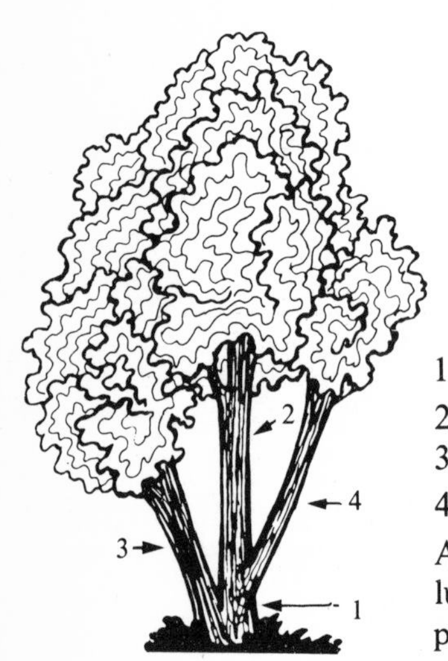

1. Original trunk, 30″ in diameter.
2. Main trunk, 15″ in diameter.
3. Sucker, 10″ in diameter.
4. Sucker, 5″ in diameter.

Add the diameters of suckers 3 and 4 and you get the lumber that is *not* growing in 2. If this tree had been pruned, 2 would be as big as 1. It's not too late—prune it, and use the suckers for firewood.

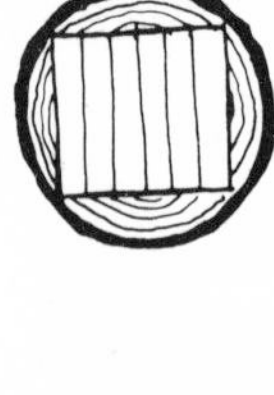

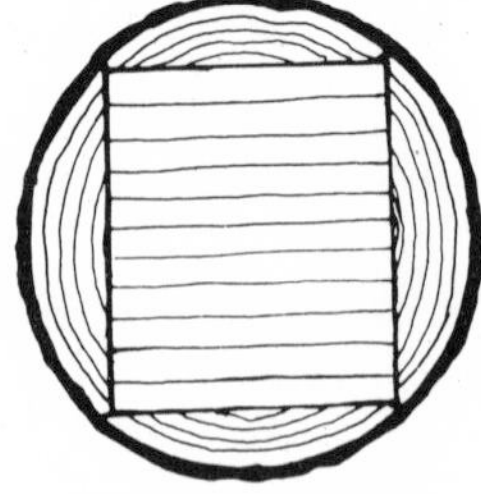

Though the volume of cut lumber would be the same, there would have been more valuable lumber in a larger single trunk.

Pruning Saplings

A *seedling* is any young tree from sprout size to about knee high, at which point it becomes a *sapling*. Once a sapling becomes head-high, prune off the limbs from the bottom one-third. Use clippers. After the tree is twice as tall as you are, prune off the limbs from the bottom half. This gives the tree a straight trunk, fifty percent crown, and encourages it to "shoot up" faster. This is particularly effective for fast-growing hybrids.

AXEMANSHIP 5

Half of America's wood energy users cut their own firewood. Many use an axe for limbing or splitting. An axe is not a toy, and its use should be taken as seriously as a chain saw. This following short course in axemanship should help make your woodlot work safer and more enjoyable.

Buying

Buy a double-bladed "Hudson Bay" type of axe if you intend to use it as a working tool. Sometimes called a "cruising axe," these are designed for professional timbermen, and are the right choice for working in a woodlot. Many people feel that a double-bladed axe is dangerous. ALL axes can be dangerous. The double-bladed axe must be treated with respect, as should all other woodcutting tools.

There is a distinct advantage in using a double-bladed axe in that you can work twice as long between sharpenings—good for the mental momentum required during long hours of swinging, and the concentration required for safety.

Axe Buying Checklist

1. *Balance*: an axe must have a balance point about three to four inches behind the head.
2. *Brand*: Pick a national brand name. The best axes have the company name stamped on the face of the axe head. Shop around and compare brands if you aren't familiar with brand names.
3. *Size*: Size is important from a safety viewpoint. Buy an axe that *you* can handle, not Paul Bunyan. An oversized axe is more prone to glancing, often right into the leg of the user.

Choosing the size: Grab the butt with your right hand, about two to three inches from the end. Hold it straight out at arm's length. If you can't do that, get a smaller axe. An oversized axe, besides being unsafe, will wear you out and put blisters on your hands.

4. *A "true" handle*: If the handle of the axe is not perfectly "true" (perpendicular to the blade), the angle will be off and the axe will be out of balance.

Before buying: Set the axe in a corner and lean it against the wall. Put your finger against the butt. Now, keep your finger in place and reverse the blades. The handle should touch your finger again in the same spot. If it doesn't, the handle isn't true. I've seen double-blades in hardware stores that were a full inch out of true; so try before you buy!

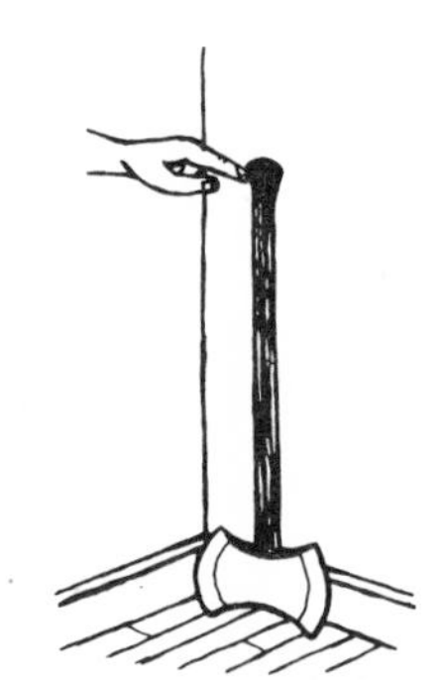

Sharpening Axes

Sharp "chisel points" cut very fast, but they also wear out fast.

GRINDING TECHNIQUE

Follow the original contour and grind the whole cutting surface. Wear safety glasses. Always grind from the edge back, especially if you have the convenience of a table-mounted grinder. This takes practice, but it is the proper way to grind axe heads, because it aligns the grind marks in the direction that the wood is forced past the edge.

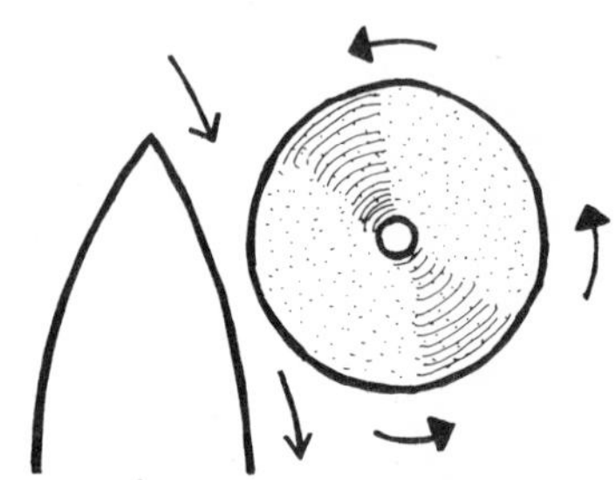

The cutting surface is from the edge back one and one-half inches.

Slightly curved axe edges cut well, and they last longer.

A small carborundum wheel, available at hardware stores, can be attached to a portable drill. (Don't press too hard or you could burn out the shaft on your drill.) Overall, this method is adequate. Grind as explained above.

After you finish grinding the cutting edge, polish it a little with #300 carborundum sandpaper mounted on a wooden block. Carefully polish in the same direction as you ground it. Polished edges stay sharp longer and cut much better.

Practicing Axemanship: "The Match Game"

Get a square-ended log about knee high. Give it a good blow with your axe right in the center. Remove the axe and insert, head up, a wooden blue tip match. Now stand squared off an arm and axe length from the match. Extend the arm and axe out to make sure that when you stand flat-footed, the axe head is directly on the match.

As you start the swing, bring your hands together. The lesson to learn is to bring the axe head and handle down *level to the ground.* The object is to light the match.

Keep your eye on the match and learn to keep it there until the axe head is sunk into the wood. This is how you learn to react to occasional glances of the axe head.

Practice with a sharp axe! Do this away from wood piles and dry grass, and don't forget to watch for flying pieces of burning match head.

Once you strike an axe, remove it from a solid bite by hitting the butt with a sharp blow from your cupped hand.

Splitting with an Axe

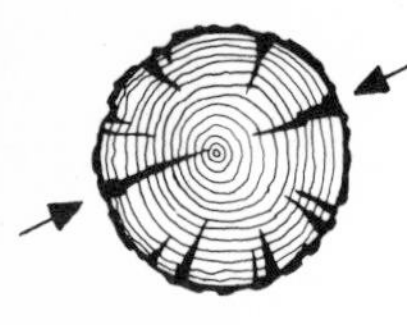

TELL-TALE CRACKS

Cracks in a chunk of wood tell you where the piece naturally wants to split. With an afternoon of "match game" practice, you'll be able to stick your axe right into any crack you choose. Remember though, check the alignment of the cracks with "impossible" knots down each side. When splitting good-sized logs, line up two large cracks opposite each other, and then hit a spot close to the center and as in line with the two cracks as you can be.

Splitting for Kindling

Each quarter of a log has a sharp corner. Just split off the corner of each quarter and you'll have good kindling (that is if the wood is dry).

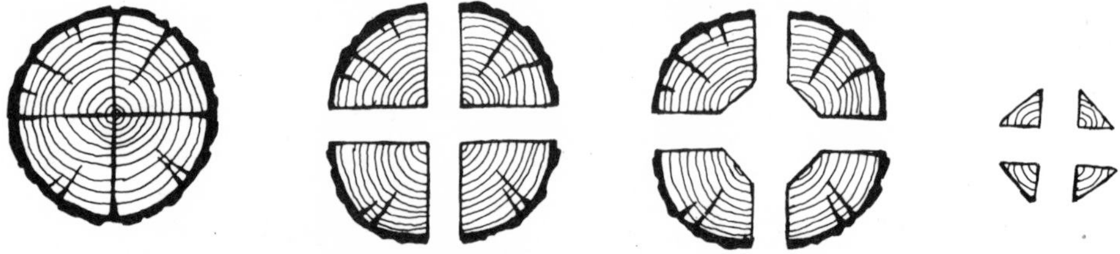

CAUTION: Never hit a single-blade axe on the flat end without wearing safety glasses. Theoretically, you shouldn't do it at all, though many people do. Axe heads are made of high carbon steel, and they chip easily. If you are going to use a single-blade axe for splitting, use a mallet to drive it through tough logs. They have soft heads and reduce the chance of steel chips. But never—*never*—strike the two axes together, or you are guaranteed to send dangerous steel chips flying through the air. You usually can strike a steel wedge with a sledge hammer and not worry about flying chips.

Mauls

Swinging a maul is the same as swinging a sledge hammer, and just as trying. Sixteen-pounders are as big as anyone should attempt to use. Just remember that a five-pounder will split just as much wood as a sixteen-pounder, but with a lot less exhaustion!

But splitting wood with a maul or a sledge and a wedge is no longer necessary. There is a newly patented light-weight "maul" type splitter with built in separators that really works. It's called the "Chopper". It is, in my opinion, a good, *safe* way to split wood, and that is the primary reason that I recommend it—safety. It still gives you good exercise, but won't wear you out unduly fast. (Note though: strictly follow the directions provided, as this is not like anything that you've ever used before. Adhere to the directions, and you'll split a lot of wood easily in a lot less time.)

Axe Maintenance

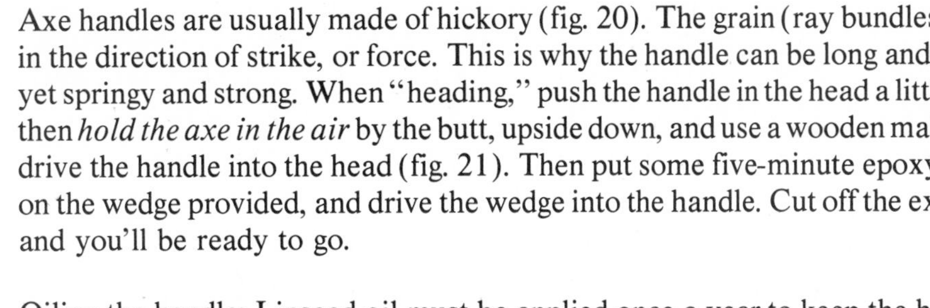
Figure 20

Figure 21

Axe handles are usually made of hickory (fig. 20). The grain (ray bundles) run in the direction of strike, or force. This is why the handle can be long and lean, yet springy and strong. When "heading," push the handle in the head a little bit, then *hold the axe in the air* by the butt, upside down, and use a wooden mallet to drive the handle into the head (fig. 21). Then put some five-minute epoxy glue on the wedge provided, and drive the wedge into the handle. Cut off the excess, and you'll be ready to go.

Oiling the handle: Linseed oil must be applied once a year to keep the handle from dry-rotting. Once dry rot begins (in five to ten years), it cannot be reversed. Drill two to four tiny (⅛") holes one to one and a half inches into the top of the handle inside the head, and not more than one or two in the wedge. Then, soak the whole axe head up to one inch past the head for twenty-four hours in raw or boiled linseed oil.

Axe Storage

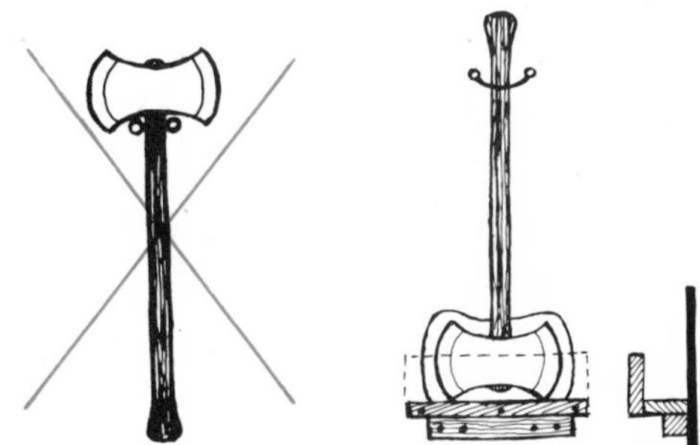

The safest way to store an axe is to put a sheath over the head and then hang it on a wall in plain view. Don't stick it in a dark corner or closet.

PRECAUTIONS

1. Always treat an axe as though it were razor sharp. Many people get cut from a "dull" axe that someone sharpened while they weren't looking!

2. Never leave a double-bladed axe stuck in a log or a stump. (Even if you use a single-blade axe, it is a bad habit, so don't do it.)

3. Axe sheaths provide maximum protection for you while carrying or storing your double-bladed axe. And if there are children around your farm or woodlot, axes should be locked up!

BUYING CORDWOOD 6

If your woodlot is too small to supply all of your firewood, then plan on being a regular buyer of firewood. I suggest that you find a good supplier and stick with him. Constant shopping around may save a buck or two, but it won't make you a steady customer of someone that *you* need. You keep him in business, and he (or they) will keep you in wood.

The best buy in wood is a semi-truck load of second grade saw logs. Most timbermen now offer this for people who can do their own bucking and splitting. You'll get an exact measure of wood in tonnage form, which is far superior to buying by the cord. The wood will often be green, so plan a year ahead. Also, this is the only alternative to the antiquated state laws (as in Pennsylvania) which require that fuelwood be sold by the cord only. One note: ask to see the weight slip that shows the tonnage as recorded by a registered scale. Overall, fuelwood bought by the semi-truck load is about one-half the cost of buying by the cord.

In some states (Vermont and New Hampshire, for example), public-owned forests are now being opened up to people who want to cut their own firewood, free or at a nominal charge. Regulations as to amounts and access vary, so check with your county or state forester for details (see pages 14–16).

If you live in evergreen country, you don't have much choice as to the fuel. But if you live in hardwood or mixed forest areas, then you will be buying either hardwood or mixed cords. If you don't know wood well, or at all, do a little looking at cordwood piles in your area. A weekend afternoon drive to three or four dealers will give you all the education that you need. Be honest and tell them that you don't know wood well.

Bring a moisture meter with you. If the wood is not bark-free and checked well, *you* select a piece to be tested. Have him split it in half. It should feel dry or have twenty percent moisture content (twenty percent or so is considered dry).

Cordwood Sizes

A cord of wood is four feet high by four feet wide by eight feet long. It should be solidly stacked between upright posts. The best cords for the money will have individual pieces that are four feet long, because that cord will be more solidly stacked; and they should be on runners, off the ground.

A half-face cord is two feet wide by four feet high by eight feet long. A third-face cord has individual pieces that are "finger tip to elbow" long, about eighteen inches, and four feet high by eight feet long. Thus, "face-cords" vary greatly in volume, and consequently in value. Your best bet in buying such cords is to compare sizes and prices from several wood dealers.

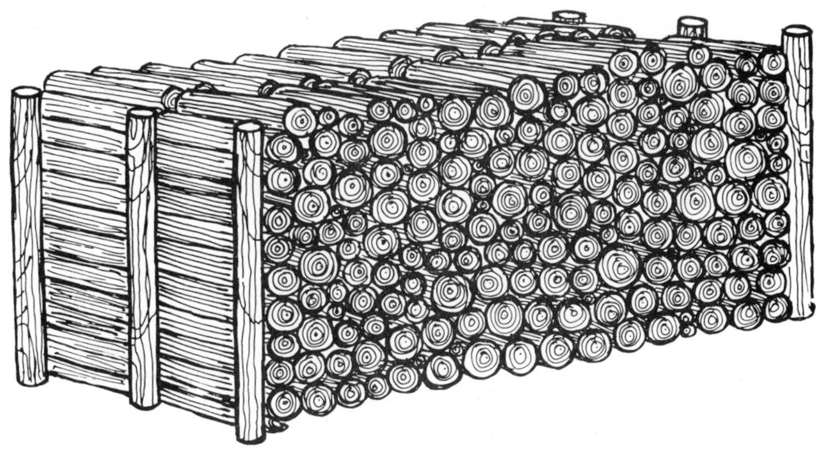

Determining Dryness

—Green wood takes one to two years to dry if not cut into firewood-sized pieces.
—If cut into firewood-sized pieces, green wood will season in six months to one year.
—Total drying can only be accomplished by keeping the wood high and dry, out of the rain and snow and exposed to air circulation. The whole process is a matter of evaporation.

"THE BARK TEST"

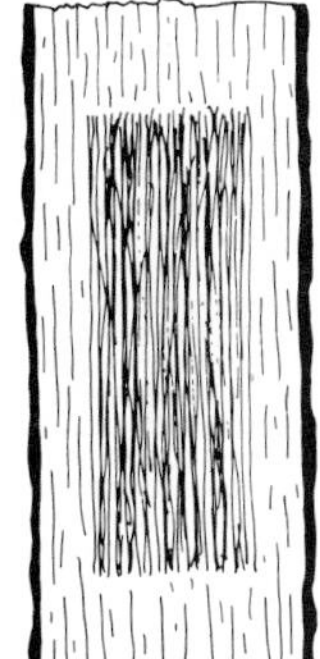

Moisture rises, so select a piece from the middle of a cord. Mark or remember which is the top of the piece as it rests. The area under the bark at this point will be damp or even wet if it is still seasoning, or if it has been exposed to excessive rain.

THE "EYE-BALL" TEST

To further check a cord for dryness, pick out a piece of wood from the middle of the cord and split it open. If there is a light colored ring around a darker colored center, then the interior of each piece of wood has not seasoned yet. Also, you probably will be able to feel moisture in the darker colored center.

Special Considerations

LENGTH

For the average fireplace, logs shoud be "fingertip to elbow" length, twelve to eighteen inches. But if you want them all short—twelve inches for easy splitting—most fuel wood cutters can accommodate you. Check your yellow pages for firewood cutters. If you are just burning occasional fires in a fireplace, twelve-inch logs—split—will stack in a square, whereas eighteen-inch logs will not.

KNOTS

The more knots that logs have, the harder the logs are to split. If you are buying wood that has a lot of knots, at least make sure that they are cut off close to the log.

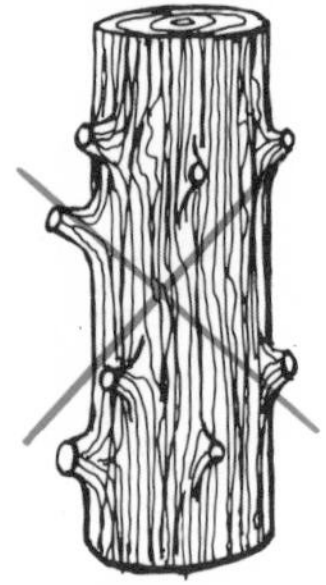

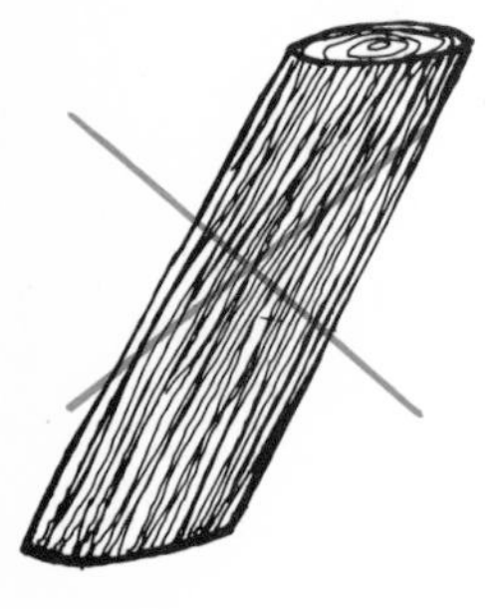

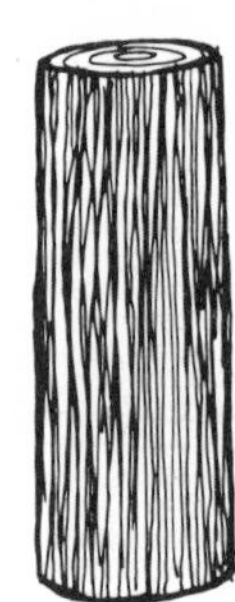

SQUARE ENDS

If a log does not have square cut ends, then the piece won't stand on end when you want to split it. That's important!

FIREWOOD STORAGE 7

There are five main procedures involved in drying and storing firewood:

1. Split open the protective bark coating.
2. Stack it bark side down for fast drying indoors.
3. Stack it bark side up for natural shelter outdoors.
4. Stack it on runners so it can breathe.
5. Shelter it from rain and snow.

Split Open the Bark

Bark is a protective coating. It keeps out damaging insects; stops the summer sun from evaporating vital water from the cambium growth layer; and it can even protect the tree from ground forest fires that burn the forest floor. Because bark forms a protective coating around a tree, it remains there after the tree is cut up into firewood. Only mildew, or the shrinking of the wood, inward, away from the bark, can loosen the bond between the bark and the wood. That usually takes one to two years if the logs are not split open. If a log is split open and then stacked bark side down, the bark no longer acts as a vapor barrier, and the wood (if sheltered) will dry to a burnable state in six months to one year, depending on the time of year that it is cut and stacked.

There are two types of water that have to be dried out of wood in order for it to be burnable: they are nutrient water and cell water.

Nutrient water is water drawn up through the ray bundles ("drinking straws stuck together with Elmer's glue" is what DOE Scientist Dr. Tom Reed calls them). That water is the "blood" of a tree. It brings minerals up from the roots and distributes them to the cambium and the leaves. When drying out, wood loses this water out of each end of a log.

Cell water, however, is locked into each and every cell. The inner ring of the cambium growth cells dies each fall when nutrient water is no longer present. The inside of a tree is all dead cells, but the lignin bonds (glue) hold all the cells in place. These cells are capable of retaining water, which is slowly released through the shrinking and cracking of cell walls.

Cell water, which evaporates *out and up*, must not be stopped by the bark. By splitting and stacking bark down and split-side up, you can cut drying time in *half.*

Also, split down large logs until the pieces are no bigger than a hand's width wide, about six inches. They dry faster, and that is a good, burnable size.

Let it Breathe

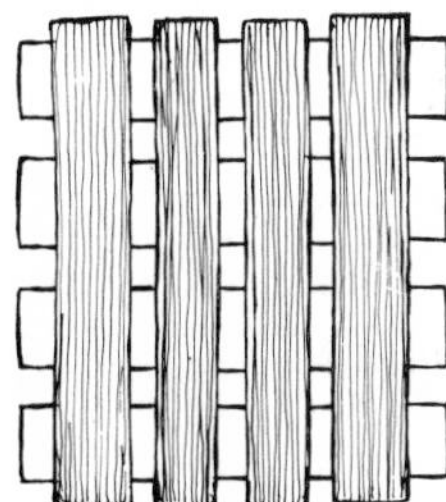

Criss-cross stacking allows more air to circulate over the top of each piece of wood than stacking tightly together. Whether you stack criss-crossed, or simply one on top of the other, you should start the bottom layer on two lengths of runners to provide an air channel underneath the stack.

The need for air circulation is obvious—it carries away the evaporating water from the surface, and that in turn allows more water vapor to seep out. If you don't understand that, try this: wet your hands and then shake off the excess water. Let them air dry by themselves. It takes many minutes. Wet them again, shake off the excess water, and then blow them dry with your breath. This same principle dries out wood, so, let the stack breathe.

Split pieces with knots in them in half, and then stack them on the bottom, or to the rear of a stack. That way, they will be the driest possible when it comes time to split them into burnable sized pieces.

Stacking Indoors

1. Don't stack more than two layers deep against a wall.
2. Don't stack in a corner, or the wood in the corner won't dry out; or it may begin to mildew if it is not thoroughly dry.

3. For seasoning green or damp wood in a basement, build a pallet of two by four runners to allow the moisture to evaporate.
4. If you're planning to build an underground wood cellar, build it rectangular, not square. Rectangular cellars allow a walkway from end to end that also helps air circulation and drying.

Outdoor Stacking

1. Stack east to west if the wind usually blows north to south—or at right angles to the prevailing wind. And, east to west stacks will be heated better by the sun, since it travels that course.
2. Place the stacks out in the open, not under trees, as trees do not protect it from rain; in fact, they further retard drying by not allowing the sun to hit it.
3. Outdoor wood sheds with dirt floors need a wooden ribbed floor added to allow air to circulate.

Shelter

You must shelter seasoned wood from rain and snow in order for it to be dry enough to burn efficiently and not give off unnecessary creosote. The burning of wet wood produces three to five times more creosote and particulate pollution.

As wood dries out, the cells shrink and crack until the piece of wood checks (tiny cracks) and cracks all the way to the center. Then, if the wood is exposed to rain or snow, these checks and cracks act like a sponge and soak up water. A simple solution to outdoor drying is to stack the wood with the protective bark up to shed the water off.

To make a solar dryer for each stack of wood, use thirty mil clear plastic to cover the top and the north side (staple it on well), plus about one foot over the south side. This solar "kiln" will hold a lot of heat on the sun side, while allowing moisture to evaporate out. However, never completely enclose a stack of green wood in plastic or canvas, or it will not dry. If you do cover a stack with a solar dryer cover, stack the wood bark down to allow the added heat to speed drying.

Insects

Termites do not live in wood—they live in the *ground*. It is not likely that you will bring termites in if you cut fresh wood. Termites and ants leave behind very obvious gnawed-out tunnels in wood, so just keep an eye on the cut end.

Black carpenter ants are a bigger worry than termites. Their prime love is wild cherry trees. That is a tree that you had better get to know if you live in the hardwood country. Ask your friends or neighbors to help you recognize them (check your library for a tree identification book). The wood is cherry sweet, and so it often houses ant nests.

Wood Pile Hazards

There are some dangers associated with wood piles:

1. Never let children play on stacks of wood. That wood is heavy enough to hurt or kill a child if a stack falls over on them.
2. In the South, scorpions live under dark, damp objects. Wood piles are no exception.
3. Rattlesnakes frequent outdoor woodpiles looking for mice, which feed on insects in wood piles. Make a little noise anytime you work around a pile; and at night, during the summer, use a flashlight, and don't reach where you can't see. (Note: the old wives' tale of "blacksnakes—no rattlesnakes" is *not* true. They can live side by side).
4. Hornets and bees like to nest in the protection of woodpiles. (It keeps skunks from tearing their nests apart.) *Look* before you disturb a wood pile.

Part 2

The Woodcutter's Chain Saw Guide

INTRODUCTION

Of all the technology that has made the present wood heat industry possible, the chain saw has been the sleeping giant. This half-century-old tool is the main ingredient in the re-establishment of home heating with wood. Its mechanical refinement has reached a level of sophistication that allows virtually anyone to learn how to use this instrument for harvesting wood fuel. Chain saws are largely responsible for making available this abundant, renewable, and relatively pollution-free fuel source, which, in turn, will help fill America's most basic need—ENERGY!

In 1973, "energy shortage" became a household word. Fireplaces, woodstoves, and chain saws were soon high on rural America's shopping lists. The desire for energy independence has catapulted the national sales volume of chain saws to over two million per year. Yet it is a fact that some 40,000[1] of these eager buyers, for the lack of proper instruction, will have a chain saw accident in the first season they work with these extremely sharp instruments. For this reason, I have emphasized *safety* in the following chapters on chain saw use.

1. National Safety Council

BUYING AND MAINTENANCE 8

Chain Saw Buyer's Checklist

The following buying tips should help in the selection of a chain saw. I recommend professional saws if you intend to harvest fuelwood, especially for cutting hardwoods. Mini-saws are great for occasional use, limbing, or cutting small trees. But if you want to maximize wood energy's potential, only a good professional saw will keep the logs rolling year 'round. Whatever size you have in mind, start with this buying checklist:

1. Buy your saw from a local, professional chain saw dealer. His main business, or a good part of it, should be chain saws.

2. He should be, or have employed, a full-time small engine mechanic.

3. Discuss with the dealer the kind of cutting that you intend to do, and then buy a saw that you both think suits your needs.

4. Buy a carrying case. It protects the cutting teeth.

5. Buy a sharpener. Sharpening is easy, once you learn how.

6. Go over the maintenance manual with the mechanic and/or dealer.

7. Ask the dealer at what intervals he should check your new saw and how much routine checks cost.

Note: Many pro shops will not service chain saws that they did not sell to you. That *can* be good business. It helps to prevent large wholesale outlets from "dumping" saws on the market and then not providing you with service. All chain saws do need occasional service.

Special Buying Considerations

1. *Thumb Operated Kill Buttons*: These are usually the fastest and the safest to operate. They immediately shut off the engine.

2. *Compression Release Buttons*: This releases the compression within the firing chamber until the magneto kicks a spark through the spark plug, firing the gasoline vapor. They make pulling the starter cord easier, which helps if you are troubled by arthritis or stiff joints, or if you just don't like yanking a pull cord.

3. *Auto-Oiler*: Oils the chain and bar each time you pull the gas trigger.

4. *Balance*: More important than bar length. It is very unlikely that any non-pro will ever need a bar longer than fourteen to sixteen inches. A sixteen-inch

bar can be used to fell thirty-inch diameter trees. Pick up several saws to test the "feel" and "balance" and choose the one that you can handle safely. That is, make sure you can muscle the saw easily into any cutting position several times, without it starting to "twist" out of your hands. (Remember that last word—HANDS!).

5. *Anti-Vibration System*: Keeps your hands from overtiring.

6. *Chain Break*: Designed to instantly stop the movement of the cutting chain, should kick-back occur.

BRAND

As far as brand goes, my recommendation is to call a couple of different timbermen that are listed in the yellow pages. Ask them for a few good brand names, and ask them which brand they use and why.

SIZE

Most people seem to think that a six-pound mini-saw is less dangerous than a ten-pound pro-saw, simply because it is so small and lightweight. NOT TRUE! My experience has been just the opposite. The "toy-like" mini-saw cuts at 8,000–9,000 rpm's, just like the pro-saw. Since they are light-weight, most people tend to handle them with a lighter grip. This is WRONG! Their light weight will make them kick back frequently if not held securely.

Pro saws have larger gas tanks and therefore run about twice as long as mini-saws. A mini-saw compared to a pro saw is like a pickup truck compared to a tractor trailer. Match the power to the load!

QUALITY

Remember that you get what you pay for! If you spend the extra money for a better quality saw, especially a pro saw, you'll recoup your investment by not having to make as many repairs. Pro saws do cost the most because they are designed for the men who make their living cutting timber by the clock. These men cut fast, hard, and nonstop—ONLY pro saws can handle this type of work load, even for fuelwood harvesting!

Before First Pull

Head Protection—hard hat—shields against kick-back and falling branches. (Modern plastic hard hats with chin straps weigh next to nothing.) Ask the dealer or a hardware store owner for one.

Eye Protection—safety glasses—shield against frequent flying splinters. They can be bought at most hardware stores.

Ear Protection—ear plugs—shield against high decibel levels; seventy decibels can permanently damage hearing. Many chain saws put out 100–125 decibels; shooters' ear plugs are the best because you can hear and talk normally with them in, when you're not running your saw. They have a built-in air pressure valve that closes when the air is vibrated past an ear-damaging level. Gunsmiths or sporting goods stores sell them.

Body Protection—sensible clothing—shields against cuts and scrapes in the woods. Leather gloves, long-sleeve shirts and long, heavy, loose-fitting pants give your legs protection against downward bar movement.

Knee Protection—loggers' leggings or loggers' knee-pads—further shield against downward bar travel. Almost one-half of all serious chain saw accident injuries occur in the area of the knee. Your chain saw dealer should carry these.

Foot Protection—heavy leather shoes (cleated soles)—help prevent slipping. (Get steel toes if you buck a lot.) Get professional chalks if you intend to do any professional work.

Maintenance Bag Checklist

Keep the following maintenance equipment in a leather or canvas bag about the size of a standard gym bag.

1. One-inch round paint brush (for cleaning fill caps).
2. Half-inch box wrench (for bar adjustments).
3. Bar oil fill can with built-in pour spout.
4. Cleaning rag tied to the outside of your bag—NEVER inside.
5. Two screwdrivers for bar and/or motor idle adjustments. Take an extra in case you lose one in the woods.
6. Chain tooth sharpener, extra files, leather gloves, and a small brass brush to clean files.
7. Rider gauge and a flat, fine-tooth mill file.
8. Ear plugs in a protective case.
9. Safety glasses in a protective case.
10. Lightweight hard hat clipped to the handle of your bag.
11. Loggers' leggings or loggers' knee-pads, especially if you are bucking a lot.
12. First aid kit, plus a space blanket for general emergencies.

Preventive Maintenance

After you buy a good chain saw, keep it clean, sharp and treat it with care. That way, cash layout for repairs—normally about once or twice a year—will be minimal. You can keep track of the maintenance requirements of your saw by drawing up a chart similar to the following one:

—Bar Oil: 30 SAE (summer); 20 SAE (winter)
—Two-Cycle Motor Oil: (mixture in oz./gal.)
—Chain Type: Chain Size:
—Tooth File Size:
—Angle Degree (for sharpening teeth):
—Number of Strokes (to sharpen each tooth):

Chain Tension and Sharpening

Read the directions and learn to sharpen the *right way*:

1. New chains should be bathed in chain and bar oil to condition the surface, as they are usually shipped in a rust preventative oil that is not intended to be a lubricant oil.
2. Set your chain tension so that the belly of the chain hangs just loose enough that the guide teeth are about one-quarter inch into the guide groove.
3. Chains on roller tipped bars do not need slack. Run the chain snug, but not tight. Grease the two roller tip holes as often as the manufacturer suggests. They usually require a special grease.
4. Sharpen with a file about as hard as you can grind your teeth together. Pressing too hard damages the file. Files have "teeth" just like a saw, so cut in one direction only.
5. File toward the cutting edge. Be consistent in the number of strokes per tooth; five is about average. Push one-way ONLY when filing; files are not designed to cut on the back-stroke.
6. If you get a saw chain back from a dealer who has sharpened it with an electric sharpener, and the silver teeth tips come back blue, he has just ruined those teeth tips. Blue steel means that he has pressed too hard and tried to sharpen it too fast, thus overheating the steel tooth tips. That takes the temper out of the steel. The blue areas will wear out unusually fast, and you're right back where you started, with a DULL chain saw.
7. How sharp? Sharp as a kitchen knife. Butter knife dull will ruin your saw. You should be able to shave your fingernail on the teeth.
8. Rider links on the chain are designed to determine how deep the teeth cut into the wood. Since each type chain has a different rider depth, your chain saw dealer is the one who should instruct you in using a rider gauge for your particular chain saw chain.

Gas and Oil Tips

1. Most chain saws use regular gas.
2. Use the motor oil recommended by the manufacturer, or one sold by the shop where you bought your saw. Follow the manufacturer's recommendations. The average mixture is fifteen to one. That means fifteen parts gas to one part oil. Mix eight ounces of chain saw motor oil in one gallon of gas. It never hurts to have a little over eight ounces of oil, or, use just a little less than a full gallon of gas. That lubricates the motor better. It's good to mix the eight ounces of oil with a small portion of the gas first, shake it well, then add the rest of the gallon of gas and shake it again.
3. Never store oily rags in your maintenance bag. That could result in spontaneous combustion and a fire.
4. *Never* store gasoline in glass of lightweight plastic containers. Use a filler can sold by your chain saw dealer, or a National Fire Protection Association approved can that has a spring loaded fill cap and a flash-back suppressor.
5. Use four layers of old nylon stocking for a spout filter.

TIGHTENING NUTS AND BOLTS

Be gentle tightening nuts or bolts on a chain saw, because the bodies are *aluminum*. That means using a torque wrench if you don't have a light touch.

After adjusting your chain, run your saw through one cut, then check the chain tension. Some saws have a tendency to allow chain tension to slip.

Cleaning

Blow out your saw after each use. Use an air compressor at your local gas station, or the industrial vacuum cleaner that you should have to clean out your chimney every month. Simply narrow the nozzle and reverse direction of the hose to blow instead of suck.

Blowing the sawdust out each time does the following:

1. Prevents stress on the machine (dirt and sawdust cause sticking and damaging friction).
2. It keeps the bar oil port open, lubricating the cutting bar and cutting chain.
3. It keeps slots and crevices in the saw body from clogging up with oil-soaked sawdust. (A saw has to be able to cool itself properly, or it will overheat quickly and burn out vital parts.)

Note: Always pull the choke fully on before removing the carburetor cover, then blow *away* from the carburetor. Most chain saw air filters can be cleaned with gasoline.

Repair

Always take your saw to a pro saw shop to be repaired, because they will, or should, along with the repair, do a complete systems check. They will occasionally find a small maintenance job that, if attended to now, will eliminate a costly repair later.

Only people living in remote areas should attempt to follow a technical repair manual (except a skilled small-engine mechanic). These are intricate machines. Care and cleaning is *your* job. Repair should be the *mechanic's* job.

Field Maintenance (brush it; shake it; feather it)

First: Brush clean the bar oil and gas fill caps, and then shake the gas can to prevent the oil from separating from the gas. My favorite gas can is one with a soft hose spout, and an air pressure release button. Put the spout in the saw's gas fill port, press the button for one or two seconds, and with a little practice, you'll get exactly the right amount of *clean* gas in the tank in seconds, instead of the usual minutes. Avoid using a funnel, because they collect dirt.

Second: When you fill the gas tank also fill the bar oil tank. While fuelwood harvesting, a chain saw will usually use about one tankful of gas per two tankfuls of bar and chain oil—BUT, by filling both the gas tank and the oil tank each time, you will be sure that your chain and bar are getting proper lubrication. Also, you'll know whether or not your bar is being automatically oiled each time you pull the gas trigger.

Third: Periodically check for a "feather" of bar oil. Hold your saw securely, aim the bar tip at a flat or smooth surface about one foot away, and pull the gas trigger full on for one second. A fine spray (feather) of bar oil should appear on the smooth surface. That indicates that your chain and bar are being properly lubricated.

Note: Adjust the high speed idle while your saw is in a cut. This can only be set properly while the saw is running at full throttle and cutting wood. Do this with *another person*, and *very cautiously*.

SAFE HANDLING 9

The most important thing to remember about handling a chain saw is KEEP BOTH HANDS ON A RUNNING SAW. Just imagine walking around carrying a running chain saw with one hand, and then having a piece of brush or limb pull the trigger of that potential gyro.

HOW TO HOLD A CHAIN SAW

1 Yaw control (side to side roll)
2 Pitch control (up and down)

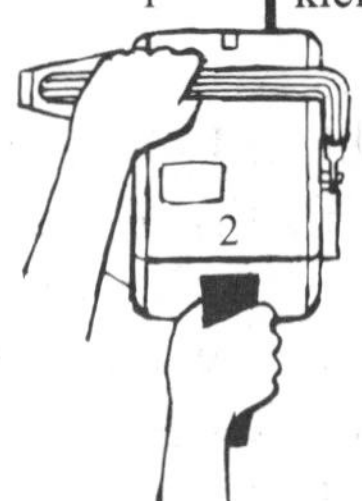

Right
This grip, and good control, will automatically guide a kick-back over your shoulder and away from your face.

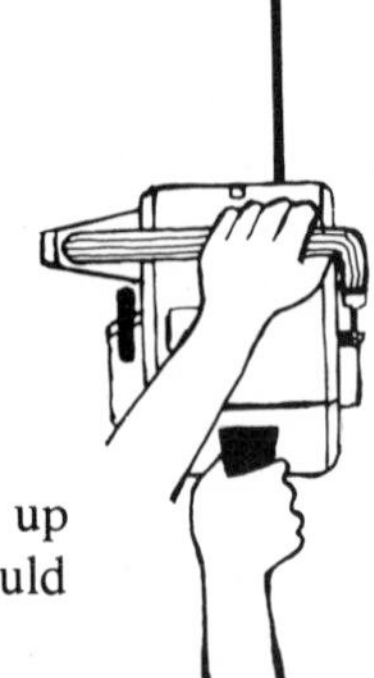

Wrong
If you grip the saw behind the cutting bar, you wind up with your face in the arc of danger. A bad kick-back would come straight back at your face.

TWO HANDLING HINTS

1. Hold and guide your saw equally with *both hands*, and keep *both feet* on the ground. *Control* does not mean *force*.

2. *Never* allow a chain to rotate while the motor is slow idling. Readjust your slow idle screw until the chain rotation ceases. (Also, never let a chain saw idle for more than one minute.)

Practice is the key to safe timbering. You must start off with small, easy jobs. A mature tree fifty to seventy-five feet tall and eighteen to thirty inches in diameter weighs 2,000 to 4,000 pounds. If you make a mistake with a tree like that, it could result in serious injury.

The Four Greatest Chain Saw Dangers

1. DOWNWARD BAR TRAVEL

The cutting bar travels downward after the cut is finished. Ease off as you near the end of a cut. Of the injuries or near misses that I've seen, over half were leg injuries, or ripped pants, because the operator stood with his legs in the downward line of bar travel. Even among professional loggers, "down time", due to injury, often slows the entire commercial chain of operation. Forty percent of loggers' injuries are attributed to the *lack* of protective clothing, namely loggers' leggings or knee-pads.

2. KICK-BACK

The cutting bar bounces back towards your body. Keep your face out of the upward line of bar travel. Injuries are usually the result of operator neglect. Here are two rules for avoiding kick-back: (a) Pull the trigger full on—always—*then* touch the wood with the chain; (b) Never tip cut.

3. FLYING SPLINTERS

The cutting teeth send splinters in all directions at high speeds! *Wear eye protection—Or risk blindness*. Flying splinters hurt, at the very least. I got hit in the left eye once because I did not put my safety glasses on. I saw the splinter coming, but it still hit my closed eye so hard that I could not see for two hours afterwards. I was lucky. Don't make the same mistake—*Wear safety glasses*.

4. GYRO EFFECT

This refers to the *self-powered* flight of the chain saw, and is a lesser known danger, but potentially the *most deadly*! Often confused with kick-back, the saw instead is travelling out of your physical control. This is most easily visualized by taking a bicycle wheel, holding the axle with both hands, then having someone spin the tire as fast as he can. Try to turn the axle left or right. You physically cannot make it go exactly where you want it to go—and it is revolving at only a few hundred rpm's! Now, imagine trying to control a chain saw that is revolving at *8,000 to 9,000* rpm's. At that speed, and with that power, you can have a potentially deadly gyro effect! For prevention, do not "swing" a running chain saw. Always move carefully, and be definite about starting and stopping each individual cut.

Basic Cutting Stances

The Arc of Danger: Draw an imaginary arc from your forehead—by the chain saw bar tip—to your toes. Do not stand in this arc when cutting.

Stand and cut so that:

A. The direction of kick-back is aimed over your right shoulder.

B. The direction of downward bar travel is aimed between your legs, or to the right of your leg.

C. Your eyes are never off the cutting bar (except when the bar is well into a felling cut).

Note: All cutting that I discuss is for *right-handed people*. If your are left-handed, the basic principles are still the same, though some need to be reversed. Also, a left-handed saw would be your best safety insurance.

HIP-CUTTING

Hip-cutting is the basic cutting stance. Work with your saw motor at the level of your hip, and use your body weight and coordination to join you and your saw into a rhythmic cutting unit. It's the safest way to fell trees, to cut crown-hung trees, and especially to limb and buck. It also is the least tiring way to handle a chain saw for a long period of time.

When cutting crown-hung trees, rest your right elbow on the front of your hip bone, and work with an extended left arm.

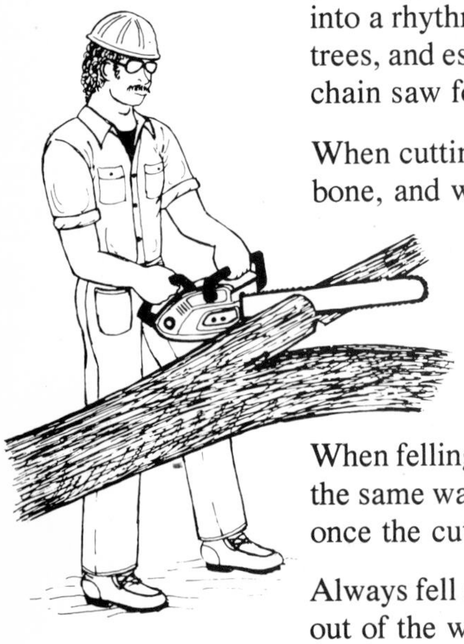

Rest your elbow on your hip while you limb and buck.

When felling, kneel on your right knee to notch the crown lean side; then kneel the same way to mark and start your fell cut. Go back to standing on both feet once the cutting bar is the bar width into the fell cut.

Always fell a tree from a standing position. Make sure that you can move back out of the way.

Cutting Pointers

Prime Rule: Always run a chain saw at full speed!

PUSHING CUT—AREA 1

Remember that excessive use of the pushing *AREA 1* puts undue strain on the whole machine. Also, *AREA 1* tends to "push" the teeth *out* of a cut, increasing the risk of downward kick-back. The way to use *AREA 1* safely is to hip-cut straight up (vertically) with your right elbow in front of your hip, keeping your feet on the ground about two feet apart, and with the direction of downward bar

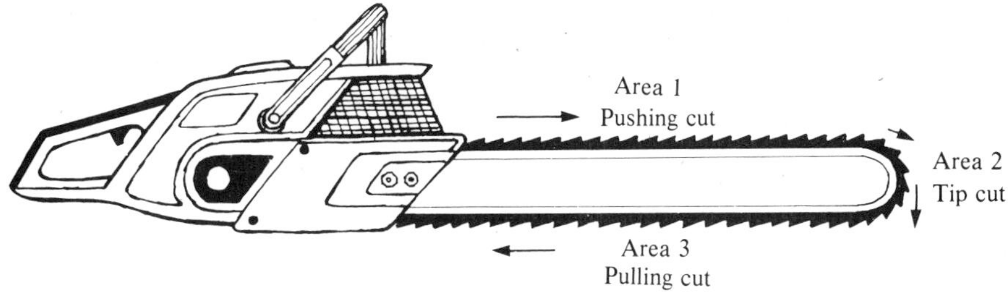

Area 1 Pushing cut: use only occasionally.
Area 2 Tip cut; the most dangerous area to cut with; don't use it.
Area 3 Pulling cut: the safest area to cut with, and the easiest on the saw.

travel aimed between your legs. If the cut is chest high, again, hip-cut with your right elbow resting on the front of your hip bone, and pull the saw up with an extended left arm.

TIP CUTTING—AREA 2

Forget it! Tip cutting is probably responsible for *most* chain saw kick-back accidents. Remember that for every action there is an equal, and opposite reaction. It is dangerously true here. The chain is travelling at 8,000–9,000 rpm's and 400 mph. But not only is it travelling *fast*, at the very tip—the tangent of its direction change—it's travelling *down*. At the same instant, the bar wants to be the equal and opposite reaction and travel upwards. So when you touch the tip to a solid object, if you don't have physical control over your chain saw, the striking friction of the teeth hitting solid matter *stops* the chain for an instant. The downward energy, which is travelling at 400 mph, is instantly transferred from the chain to the bar, sending the bar upward at a theoretical 400 mph. That is *kick-back*!

PULLING CUT—AREA 3

This pulls the teeth *into* a cut, and that makes the bottom of the bar the *safest area* to cut with.

FELLING 10

The Direction of Fall

The direction of fall is pre-set in most trees by what is called "crown lean" (the result of a tree's crown having grown off center). This one-sided or angled growth causes the tree to be "weighted" in the same direction. This weighted side is the *only* direction a tree will fall.

A tree develops its crown lean during its many years of growth, and the main influence in that development is the sun. Since the crown is the tree's food producer, and since it makes its food from ground nutrients and sunlight, crowns will usually grow (in our hemisphere) reaching out to the south sun. This is the most common lean direction. Or, the crown will grow limbs out into a newly formed opening in the forest canopy, to expand the tree's growth potential by capturing more solar energy. This "lean" can be in any direction.

Once the crown lean has been established (especially in wolf trees), the tree's center of gravity can be likened to the Leaning Tower of Pisa. That is, the crown, which is about equal in weight to the tree's main trunk, has grown off to one side of the tree's center of gravity. And only the tree's root system, which usually matches the crown in diameter and depth, keeps it from falling over. Thus, the only direction that a tree can be felled is in the general direction of crown lean.

Procedures for Felling

1. *Clear the Brush* Clear the brush from around the base of the tree. A trip at the wrong time can be disastrous. But, don't try to cut brush with a chain saw. The chain teeth can slap the brush into your body, particularly your hands and face. And too, pencil-thin brush can foul your chain saw drive mechanism. Special brush cutter attachments are made for chain saw bars, but hand cutting with clippers is faster and simpler.

2. *Determine Direction of Crown Lean* Fell the tree in the general direction of crown lean. Felling the tree in any other direction must be done with the aid of a bulldozer or professional logger's skidder. Ropes or cables generally won't do it!

The only other alternative to altering a natural lean is by topping the tree (cutting the top before the base). But there is no need for it in fuelwood harvesting. It requires the use of tree climbers. I have topped and dismantled trees from the crown to the ground. My advice about topping with climbers is—LEAVE IT TO A PRO—or get professional instruction from a tree surgeon or pro-topper, who actually does it for a living. Topping is the most dangerous part of harvesting big timber.

3. *Check the Landing Zone* Try to avoid crushing young trees. And don't forget that a big tree's potential power is tens of thousands of pounds of force upon landing. That force can snap off dead branches and send them flying long distances.

4. *Check Your Gas* Make sure that your saw is full of gas and oil and running properly before you attempt felling any large tree. You can get into a dangerous situation if you are within several inches of severing the base of a tree, and suddenly your chain saw runs out of gas! The precarious balance that the tree may be in while you re-gas your saw can be offset by a sudden gust of wind. If the tree is straight and tall, with no crown lean, it can be blown over in any direction, including backwards onto you.

Notch cut position

5. *Notch on Crown Lean Side* Never walk in front of a notched tree. The notch need never be deeper than one-quarter of the tree's diameter, but it should not exceed one-third of it. At that point, you are nearly severing the base, and the tree can begin to fall, closing the gap you just created and locking your chain saw bar tight in the cut. If that happens, stop your saw and take out your ear plugs. This can be a dangerous situation! Again, that tree can blow over by any sudden gust of wind. Or a hollow or rotten-centered tree can snap and go over. So your best defense is to be able to *hear* what is going on, until you can re-cut the base with another saw or good axe. (Keep in mind that one bad axe bite can cut right through a chain and ruin the bar. The chain can be fixed, but not the bar.)

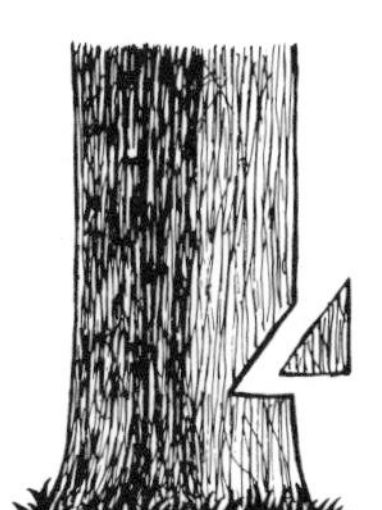

Wolf trees with two or more trunks may separate unexpectedly when you attempt to fell them. Use caution when felling them, because you may not be able to tell how deep the natural trunk separation goes.

6. *Start Your Fell Cut* If you do your fell cut from the same hip-cut position that you used to notch the crown lean side, your cuts should be parallel. This is necessary, or the following things could happen:

Fell cut position

—You may have to re-cut.
—Non-parallel cuts can cause you to go in too deep before the tree begins falling, and then it "lags" in flight, causing frequent crown hang-ups.
—Straight trees facing a breeze can lean back and lock up your saw.
—It may not fall exactly where you want it to.
—Worst of all, the trunk can split upwards and hit you. That's called a "barber chair". After your feet are set in position, cut a mark where you want to fell cut. The mark should be two to three inches above the flat cut of the notch. It takes a lot of practice to be able to walk up to big trees, notch them, and fell cut them perfectly each time. (A good timberman cannot be made in one day).

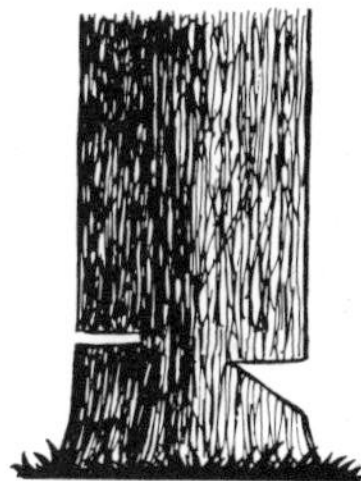
Timberman's Cut

The *timberman's cut* is unduly dangerous because you must use the top of the bar to back-cut the notch. It's designed to give a log a square butt, because sawmills won't buy them unless they are square cut, and fresh from the stump.

7. *Guide the Crown* Start your fell cut slowly at first. That is, use light cutting pressure but with the motor still running at full speed. If all looks OK once the bar width is completely into the cut, *watch the crown—then "bore into it"*. Cut as fast as your saw can work without straining, because the faster you cut the butt out from under it, the faster "she" falls, reducing the chances of a crown hang-up. Control the precise direction of fall by counter-cutting. (*Caution*: Be

extremely careful when felling on a windy day.) From the second the crown starts to move, cut and counter-cut for NO MORE than three seconds. Always keep your eyes on the crown to control direction of fall, and to guard against dead limbs falling down on your head. After three seconds of cutting and counter-cutting—*kill your saw motor and stand clear*—in the opposite direction of fall (at least five feet from the butt).

ADDITIONAL FELLING NOTES

Counter-cutting: Direct your notes cut in the direction of unwanted fall (like counter-steering a skidding car). If it's pulling too far to the right, cut only the right side of the butt, and vice-versa.

Normal cut

Pulling left, cut left

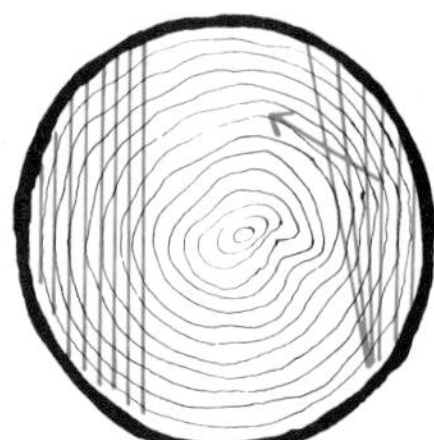

Pulling right, cut right

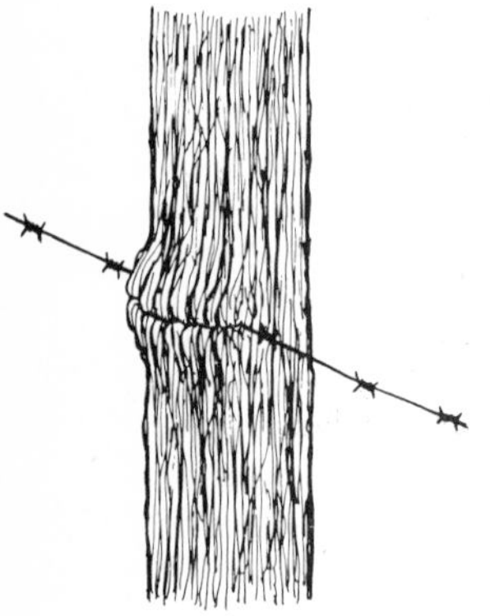

Timing Yourself: To gauge the three seconds of fall time, use a clock's second hand to practice. Count in rhythm: one thousand—two thousand—three thousand.

Farm Trees: Trees that grow around old farm houses, barns and the edges of fields will almost always have some hardware in them—nails, parts of fences, old sap spouts, to name a few things.

Crown Hang-Ups

Crown hang-ups (timbermen call them hangers) and wind-falls (trees that have been partially blown over by a gust of wind) are easy to deal with. By using the hip-cut, you simply cut the trunk of the tree once or—if necessary—two or three times, until the tree comes down. You're not cutting for lumber, so go ahead and buck it up where it leans.

Caution: On rare occasions, a crown-hung tree will stay locked up in the other tree's crown as you buck it. The trunk will become short enough so that the tree is nearly vertical again. I once had this happen while working on top of a pile of tree tops left behind by timbermen. *The crown suddenly fell backwards towards me.* I had to dive out of the way to avoid being hit. So use extra caution when they remain hung.

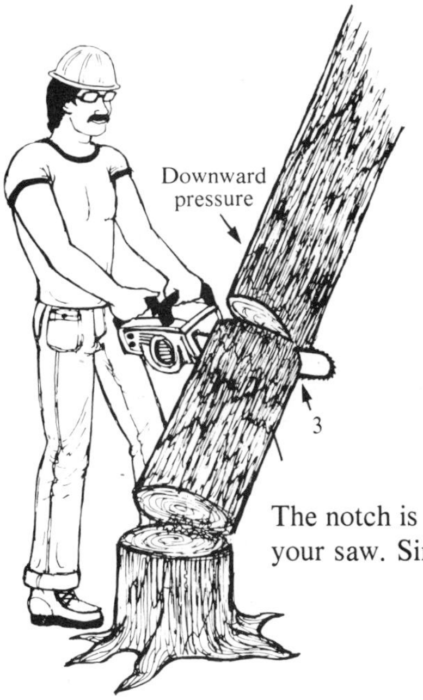

Downward pressure

1 First cut
2 Second cut
3 Hip-cut up last

The notch is slightly exaggerated for this diagram. Make them shallow or you'll bind your saw. Since the pressure of the tree is down, hip cut up into it last (3).

When a tree (1) is crown-hung in two other trees (2) & (3), *don't* try to fell (2) or (3) until (1) is unhung and down.

FRESH WINDFALL

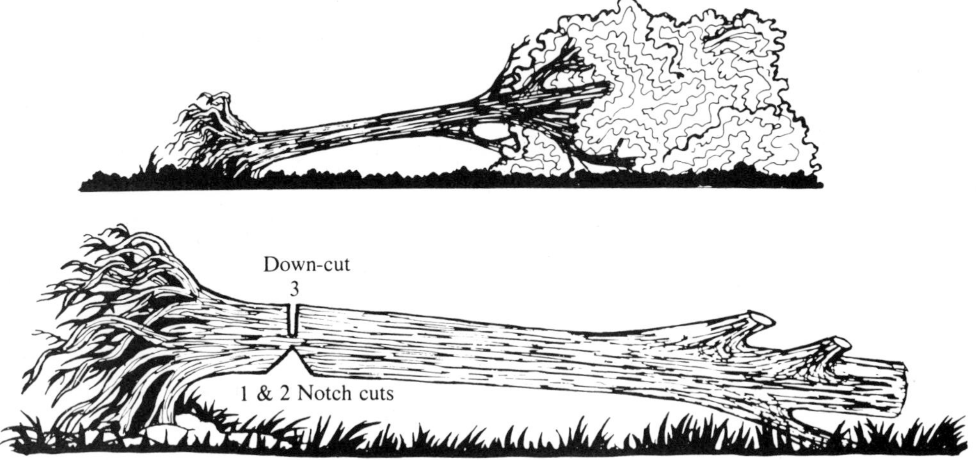

The roots of a fresh windfall anchor the stump to the ground, so make the last cut (3) down.

FELLING ON A HILLSIDE

Usually the crowns will lean towards the bottom of a hill. Start from the bottom and work *up* the hill one tree at a time. Fell one; limb it—buck it—remove it. If you cut them all down one on top of the other, you'll wind up with a dangerous mess of widow-makers that can roll unexpectedly.

BUTT WHIP

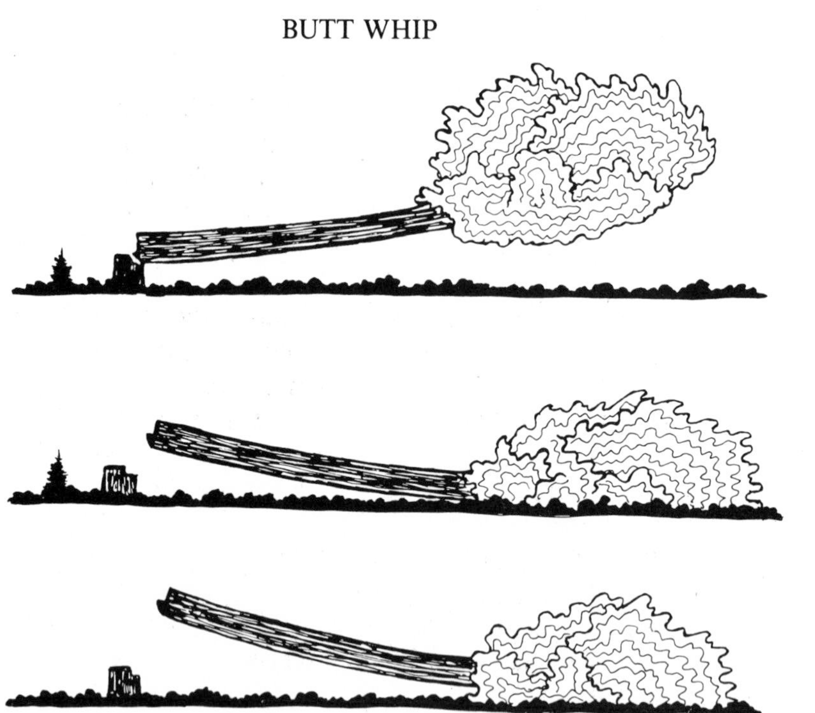

Sometimes trees hit the ground like a rocking chair. Stand back *always*.

LIMBING AND BUCKING 11

Limbing and bucking can be tiring and hazardous work. Professional loggers develop stamina simply by doing it every day. Lacking the physical conditioning and/or the experience, the weekend cutter should *keep his mind on what he is doing* at all times and know when to quit.

Limbing and Bucking Checklist

The following section is not intended to be a complete explanation of limbing and bucking safety. You will have to learn the hard way what you CAN and CAN'T do with a chain saw and a felled tree. But here are some points worth keeping in mind:

1. Wear pro-timberman shoes that, like soccer or football shoes, have metallic cleats built into the soles for gripping logs. They're called *chalks*. Or at least wear lug soled boots. (Stay off logs when it is raining.)
2. Make sure that the felled tree is "settled". Walk up on the butt of the log (the end next to the stump), without your saw, and bounce up and down to make sure that the tree is settled. Use *extreme caution* when working trees off a hillside. If the tree remains stable, walk out to where the limbs start. Again bounce up and down. Always stand facing the limbs and crown while doing this. And always walk on the logs straight on.
3. Never stand sideways on a log. If you do, and it suddenly rolls in the direction that you're facing, it will likely buckle your knees right out from under you.
4. Limb and buck from the butt to the crown. The crown anchors the tree.
5. Never saw off short dead limbs or limb base stubble. They can snap and fly back at you. Knock them off with a club.
6. On hillsides, never work on the downhill side of a felled tree or large log.
7. Never step into the crotch of a limb to work.
8. Never step on cut off limbs, or on short logs that can roll out from under your feet.
9. Use a log jack if you keep hitting the ground when bucking. These are log rollers with a triangular lifting cantilever built on.
10. Ecologically, it is best to buck a tree where it falls. It's even better to fell and buck during the winter when there is snow on the ground to protect the forest floor.
11. If you intend to drag logs out of the woods to work on them, limb them first. Use chains *only* to drag logs, not ropes or cables, as they can stretch, snap, and fly back with dangerous speed.
12. If you use a trailer for removing short, liftable logs, make a bucking stick measured the same length as your trailer bed.
13. Never use a metal sawbuck. If the kick-back danger isn't enough reason, the inevitability of chipped or broken saw teeth should be.

LIMBING AND BUCKING CUTS

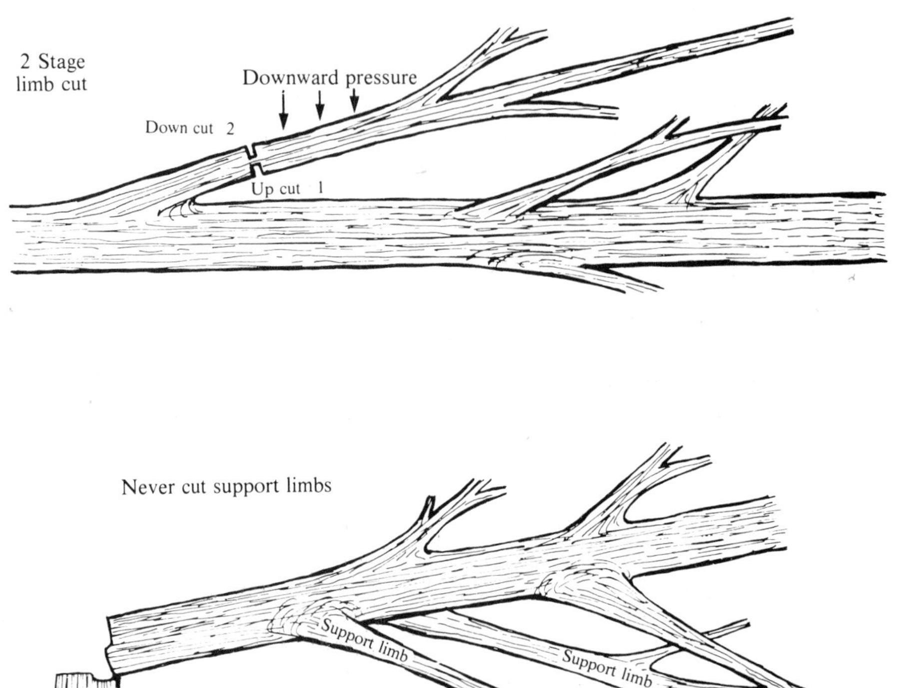

Don't ever cut the limbs that keep a tree suspended off the ground. The tree could roll onto you. Pine trees are the most notorious for snapping and rolling unexpectedly. First limb the top, then one side (never vice-versa), then use a log roller (peavey) to roll and level the tree.

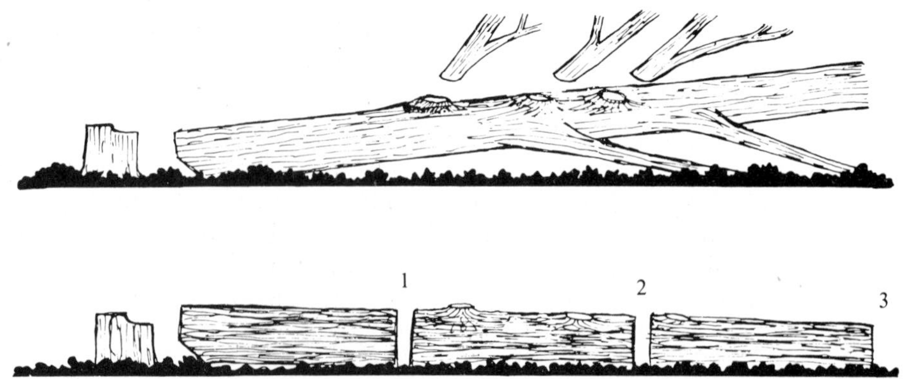

First cut the limbs that are upright, then cut the limbs on the sides. It is usually easier to buck from the butt to the smaller end.

14. When limbing and bucking a lot you will use much more bar oil than usual, so much so that you could run out of bar oil before you run out of gas. *Check your oil often*. Here's a useful tip: don't fill the gas tank full. Leave an inch or so unfilled. That pint or so should make you run out of gas before you run out of bar oil.

Carrying Wood

Now that you have your fuelwood cut up and ready to haul away, remember that that tree *still weighs the same* after it's cut up.

I use a small garden tractor with a pull behind trailer to haul short logs out of my parents' woodlot. It's easy, and ecologically sound, since its rubber tires don't rip up the forest floor.

If you plan to haul wood in the trunk of your car, remember that a trunkload of oak (or any other hardwood) can weigh 300–500 pounds or more. That could break your rear car springs. A load of pine or other softwood should weigh about two-thirds that much. Also, that much weight can lift your car's front end a little, and make steering unsure under slippery road conditions.

A cord of hardwood weighs in at about 5,000 pounds. Pickup trucks are usually half-ton. That means that they are designed to *safely* carry only 1,000 pounds of cargo. If you pile a pickup truck box full of hardwood, you could wind up with 5,000 pounds on those 1,000-pound springs. That can break them and blow out tires. So *take it easy with the loads*.

Chain Saw Storage

Store your chain saw in its carrying case. That protects the entire saw, especially the cutting teeth. And store it *flat*, base down, to keep the gas and bar oil from spilling.

Build yourself a storage shelf to house your saw, maintenance bag and maintenance chart. Gas and oil cans should always be stored outside in a well ventilated shed. Never store gas or oil in glass or plastic containers. Use safe, non-breakable, non-spillable, National Fire Protection Association approved cans that have spring loaded spouts and a flash-back guard.

Reread this *chain saw guide* several times before you attempt to use a chain saw for the first time. If you know someone who is buying, or has just bought, a new chain saw, suggest that they read through this guide. Please don't become one of the 40,000 people that seriously injure themselves each year with chain saws.

Part 3

Wood Heat Units: Design and Function

THE FIREPLACE: PAST AND PRESENT 12

Wood energy is solid solar energy. Solar energy is an uncontrolled hydrogen explosion that burns at the temperature of an atomic bomb. Wood burns at a temperature of 1400° Fahrenheit, and if not properly *contained* during the combustion process, it can become an uncontrolled reaction because the function of wood is to store and then release the energy that the atomic hydrogen reaction—from the sun—gave it in the first place.

Prehistoric man devised a way to contain fire to cook and to prevent the onslaught of predatory animals. He designed a simple, crude place-for-fire. The discovery that fire could be brought back from the cracks in volcano lava fields, put into fireplace containments, and then used to serve man, made man the most superior predator on earth. Man was then learning to *think* in order to survive better in his environment; by designing the fireplace and then refining it, he made this form of energy work for him, not against him. In his environment, birds built nests to contain and protect their offspring; and many animals dug holes for protection from the elements. But only man put nature's energy—fire—*into* a container—a fireplace—and by doing so, was able to remain outside of containment (caves), yet protected from predators. In practically the blink of an eye, the design and function of the fireplace changed the course of history.

Today the design and function of fireplaces and woodstoves is good and rapidly getting better. Auburn University, the Fireplace Institute, and Corning Glass Works are each involved in revolutionizing the prehistoric principles of simple fire containment.

At Auburn University, the Auburn Woodburning Laboratory—AWL for short—is analyzing the process of controlled combustion within the containment structure. The mechanics of containment must be designed to fit the process; and since no one before this has ever fully analyzed the process of burning wood for energy, the design of fireplaces and woodstoves has been based mostly on theory. Now, the data that AWL are compiling, concerning the best way to release the energy from wood while burning it, are being used to design fireplaces and woodstoves that best promote maximum utilization of the energy contained in each pound of wood—8,600 BTUs of heat. Auburn University's Woodburning Laboratory is also doing ongoing wood energy research work, under grant, for the U. S. Department of Energy.

The Fireplace Institute has designed and built the first efficiency test center at Auburn University. The center is now testing fireplaces and wood stoves, and upon completion of the testing of a unit, a Fireplace Institute label is attached that gives the industry's first standard efficiency rating. Dr. David Dyer, Professor of Engineering at Auburn, says, "The rating system will use the

A manufactured fireplace is examined in Auburn University's woodburning facility by (left to right) Professors Glen Maples, Tim Maxwell, and David Dyer. The three engineers have over thirty years combined experience in the heat efficiency field.

energy efficiency ratio now used on air conditioners and similar products. This will help the consumer to know how much wood is required, and how many rooms can be heated with the product being purchased." This pioneering effort by the Fireplace Institute, and the 325 manufacturers, distributors and dealers that it represents, will give wood energy consumers reliable performance records for products that are safe and efficient.

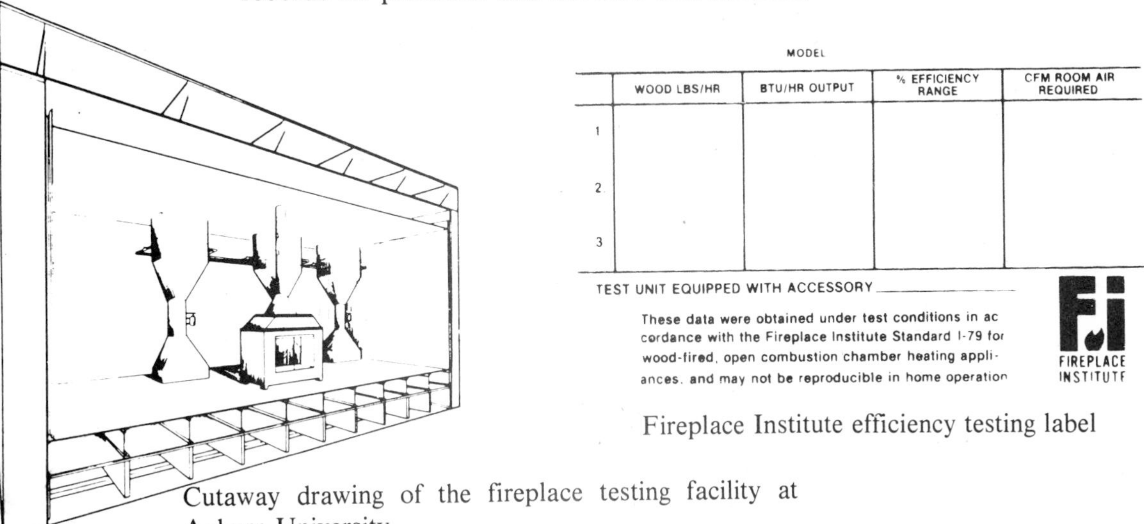

MODEL

	WOOD LBS/HR	BTU/HR OUTPUT	% EFFICIENCY RANGE	CFM ROOM AIR REQUIRED
1				
2				
3				

TEST UNIT EQUIPPED WITH ACCESSORY ________

These data were obtained under test conditions in accordance with the Fireplace Institute Standard I-79 for wood-fired, open combustion chamber heating appliances, and may not be reproducible in home operation

Fireplace Institute efficiency testing label

Cutaway drawing of the fireplace testing facility at Auburn University.

Corning Glass Works, the inventor of Pyrex™ glass in 1915, has designed a high quality fireplace glass called Vycor™ that can withstand an *instant* "thermo-shock" temperature change from 1600° F down to 0° F without breakage or damage. That means that large pieces of fireplace or woodstove glass can be very safe. In addition, Pyrex™, PyroCeram™, and Vycor™ glasses transmit twenty-five percent more heat than metal.

Several companies are now developing a product that will increase the efficiency of wood heat units: the catalytic convertor for wood stoves. This device is designed to convert the unused energy in wood smoke into usable heat by *lowering* the combustion temperature of methane (which accounts for 50% of a wood fire's flame), creosote and hydrocarbons. That will allow true secondary combustion to take place, while at the same time eliminate almost all creosote buildup in chimneys—a feat that fire insurance companies will applaud. These units are intended for use in new stoves as well as to retrofit to existing stoves by way of a special stovepipe attachment.

Overall, the wood energy industry is conscious of the health and safety needs of American consumers; and indeed, manufacturers are responding with the finest wood heat units made anywhere in the world today.

WOOD HEAT FIRES 13

Fire

Fire is matter in high speed motion in the process of changing its physical form. Example: If you throw a piece of butter into a hot frying pan, it melts, because you have started fast molecular movement by supplying a "push" of concentrated moving energy—heat. The push begins the process of accelerating molecular movement within the butter. The more push that is added, the faster the molecules of butter move, and the hotter they become. The friction of molecule banging into molecule raises its temperature. The more concentrated the push of energy, the faster the molecules move until they are pushed past a point where they change their physical form and release their stored energy. That change is called *fire*. It is irreversible and self-feeding, and it continues until the entire body of matter changes (consumes) itself. The release of stored energy during this change is so intense that it emits visible electromagnetic energy, which we see as flames.

The Three Stages of Wood Combustion

Stage I Flame: the ignition or "push", where the temperature of the wood causes it to change its physical form into FIRE. The releasing energy source, usually a match, touches the outer layer of wood matter and transfers the reaction.

Stage II Distillation occurs as gradually increasing depths of wood matter are heated up until the water and gases begin to evaporate.

Stage III Charcoaling happens after the water vapor and gases are driven off. The wood matter that remains is nearly pure carbon. A high temperature alone can cause charcoal to be pushed to the point of ignition. Heat from wood stoves that are placed too close to wood walls can push charcoaled wood into spontaneous combustion at temperatures as low as 225° Fahrenheit.

Burning wood goes through the three stages of combustion in a 1—2—3, 1—2—3 continuous cycle as the flame advances on an irreversibly forward course. External factors, such as the lack of oxygen, can halt the process, but the process cannot stop itself. However, the process of combustion can proceed from 2 to 3 to 1: 2—distillation, 3—charcoaling, 1—ignition = FIRE.

Fire Wood: How Dry Should It Be?

Green growing wood is ninety percent water. In order for wood to burn well, it should be dried to twenty percent moisture, or simply dry to the touch. If you split a piece of firewood open and can feel dampness, sometimes even wetness, it has not yet reached a burnable state. Tell-tale cracks indicate that it is seasoned, but the rain can soak in, and that can raise moisture content to fifty percent or higher. In simple terms, burnable means dry to the touch inside of a split piece.

BTU Output Per Pound

BTU means the volume of heat or the total heat output capability. BTU's per pound of wood is fixed at 8600 units *for any wood*. But, if your wood isn't *dry* (bone dry to the touch inside), you will not be able to extract all 8600 BTU's of energy. Smoke is BTU's lost! The more wood smokes, the more BTU's are lost and the less efficient your wood heat unit is. If you buy wood that smokes badly, then you are losing money. A sure sign of BTU's lost is wood that hisses when it burns. Sometimes any wood will hiss a bit, but if it hisses as loud as you yourself can hiss, it's too wet. Give that load full draft at that point. And then season the rest of that cord before you burn it.

Ember Cleavage

Often times called "coaling," ember cleavage is the innate ability of wood to cleave off (or drop off) a hot burning ember, and build up a stack of red hot coals (hence the term coaling). But, ember cleavage is easier for most people to understand.

As burning wood goes through stage II distillation, the twenty percent remaining water, methane gas, and natural chemicals such as ammonia and alcohol, are distilled out, and the wood totally dries out. Methane gas from stage

II distillation is responsible for about one-half of the flame and heat from burning wood. Accelerated drying results, and accelerated shrinking of the wood fiber, cellulose and lignin takes place. At this point you have small embers of real, natural, charcoal (which is stage III of combustion). These embers cleave, fall off, and form a red hot bed of coals. Ember cleavage gives you the hottest, most efficient stage of the combustion process.

Ash Beds

Ash beds are the secret to good, longlasting fires. They are layers of ash and spent charcoal underneath a fire. They are used to your advantage in two ways:

—The ash bed gets red hot and holds heat underneath the fire. It regenerates heat for continuous Stage II of combustion—getting the wood above it hot and keeping it hot. Without heat from below, you won't have good flame on large pieces of wood.

—It can be formed into a channel, wide in front and narrowing upward toward the rear. This channels air—especially in fireplaces—under the center of the fire and up the "fireback"—the back wall—which is usually slanted forward to create a "draw" of air upward.

HOW TO BUILD AN ASH BED

A bed of ash is a fused layer of spent ash and coals three to six inches deep. To begin building a bed, burn pine (especially for covering furnace grates), because pine leaves behind large pieces of spent charcoal. Hardwoods burn to a powder, and therefore won't build a bed of ash. After each fire, leave the coals alone. Build each new fire on the old layer of ash. The high heat from the fire above will fuse the ash and new coals together. Don't poke it, and don't rake the grates. After several days to several weeks of fires, the ash and half-burnt coals will fuse into an airtight, heat-retaining ash bed.

THE FUNCTION OF AN ASH BED IN A FURNACE

2″ loop handle

4′ long, curved

2″ hook

In order to manually operate a furnace properly and conserve fuel, you must have an ash bed. You cannot turn down (damper off) a manually operated furnace at night and then slow-burn stacked dry logs all night, unless it's done on an ash bed.

Don't rake a manually operated furnace—it is not necessary. The ash bed should be three to six inches thick, with one air hole, poked in the same spot each time. Angle the poker down in front. If the bed gets too thick, scoop or shovel the excess off the top. If you rake it, you'll probably ruin the ash bed. You'll wind up with all or most of it down in the ash pit. Night fires can only have a small amount of air, and they should be laid out on a bed of red hot coals. Do this with hardwoods, and you'll have hot, glowing coals left six to eight hours later. A small pile of tinder and kindling, fanned by a bellows, will then start a morning fire.

THE AIR HOLE

An ash bed is not as delicate as a sand castle, but the air hole is. It can meander around the bed, but a little care will keep it in front, just inside the door. If it gets a little too big, flatten out a tin can and wedge it in the rear of the enlarged opening; or use a piece of terra cotta tile to close it up. Don't poke in the side walls; that will only make the hole bigger.

Burning Characteristics

HARDWOOD

Hardwood is good as a fuel source because it is very dense, burns hot and slow, and leaves behind almost no ash. However, it takes a little longer to get started, does not cleave enough to give a quick bed of ash, and takes a little longer to give off high sustained heat. So, start a fire off with a stack of soft wood, and then add on the hardwood.

SOFTWOODS

Pines and other evergreens burn hot and fast because of the pine pitch content. If used for kindling, they give quick flames, they cleave very fast, and they give you a good bed of coals to put hardwood on.

Pines, evergreens and poplars (aspens) won't last as long at night (during turn down) as will oak or hardwoods. So, if you live in the northwestern United States or any region where the only wood available is softwood, get a medium or large size stove that accommodates a large load of wood.

Basic Stacking Rules for Fireplaces and Woodstoves

1. *Base*: Two large pieces of wood laid parallel with the direction of draft, usually front to rear, and no farther apart than your logs are long. About one foot is good.

2. *Tinder*: Sometimes called starter, it burns very fast and lights the kindling. (Fill the ash bed channel between the two base logs with it.)

3. *Kindling*: Lay crosswise, over the base logs, finger size up to wrist size pieces of wood, close together (touching each other), then repeat with another layer crosswise in the opposite direction.

4. *Split logs* or quartered logs: Lay them close together, about a finger width apart, crosswise in the opposite direction of the last layer of kindling.

Tinder: Starts the Kindling

Any fine, very dry, natural fiber can be used as tinder. It should be so fine and dry that it crackles when you ball it up. It can be pine needles, very fine pine limb tips, or a ball of dry grass or hay. Best of all are dry, brittle pine cones. The pine pitch makes them burn very hot, and quite long.

Around the household, use the following:

—Brown paper bags. They burn slow and hot. Tear the bags into dinner plate sized pieces, and crush each piece into a ball.

—Corrugated cardboard box. Also very good. Tear it into hand-sized pieces and crush into balls.

—Newspaper. It will work well if you unfold the paper, lay it flat on the floor, grab the center of each sheet, and then crumble it into a ball by drawing the sheet into the center.

Kindling

Kindling lights the stack of wood from the inside out. The best kindling is pine, split down to the size of your finger.

—You should use at least a double hand full.

—If you have trouble stacking kindling, tie it into a bundle with some string, lay it over the tinder in the ash bed channel between your two base logs, then stack the rest of your split logs on top.

KINDLING FEEDER STICKS

If the fire in your fireplace lags, or if your wood is a bit green or damp, you need to make long, kindling-thick pieces of pine called feeder sticks. When the flame dies off a stack of wood, slide two or three of these sticks into the hot coals in the channel and they will feed flames back into your stack.

Fireplace Basics

Fireplaces are usually a focal point for a party or an evening of relaxation. Follow the stacking rules that we have previously outlined and, when starting a new fire, use very dry halved or quartered pieces, not more than six inches in diameter.

Since fireplace heat is not well contained, you must stack the pieces close together, about one finger width apart, because in simplest terms, it takes fire to make fire. Logs feed off each other, so unless close contact with flame is maintained, a log will go out as soon as the outside is charred. Don't skimp on wood. Stack your fires about one cubic foot in size.

Many people have trouble getting fires going in a fireplace simply because they use small round logs with the bark on. Since bark is a protective coating, and since the round shape resists ember cleavage, split the logs, stack them flat side down, and they will burn better.

AIR FLOW

To get the best results from your fireplaces, you must have a bed of ash around the andiron arms, or under the grate basket. The bed should then be formed into

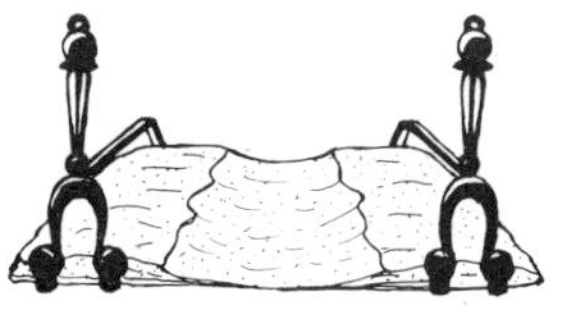

a channel or trough. This directs the draft under and then up the back of your stack of wood.

Note: A good way to start the draft going is to put a row of newspaper balls along the fire back. Light each end of the row, then light your tinder. The tall flames from the newspaper balls will send a good jet of air up the chimney that will start your upward draft.

Fireplace Stacking

—Keep the stack of wood near the fireback. It doesn't matter whether you use grates, andirons, or build it on the ash bed. The best draft is near the rear.
—Always put the split side of a log toward the center of the fire, or put the split side down if the log is split in half.
—If you stack wood right on the ash bed, lay two six-inch diameter pieces front to rear (flat side down to keep them from rolling) about a foot apart. These pieces help channel the draft to the rear, and allow the channel to stay open, even after the fire is going well and the coals begin building up beneath the stack. Also, the channel can be filled with tinder after the kindling and split logs are stacked.
—Always stack in a square. Lay two or three pieces one way, then two or three pieces the opposite way.
—Andiron stacking is slightly different, because you only have four small points of contact to hold the stack of wood up. Stack two large pieces on the bottom, across the andirons and over the ash bed trough, and then decrease the size of each piece as you stack upward. This way, your points of contact won't burn out and collapse the stack.
—In a grate basket, put in several inches of kindling, then add on several four-inch diameter pieces of wood, split side down. In grates, small pieces of split wood burn better than large unsplit logs. Always put the tinder *underneath* a grate, because the weight of the kindling and logs will crush tinder and prevent it from burning.
—When adding new wood, or when restacking a seemingly burnt out fire, don't stomp the old coals with a poker. Just because you don't see bright flame, don't think you've lost the fire. As the flames die away and embers and coals build a mound, you now have stage III of combustion—charcoal. It's the hottest, most efficient phase of burning. If you beat it down with a poker, as most people like to do, you actually hurt the process. Use the poker to gently move most of the large pieces to the center, build a new stack on top of that, then gently fan it with a bellows. The heat from the mound of glowing charcoal will put a blaze up the center of a new stack of wood.

THE "LONG BURNER" LOG

The large log near the fireback will burn slowly and will keep the area hot enough so that stack after stack of smaller pieces will light easily and continually burn with good flame.

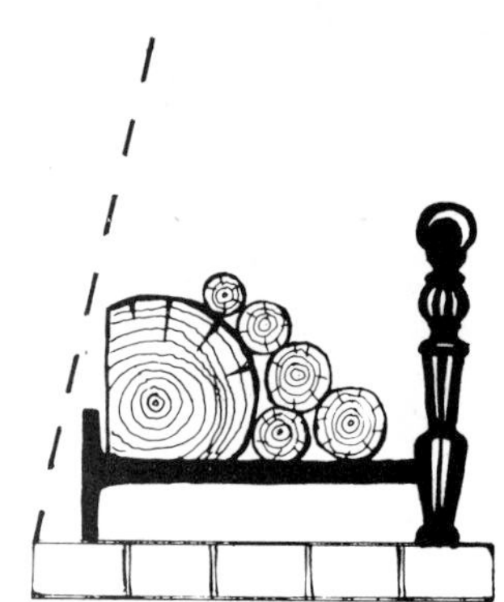

To make a long burner log, start off with a very dry log a foot longer than your andirons are wide. It should be about twelve to fifteen inches in diameter. Split or saw off two sides as shown, and you'll have a good long burning log that won't roll forward, and that will generate heat to ignite subsequent additions of wood.

THE ALL-NIGHTER STACK

If you are using a large masonry fireplace with built-in electric or a natural hot air flow circulators, and if you want to use it to supply heat during the night, there are a few necessary rules to follow:

—Because of its *mass*, a masonry fireplace and its rock or concrete slab mantle stores heat and then slowly releases it all night long. So, start heating up the fireplace six hours before you go to bed.
—You must have fairly airtight glass doors on it, with a good, built-in draft door on the bottom.
—Fires right on the ash bed always last longest. Several hours before you retire, build up a bed of red hot coals, three to four inches deep. Then stack three large, very dry oak logs on it, back against the fireback. Close the glass doors, adjust the bottom draft, and the fire will glow well into the night.

Apartment Fireplaces

Many apartment fireplaces are not designed to safely sustain a roaring fire for long periods of time. I have seen apartment fireplaces that had wood facing installed as close as four inches from the opening of the front of the firebox. It should be eighteen inches away, according to National Fire Protection Association standards. If you have an apartment house fireplace, keep your fires small and in the center. Keep the fire away from the walls as you cannot tell how well the side and back walls have been insulated. If it is an approved "zero-clearance" fireplace, then you probably will not need to worry; but still, keep the size of your fires reasonable.

Wood Stove Fires

To initially heat up a unit, stack small kindling-size pieces in your stove until it is *no more than* one-third full. The larger the volume of the flame, the faster the energy is released. This gives you high combustion efficiency and a very intense generation of heat. After a fast burn, you will have raised the temperature of your stove to a safe operating level, and you will have a bed of hot coals to sustain larger pieces of wood. Now put logs or quartered pieces on; and the slower burning logs will maintain heat output.

Two cautions:

1. Don't over-fire a brand new cast iron stove.
2. Keep your chimney clean, especially the throat area, or fast-burning fires will cause a chimney fire in a creosote-lined chimney.

AIR FLOW

Fire results in the expansion of gases and hot air. Thus, a jet of air is pushed up the chimney as long as there is fire in the firebox. This push of air up also creates a pull through the bottom draft door. You must regulate both draft and damper equally, or you'll disrupt the flow.

If you close the top damper but not the bottom draft, you'll get smoke in the firebox and possibly into your house. Open the top damper before you open the door. If you close the bottom draft but not the top damper, you cut off your combustion air; and also, you won't contain some necessary back-pressure, which gives you high heat. Without a certain amount of back-pressure to maintain high heat, you'll lose your fire faster. Normal settings for damper and draft are only two-thirds open.

It is this push-pull principle that makes airtight stoves so efficient, and thus superior heating units.

HOT BURNING

When you burn softwoods, split the pieces small, hot burn them fairly fast, and reduce them to stage III charcoal; then dampen off the air and let them smolder. The creosote is thereby burned off, and the coals will produce a long, *hot* release of heat. But you must turn down the push-pull draft and damper on a stove full of coals, or you'll needlessly lose half of your heat. This simple principle can be used for hardwood, especially if the wood is wet or a bit green. For people who live in the West, Auburn University has found that fir gives off less creosote than pine.

DAMPER SETTINGS AND DRAFT

At night, the top damper should be set at a maximum of three-quarters closed, or you may get smoke in your house, and you may smother your fire. The bottom draft should be about three-quarters closed too. Dry wood needs less air, while damp or unseasoned wood needs more air.

Note: Roaring hot fires should *never* be left unattended. If you leave your house, damper down the fire.

LOAD LIMITS

A stove glowing red hot is 1400° Fahrenheit. That is a dangerous situation. Wood stoves and fireplaces are not designed to operate red hot. Some stove pipe will warp from such excessive heat. Also, there will almost certainly be a chimney fire if there is one-quarter inch or more of creosote inside the chimney (a one-month build-up). *Never overload a wood stove or fireplace.* Follow the load limits suggested here:

—Never load a wood heat unit over three-quarters full, inside height.
—Never load a wood heat unit more than half full in solid volume. In other

words, for hot fires with a full draft, logs inside should not equal more than half of the total inside volume of the load capacity of the unit.

—Never fire a wood heat unit that is full of kindling. The heat intensity of kindling is ten times that of solid wood.

—Never burn more than one "sterno-type" compressed log at a time. Many contain petroleum in the form of paraffin, which bonds the wood chips together. These compressed logs burn three times as hot as ordinary wood.

"RED HOT" STOVE SHUTDOWN

1. Close the bottom draft. (Eliminate all intake air).
2. Close the top damper. (Keep the smoke in the stove to kill the flame).

This is the same procedure that you use to stop a chimney fire. But, while most chimney fires will go out if all intake air is shut off, the overheated stove is in danger of being warped. So, let it cool down *slowly*, by itself.

—Never throw water on the stove.

—Never use a CO_2 fire extinguisher on it.

Either of the above will severely warp and damage the unit.

How to Use a Coal Grate

If your wood stove is designed for burning both wood and coal, using a coal grate to carry a fire long into the night is relatively simple. After the unit is hot and the chimney draw is sufficiently strong to be safe for coal use, spread the hot wood embers under the grate to form an air channel. That's important because, as Benjamin Franklin discovered, coal needs air from *below* or it won't burn. Next, line the bottom of the grate with fresh dry kindling, and on top of that put a thick layer of nut grade coal. Light the kindling, give it full draft with the damper open, and it should catch fire. After about thirty minutes you can reduce the draft, but *never* close off the damper completely, or coal gas will seep into your house.

Coal Gas

"Coal gas" is carbon monoxide plus sulfur gas, and the very words strike a note of alarm in people who have used parlor stoves to heat their homes. Coal gas is deadly, and it has killed entire families while they slept. The statistics are grim.

The growing number of wood stoves will bring back the use of coal to carry a fire long into the night. But the dangerous lack of knowledge about the carbon monoxide that solid fuel heaters can generate is also going to make "coal gas" a household word again. The improper venting of wood stoves is the cause. Coal should *not* be used in a wood stove that does not have an airtight, unified chimney system. Further, remember these rules before using coal:

1. Keep the chimney *free* of creosote, or the carbon monoxide will be forced into your house, rather than up the chimney.
2. If your stove "back-puffs" constantly, don't use coal.
3. If your stove has a top loading door or lid, install an "ideal" flow chimney to vent the gases quickly and smoothly.

4. Always close the doors when burning coal.
5. Always use a coal grate.
6. Never close the top damper while the bottom draft is open, or you'll force coal gas into your house.

Ten Commandments of Wood Burning Safety

1. Open the damper, full on, before building the fire.
2. Do a visual inspection every time before lighting a fire.
3. Never overload the unit—half to two-thirds is maximum.
4. Never use flash-flammable liquids to light a fire.
5. Never keep any burnable item within eight feet of a fireplace or stove.
6. Always keep a door or spark guard across the front of a wood heat unit.
7. Keep small children away from woodstoves and fireplaces.
8. Never leave a roaring fire unattended in either a fireplace or wood stove.
9. Dispose of ashes *safely*. Do not put them in a cardboard carton, for example.
10. Do a monthly chimney inspection for creosote buildup.

Summary

The design of safe wood heat units is the responsibility of a manufacturer; but the operation and sustained use of a unit is the responsibility of its owner.

A wood heat unit can be safe and efficient if the person using it follows the procedures mentioned in this book; and building efficient fires is no more difficult than reading this chapter.

MAINTENANCE 14

Daily Maintenance Checklist

1. Clean away any combustible material from within eight feet of the unit.
2. Sweep the floor and hearth area to prevent burnable wood-dust and woodchips from accumulating in front of the firebox opening. (Resin sparks can go through even a tiny mesh screen.)
3. Rotate the damper 360° to check for a "sandpaper" sound when turning. This usually means creosote buildup in the chimney.
4. Check the throat of the chimney (where it joins the woodstove) for crusty creosote buildup.
5. Check the ash bed layer (and the air intake hole in a furnace).
6. Before building the fire, light a match and hold it up in the chimney throat or in the door opening. If the house is warmer than the outside, air should be moving up the chimney, and that means that the chimney is open.
7. Double check the door, damper, and air controls before leaving the newly lighted fire.

Once-a-Month Maintenance Checklist

1. Inspect the entire wood heat system, inside and outside of your house. Look for any cracks, burned out bolts, any odd-looking defects; and especially, check for any pre-fab metal chimney supports that may have been blown loose by the wind.
2. Check the door for warpage. It must fit tight to be safe.
3. Check all of the chimney joints.
4. Clean out the chimney throat, and clean it well!
5. Run a snug-fitting chimney brush down and back up the chimney at least two times.
6. Check next month's stack of firewood for dryness.

Accessories Needed for Daily Use

1. A four-foot long poker (especially if you have a wood furnace).
2. A long pair of tongs for rearranging a burned out fire which has left behind hot, smoldering end pieces.
3. A bellows.
4. A Cape Cod kerosene lighter pot, if you live along the damp sea coast.
5. A four-foot scoop shovel.
6. An ash/coal bucket (called a scuttle).
7. Three chimney fire extinguisher flares.

Note: All of the above are usually available from a good wood energy retailer.

Choosing and Using a Chimney Brush

If you have an eight-inch flue, then you'll normally get one-quarter to one-half inch of flake creosote inside each month. You'll also have about one-eighth to one-quarter inch of hard black glossy creosote on each chimney wall. The inside dimensions will be reduced by anywhere from a half inch to an inch because of the buildup of creosote.

Creosote may seem soft, but it flakes off in quarter or half-dollar sized pieces and clogs up an eight-inch brush within about five feet of the start of the monthly cleanout. The brush's spring steel bristles sweep the flakes off as they pass by, so an excessively tight-fitting brush will clog quickly. In this case, use two brushes, a seven-inch and an eight-inch; make two passes with the seven-inch and then two passes with the eight-inch.

Safety Note: Never use chains, tire chains, or anything other than a proper fitting chimney brush to clean a chimney. Chains can break the tile flue lining.

Chimney brushes usually can go one way only. If the fit is tight, as in an eight-inch brush going through a dirty eight-inch chimney, it is nearly impossible to reverse direction, because the spring steel bristles will not bend (bow in) and snap back in the opposite direction. If you have a chimney brush that is just a bit too tight to go easily through the chimney, then use a steel nail cutter to trim one-quarter inch off two adjoining sides.

VACUUM CLEANERS

Industrial grade vacuum cleaners are useful for cleaning out chimneys; blowing sawdust out of chain saws; vacuuming around a wood heat unit; and vacuuming up water spills. They cost fifty to seventy-five dollars at most hardware stores.

Checklist of needed features:

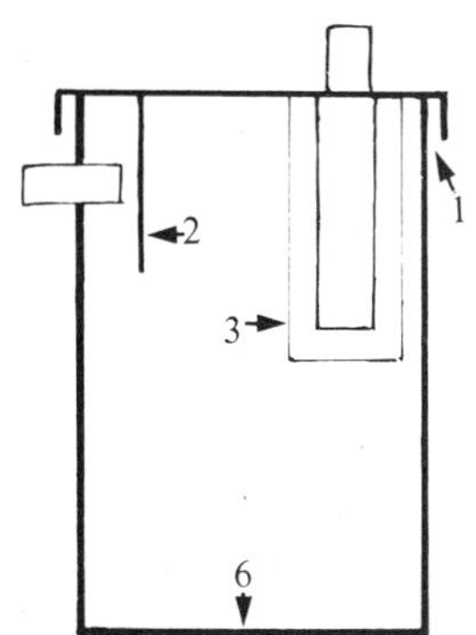

1. Good seal.
2. Water stop.
3. Large polyfoam filter.
4. Extra lengths of flexible exhaust hose. (The polyfoam filter will catch large pieces of creosote flakes, but the airborne dust must be blown out of the nearest window.)
5. Extra lengths of narrow, stiff hose for reaching to the inside of the chimney base.
6. Two-gallon canister.

Reducing Creosote Buildup

—Match the inside chimney flue diameter to the flue port size of the unit.
—Avoid ninety-degree elbows, if at all possible. Build an "ideal flow" chimney for best performance (see typical installations).
—Install your chimney *inside* your house, whether it is pre-fab metal or masonry.
—Maintain a high chimney flue temperature, 300° to 400°F (which is half as hot as the 700° on the inside of your stove). Hot fires and/or a chimney thermometer make it easy to accomplish that. Creosote is condensed smoke, so a well-insulated, hot chimney, will keep the smoke moving outside where it is supposed to go. Use class A, triple-wall, air insulated, or double-wall asbestos-insulated pre-fab chimney sections (whatever local codes require), or have a *vermiculite-insulated* masonry chimney built.
—Avoid green wood, wet wood, or pines and softwoods at night during turndown. If you must use any of these, vacuum your chimney throat every week, and clean the entire chimney every month.

The more creosote you allow to build up inside a chimney, the hotter a chimney fire will be, and thus the more damaging it can be to flue tiles or a metal, pre-fab chimney. A chimney fire from a creosote buildup of about a half-inch will generate temperatures of about 1600°F[1]. *But*: a creosote buildup that is an inch or more thick can generate temperatures in excess of 3,000°F[2]; and that can melt metal, or expand chimney flue linings until they crack and break. Further, "Because of its acidity, creosote is corrosive to steel and other materials (all types of flue linings). And, the corrosive effect of creosote was observed to be most severe after chimney fires."[3] The National Fire Protection

1. Auburn Woodburning Laboratory.
2. Dura Vent Corporation.
3. Auburn Woodburning Laboratory.

Association says that the first chimney fire can be bad, the second serious, and the third often burns the house down, because each chimney fire deteriorates the metal or tile flue lining until a fire of 3,000° generates enough heat to leave the containment of the chimney and ignite wood directly, or it heats up nearby combustible wood walls until they ignite through quick charcoaling and spontaneous combustion.

Chimney Fires

Dense, light grey smoke pouring out of the top of a chimney usually means a chimney fire. And if you hear a roar, or a snap-crackle-pop "Rice Krispies" sound inside the chimney, *it is a chimney fire.*

A chimney fire is exactly like a charcoal fire, and just as hot. And like a charcoal fire, there is no readily visible flame, only an intense red glow. Because there is no flame to spread the fire, it takes a movement of air to keep it going. The jet of air going up the chimney from the push-pull effect of the entire wood heat system keeps the chimney fire going—hotter and hotter the longer it lasts. But, if you stop the jet of air, the fire usually is arrested and will burn itself out.

PREVENTING CHIMNEY FIRES

1. Never use a fireplace, woodstove, or furnace for a trash incinerator.
2. Never start a fire in a wood heat unit that is full of kindling.
3. Never stuff a dried-out Christmas tree into a wood heat unit.
4. Never put full draft on a large, restacked fire, because once the chimney is hot, the shot of flame and sparks from a new fire will set excess creosote on fire.

PUTTING OUT A CHIMNEY FIRE

1. Close the air intakes.
2. Close the damper.
3. Close the chimney cap damper if your masonry chimney has one.
4. Put a lighted chimney fire extinguisher in the stove. (Read the manufacturer's directions the day you buy the extinguisher flare.)
5. If the chimney fire isn't out in three to five minutes, call your local fire department.
6. If it does go out, don't open the door or damper for at least thirty minutes, or it will start up all over again.

TYPICAL CHIMNEY INSTALLATIONS 15

Ideal Flow Installation

Always install with maintenance in mind. That means installing stovepipe in a way that does not resist smoke flow out of the chimney. The faster smoke leaves the chimney, the less creosote that will build up. Less creosote buildup means less maintenance, although a monthly inspection and/or clean-out should be part of wood energy use. The use of forty-five degree joints instead of ninety degree elbows allows the hot gases and creosote to leave the chimney smoothly and quickly, and that insures less creosote buildup. If the stove or fireplace does not allow you to run a chimney brush up into the forty-five degree slope, than make the section removable for cleaning.

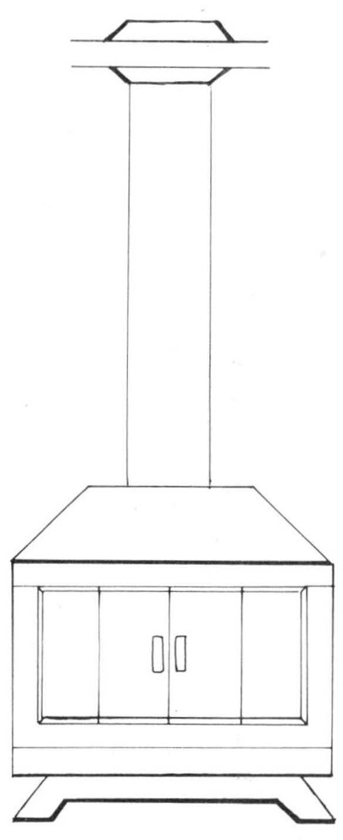

Vertical installation is preferable.

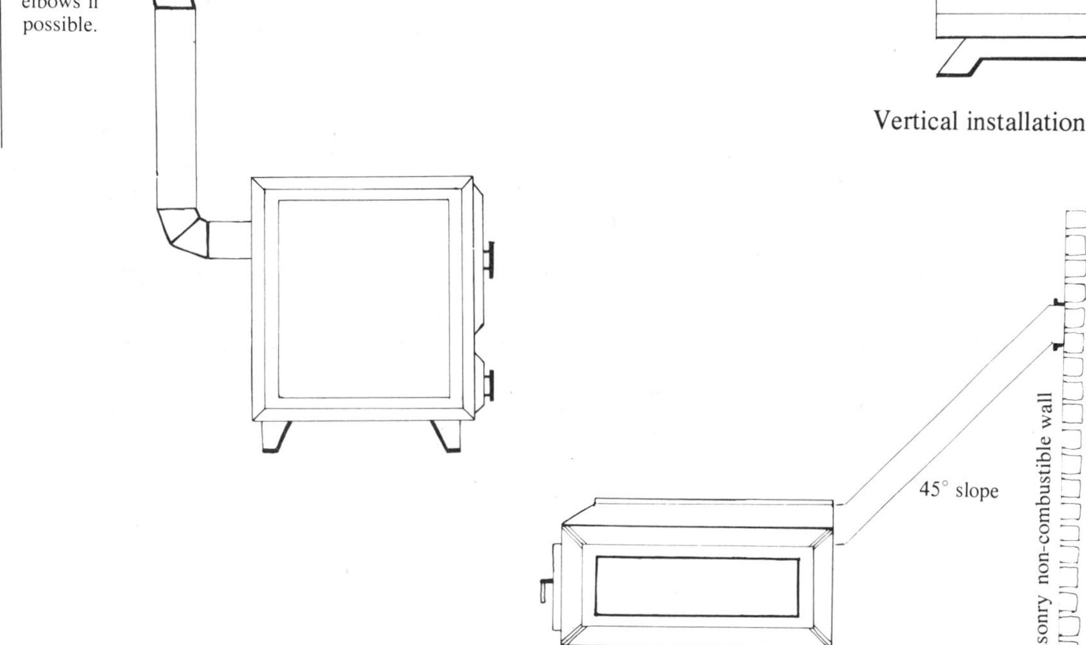

Safety note: do not use this type of hook-up with a combustible wall unless NFPA approved protection can be applied to the walls.

National Fire Protection Association Recommended Minimum Clearances for Combustible Walls and Ceilings

	Freestanding Fireplaces and Stoves	Stovepipe
Unprotected	36″	18″
¼″ asbestos millboard spaced out 1″	18″	12″
28 ga. sheet metal on ¼″ asbestos millboard	18″	12″
28 ga. sheet metal spaced out 1″	12″	9″
28 ga. sheet metal on ⅛″ asbestos millboard spaced out 1″	12″	9″
¼″ asbestos millboard on 1″ mineral fiber batts reinforced with wire mesh or equivalent	12″	6″
22 ga. sheet metal on 1″ mineral fiber batts reinforced with wire mesh or equivalent	12″	3″

(Adapted from Tables 1 and 2, NFPA Bulletin HS-10)

Author's Note: Asbestos millboard is soft like thick paper board. Some asbestos sheeting is hard and brittle, which is *unacceptable* for this application because its density transfers heat, whereas soft millboard does not.

STOVE PIPE INSTALLATION

Stove pipe is single-walled pipe. It should be a stainless steel or galvanized steel pipe. If used, it must only be used from the stove to the thimble (which protects the wall where the pipe passes through). *Never* use it outside a house, or up through an attic. Stove pipe clearances are less than for stoves because the area facing the combustible wall or ceiling is smaller.

—Stovepipe thickness should be at least 24 gauge.

—Secure each stovepipe joint with three sheet metal screws.

—Support stovepipe if length of unsupported run is six feet or more.

—Stovepipe should only extend into the chimney to the inner surface of the flue liner.

—Secure chimney connection with high temperature furnace cement.

—Never pass an uninsulated stovepipe through a ceiling (a thimble must be used for all walls and ceilings).

—Pass uninsulated stovepipe through an outside wall by using an approved thimble.

VENT CLEARANCES

We recommend that a factory designed and tested thimble be used to vent a fireplace or wood stove through a wall. The thimble can be fire clay or metal. The dealer that you purchase the thimble from will tell you what the exact installation requirements are for that particular model.

Safety Note: Do not chisel a hole into an existing masonry chimney to vent a stovepipe into it. You could damage the tile flue, a potentially dangerous situation. Consult a licensed chimney builder for help.

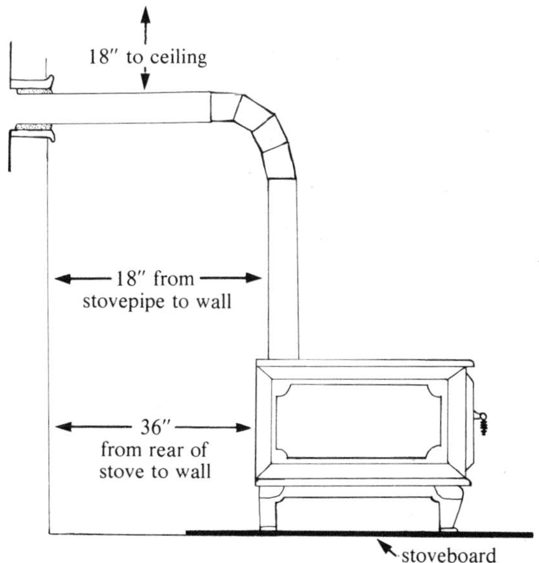

Clearances from NFPA Bulletin HS-10.

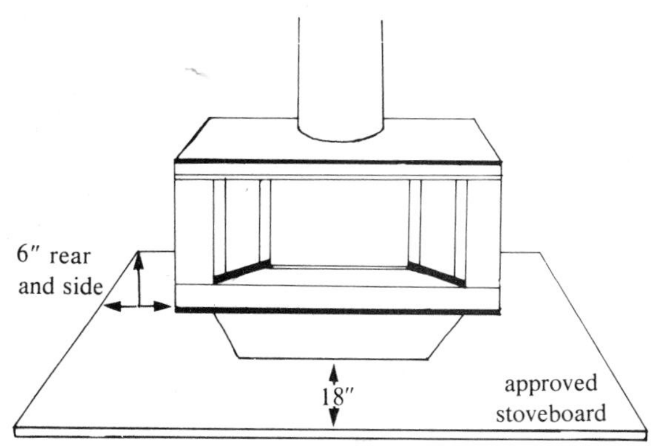

The front is the most important area to protect from sparks, though all sides should be well protected. *Clearances from NFPA Bulletin HS-10.*

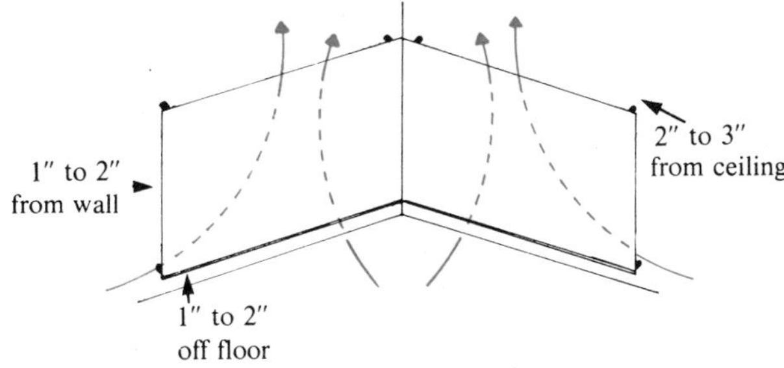

The purpose of the 1″ to 2″ airspace is to allow the air to rise and carry the heat up and away. Since nails conduct heat directly into wood, they should not be used directly opposite the hottest or nearest point of a stove.

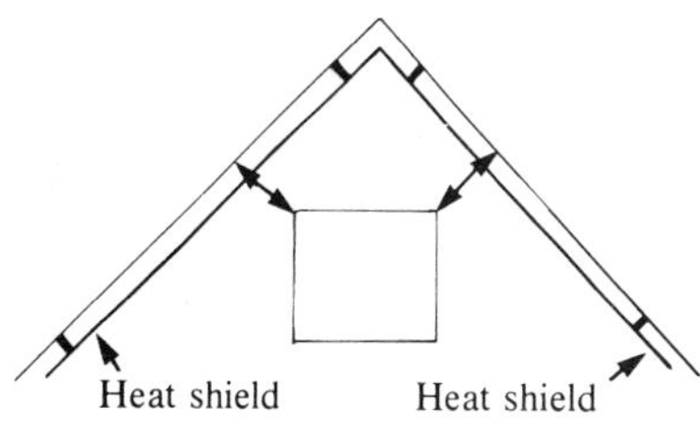

The clearance of a unit is measured from the point of the unit that is closest to the wall.

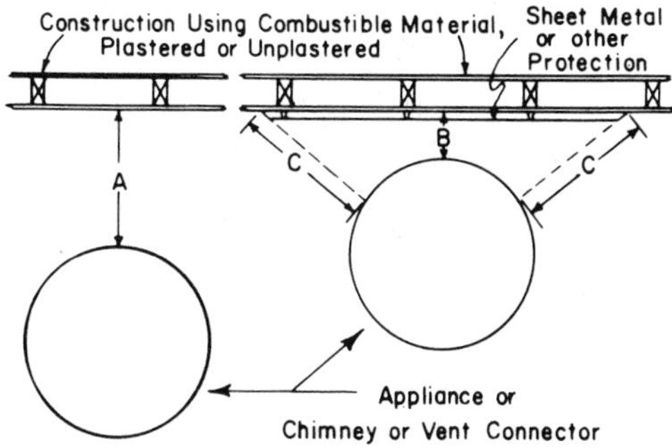

A equals the required clearance with no protection as specified in "National Fire Protection Association Minimum Clearances for Combustible Walls and Ceilings." *B* equals the reduced clearances permitted in accordance with NFPA minimum clearances. The protection applied to the wall should extend far enough in each direction to make C equal to A. *From Figure 5, NFPA Bulletin HS-10.*

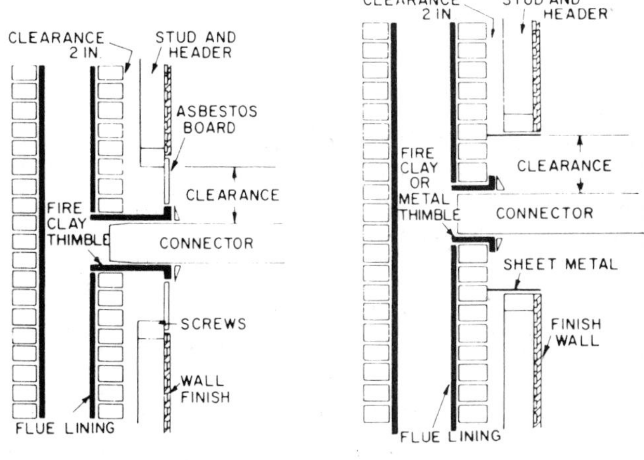

Figure A   Figure B

For chimney connectors passing through combustible walls, asbestos millboard (fig. A), sheet metal, or a metal lath and plaster finish may be used. In Figure A, the minimum clearance on all sides is 18″ from combustibles. In Figure B, surround the thimble with 8″ or more of brickwork or equivalent fireproof material. *From Figure 7, NFPA Bulletin HS-10.*

CHIMNEY CLEARANCES FOR REDUCED CLEARANCE STOVES

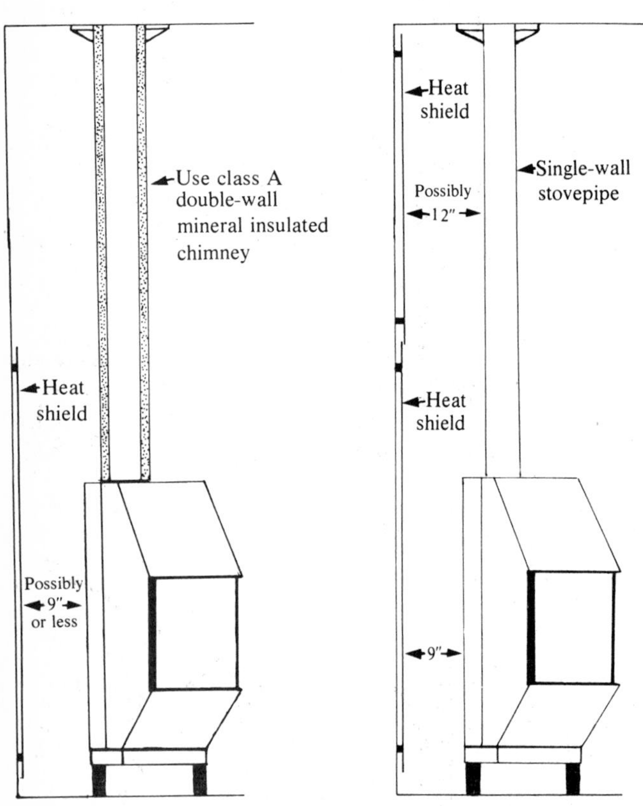

If you install a reduced clearance unit that brings the chimney closer than 18" to the wall, then the chimney must be Class A, insulated; or, you must use an approved heat shield behind the stovepipe. (From Tables 1 and 2, NFPA HS-10)

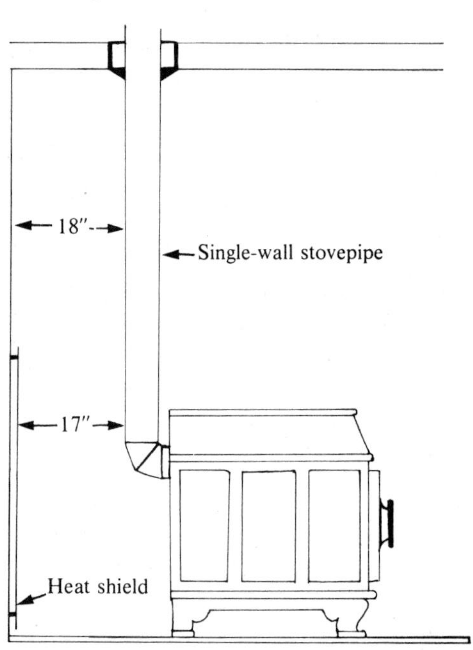

If you install an approved heat shield to reduce the wall clearance of a *rear vented* stove, don't forget that uninsulated stovepipe must still be 18" from the wall. *Clearances from Table 2, NFPA Bulletin HS-10.*

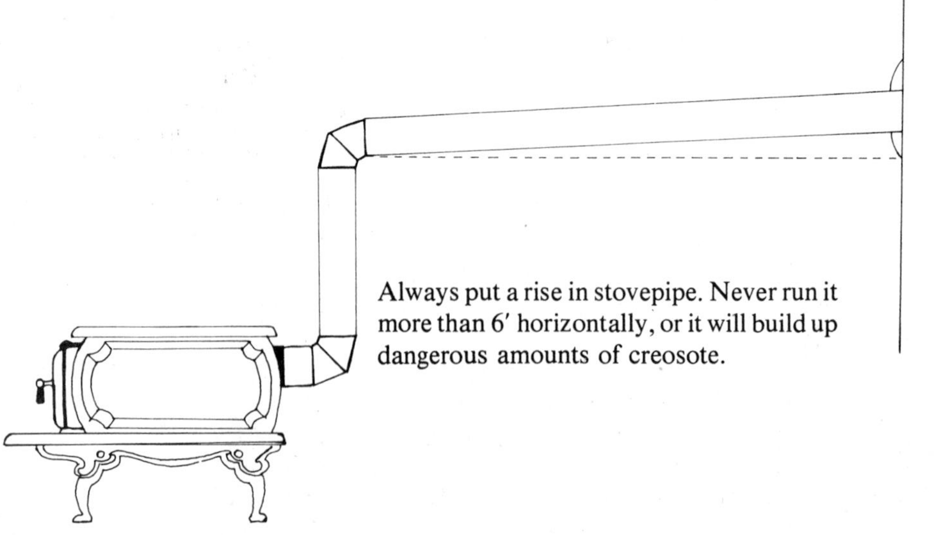

Always put a rise in stovepipe. Never run it more than 6' horizontally, or it will build up dangerous amounts of creosote.

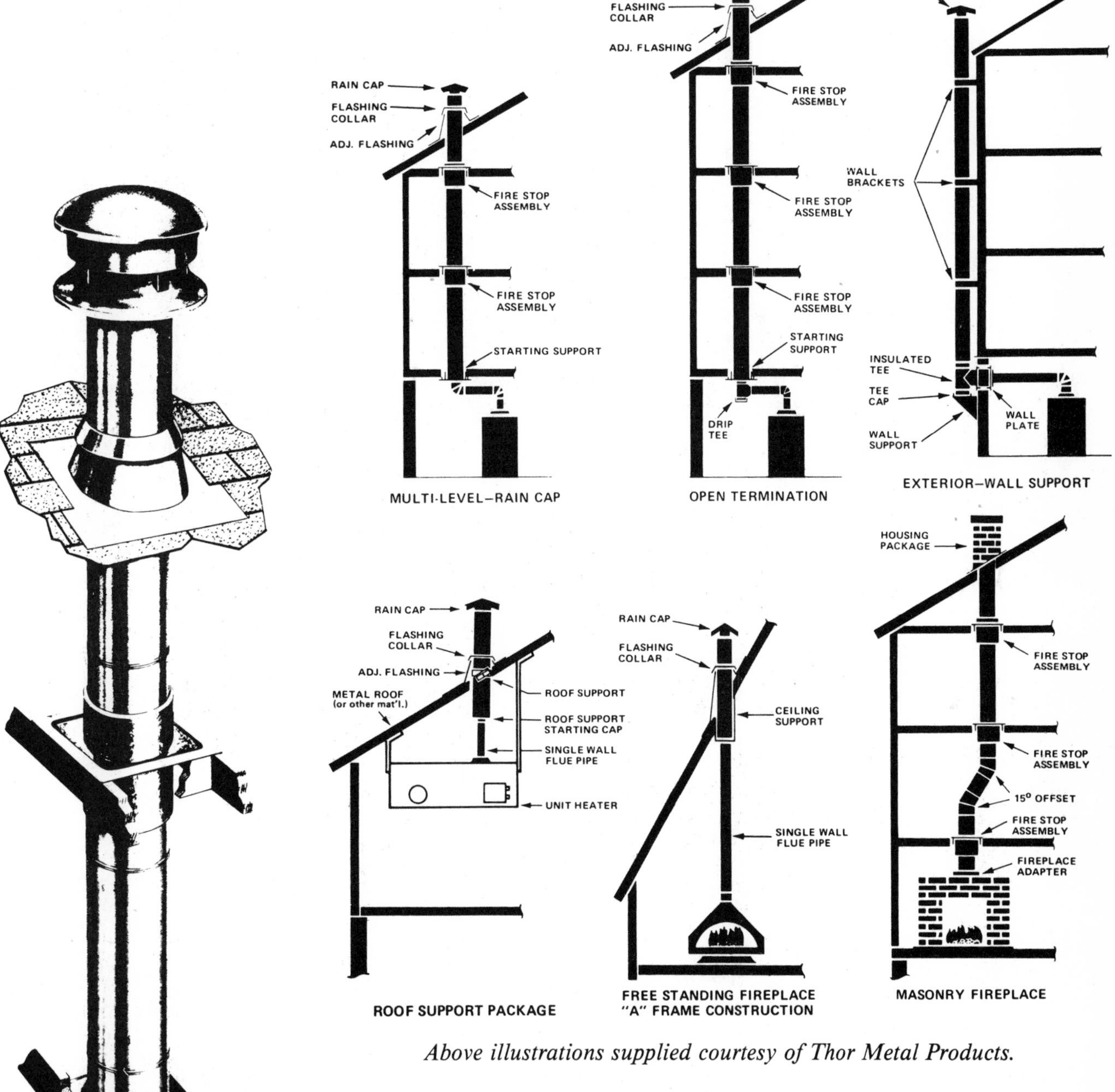

Above illustrations supplied courtesy of Thor Metal Products.

Note the 2″ clearance between the chimney shaft and the wood. Also, the heavy bands around the joints are locking bands, which are a good safety addition to any chimney. *Illustration supplied courtesy of Metalbestos Chimney Systems.*

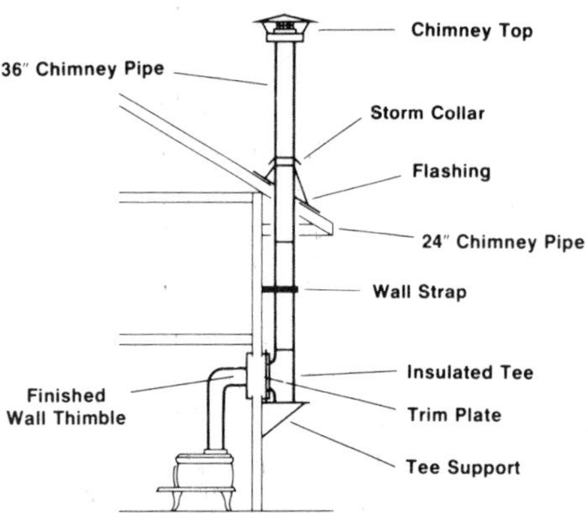

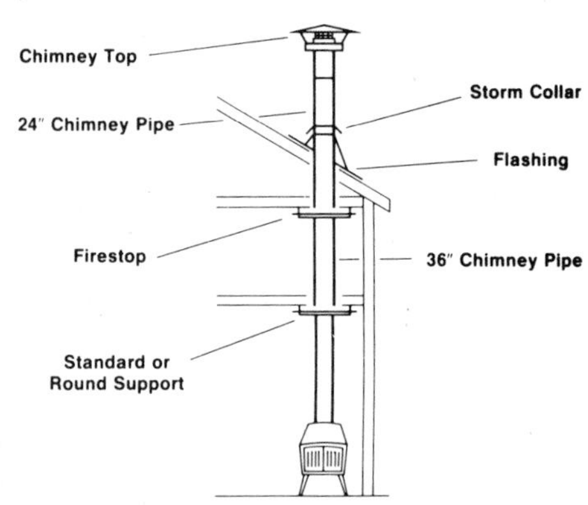

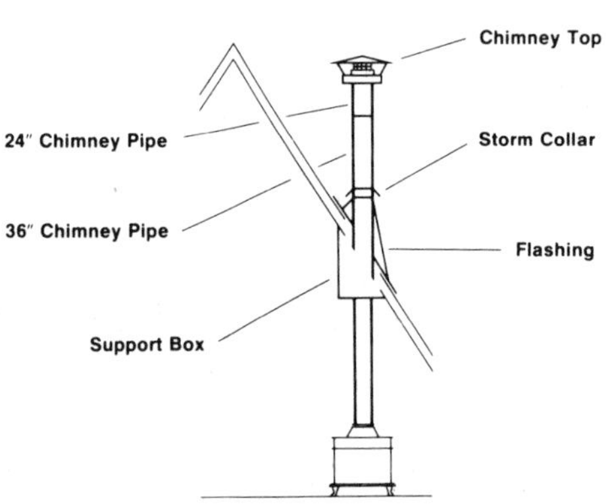

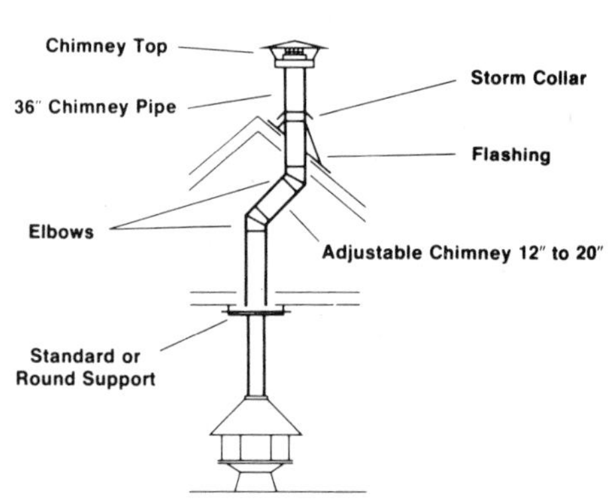

Above illustrations supplied courtesy of Dura-Vent Corporation.

Masonry Chimney Basics

A masonry chimney must be a solid structure, standing two inches away from, and independent of, the wood frame of a house. Unless it is part of the footing (concrete support wall) of a house, it must have an approved building code base below the frost line, matched to the weight bearing capacity of the soil on which it stands. Only an experienced, licensed chimney builder should do the construction, or you could void your fire insurance coverage in the event of a fire that is traced to an improperly built chimney system. Ask the mason to build a chimney with a *round* flue, because round flues resist creosote build-up better than square flues.

Call your local building code official to obtain the necessary requirements for your area.

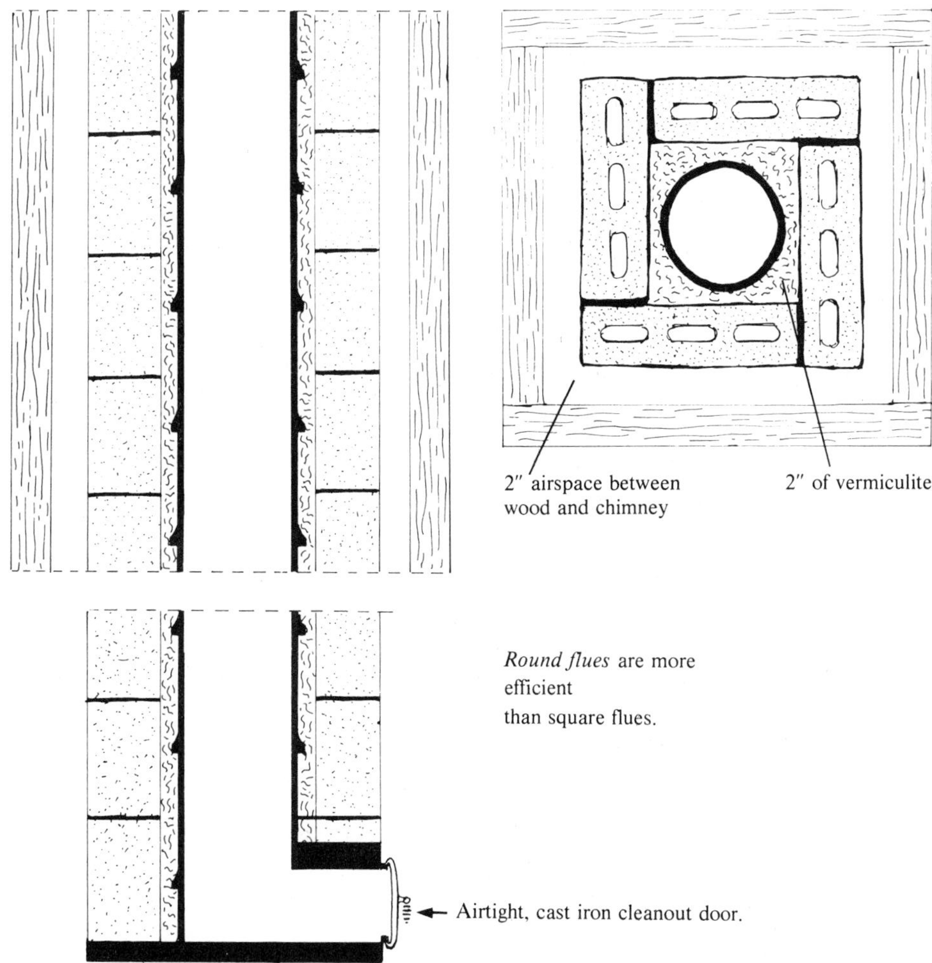

Inserts and Wood Stoves in Masonry Fireplaces

CAUTION: Improper installation of this type of unit can be dangerous. Fireplace inserts, and wood stoves installed in a masory fireplace, do not allow for a unified chimney system. The lack of an airtight connecting pipe between the flue port (flue collar) and the throat of the masonry chimney causes eddies of turbulent and stagnant smoke to condense into creosote, which begins to build up on the inside walls of the old fireplace, and in the entire chimney. Unless an airtight seal is created around the face shield, or around the frame of the unit where it rests against the face of the masonry, cool air filtering in along the body of the unit will further cause smoke to cool and condense into creosote. Thus a dangerous build-up can occur in the chimney *and* in the old fireplace itself. At the summer Wood Energy Institute meeting in St. Louis on September 11, 1979, chimney sweeps reported a growing number of dangerous chimney fires being caused by improper installation of fireplace inserts and wood stoves that are simply "pushed" into a masonry fireplace.

Therefore, *FireFacts* recommends that you consider the following guidelines when purchasing or using fireplace inserts or wood stoves installed in an existing masonry fireplace, where the use is intended to be for primary or secondary heating of your home.

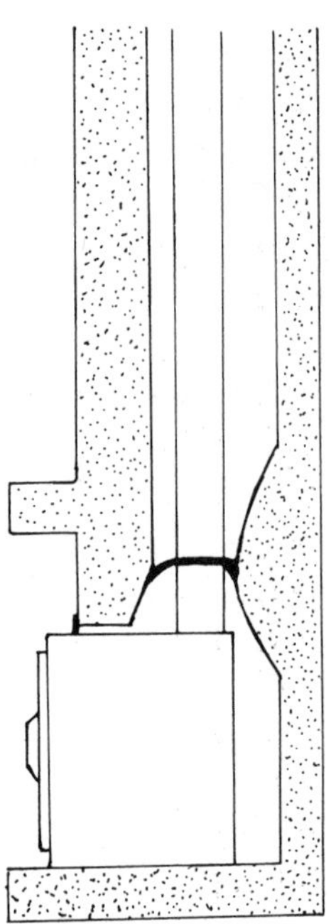

First: The unit should have an airtight, *unified* chimney system, preferably insulated bottom to top (see "Upgrading for Safety and Efficiency.")

Second: The outside flange, where the unit rests against the face of the masonry fireplace (sides, top, and bottom) must be sealed. Fiberglass in itself is not a sealer, so in conjunction with that, use a high temperature sealant sold at a heating supply retail outlet.

Third: If a unit has a hole simply cut into the back or top, and thus does not have a flared flange to accept a tight-fitting flue pipe, you probably will not be able to install an airtight, unified chimney system. Units that have a square flue hole, even if it has a flared flange, require a handmade adapter to hook it up to a round chimney.

Fourth: Check the size and shape of the throat damper in your fireplace before you buy an insert or wood stove that is to be vented through it. If it is narrow—four inches or so—and long—eighteen to twenty-four inches—then a flue pipe will not fit through it. It will have to be removed, and some masonry or brick may have to be chiseled away before a flue pipe will pass through and above the throat.

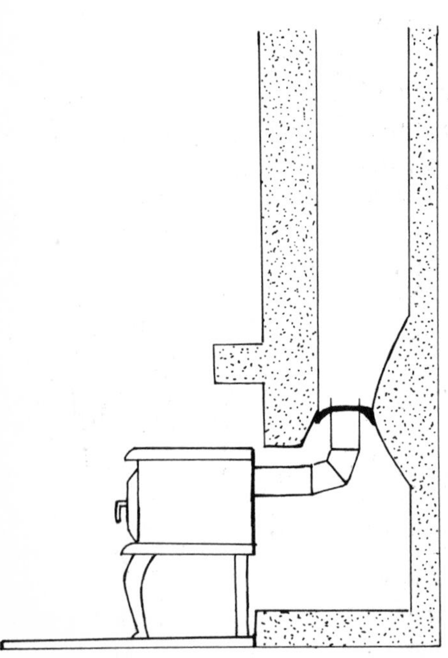

Fifth: Where a unified chimney system is not possible, connect enough flue pipe to reach *past* the damper, preferably through a collar as described in the section "Upgrading for Safety and Efficiency." In some counties and cities, this is required by the local building codes.

Sixth: Do not smolder logs at night in a system that does not have an airtight seal and unified chimney. Instead, burn only seasoned wood with enough draft to keep the logs from smoking excessively; this will also keep the chimney hot enough to draw smoke out before it can condense into creosote.

Upgrading for Safety and Efficiency

Before putting old fireplaces with unlined chimneys into use, the firebox should be converted to a safe, steel insert, and the chimney should be lined with vitrified tile or stainless steel. Stainless steel lining is the simplest to install.

Follow this method:

1. Buy a fireplace insert that fits into the old fireplace.
2. Buy enough stainless steel lining to reach from the top of the insert to the top of the chimney.
3. Make a sheet metal collar out of 24-gauge stainless steel that will seal off the throat of the chimney. The stainless steel lining will pass through it in a hole cut to size, and the collar will catch and hold the vermiculite insulation that will be poured in between the lining and the old chimney. Use a masonry bit to drill into the stone, brick, or masonry joints to secure the collar into place. If the old chimney has a damper, then the damper has to be removed, because the liner must be assembled section by section and then lowered down through the collar and onto the insert. To measure the hole in the collar, bolt it temporarily into place and slide in the insert. Tape a thin magic marker to a yardstick and run it up the inside of the insert's flue port with the tip of the marker touching the collar. If the hole does not line up well, then you can use the flexible elbows to work the system into alignment.
4. Measure the height of the flue flange (usually two or three inches). Scribe a mark that high on the inside of the bottom piece of lining (the first to be lowered). That mark will insure that you get the lining far enough over the flange.
5. Assemble the liner pieces using three sheet metal screws and high temperature furnace cement. The cement seals out air which could cause excess creosote buildup, and it helps seal the lining in the event of a chimney fire.
6. Slide in the insert and carefully pull the liner over the flange.
7. Pour loose vermiculite into the space between the new liner and the old chimney. This is necessary to insulate the liner and prevent smoke from condensing into creosote. (Bags of vermiculite can be bought at most hardware stores.)
8. Install a rain cap over the top, and you're all set.

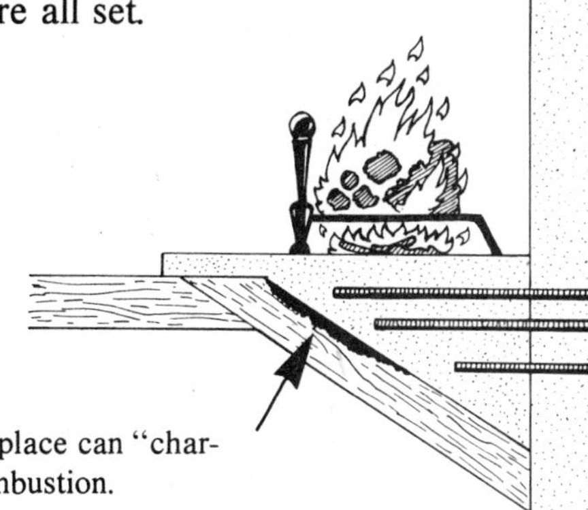

This is dangerous! The wood beneath the fireplace can "charcoal" and catch fire through spontaneous combustion.

Many old fireplaces (even some that were built during the 1950s) were built with wood too close to the firebox or chimney. If you have *any* wood beneath your fireplace, or if the floor joists get hot when you burn a fire, have it checked by a building code inspector or local fire marshal (locate them through your county courthouse). The presence of wood beneath an old chimney could result in charcoaling of the wood and then spontaneous combustion. That can take place as quickly as one year, or over as long as twenty years.

Removable Cleanout Section

If you have, or intend to install, a furnace or wood stove that does not allow a vacuum cleaner hose to go all the way to the chimney, then you should install a removable section between the unit and the chimney.

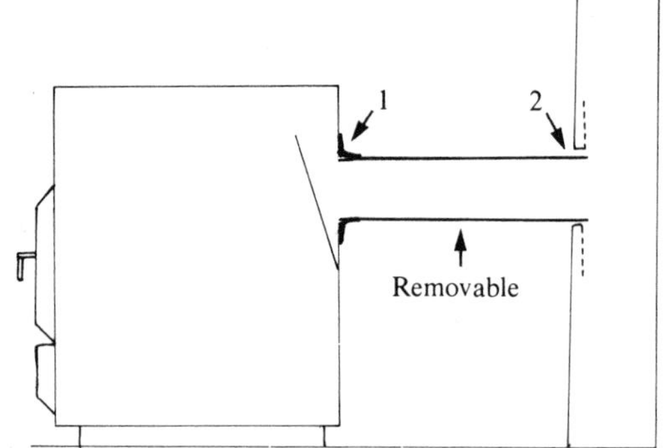

Joint #1 should be tight. Joint #2 must be hand tapered to allow the section to slide into the thimble of the masonry chimney. Pack joint #2 with fiberglass or use non-hardening furnace cement.

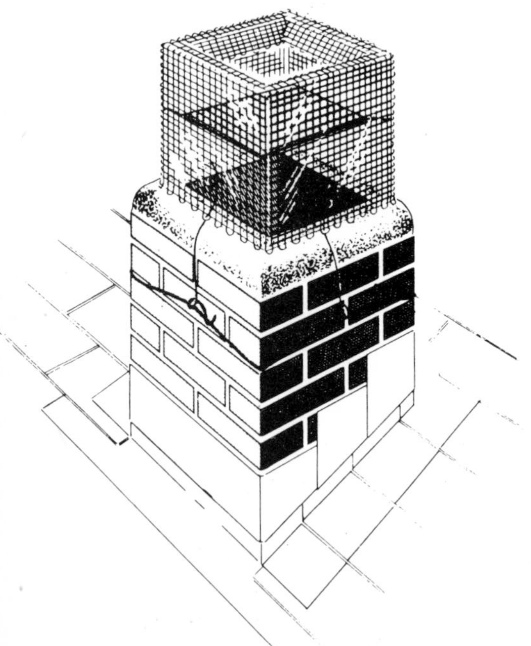

Spark arrestors on chimneys prevent sparks from flying out and falling on the roof.

Chimney Caps

For masonry chimney caps, use a slab of slate that slips down into a border of brick. That way, it can be lifted off to clean the chimney. A cap over a nice (or expensive) masonry chimney prevents rain from entering small cracks, freezing, and thereby loosening the top layer of masonry. There are many types of caps for metal chimneys available at your local wood energy retailer; but whatever type of cap you install, make sure that it is removable. You must be able to clean out your chimney, and that is usually done from the top down.

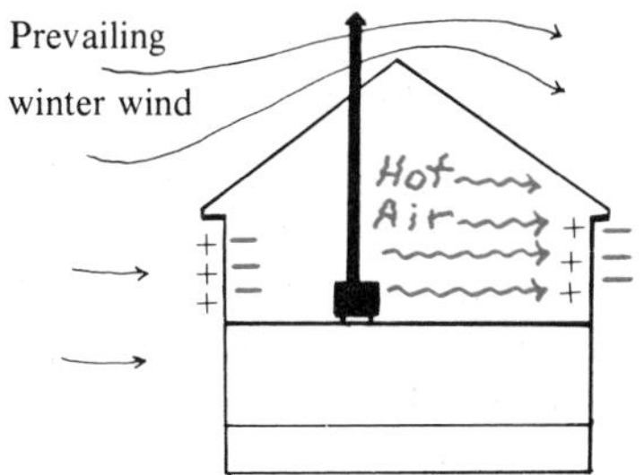

Wind draw on a house is a natural phenomenon that you should take advantage of. The minus (−) signs show where a partial vacuum is forming on the lee side of the house. Wind sucks warm air out of a house—it is not blown out. Thus warm air is drawn through a house in the direction that the winter wind blows.

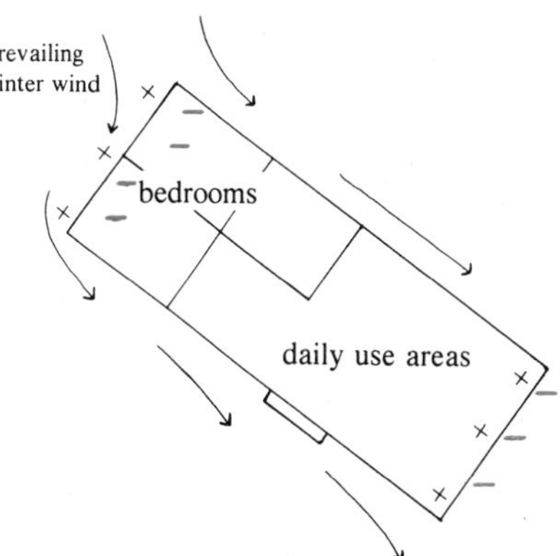

Angle a new ranch style house into the prevailing winter wind (your county weatherman can tell you the direction). Install your heating system in the uppermost corner, under the bedrooms where it will allow heat to rise up and be carried throughout the rest of the house.

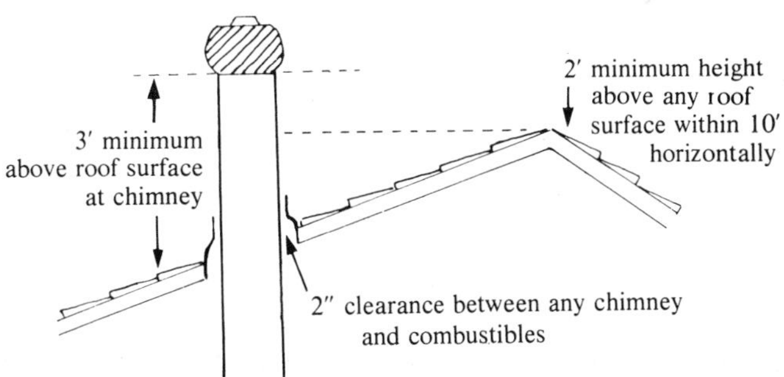

REQUIRED CHIMNEY HEIGHT ABOVE ROOF
(From NFPA Bulletin 211)

Final Chimney Notes

—If you have a wood shingle roof, extend the chimney at least four feet above the peak, and install a spark guard.
—If a metal chimney doesn't draw well, try adding one more section of chimney to increase the jet of air up.
—If you live in a hilly "washboard" area that causes winds to stop the smoke from rising out of the chimney, install a chimney cap that uses the wind to suck the smoke up. All wood energy retailers carry them, or they can order one for you.

Installation Safety Checklist

Call your fire insurance company and, where necessary, your local building code inspector and ask for:

1. Their requirements for laboratory certification of wood heat units.
2. Their clearance requirements.
3. Their chimney construction and installation standards for both pre-fab and masonry (pre-fab chimney requirements can state either double-wall or triple-wall).

After installation, have your insurance company and/or local building code official make an inspection. Failure to do so could void your fire insurance coverage.

How To Use the *FireFacts* Buying Guide 16

The *FireFacts* buying guide is the first uniform, consumer-oriented guide to the products of the wood energy industry. All products listed were voluntarily submitted by the manufacturers. We have included the majority of the American manufacturers, and many of the Canadian manufacturers that export to the United States. There are also a few European and Asian imports. We have selected products from a broad market, based on aesthetics, efficiency, and innovative design. The uniform specification charts should allow you to compare different models easily. The specifications are as factual, consistent, and accurate as possible. Each "special feature" entry was edited to help insure objectivity in presentation. However, should a specification be incorrect or outdated, the error is unintentional. A few notes on "special features": most products carry a warranty, even if we do not state that; most units are firebrick-lined; the majority of the units are hand-welded (except cast iron units); finally, these entries are only a sample of the features of a particular unit.

More models are available than we have listed here. We have surveyed the market and selected what we consider to be some of the best products *available nationally*. Most manufacturers produce one or more simple, less expensive models. Since the national market is becoming saturated with "plain black boxes," we would do you no service by including them.

Since mobile home owners are now able to buy and install units designed specifically for them, we have indicated such approved units by printing MHA to the right of "Function" in the specification chart. This annotation stands for mobile home approved, and means that the unit has been designed and tested according to Federal HUD regulations.

A manufacturer is allowed by law to make outside, aesthetic changes and still market a unit as laboratory listed, as long as there was a prior testing by that laboratory for that unit. Therefore you may find some minor alterations in a model in the subsequent year.

The model names are, in most cases, registered trade names, and thus the use of them by another person or company could be in violation of applicable laws. Also, it *must* be assumed that each product is patented or carries a patent pending on design and/or mechanical function. It is unlawful for any person or company to reproduce any product under patent.

No illustration, drawing, or diagram may be reproduced without the permission of *FireFacts* or the manufacturer.

Photograph — The photo that the manufacturer has provided us is often the deluxe version of a product. We advise that it should be used only as a general guide to that product, since aesthetic changes or refinements may have been made from the time of our press deadline to the time of your purchase of the unit.

Schematic

Study the schematic carefully if you are comparing units by function. A schematic may not be revealing the first time that you glance at it. Ask a friend for some help if you don't have a knack for understanding mechanical drawings.

Manufacturer

Write to the manufacturer for information. *Do not write to FireFacts* as we cannot answer inquiries about products. That is the responsibility of the manufacturer. In some cases, the company listed is the importer, not the manufacturer.

Model

One model may come in two or three sizes, and may vary in function depending on the options available. Also, the manufacturers usually produce more models than we have listed here.

Function

The function of a unit as indicated on the specification sheet is usually self-explanatory. To further assist you in determining the meaning of the entry, we have provided a glossary of *FireFacts* terms, and industry terminology as well. *Safety note*: The add-on furnaces that we list *must* be vented into a separate chimney. The term "add-on" refers to a unit's ability to supplement your heating or hot water system. NFPA standards and most building codes require a separate flue for each solid fuel appliance.

Size

The size of a unit will occasionally limit its placement in a house. Measure the installation site, then buy the unit accordingly. Don't forget about clearance standards. The inside of an old fireplace can dictate the size of the insert. An odd sized fireplace may require a few alterations by the manufacturer of the insert.

Weight

If you plan to add any brick or masonry work to your woodstove or free-standing fireplace, you should keep it under 500 pounds total (stove and masonry), or else install a column support beneath the floor joists, down in the basement. (The floor joists should be 2″ × 10″ with 16″ centers between each one. If not, consult a carpenter before you go over 500 pounds.) Where two weights are separated by a slash, then the second figure is the shipping weight. Where two or more figures are separated by commas, then each successive figure is the weight of the next larger model.

Color

Porcelain enamel finishes are usually permanent as long as you don't get your stove red hot. A disadvantage of porcelain is that it can't be fixed if it gets scratched or chipped. Many units now have the new high temperature paints, such as we have listed in our accessories for the do-it-your-selfers. These are quality, lasting products—good to 1200°—a much hotter temperature than you normally run a stove or fireplace.

Airtight

Airtight means that the unit can be closed up so tight than no air can enter. A fire can thus be extinguished as soon as all controls are closed. Chimney fires are put out by shutting off all the intake air. (Since a leaky chimney system can still allow a chimney fire to burn, use furnace cement on the joints of prefab chimneys to seal them up.) Just because a stove or fireplace insert has a lock handle and gaskets, don't assume that it is airtight. Run this check:

1. Look for it in writing.
2. Physically check the doors for obvious gaps when they are closed.
3. If a door (or doors) has to be forced closed to make the sealing gasket touch the lip of the stove opening, then you may not get an airtight fit even when the lock handles are closed.

Try this test: Put a new dollar bill in each area that doesn't seem to close tight, lock the doors and try to remove the dollar bill. If it resists being pulled out, then that area of the door is reasonably airtight. If the dollar bill slips out with the doors locked shut, then it isn't airtight.

Airtightness is not necessary for efficiency. It simply adds a margin of safety in the event of a chimney fire. Since there is no industry-wide or government standard for determining airtightness, the term can be used at the discretion of the manufacturer.

Reduced Clearance

Reduced clearance means installing a wood heat unit closer than the "National Fire Protection Association, recommended minimum clearances for combustible walls and ceilings."

Some units are designed to be installed closer to walls than the thirty-six inch clearance recommended by the NFPA. Heat shields that are often available as standard equipment, or as an option, can greatly reduce the distance between a wall and a stove or fireplace. Every manufacturer is required by law—as of June 1980—to furnish clearance standards for their products. Follow those standards exactly or you'll be installing a unit in a way that does not meet the established criteria for safe installation.

Zero-clearance fireplace units can be installed with the unit touching a wall and the floor. However, you must still maintain an eighteen-inch clearance from wood or combustible materials from the outside opening of the unit to that material.

Floor clearance: A six-inch airspace is minimum beneath a wood stove or free-standing fireplace. Always place a certified stove-board beneath, twelve inches on each side and rear, and eighteen inches in front of a stove or free-standing fireplace. Again, follow the manufacturer's recommendations. Never build up the area beneath a fireplace or woodstove with brick, because the brick will transmit heat to the wood floor and that's unsafe.

Outside Combustion Air

Outside combustion air is air that is drawn in from outside of your house through a pipe or vent to the fireplace or woodstove fire chamber. Many companies now offer this option because—with most fireplaces and woodstoves—the air that you are spending money to heat goes up your chimney, and cold outside air is sucked into your house to replace it. That is inefficient and creates drafts. Federal HUD regulations state that mobile home fireplaces and woodstoves must be designed for such use. Using cold outside combustion air for your fireplace or woodstove greatly increases the overall efficiency of your wood heat unit, perhaps by as much as twenty percent. The manufacturers usually supply adequate installation instructions for hookup of these units.

Glass

The quality of glass doors is a measure of its thermal shock resistance (TSR), which is its resistance to breakage from high heat or sudden temperature change. For fireplace glass that simply encloses a firebox that gets only occasional use, a glass with a TSR of 480° F and up is usually adequate. This category includes tempered glass (soda lime glass), borosilicate, Pyrex™, tempered Pyrex™, Pyroceram™, and Tempax™. However, the fire, or even a red hot smoldering log, should not be allowed to come in contact with the glass. Pyroceram™ and Rubex™ have a TSR of over 1100° F and can be used in close proximity to a fire. But if the fire of a wood stove is in contact with the glass, then a glass with a much higher TSR should be used. Red hot logs and their flame are approximately 1400° F. Therefore, the safest glass will have a TSR of up to 1600° F. Currently, Vycor™ is the only glass on the market that attains this margin of safety. This safety margin is important should a child splash water against a hot wood stove or freestanding fireplace. Quality glass should not break. Also, high quality glass radiates up to 25 percent more heat than metal. (See our presentation on Corning Glass Works for more information.)

Cooking Surface

Cooking on a wood stove, especially a two-level step stove, can be an added convenience. However, if you intend to do a lot of cooking with a wood stove, we recommend that you consider one of the kitchen ranges that are designed primarily for cooking.

Construction

Metals Used in Wood Stoves and Fireplaces

Since cast iron has long been the primary material used in the construction of wood stoves and fireplaces, let us look first at the properties of iron.

Pure iron in its raw state is called pig iron. The purer the iron (the more "slag" or dirt that is removed) the better the quality, the higher the cost, and the better the cast product. Iron from different parts of the world differ in quality. American grey iron is considered to be among the best. Slag, or scrap iron is the poorest. Cast irons are rated as grey iron (#1), pig iron (#2), and scrap iron (#3). Under the relatively low temperatures at which wood stoves operate, grey iron and pig iron are about equal in performance. There are other types and qualities of iron, such as malleable and ductile, but they are not usually used in wood stove construction. If cast products such as stoves, door frames, or doors are made from quality iron, and cast with *good quality control*, then the product should never warp or "burn out." Conversely, if the casted product is made from scrap iron, and/or the manufacturer does not inspect the products for defects, the chances are that some products from that manufacturer may warp and/or crack. Since even the label of a testing laboratory simply means that the *design* has been tested (not each individual unit), the quality control check of a unit is up to you.

Note: All cast iron stoves must be seasoned before being put into high-temperature use, or cracks and warps can occur. Start off with *small* fires that only "warm up" the stove, and then let it cool completely, repeating several times. Gradually build up to a hot fire about the seventh time. This breaks in the metal to where it can expand and contract a bit more each time. The principle is similar to marathon running: no one should ever buy a brand new pair of running shoes and go out and run ten miles the first day. If you want your brand new cast iron wood stove to be around "for a long run," train it for the marathon job of heating your home by seasoning it first.

As to the question of heat transfer of cast iron vs. that of steel, the basic difference is as follows: sand cast iron wood heat units have nearly twice the surface area as that of smooth walled steel units. That's because sand cast iron is very granular. Therefore the heatability of the *surface* of cast iron is better than steel. Also, cast iron has a lighter molecular structure than steel which distributes heat a bit more evenly. But, some steel—such as boiler plate alloy—moves heat through its molecules faster than cast iron, so steel can radiate heat faster, though in smaller volume. All things considered, they are virtually equal in their ability to transfer heat from the firebox to air in your house. The design and function of the unit is much more important. Actually, the only major difference between cast iron and steel is the potential shape of the unit. One advantage of cast, from the point of view of design, is that it can be molded into almost any shape. The only other fireplace/wood stove material that can be molded is ceramic silicone carbide. Steel stoves are limited to linear shapes.

One advantage of steel is that it can be repaired. (Cast iron can crack and usually cannot be repaired).

There is a wide variation in the types of steel used in the manufacturing of wood stoves and fireplaces, and the usable life of any steel can vary greatly depending on its proximity to the fire. If you wish to investigate the properties of steel used in a unit, get a book on metallurgy from your local library, or talk to a local sheetmetalsmith.

The following is a brief explanation of the most common types and thickness of steel: any steel can be called plate steel if it is ¼″ thick, any steel that is less than ¼″ thick is usually refered to as sheet steel; high carbon steel is .09% carbon, and is the type that boiler plate is made from; mild steel is .05% carbon; low carbon is .01% carbon, and is flexible enough to be bent easily. Boiler plate, annealed (hardened or tempered) cold rolled, hot rolled steel, and cold rolled steel all have qualities that make them suitable for wood stove and fireplace construction. If you desire information on the quality of a particular type, ask the manufacturer for details of the steel used in their products. Overall, the purchase of a wood heat unit should not be based on cast iron versus steel, but rather on quality, efficiency, function and your own aesthetic requirements.

Gauge or Thickness

There are no thickness standards for a wood heat unit's metal contruction, but by comparing the many different stoves and fireplaces that we list, you can get an idea of what is commonly considered safe. The thicknesses given in the buying guide specification chart are usually for steel only since cast iron thicknesses are not measured. The thicker figure is usually the top of the unit, and the smaller thicknesses refer to the stove body and outer walls.

GAUGES AND THICKNESSES
(Approximate equivalents)

Inches		*Gauge*
Fraction	*Decimal*	
3/8″		
5/16″		
1/4″		
1/5″	.2092	5 ga.
3/16″	.1875	6.5 ga.
	.1793	7 ga.
4/25″	.1345	10 ga.
1/8″	.1250	11.5 ga.
1/10″	.1046	12 ga.
7/100″	.0747	14 ga.
		16 ga.
		18 ga.
		20 ga.
3/100″	.0299	22 ga.

Air Blowers

If you want your wood heat unit to heat your whole house or a large part of it, you should get a unit that has a blower of around 1,000 CFM (cubic feet per minute). Your house "breathes" in and out at a rate of 200 CFM, so it takes a large blower to keep it warm.

Flue — The flue begins where the exhaust opening directs smoke out of a wood stove or fireplace. It then extends into the chimney and becomes the inside lining of a chimney. The function of a flue is to get hot from the smoke and create a jet—or push—of air up the chimney.

Flue Size — As the hot flue causes the expanding gases, to go up the chimney, the jet of air pushing up also pulls air from beneath. So, smoke is actually *pulled* up out of a fireplace or woodstove.

If the unit has a six inch flue, then the chimney should also be six inch inside diameter. Modern woodstoves and fireplaces are designed to burn wood at a specific rate, which is determined by the unit's size; and so the "push-pull" system of cold air intake and hot gas and smoke outflow give the most efficient unit heat output if the system is uniform in size and design. If you put a six inch round pipe into an eight inch or ten inch round chimney flue, you decrease the velocity of existing smoke and gases and increase creosote buildup. Note, however: when venting round stovepipe into *square* or *rectangular* flue tile, the inside dimensions of the flue should be twenty five percent larger than the stovepipe to assure a good draft and to help guard against back-puffing. Do not put an eight inch flue into a six inch chimney or you'll be producing more smoke and gas than the chimney can expel. This is especially important in burning coal. And, each wood heat unit must have its own flue, although one masonry housing can be built with two flues in it.

Efficiency — There are two types of efficiency: heat output efficiency and combustion efficiency. The most common rating percentage is the amount of radiant heat output, or rather, the heat generated out into the room versus the heat locked inside the unit. But, this is measured under ideal laboratory conditions with a charge of dry wood in the form of bran. In laymen's terms, a bran is a stack of cut and dried fir lumber, each piece usually 1″ × 3″ × 2′ long, stacked in a waffle shape and nailed together. This rating gives you an idea of how well the unit generates heat for your house; though this should only be used as a guide, not as the "Gospel Truth." It is, in most cases, the percentage rating that the manufacturers have supplied us with. Sixty percent is a good heat output range, and, in general, sixty percent is about as high as *any* stove is capable of achieving. The only stoves capable of eighty to ninety percent combustion efficiency are thin-walled, laboratory test units; and unless a catalytic convertor is installed to eat up the smoke, these units are high creosote producers.

The other type of efficiency rating percentage is combustion efficiency. It is the ratio of potential heat output per pound of wood (8,600 BTU per pound) versus the amount of actual heat that the unit can get the wood to give up. If the unit cannot get dry wood to burn without smoking, then the smoke is unburned wood and that is heat lost up the chimney. Again, sixty percent combustion efficiency is good. That applies to any heating unit, whether it is wood, oil, or coal. Gas is rated ninety percent efficient in combustion efficiency. The efficiencies in the buying guide that are in the seventy to eighty percent range are in most cases combustion efficiencies. The catalytic convertor stoves now under development promise to achieve an even greater combustion efficiency—perhaps in the seventy to eighty percent range—and will work best during "turndown."

Some manufacturers will mention *total efficiency*. That is usually a low number because it is heat output efficiency times combustion efficiency. Example: sixty percent × sixty percent = thirty-six percent Total Efficiency, because if sixty percent of the potential heat is extracted from the wood, and if sixty percent of the extracted heat gets into the room, then thirty-six percent gets used; sixty-four percent gets wasted. The same holds true for oil or coal burners.

Heat Output

Some ratings are in BTUs per hour. An average house usually needs about 100,000 BTUs per hour from a central heating unit. Domestic hot water tie-in requires another 10,000 to 15,000 BTUs per hour.

The average house is about 1500 square feet in area. Simply multiply the length and the width of each room, and then add them all up to get the square footage of your house. A strategically placed wood heat unit that is designed to heat 2,000 to 3,000 square feet should keep the average house well heated.

Tested by

We only list certified testing laboratories. These laboratories are licensed under one of the three regional building code organizations: ICBO, the International Conference of Building Code Officials; BOCA, the Building Officials and Code Administrators International; and SBCCI, the Southern Building Code Congress International. These organizations oversee testing labs.

When a certified testing lab puts its label on a unit, that means that they have tested that *model*, not each individual unit. They usually test them according to Underwriters Laboratories specifications, usually UL*737* and/or UL*1482*. That certification label means that that unit is safe; and not that it is a "good buy." *You* must decide whether or not it is worth the money. However, just because a unit is not listed as tested, that does not necessarily mean that it is an inferior unit. Testing can cost $5,000 to $10,000 per model, and it can take from six months to a year to finalize. If you like the looks of a product in the buying guide which lacks test data, write or call the manufacturer and ask for the test status of his unit.

Consumer Product Safety Commission Labels

By mid-1980, all new, wood heat units will be coming off the assembly lines with a Consumer Product Safety Commission label that will give the minimum clearance requirements for that unit. The petition for such a label was granted on 7 July 1979. The label is intended to make wood heat unit installation and use safer.

If you have a safety problem with a wood heat unit, call the Consumer Product Safety Commission in Washington, D.C. The call is *free*. The numbers are: in the U.S., 800-638-8326; in Maryland, 800-492-8363; in Alaska, Hawaii, Puerto Rico, Virgin Islands, 800-638-8333. They also have electronic relays enabling deaf people to receive a message and communicate a response.

Suggested Retail Price

The picture of a product may not be exactly the same model or product that the suggested retail price refers to. Before you write out a check and order a unit via mail order, we strongly urge you to check the manufacturer's brochure, or call them and ask whether or not the picture and the price that we list correspond. Prices, of course, are subject to change without notice.

Brochure

If you write for fifteen or so brochures, you will get quite an education in buying, far more than we can present in any one book. If you intend to put $1,500 to $3,000 into a good masonry fireplace, by all means, write to *every* manufacturer that we list masonry products for. The brochures contain *dozens* of design ideas, often in full color. And usually, if a brochure costs a dollar or two, it will be worth it.

Mail Order

Many of the units that we list can be ordered by mail but only if there is no dealer in your area. Shipment is usually by common freight carrier. However, we strongly recommend buying through a reputable dealer whenever possible.

Part 4

The FireFacts Buying Guide

Manufacturer	Double Eagle Fireplace Mfg. Inc. Dept. FF 410 S. 96th Seattle, Wash. 98108
Model	Zero Clearance
Function	Built-in fireplace (MHA)
Size (H, W, D)	41″, 45″, 25″
Weight	200 lbs.
Colors	Black and brass
Airtight?	N/A
Reduced clearance	Zero clearance
Outside combustion air?	Yes
Glass? (type)	Yes
Cooking surface?	N/A
CONSTRUCTION *Material*	Stainless steel
Gauge or thickness	14 ga.
Air blower? (output)	Optional, 180 CFM
Flue size	8″
Special features	Three-wall stainless steel interior. Outside air for heat exchanger. 25 year warranty against burn out. Class A Metal Fab pipe.
Options and accessories	Unit complete
Efficiency	80%
Heat output (or area)	3,000 sq. ft.
Tested by	Northwest Laboratories
Suggested retail price	$895.00
Brochure	Free
For nearest dealer call	206-767-3440
Mail order, if no dealer?	Yes

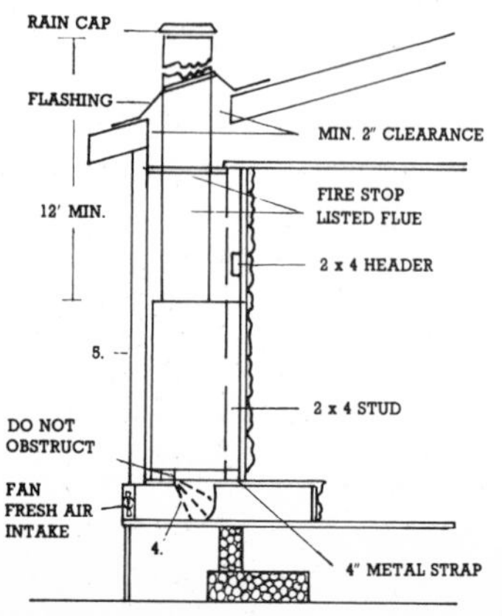

Manufacturer	Ember Box Fireplaces Dept. FF 1012 So. Agnew Oklahoma City, OK 73148
Model	Chalet 541 R
Function	Fireplace hood
Size (H, W, D)	58″ H, 41″ dia.
Weight	280 lbs., 315 lbs.
Colors	Black (copper optional)
Airtight?	N/A
Reduced clearance	N/A
Outside combustion air?	Possible
Glass? (type)	Optional
Cooking surface?	N/A
CONSTRUCTION *Material*	Steel
Gauge or thickness	16 gauge
Air blower? (output)	N/A
Flue size	14″
Special features	Can be hung from chains. 20 yr. warranty against burnout. Price includes flue to 8′ ceiling.
Options and accessories	Firepit. Smooth or ribbed steel, Glass cage. (4 sizes, up to 72″)
Efficiency	N/A
Heat output (or area)	N/A
Tested by	N/A
Suggested retail price	Base price $839.00 (ribbed steel)
Brochure	Color, free
For nearest dealer call	405-236-0404
Mail order, if no dealer?	Yes

Manufacturer	Ember Box Fireplaces Dept. FF 1012 So. Agnew Oklahoma City, OK 73148
Model	Chateau
Function	Fireplace hood
Size (H, W, D)	48″ or 60″ W
Weight	Varies (200-350 lbs.)
Colors	Black or copper
Airtight?	N/A
Reduced clearance	N/A
Outside combustion air?	Possible
Glass? (type)	Optional
Cooking surface?	N/A
CONSTRUCTION *Material*	Steel or hammered copper
Gauge or thickness	N/A
Air blower? (output)	N/A
Flue size	14″
Special features	Can be made as freestanding (on legs), or center hung. 20 yr. warranty.
Options and accessories	Hand hammered copper. Square body. (Copper: add 120% to base price.)
Efficiency	N/A
Heat output (or area)	N/A
Tested by	N/A
Suggested retail price	Base price $1,088.00
Brochure	Color, free
For nearest dealer call	405-236-0404
Mail order, if no dealer?	Yes

Manufacturer	Ember Box Fireplaces Dept. FF 1012 So. Agnew Oklahoma City, OK 73148
Model	Copper Chalet 595
Function	Fireplace hood
Size (H, W, D)	58″ H, 48″ dia.
Weight	915 lbs., 1100 lbs.
Colors	Copper (steel optional)
Airtight?	N/A
Reduced clearance	N/A
Outside combustion air?	Possible
Glass? (type)	Optional
Cooking surface?	N/A
CONSTRUCTION *Material*	Hand hammered copper
Gauge or thickness	16 ga. (¼″ band)
Air blower? (output)	N/A
Flue size	14″
Special features	Can be hung from chains. 20 yr. warranty against burnout. Price includes flue to 8′ ceiling.
Options and accessories	Glass cage. (Sizes from 41″ to 72″ in dia.)
Efficiency	N/A
Heat output (or area)	N/A
Tested by	N/A
Suggested retail price	Base price $1,973.00
Brochure	Color, free
For nearest dealer call	405-236-0404
Mail order, if no dealer?	Yes

Manufacturer	Ember Box Fireplaces Dept. FF 1012 So. Agnew Oklahoma City, OK 73148
Model	La Casa
Function	Fireplace hood
Size (H, W, D)	44″ wide, 26″ deep
Weight	300 lbs./340 lbs.
Colors	Black, copper
Airtight?	N/A
Reduced clearance	N/A
Outside combustion air?	Possible
Glass? (type)	Yes
Cooking surface?	N/A
CONSTRUCTION *Material*	Steel, or hammered copper
Gauge or thickness	16 gauge
Air blower? (output)	Optional
Flue size	10″
Special features	Hand welded. Baffled heat exchanger. Interior flue to ceiling. 20 yr. warranty against burnout. Screen. Draft control.
Options and accessories	Blower. Medallion. Can be ordered double-sided to serve, or divide, two rooms.
Efficiency	N/A
Heat output (or area)	N/A
Tested by	N/A
Suggested retail price	$1,370 steel; $3,014 copper
Brochure	Color, free
For nearest dealer call	405-236-0404
Mail order, if no dealer?	Yes

Manufacturer	Ember Box Fireplaces Dept. FF 1012 So. Agnew Oklahoma City, OK 73148
Model	Lodge
Function	Fireplace hood (corner unit)
Size (H, W, D)	71″ W, 25″ H doors, 24″ H hood
Weight	165 lbs.
Colors	Black
Airtight?	N/A
Reduced clearance	N/A
Outside combustion air?	Possible
Glass? (type)	Optional, 46″ wide
Cooking surface?	N/A
CONSTRUCTION *Material*	Steel
Gauge or thickness	16 gauge
Air blower? (output)	N/A
Flue size	10″ or 12″
Special features	Hand welded. Interior (class "A") flue to ceiling. 20 yr. warranty against burnout.
Options and accessories	Glass doors.
Efficiency	N/A
Heat output (or area)	N/A
Tested by	N/A
Suggested retail price	$469, $689 with glass
Brochure	Color, free
For nearest dealer call	405-236-0404
Mail order, if no dealer?	Yes

Manufacturer	F & W Econoheat, Inc. Route 2, Box 485 (FF) 7 Andrea Drive Bruce Industrial Park Belgrade, MT 59714
Model	BHV System, Model B
Function	Built-in fireplace
Size (H, W, D)	52", 38", 34"
Weight	880 lbs.
Colors	Gold
Airtight?	Yes
Reduced clearance	Yes
Outside combustion air?	Yes
Glass? (type)	Yes
Cooking surface?	No
CONSTRUCTION *Material*	Steel
Gauge or thickness	10 and 12 gauge
Air blower? (output)	Yes, (2) 2,000 CFM each
Flue size	10"
Special features	Factory built chimney included. Thermostatically controlled. Connects to central duct work. Barometric damper. Replaceable fire walls. Wood/coal use.
Options and accessories	Domestic hot water coil
Efficiency	46%
Heat output (or area)	108,000 BTUs / hr.
Tested by	Testing Consultants, Inc.
Suggested retail price	$2,999.00
Brochure	Color, 4 page, 50¢
For nearest dealer call	406-388-4911
Mail order, if no dealer?	Yes

Manufacturer	George Mayer Mfg. Inc. P.O. Box 1468 (FF) Miami, OK 74354
Model	QA-36-WTD
Function	Built-in or free standing fireplace
Size (H, W, D)	54½", 40½", 23½"
Weight	586 lbs.
Colors	Black
Airtight?	N/A
Reduced clearance	N/A
Outside combustion air?	Yes
Glass? (type)	Yes
Cooking surface?	N/A
CONSTRUCTION *Material*	Plate steel
Gauge or thickness	3/16", 1/16"
Air blower? (output)	Yes, (2) 500 CFM (ea)
Flue size	12"
Special features	Will duct up to ten rooms. Blowers and housing. Grills. Thermostatic limit switch. Clean out door. Ash dump. Lintels. Wall switch. Over 20,000 sq. in. of heat exchanger area.
Options and accessories	Four models.
Efficiency	50%
Heat output (or area)	175,000 BTUs/hr.
Tested by	Gas Appliance Lab
Suggested retail price	$950.00
Brochure	Free
For nearest dealer call	918-542-8411
Mail order, if no dealer?	N/A

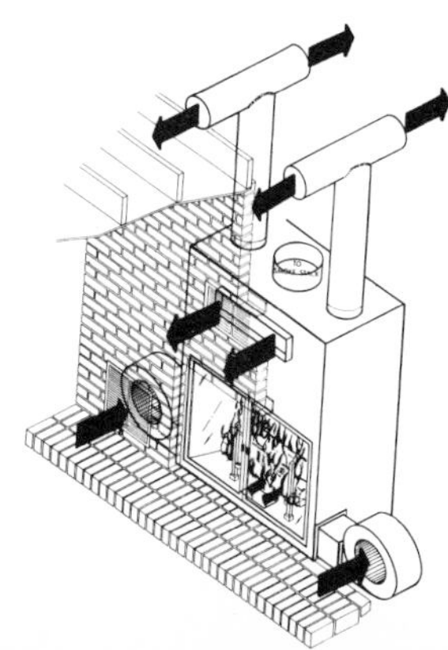

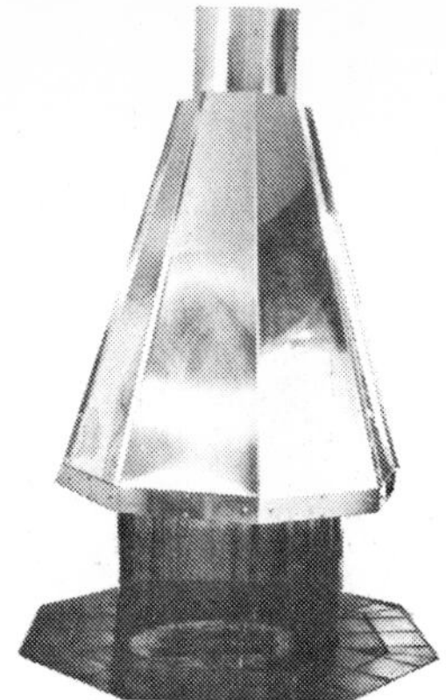

Manufacturer	Goodwin of California Dept. FF 1075 2nd Street Berkeley, Calif. 94710
Model	Fireplace Hoods
Function	Open hearth fireplaces
Size (H, W, D)	Custom sizes and shapes
Weight	Varies
Colors	See special features
Airtight?	N/A
Reduced clearance	N/A
Outside combustion air?	Possible
Glass? (type)	N/A
Cooking surface?	N/A
CONSTRUCTION *Material*	See below
Gauge or thickness	Varies
Air blower? (output)	N/A
Flue size	Varies
Special features	Stainless steel, polished copper, polished brass, black iron. Any architectural design can be custom made. Special colors available.
Options and accessories	Firebowls. Western, Malm, Majestic, and other pre-built fireplaces can be clad in solid copper or solid brass.
Efficiency	N/A
Heat output (or area)	N/A
Tested by	N/A
Suggested retail price	Usually under $1,000
Brochure	Free
For nearest dealer call	415-525-1515
Mail order, if no dealer?	Yes

Manufacturer	Hydroheat Div. Ridgway Steel P.O. Box 382 (FF) Ridgway, PA 15853
Model	Hydroplace
Function	Built-in hydronic fireplace
Size (H, W, D)	56½", 42", 25"
Weight	475 lbs.
Colors	Black
Airtight?	N/A
Reduced clearance	N/A
Outside combustion air?	N/A
Glass? (type)	N/A
Cooking surface?	N/A
CONSTRUCTION *Material*	Low carbon steel
Gauge or thickness	3/16", 1/8"
Air blower? (output)	N/A
Flue size	13" × 13"
Special features	3/4" schedule 40 hot water pipe. Pressure relief valve. Can hook up to hot air, or any hot water heat system.
Options and accessories	Heat exchange coils for hot air systems. Aquastat. Expansion tanks. Stainless steel water pump.
Efficiency	40%
Heat output (or area)	50,000 BTUs/hr.
Tested by	N/A
Suggested retail price	$1,095.00
Brochure	Free
For nearest dealer call	814-776-1323
Mail order, if no dealer?	Yes

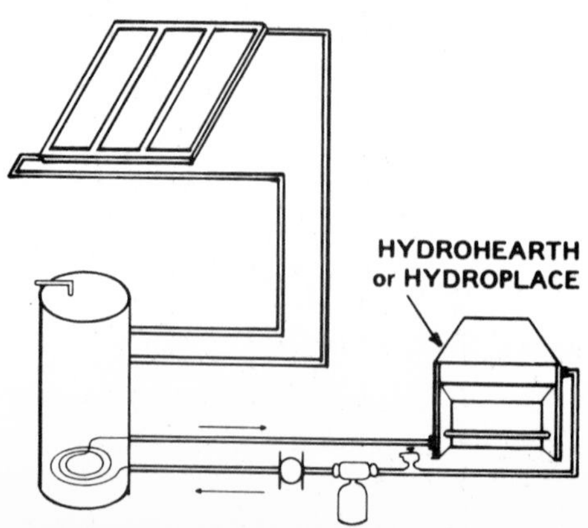

Manufacturer	IN-FURN-O Dept. FF Div. Amer. Rd. Equip. Co. 4201 North 26th St. Omaha, Neb. 68111
Model	IF 36-L
Function	Built-in fireplace
Size (H, W, D)	48″, 36″, 25″
Weight	487 lbs.
Colors	Black
Airtight?	N/A
Reduced clearance	N/A
Outside combustion air?	Optional
Glass? (type)	Yes, customer's choice
Cooking surface?	N/A
CONSTRUCTION *Material*	Steel
Gauge or thickness	3/16″, ¼″
Air blower? (output)	Yes (2), total 980 CFM
Flue size	10″
Special features	Twin blowers. Grills and registers. Duct connections. Thermostat. Limit switch. Insulation. Ash dump. Hot air baffle system. 25 year limited warranty.
Options and accessories	Unit complete.
Efficiency	42% without glass doors
Heat output (or area)	68,000 BTUs/hr.
Tested by	Gas and Mechanical Lab.
Suggested retail price	$800.00 base price
Brochure	Color, free
For nearest dealer call	402-451-2575
Mail order, if no dealer?	N/A

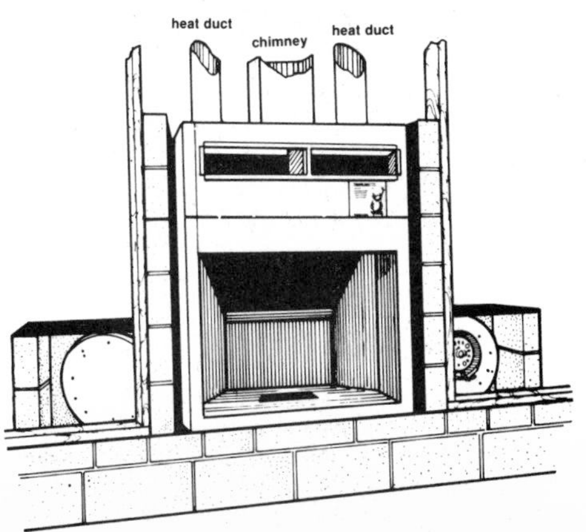

Manufacturer	J.L. Metal Fabricating, Inc. Rt. 2 Box 252 (FF) Grantsburg, Wis. 54840
Model	Furnaceplace #24
Function	Built-in fireplace (MHA)
Size (H, W, D)	Wall opening 30½″ × 27 3/8″
Weight	315 lbs./340 lbs.
Colors	Black
Airtight?	N/A
Reduced clearance	Zero clearance
Outside combustion air?	Yes
Glass? (type)	N/A
Cooking surface?	N/A
CONSTRUCTION *Material*	Steel
Gauge or thickness	10 gauge
Air blower? (output)	N/A
Flue size	8″
Special features	Designed for mobile home; or retrofit through any house wall. Unit and 9′ chimney ready to install. Firebrick lined on bottom. Screen. Metal door for front close-off. 5 year limited warranty.
Options and accessories	Grate
Efficiency	N/A
Heat output (or area)	N/A
Tested by	N/A
Suggested retail price	N/A
Brochure	Color, free
For nearest dealer call	715-463-5611
Mail order, if no dealer?	N/A

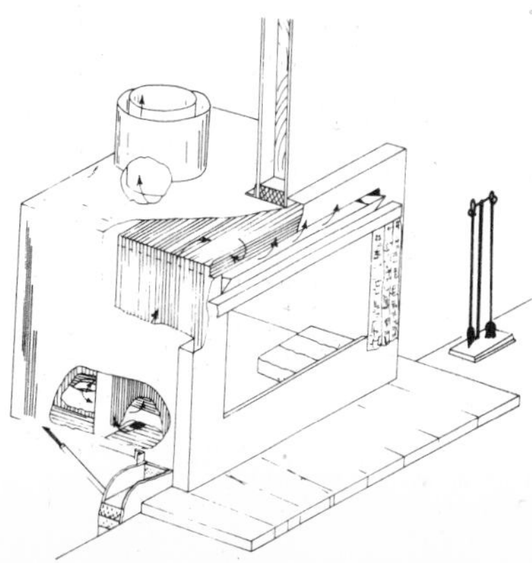

Manufacturer	Juca, Inc. P.O. Box 68 (FF) No. Judson, Ind. 46366
Model	C-6
Function	Fireplace hood
Size (H, W, D)	56″, 41″, 31″
Weight	420 lbs./460 lbs.
Colors	Red, gold, orange, black
Airtight?	N/A
Reduced clearance	N/A
Outside combustion air?	Possible
Glass? (type)	Yes (3 sides), tempered
Cooking surface?	N/A
CONSTRUCTION *Material*	Steel
Gauge or thickness	11 ga. to 14 ga.
Air blower? (output)	Yes, 465 CFM
Flue size	10″
Special features	7 tube heat exchange system. Metal panel inserts protect glass when unattended. Remote blower possible.
Options and accessories	Blower-865 CFM. Belt-drive blowers from 1790 CFM to 2500 CFM. (Note: masonry base not included).
Efficiency	80%
Heat output (or area)	180,000 BTUs/hr
Tested by	N/A
Suggested retail price	$795.40
Brochure	Color, free
For nearest dealer call	219-393-5506
Mail order, if no dealer?	Yes

10″ FLUE
OFFSET FOR FACEBRICK
HEAT OUTLET TO FURNACE HOT AIR DUCTS
TEMPERED GLASS DOOR
HEAT OUTLET FOR ROOM
FIRE DRAFT CONTROL

Manufacturer	Juca, Inc. P.O. Box 68 (FF) No. Judson, Ind. 46366
Model	F9
Function	Built-in fireplace
Size (H, W, D)	41″, 42″, 26″
Weight	375 lbs./500 lbs.
Colors	Black
Airtight?	N/A
Reduced clearance	Yes
Outside combustion air?	Possible
Glass? (type)	Yes, tempered
Cooking surface?	N/A
CONSTRUCTION *Material*	Steel
Gauge or thickness	11 ga. to 14 ga.
Air blower? (output)	Yes, 465 CFM
Flue size	10″
Special features	Tubular heat exchange system. Door assembly is extended 4″ out. Bottomless to accommodate ash dump, outside air.
Options and accessories	Larger blower (see other Jucas). Rear feed door. See-through model. (Other models available.)
Efficiency	65%
Heat output (or area)	140,000 BTUs/hr.
Tested by	Arnold Greene Test Lab
Suggested retail price	$621.96
Brochure	Free
For nearest dealer call	219-393-5506
Mail order, if no dealer?	Yes

Manufacturer	Majestic Company P.O. Box 800 (FF) Huntington, Ind. 46750
Model	Energy Saving ESF-IIB
Function	Built-in fireplace
Size (H, W, D)	52″, 58¼″, 27½″
Weight	263 lbs.
Colors	Black
Airtight?	N/A
Reduced clearance	Zero clearance
Outside combustion air?	Optional
Glass? (type)	Optional
Cooking surface?	N/A
CONSTRUCTION *Material*	Steel
Gauge or thickness	N/A
Air blower? (output)	Optional
Flue size	8″
Special features	Cast refractory bottom. Double wall construction. Screen.
Options and accessories	Hearth extension. Hot air duct kit.
Efficiency	34%
Heat output (or area)	N/A
Tested by	Underwriters Laboratories
Suggested retail price	N/A
Brochure	Color, free
For nearest dealer call	800-348-2835
Mail order, if no dealer?	N/A

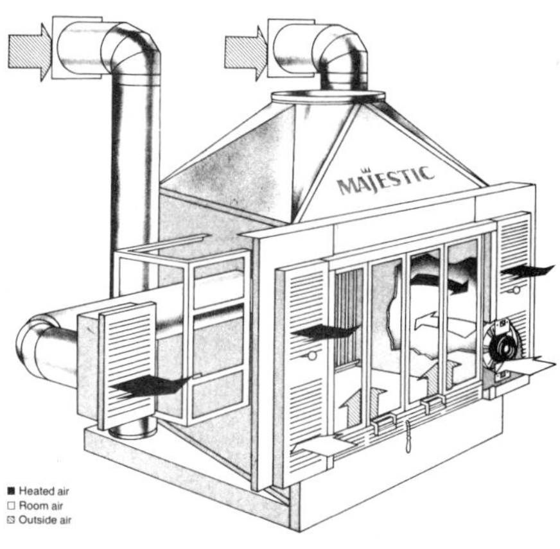

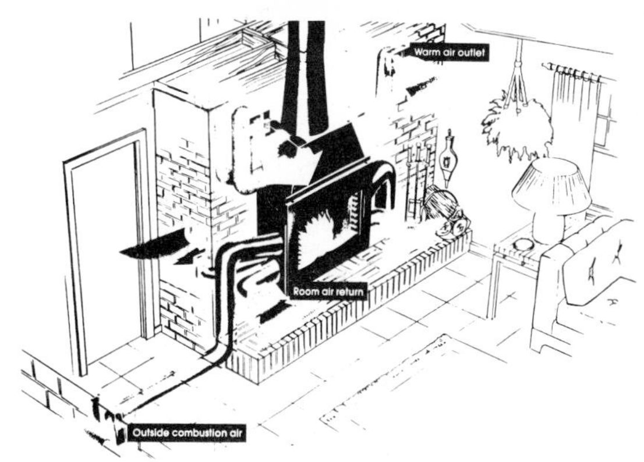

Manufacturer	Martin Industries P.O. Box 128 (FF) Florence, Alabama 35630
Model	Octa-Therm BWH-36
Function	Built-in fireplace
Size (H, W, D)	49½″, 45″, 25″
Weight	298 lbs.
Colors	N/A
Airtight?	N/A
Reduced clearance	Zero clearance
Outside combustion air?	Yes
Glass? (type)	Optional
Cooking surface?	N/A
CONSTRUCTION *Material*	Steel
Gauge or thickness	12 ga.
Air blower? (output)	Optional, 200 CFM
Flue size	9″
Special features	Aluminized and galvanized firebox. Positive seal damper. 2″ cast refractory bottom. Outside damper. Screen. Enamelled outside air inlet.
Options and accessories	Grills. Duct sections & connectors. 24″ flue starter section. Fire-stop.
Efficiency	N/A
Heat output (or area)	42,600 BTUs/hr.
Tested by	Underwriters Laboratories
Suggested retail price	N/A
Brochure	Color, 6 page, 25¢
For nearest dealer call	Write to above
Mail order, if no dealer?	N/A

Manufacturer	Martin Industries P.O. Box 128 (FF) Florence, Alabama 35630
Model	Quadra-Therm LF-36
Function	Built-in fireplace
Size (H, W, D)	41″, 44″, 25″
Weight	225 lbs.
Colors	N/A
Airtight?	N/A
Reduced clearance	Zero clearance
Outside combustion air?	Yes
Glass? (type)	Optional
Cooking surface?	N/A
CONSTRUCTION *Material*	Steel
Gauge or thickness	12 ga.
Air blower? (output)	N/A
Flue size	8″
Special features	Positive sealing damper. 2″ cast refractory bottom. Aluminized and galvanized firebox. Outside damper. Screen. Enamelled outside air inlet. No starter flue required. Stainless steel flue.
Options and accessories	Brass door frame and door.
Efficiency	N/A
Heat output (or area)	N/A
Tested by	Underwriters Laboratories
Suggested retail price	N/A
Brochure	Color, 6 page, 25¢
For nearest dealer call	Write to above
Mail order, if no dealer?	N/A

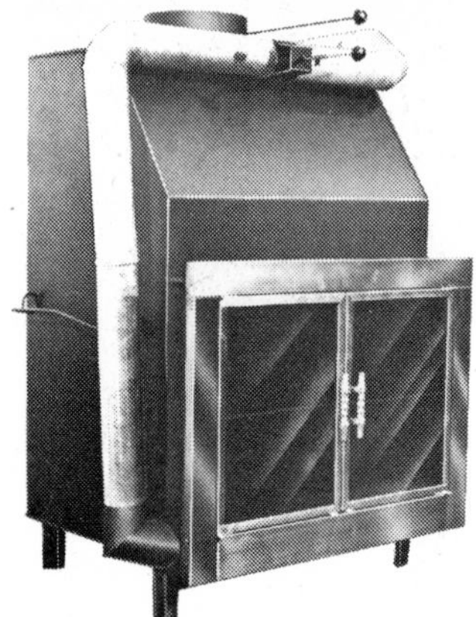

Manufacturer	Messer Mfg. Co. Dept. FF Hwy. 60-71 North Windom, MN 56101
Model	Timberland Fireplace Furnace
Function	Built-in fireplace
Size (H, W, D)	58″, 35½″, 30″
Weight	750 lbs./800 lbs.
Colors	Brass
Airtight?	N/A
Reduced clearance	N/A
Outside combustion air?	Yes
Glass? (type)	Yes, tempered
Cooking surface?	Optional
CONSTRUCTION *Material*	Plate steel
Gauge or thickness	3/16″
Air blower? (output)	N/A
Flue size	12″
Special features	Solid brass doors, Natural convection of hot air. (See schematic for additional information.)
Options and accessories	Cooking grill. Available with or without 4″ lightweight outer wall. ("See-thru" model available.)
Efficiency	N/A
Heat output (or area)	1,500 sq. ft.
Tested by	ICBO
Suggested retail price	N/A
Brochure	Color, free
For nearest dealer call	507-831-1904
Mail order, if no dealer?	Yes

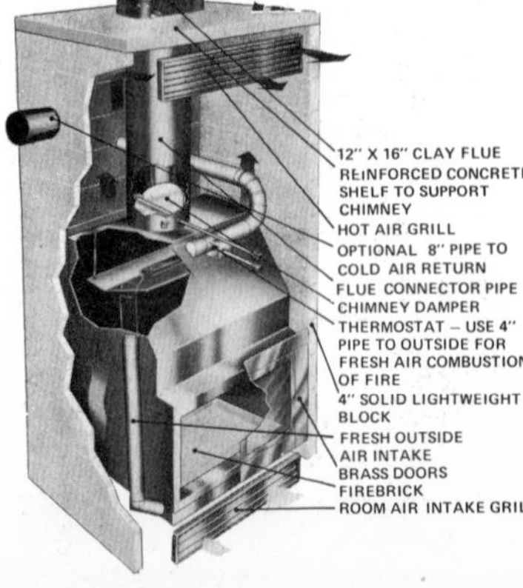

Manufacturer	Preway, Inc. Dept. FF 1430 Second St. N. Wisconsin Rapids, WI 54494
Model	B142R
Function	Built-in fireplace
Size (H, W, D)	42″ firebox
Weight	363 lbs.
Colors	N/A
Airtight?	N/A
Reduced clearance	Zero clearance
Outside combustion air?	N/A
Glass? (type)	Optional
Cooking surface?	N/A
CONSTRUCTION *Material*	Steel
Gauge or thickness	N/A
Air blower? (output)	Optional
Flue size	N/A
Special features	Double walled, circulates hot air. Refractory base, firebrick back. Porcelain side walls.
Options and accessories	Left or right open end. Glass doors. Blower. Grate.
Efficiency	N/A
Heat output (or area)	N/A
Tested by	UL (ICBO) (BOCA) (SBCC)
Suggested retail price	$519.40
Brochure	Color, free
For nearest dealer call	715-423-1100
Mail order, if no dealer?	N/A

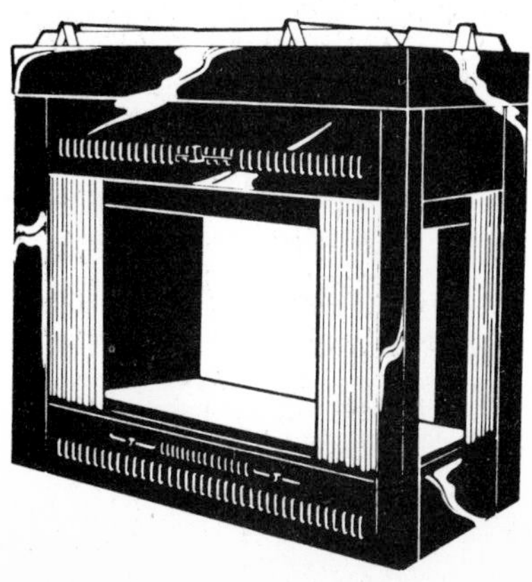

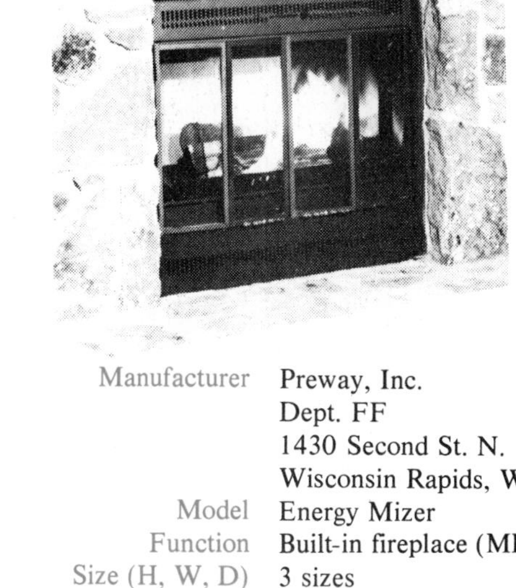

Manufacturer	Preway, Inc. Dept. FF 1430 Second St. N. Wisconsin Rapids, WI 54494
Model	Energy Mizer
Function	Built-in fireplace (MHA)
Size (H, W, D)	3 sizes
Weight	N/A
Colors	N/A
Airtight?	N/A
Reduced clearance	Zero clearance
Outside combustion air?	Yes
Glass? (type)	Yes
Cooking surface?	N/A
CONSTRUCTION *Material*	Steel
Gauge or thickness	N/A
Air blower? (output)	Optional
Flue size	8″
Special features	Double wall construction, hot air circulating. Refractory base, firebrick back. Triple wall chimney.
Options and accessories	Blower.
Efficiency	N/A
Heat output (or area)	N/A
Tested by	Underwriters Laboratories
Suggested retail price	Base price, $634.95
Brochure	Color, free
For nearest dealer call	715-423-1100
Mail order, if no dealer?	N/A

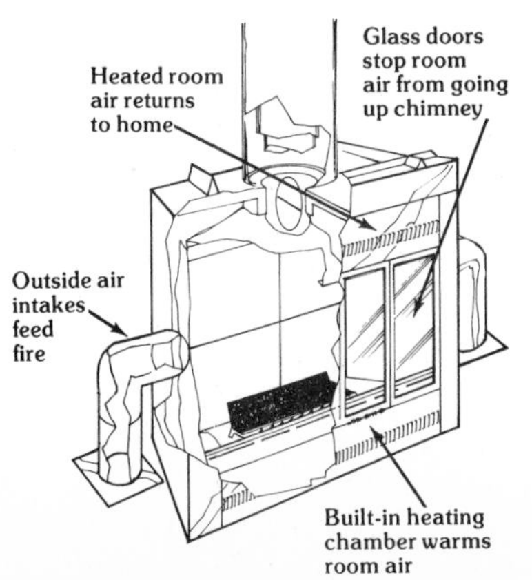

Manufacturer	Pyrosolar Industries, Inc. Hwy. CC, Box 858 (FF) Rolla, MO 65401
Model	CC Standard
Function	Built-in fireplace
Size (H, W, D)	44″, 44″, 28″
Weight	400 lbs.
Colors	N/A
Airtight?	N/A
Reduced clearance	N/A
Outside combustion air?	Yes, 3″ duct
Glass? (type)	Optional
Cooking surface?	N/A
CONSTRUCTION *Material*	Steel
Gauge or thickness	11 ga., 22 ga.
Air blower? (output)	Yes, 650 to 1,600 CFM
Flue size	8″
Special features	Wood/coal grate. Ash pan.
Options and accessories	Glass doors
Efficiency	75%
Heat output (or area)	50,000 to 100,000 BTUs/hr.
Tested by	N/A
Suggested retail price	$825.00
Brochure	Free
For nearest dealer call	314-341-3612
Mail order, if no dealer?	Yes

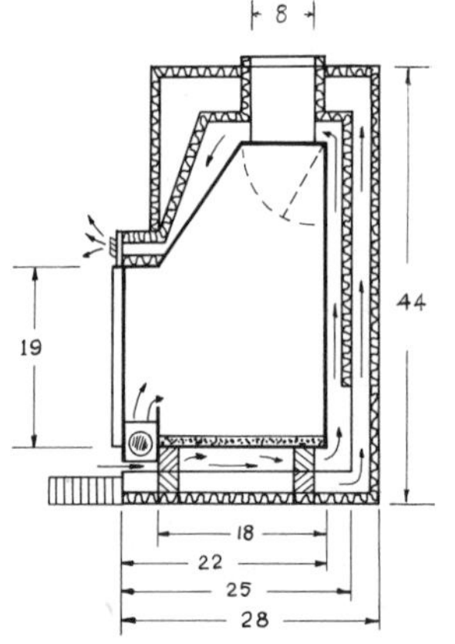

Manufacturer	Pyrosolar Industries, Inc. Hwy. CC, Box 858 (FF) Rolla, MO 65401
Model	CC/2 See-through
Function	Built-in fireplace
Size (H, W, D)	44″, 44″, 32″
Weight	400 lbs.
Colors	N/A
Airtight?	N/A
Reduced clearance	Yes
Outside combustion air?	Yes, 3″ duct
Glass? (type)	Optional
Cooking surface?	N/A
CONSTRUCTION *Material*	Steel
Gauge or thickness	11 ga., 22 ga.
Air blower? (output)	Yes, 650 to 1,600 CFM
Flue size	10″
Special features	Wood/coal grate. Ash pan.
Options and accessories	Solid back door. Glass doors.
Efficiency	75% (with doors)
Heat output (or area)	35,000 to 75,000 BTUs/hr.
Tested by	N/A
Suggested retail price	Base price, $875.00
Brochure	Color, free
For nearest dealer call	314-341-3612
Mail order, if no dealer?	Yes

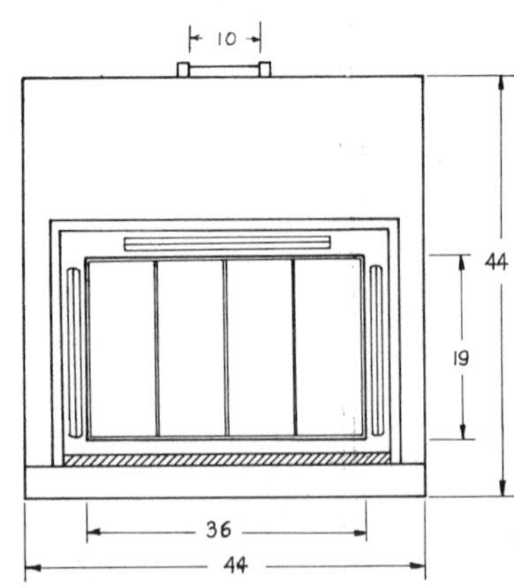

Manufacturer	Pyrosolar Industries, Inc. Hwy. CC, Box 858 (FF) Rolla, MO 65401
Model	ZPY-32
Function	Built-in fireplace
Size (H, W, D)	45″, 45″, 26″
Weight	450 lbs.
Colors	N/A
Airtight?	N/A
Reduced clearance	Zero clearance
Outside combustion air?	Yes, 2″ × 12″
Glass? (type)	Optional
Cooking surface?	N/A
CONSTRUCTION *Material*	Steel
Gauge or thickness	11 ga., 22 ga.
Air blower? (output)	Yes, 600 to 1,600 CFM
Flue size	10″
Special features	Can be hooked up to your existing central hot air system. Can also burn coal with grate.
Options and accessories	Custom sizes. Wood/coal grate. Glass doors.
Efficiency	50% to 75%
Heat output (or area)	50,000 to 100,000 BTUs/hr.
Tested by	Underwriters Laboratories
Suggested retail price	Base price $950.00
Brochure	Free
For nearest dealer call	314-341-3612
Mail order, if no dealer?	Yes

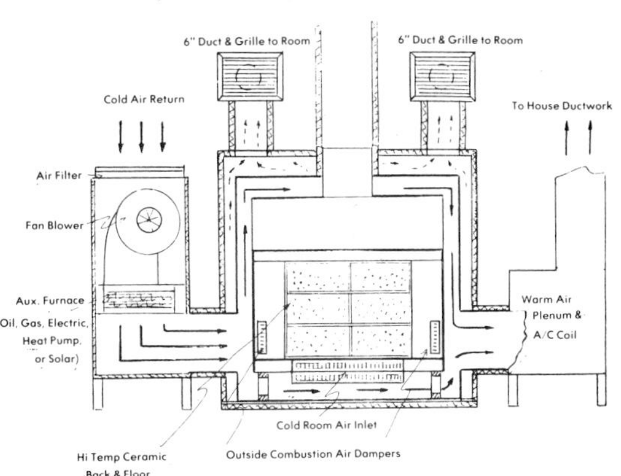

Manufacturer	Superior Fireplace Co. Dept. FF 4325 Artesia Ave. Fullerton, CA 92633
Model	E-Z Energizer
Function	Built-in fireplace
Size (H, W, D)	2 sizes
Weight	247 lbs., 280 lbs.
Colors	N/A
Airtight?	N/A
Reduced clearance	Zero clearance
Outside combustion air?	Yes
Glass? (type)	Optional
Cooking surface?	N/A
CONSTRUCTION *Material*	Stainless steel
Gauge or thickness	N/A
Air blower? (output)	Optional, 180 CFM
Flue size	10″
Special features	Aluminized, galvanized stainless steel body. Flexible ducting. Screen. 25 yr. limited warranty.
Options and accessories	Glass doors. Blower.
Efficiency	(FI test in progress)
Heat output (or area)	N/A
Tested by	Underwriters Laboratories
Suggested retail price	$696.00, $792.00
Brochure	Color, free
For nearest dealer call	714-521-7302
Mail order, if no dealer?	N/A

Manufacturer	Superior Fireplace Co. Dept. FF 4325 Artesia Ave. Fullerton, CA 92633
Model	E-Z Set
Function	Built-in fireplace
Size (H, W, D)	3 sizes
Weight	251 lbs. to 358 lbs.
Colors	N/A
Airtight?	N/A
Reduced clearance	Zero clearance
Outside combustion air?	N/A
Glass? (type)	N/A
Cooking surface?	N/A
CONSTRUCTION *Material*	Stainless steel
Gauge or thickness	N/A
Air blower? (output)	Optional, 250 CFM
Flue size	10″
Special features	Aluminized, galvanized stainless steel. Screen. 25 year limited warranty.
Options and accessories	Blower. (corner models available.)
Efficiency	(FI test is in progress)
Heat output (or area)	N/A
Tested by	(ICBO)(BOCA)(SBCC)(UL)
Suggested retail price	$330.00 to $446.00
Brochure	Color, free
For nearest dealer call	714-521-7302
Mail order, if no dealer?	N/A

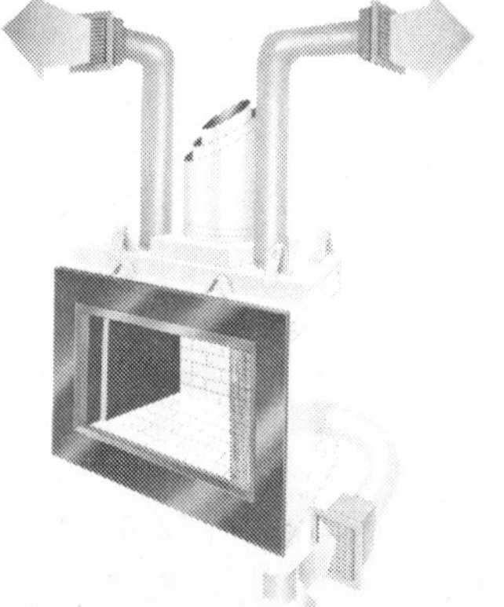

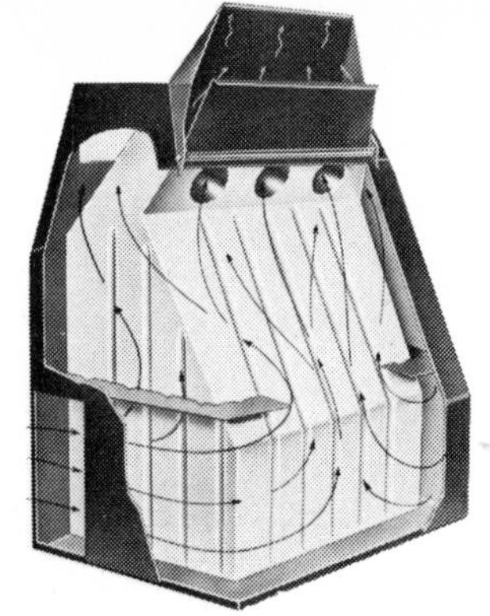

Manufacturer	Superior Fireplace Co. Dept. FF 4325 Artesia Ave. Fullerton, CA 92633
Model	Heatform
Function	Built-in fireplace
Size (H, W, D)	7 sizes
Weight	168 lbs. to 411 lbs.
Colors	N/A
Airtight?	N/A
Reduced clearance	N/A
Outside combustion air?	Optional
Glass? (type)	N/A
Cooking surface?	N/A
CONSTRUCTION *Material*	Steel
Gauge or thickness	7 ga., 11 ga., 16 ga.
Air blower? (output)	N/A
Flue size	(masonry flue only)
Special features	Positive seal damper. Heat tube heat exchange system. 20 year limited warranty.
Options and accessories	Outside air kit. Grills. Ash dump Clean out door. (See-thru or corner model.)
Efficiency	(FI test in progress)
Heat output (or area)	N/A
Tested by	ICBO
Suggested retail price	$244.00 to $1,068.00
Brochure	Color, free
For nearest dealer call	714-521-7302
Mail order, if no dealer?	N/A

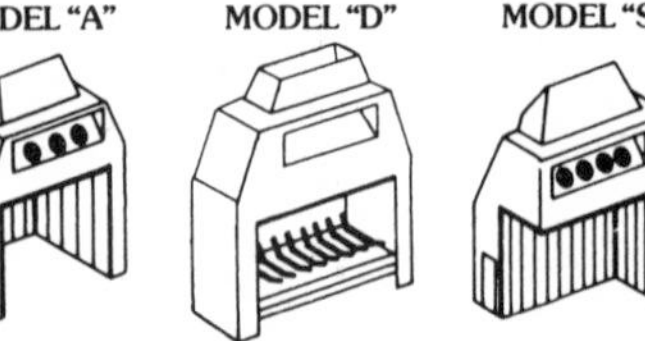

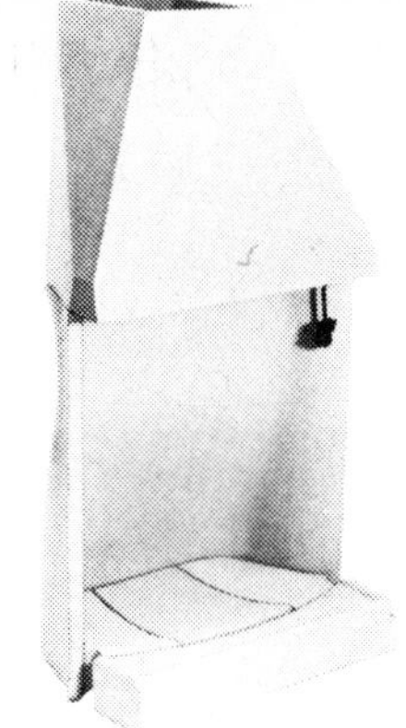

Manufacturer	Survival Heat Inc. Dept. FF 10491 135 A Street Surrey, B.C., Canada
Model	Bellfires S-25
Function	Built-in fireplace
Size (H, W, D)	48", 26¾", 19½"
Weight	378 lbs. (shipping weight)
Colors	Firebrick grey
Airtight?	N/A
Reduced clearance	Yes
Outside combustion air?	N/A
Glass? (type)	N/A
Cooking surface?	N/A
CONSTRUCTION *Material*	Cast refractory
Gauge or thickness	Varies
Air blower? (output)	N/A
Flue size	8"
Special features	2500° refractory, cast with steel alloy fibers, has 130,000 psi tensile strength. 25 yr. warranty.
Options and accessories	Metal chimney adapter. Screen. Grate. (Smaller, larger, and corner models available.)
Efficiency	73%
Heat output (or area)	3,500 cu. ft.
Tested by	Warnock Hersey (CMHC)
Suggested retail price	$350.00
Brochure	Free
For nearest dealer call	604-585-2377
Mail order, if no dealer?	N/A

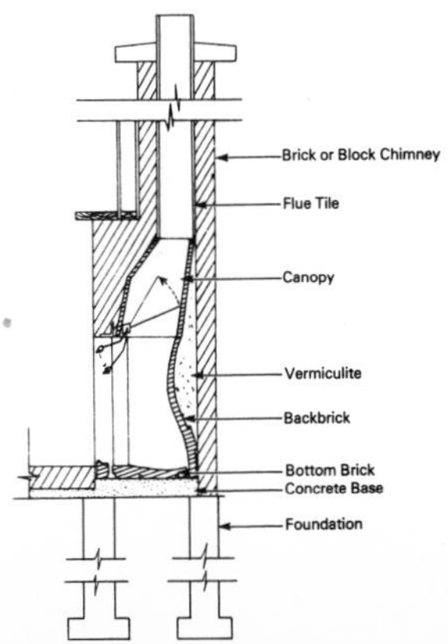

Manufacturer	Survival Heat Inc. Dept. FF 10491 135 A Street Surrey, B.C., Canada
Model	Bellfires TSO
Function	Built-in fireplace
Size (H, W, D)	48", 26¾", 17¾"
Weight	310 lbs.
Colors	Firebrick grey
Airtight?	N/A
Reduced clearance	Yes
Outside combustion air?	N/A
Glass? (type)	N/A
Cooking surface?	N/A
CONSTRUCTION *Material*	Cast refractory
Gauge or thickness	Varies
Air blower? (output)	N/A
Flue size	8"
Special features	3 sides open. (See model S-25 about refractory.) Can be installed on wood floors.
Options and accessories	Metal chimney adapter. Screens (frame or lintel hung). Smaller or larger size available.
Efficiency	73%
Heat output (or area)	3,500 cu. ft.
Tested by	Warnock Hersey (CMHC)
Suggested retail price	Base price $350.00
Brochure	Free
For nearest dealer call	604-585-2377
Mail order, if no dealer?	N/A

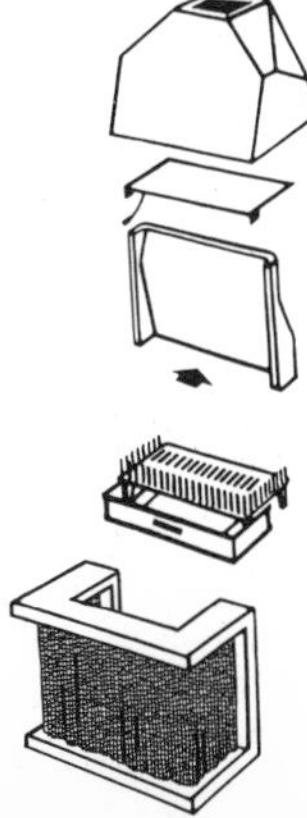

Manufacturer	Tropicana Marketing Inc. Dept FF 7419 North St. N.W. Tacoma, WA 98498
Model	Tropicana Fireplace
Function	Built-in fireplace (MHA)
Size (H, W, D)	43", 46¾", 24"
Weight	160 lbs.
Colors	Black w/ brass doors
Airtight?	N/A
Reduced clearance	Zero clearance
Outside combustion air?	Yes
Glass? (type)	Yes
Cooking surface?	N/A
CONSTRUCTION *Material*	Stainless steel
Gauge or thickness	N/A
Air blower? (output)	Yes, 180 CFM
Flue size	8"
Special features	Double wall, stainless steel firebox, galvanized steel oven insulation. Wood/coal use. 25 yr. warranty.
Options and accessories	Unit complete. (Smaller model available.)
Efficiency	75%
Heat output (or area)	3,000 sq. ft.
Tested by	Warnock Hersey (ICBO) (UL)
Suggested retail price	N/A
Brochure	Free
For nearest dealer call	206-581-4312
Mail order, if no dealer?	N/A

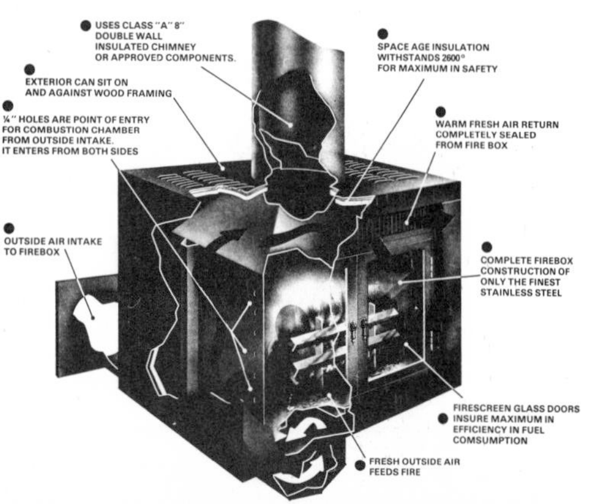

Manufacturer	Woodside Fireplaces P.O. Box 2249 (FF) Redwood City, CA 94064
Model	Heatsaver II
Function	Built-in fireplace (MHA)
Size (H, W, D)	43", 46 3/4", 24"
Weight	321 lbs.
Colors	Black
Airtight?	N/A
Reduced clearance	Yes
Outside combustion air?	Yes
Glass? (type)	Yes, tempered
Cooking surface?	N/A
CONSTRUCTION *Material*	Steel
Gauge or thickness	N/A
Air blower? (output)	Optional, 140 CFM
Flue size	8"
Special features	Double wall construction. Firebrick back and bottom. 25 yr. warranty.
Options and accessories	Blower. (Woodside also makes zero clearance open end fireplaces.)
Efficiency	N/A
Heat output (or area)	N/A
Tested by	Underwriters Laboratories
Suggested retail price	$613.00
Brochure	Color, free
For nearest dealer call	415-368-2912
Mail order, if no dealer?	N/A

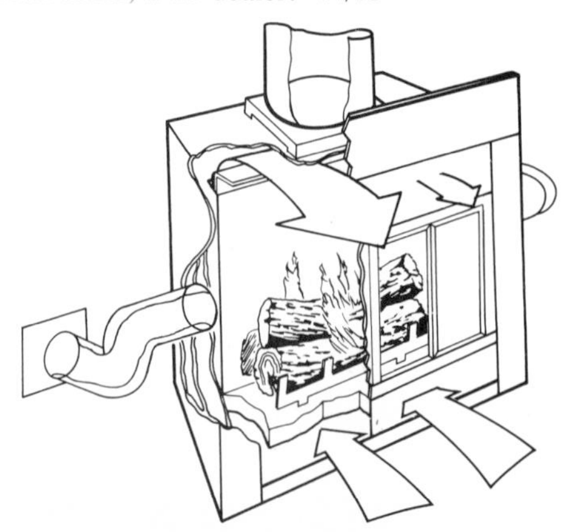

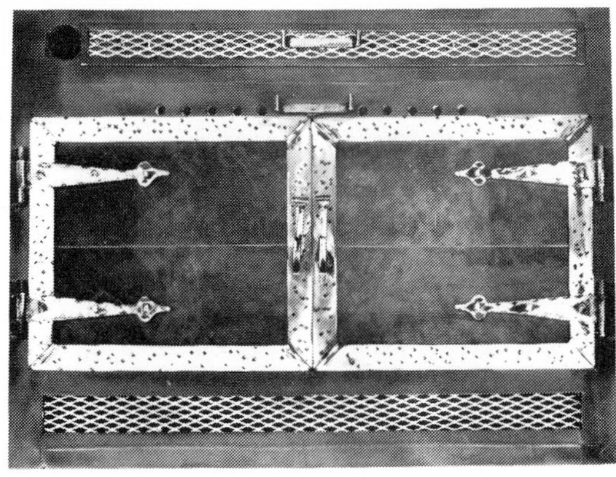

Manufacturer	All Nighter Stove Works Dept. FF 80 Commerce St. Glastonbury, CT 06033
Model	Overnight Fireplace Heater
Function	Fireplace insert
Size (H, W, D)	27″, 37″, 19″
Weight	350 lbs.
Colors	Black/steel
Airtight?	N/A
Reduced clearance	N/A
Outside combustion air?	N/A
Glass? (type)	Yes, Pyroceram
Cooking surface?	N/A
CONSTRUCTION *Material*	Steel
Gauge or thickness	¼″
Air blower? (output)	Optional, 60–100 CFM
Flue size	Rectangular
Special features	"Hammered look" doors and hinges. Double wall construction.
Options and accessories	2-speed blower
Efficiency	N/A
Heat output (or area)	3–5 rooms
Tested by	In progress
Suggested retail price	$699.00
Brochure	$1.00
For nearest dealer call	203-659-0344
Mail order, if no dealer?	N/A

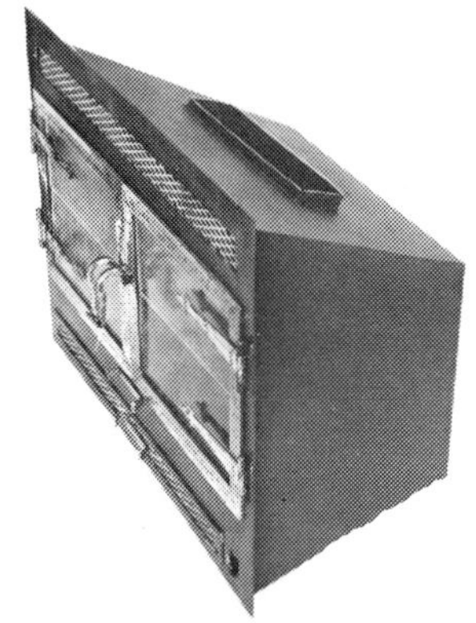

Manufacturer	Aquappliances, Inc. Dept. FF 315 Sunshine Lane San Marcos, Calif. 92069
Model	The Free Heat Machine
Function	Glass fire screen (hot air)
Size (H, W, D)	5 sizes
Weight	N/A
Colors	Black with brass trim
Airtight?	N/A
Reduced clearance	N/A
Outside combustion air?	N/A
Glass? (type)	Yes
Cooking surface?	No
CONSTRUCTION *Material*	Steel
Gauge or thickness	N/A
Air blower? (output)	Yes (2) 2-speed, 160 CFM (ea)
Flue size	N/A
Special features	Draft control, One year limited warranty. Removable ash pan. 12 heat exchanger tubes, each 1½″ in diameter.
Options and accessories	Screen.
Efficiency	N/A
Heat output (or area)	38,000 BTUs/hr., 1,500 sq. ft.
Tested by	UL listed and Canadian Standards Assoc.
Suggested retail price	N/A
Brochure	Free
For nearest dealer call	714-744-1610
Mail order, if no dealer?	N/A

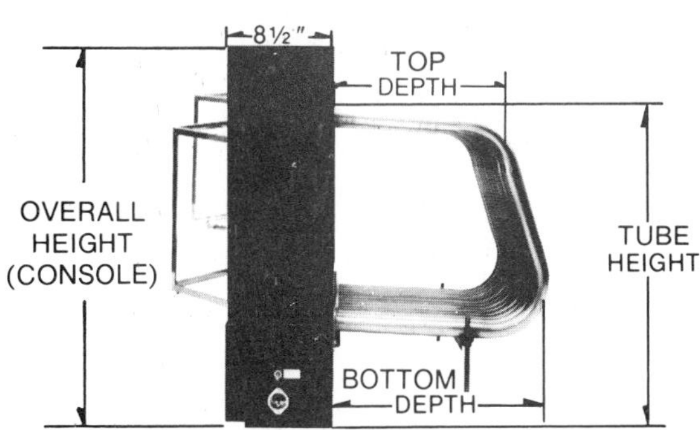

Manufacturer	ARC Industries, Inc. P.O. Box 718 (FF) Middletown, Conn. 06457
Model	Fyrdor
Function	Glass fire screen (hot air)
Size (H, W, D)	4 sizes, 24″-34″ H, 32″-48″ W
Weight	100 lbs.
Colors	Black with brass trim
Airtight?	Can be made airtight
Reduced clearance	N/A
Outside combustion air?	N/A
Glass? (type)	Yes, tempered
Cooking surface?	N/A
CONSTRUCTION *Material*	Steel and stainless steel
Gauge or thickness	16 ga.
Air blower? (output)	Yes, 60 CFM (R or L side)
Flue size	N/A
Special features	All welded construction. Burn area of grate is 18 ga. stainless steel tube over 14 ga. steel tube. 3 yr. guarantee against burnout. Brass plated strap hinges. Air is heated to 700° F.
Options and accessories	Unit complete.
Efficiency	N/A
Heat output (or area)	1,200 sq. ft.
Tested by	N/A
Suggested retail price	$395.00
Brochure	Color, free
For nearest dealer call	203-347-5211
Mail order, if no dealer?	N/A

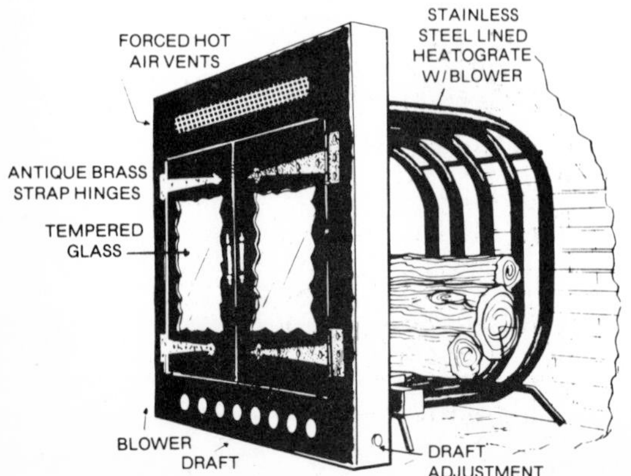

Manufacturer	Bennett-Ireland Dept. FF 23 State Street Norwich, New York 13815
Model	Benefire #1000
Function	Fireplace insert
Size (H, W, D)	24″, 24″, 16″ (firebox)
Weight	220 lbs.
Colors	Ant. brass w/black trim
Airtight?	Yes
Reduced clearance	N/A
Outside combustion air?	N/A
Glass? (type)	Yes, tempered
Cooking surface?	N/A
CONSTRUCTION *Material*	Steel
Gauge or thickness	3/16″
Air blower? (output)	Yes
Flue size	N/A
Special features	5-flue heat exchanger. Draft control. Log retainers. Metal door shields slip behind glass at night.
Options and accessories	Unit complete.
Efficiency	N/A
Heat output (or area)	50,000 BTUs/hr
Tested by	N/A
Suggested retail price	$599.95
Brochure	Color, free
For nearest dealer call	607-334-3216
Mail order, if no dealer?	N/A

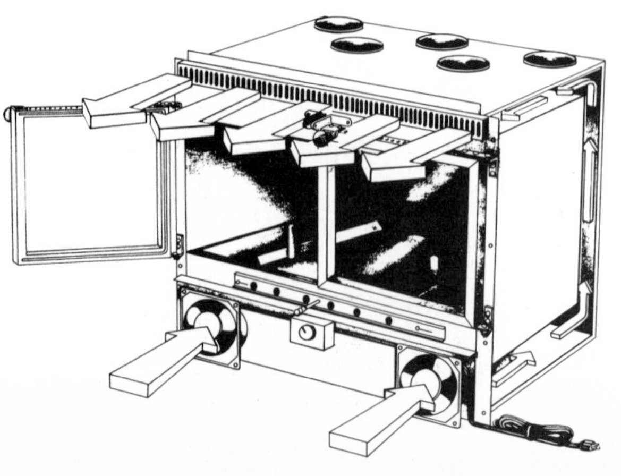

Manufacturer	C.E.M.I. Box 290 (FF) Ashland, Ohio 44805
Model	Concept II
Function	Fireplace insert
Size (H, W, D)	25″, 26″, 19″ (firebox)
Weight	330 lbs.
Colors	Swedish steel (blue), or black.
Airtight?	Yes
Reduced clearance	N/A
Outside combustion air?	N/A
Glass? (type)	Yes, mica
Cooking surface?	N/A
CONSTRUCTION *Material*	Steel, cast iron.
Gauge or thickness	¼″
Air blower? (output)	Yes, 105 CFM
Flue size	N/A
Special features	Baffled heat exchanger. Double-wall construction. Pre-heated combustion air. Firebrick lined. Damper. 25 yr. limited warranty.
Options and accessories	"Picture" trim frames in 3 sizes.
Efficiency	78%
Heat output (or area)	120,000 BTUs/hr.
Tested by	In progress
Suggested retail price	$650.00
Brochure	Color, free.
For nearest dealer call	419-289-2224
Mail order, if no dealer?	N/A

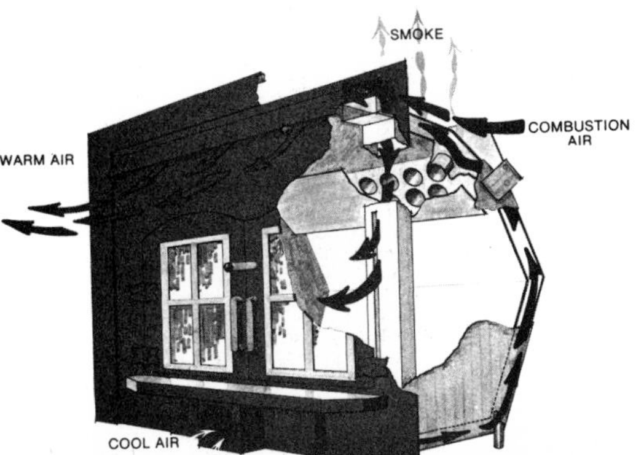

Manufacturer	C & H Manufacturing Dept. FF 654 N. Colony Road Wallingford, Conn. 06492
Model	Fire Rite Insert
Function	Fireplace insert
Size (H, W, D)	25½″, 30½″, 18″
Weight	200 lbs.
Colors	Black
Airtight?	Yes
Reduced clearance	N/A
Outside combustion air?	N/A
Glass? (type)	Yes, Pyrex
Cooking surface?	N/A
CONSTRUCTION *Material*	Boiler plate steel
Gauge or thickness	3/16″
Air blower? (output)	Optional
Flue size	8″
Special features	Firebrick lined. Takes 26″ logs.
Options and accessories	Blower. Screen. Stove boards. Fireplace cover panels. (C & H has five different inserts and stoves.)
Efficiency	N/A
Heat output (or area)	1,250 sq. ft.
Tested by	N/A
Suggested retail price	$459.00
Brochure	Free
For nearest dealer call	203-269-6644
Mail order, if no dealer?	Yes

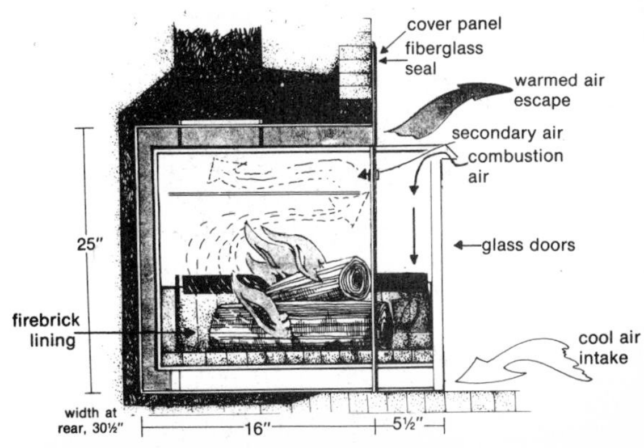

Manufacturer	DeVault Fab-Weld P.O. Box 98 (FF) DeVault, PA 19432
Model	Old Mill 55
Function	Fireplace insert/wood stove
Size (H, W, D)	22¼″, 25″, 28″
Weight	395 lbs.
Colors	N/A
Airtight?	Yes
Reduced clearance	N/A
Outside combustion air?	N/A
Glass? (type)	N/A
Cooking surface?	Yes, 18″ × 25″
CONSTRUCTION *Material*	Steel, cast iron
Gauge or thickness	¼″
Air blower? (output)	Optional, 140 CFM
Flue size	8″ (top)
Special features	Cast iron door, 25 year limited warranty. Firebrick lined. Double baffle. Takes 24″ logs.
Options and accessories	Blower. (Small single door model available.)
Efficiency	N/A
Heat output (or area)	2,200 to 2,500 sq. ft.
Tested by	Arnold Greene Test Lab
Suggested retail price	$432.00
Brochure	Free
For nearest dealer call	215-647-5590
Mail order, if no dealer?	Yes

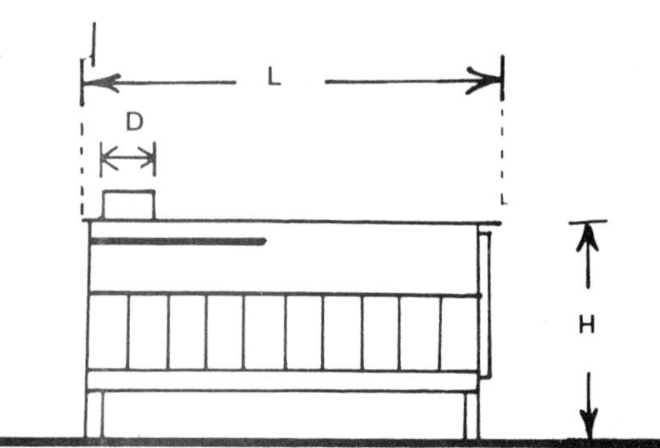

Manufacturer	Double Eagle Fireplace Mfg. Dept. FF 410 S. 96th Seattle, Wash. 98108
Model	Insert
Function	Fireplace insert
Size (H, W, D)	22″, 31″, 18″
Weight	150 lbs.
Colors	Black and brass
Airtight?	N/A
Reduced clearance	N/A
Outside combustion air?	Yes
Glass? (type)	Yes, tempered glass
Cooking surface?	N/A
CONSTRUCTION *Material*	Stainless steel
Gauge or thickness	14 ga.
Air blower? (output)	Yes, 180 CFM
Flue size	N/A
Special features	25 year warranty against burnout. Uses outside air for heat exchanger. Draw screen.
Options and accessories	Unit complete.
Efficiency	80%
Heat output (or area)	2,000 to 3,000 sq. ft.
Tested by	N/A
Suggested retail price	$725.00
Brochure	Free
For nearest dealer call	206-767-3440
Mail order, if no dealer?	Yes

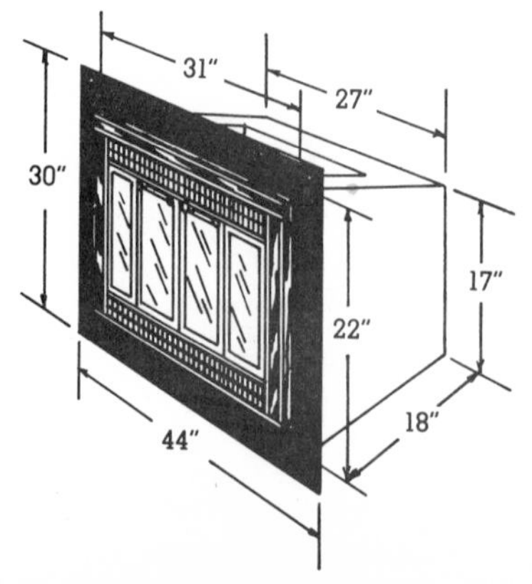

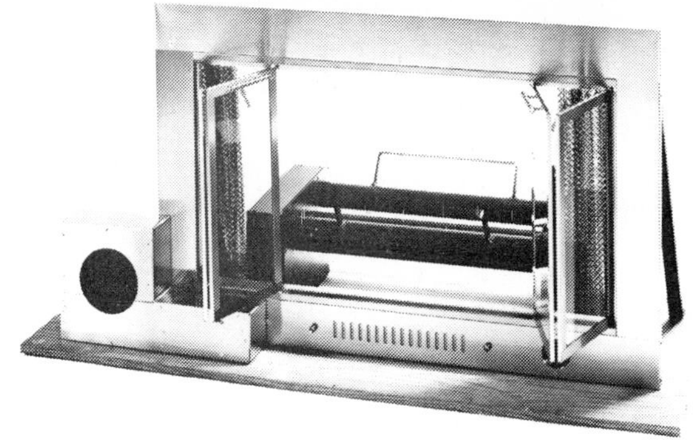

Manufacturer	Fireguard, Inc. P.O. Box 413 (FF) 352 Sackett Pt. Rd. North Haven, Conn. 06473
Model	Heatmaster
Function	Glass fire screen (hot air)
Size (H, W, D)	5 sizes
Weight	N/A
Colors	Antique brass
Airtight?	N/A
Reduced clearance	N/A
Outside combustion air?	N/A
Glass? (type)	Yes, tempered
Cooking surface?	N/A
CONSTRUCTION *Material*	Steel
Gauge or thickness	14 ga. heat exchanger
Air blower? (output)	Yes, 105 CFM
Flue size	N/A
Special features	Draw screen. Variable speed noiseless fan. Adjustable grate.
Options and accessories	Unit complete.
Efficiency	N/A
Heat output (or area)	20,000 BTUs/hr., 1,500 sq. ft.
Tested by	N/A
Suggested retail price	$300.00
Brochure	Free
For nearest dealer call	203-248-9308
Mail order, if no dealer?	N/A

Manufacturer	Fisher Stoves Int'l., Inc. P.O. Box 10605 (FF) Eugene, Oregon 97440
Model	Fireplace Insert
Function	Fireplace insert
Size (H, W, D)	21 ¾", 24¾", 36¾"
Weight	610 lbs., 620 lbs.
Colors	Black with nickel trim
Airtight?	Yes
Reduced clearance	N/A
Outside combustion air?	N/A
Glass? (type)	N/A
Cooking surface?	Yes, 24¾" × 13"
CONSTRUCTION *Material*	Steel, cast iron
Gauge or thickness	¼", 5/16"
Air blower? (output)	Optional
Flue size	8"
Special features	Cast iron doors. Chromium fire screen. Firebrick lined. Takes 27" logs.
Options and accessories	Nickel trim doors. Flashing to fit fireplace opening. Blower. (Five other models available.)
Efficiency	N/A
Heat output (or area)	1,750 sq. ft.
Tested by	UL and ICBO
Suggested retail price	$699.00
Brochure	Free
For nearest dealer call	Write to above
Mail order, if no dealer?	N/A

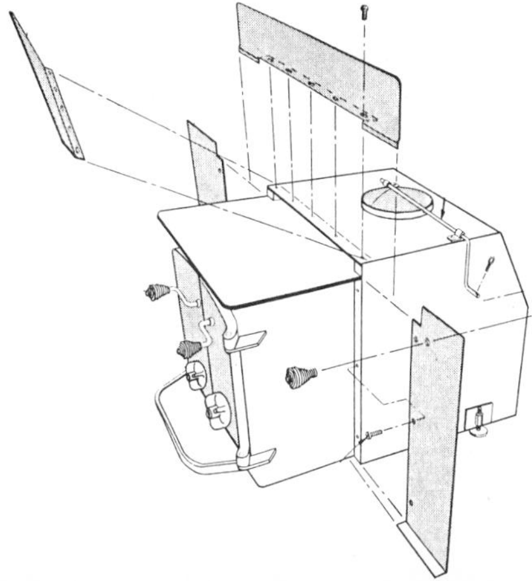

Manufacturer	Grizzly Stoves/Derco Inc. P.O. Box 9 (FF) Blissfield, Michigan 49228
Model	Fireplace Furnace
Function	Fireplace insert
Size (H, W, D)	3 sizes
Weight	300 lbs., 345 lbs., 385 lbs.
Colors	Black with nickel trim
Airtight?	Yes
Reduced clearance	N/A
Outside combustion air?	N/A
Glass? (type)	Yes, Vycor
Cooking surface?	Yes
CONSTRUCTION *Material*	Plate steel
Gauge or thickness	¼", 14 ga.
Air blower? (output)	Yes, 265 CFM
Flue size	8"
Special features	Thermostat controlled blower. Fireclay lining. Baffled. Double wall. 25 year limited warranty. Takes 24" logs.
Options and accessories	Can be converted (with legs) to free-standing unit. Solid doors optional.
Efficiency	80%
Heat output (or area)	50,000 BTUs/hr
Tested by	N/A
Suggested retail price	$537.00 to $737.00
Brochure	Color, free
For nearest dealer call	517-486-4337
Mail order, if no dealer?	Yes

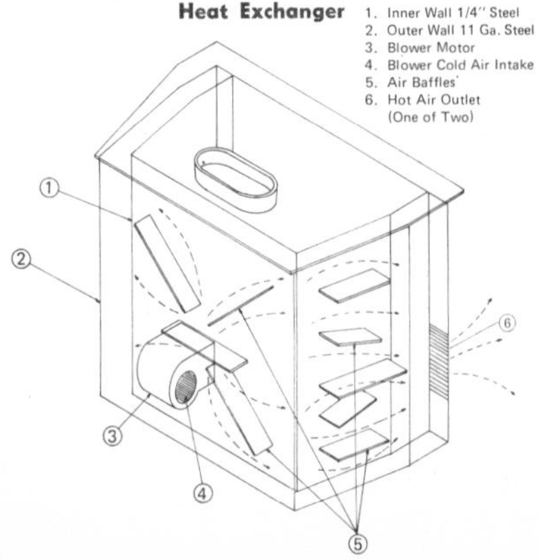

Manufacturer	Hayes Equip. Corp. P.O. Box 526 (FF) Unionville, Conn. 06085
Model	Better 'N' Ben's 701
Function	Fireplace insert/woodstove
Size (H, W, D)	23¼", 30", 24¾"
Weight	525 lbs./535 lbs.
Colors	Black
Airtight?	Yes
Reduced clearance	N/A
Outside combustion air?	N/A
Glass? (type)	N/A
Cooking surface?	Yes, 10½" × 30"
CONSTRUCTION *Material*	Plate steel, cast iron
Gauge or thickness	¼"
Air blower? (output)	Optional, 135 CFM
Flue size	7"
Special features	Cast iron door. Baffled. Damper. Firebrick lined. Back panels insulation. Screen. Heat deflector. Takes 22" logs.
Options and accessories	Nickel trimmed doors. Broiler grill. Top mounted baking oven.
Efficiency	60%
Heat output (or area)	55,000 BTUs/hr. (w/blower)
Tested by	Arnold Greene/BOCA/ICBO
Suggested retail price	$599.00
Brochure	Color 12 page, free.
For nearest dealer call	203-673-2557
Mail order, if no dealer?	N/A

Manufacturer	Hydro-Temp RD #1 Box 14 (FF) Lewisberry, PA 17339
Model	Conestoga Insert
Function	Fireplace insert
Size (H, W, D)	26", 44", 19"
Weight	375 lbs.
Colors	Black
Airtight?	Yes
Reduced clearance	N/A
Outside combustion air?	N/A
Glass? (type)	N/A
Cooking surface?	N/A
CONSTRUCTION *Material*	Steel, cast iron
Gauge or thickness	11 gauge
Air blower? (output)	On hot air model, 167 CFM
Flue size	N/A
Special features	Bi-fold cast iron doors. Cast iron front. Pre-heated draft. Slide damper. 1¼" water jacket on hydronic unit. 15 yr. limited warranty. Firebrick lined.
Options and accessories	Hot air or hot water. Screen. (Built-in units available.)
Efficiency	72%
Heat output (or area)	100,000 BTUs/hr.
Tested by	N/A
Suggested retail price	$625.00 (air), $675.00 (hydronic)
Brochure	Free
For nearest dealer call	717-938-2673
Mail order, if no dealer?	Yes

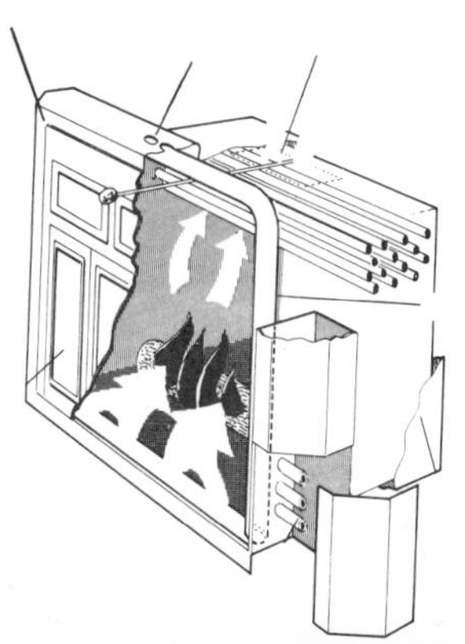

Manufacturer	Jackson Frontier Dept. FF 4065 W. 11 Steet Eugene, OR 97402
Model	Frontier FI-24-8
Function	Fireplace insert
Size (H, W, D)	22¼", 25¼", 20½"
Weight	295 lbs.
Colors	Black
Airtight?	Yes
Reduced clearance	N/A
Outside combustion air?	N/A
Glass? (type)	N/A
Cooking surface?	N/A
CONSTRUCTION *Material*	Plate steel
Gauge or thickness	5/16", 1/4", 3/16"
Air blower? (output)	Yes, 80 CFM (2)
Flue size	8"
Special features	Has no bottom; instead, two ¼" thick tubular heat exchangers; fire burns on existing fireplace floor. Double wall top and rear. Screen. Takes 24" logs.
Options and accessories	Unit complete.
Efficiency	40%
Heat output (or area)	1,500 sq. ft.
Tested by	N/A
Suggested retail price	N/A
Brochure	Free
For nearest dealer call	503-484-2877
Mail order, if no dealer?	Yes

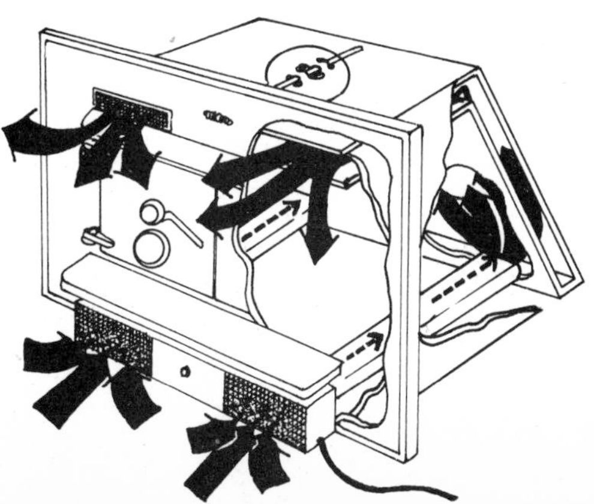

Manufacturer	Lauderdale-Hamilton Box 45 (FF) Main St. Shannon, MS 38868
Model	Standard
Function	Glass fire screen (hot air)
Size (H, W, D)	32", 48", 20"
Weight	60 lbs.
Colors	Black
Airtight?	N/A
Reduced clearance	N/A
Outside combustion air?	N/A
Glass? (type)	Tempered
Cooking surface?	N/A
CONSTRUCTION *Material*	Steel
Gauge or thickness	16 ga., 10 ga.
Air blower? (output)	Yes, 60 CFM
Flue size	N/A
Special features	16 ga. frame, 10 ga. bottom. Damper door.
Options and accessories	Custom sizes. Decorative blower covers.
Efficiency	N/A
Heat output (or area)	30,000 BTUs/hr
Tested by	N/A
Suggested retail price	$199.95
Brochure	Free
For nearest dealer call	601-767-3928
Mail order, if no dealer?	Yes

Manufacturer	National Stove Works. Inc. Dept. FF Howe Caverns Road Cableskill, N.Y. 12043
Model	Insider
Function	Fireplace insert
Size (H, W, D)	25", 34", 26"
Weight	390 lbs./400 lbs.
Colors	Black
Airtight?	Yes
Reduced clearance	N/A
Outside combustion air?	N/A
Glass? (type)	Yes, Vycor
Cooking surface?	N/A
CONSTRUCTION *Material*	Hot rolled steel
Gauge or thickness	3/16"
Air blower? (output)	Yes, (2), total 220 CFM
Flue size	N/A
Special features	Double-walled continuously welded body. Built-in blowers. Takes up to 28" logs.
Options and accessories	Unit Complete. (Smaller and larger size available.)
Efficiency	50% to 75%
Heat output (or area)	75,000 BTUs/hr, 1,400 sq. ft.
Tested by	Arnold Greene Lab (UL)
Suggested retail price	$749.00
Brochure	Color, free
For nearest dealer call	518-292-8517
Mail order, if no dealer?	N/A

Manufacturer	Peacock Stove Works Rt. 2 Box 2431 (FF) Baldwin, MI 49304
Model	Sunspirit
Function	Fireplace insert
Size (H, W, D)	25″, 24″, 30″
Weight	N/A
Colors	Black
Airtight?	Yes
Reduced clearance	N/A
Outside combustion air?	N/A
Glass? (type)	N/A
Cooking surface?	Yes
CONSTRUCTION *Material*	Plate steel
Gauge or thickness	7 ga.
Air blower? (output)	Yes, 265 CFM
Flue size	8″ (top)
Special features	Secondary combustion air system. Screen. Firebrick lined. 25 year warranty.
Options and accessories	Unit complete.
Efficiency	88%
Heat output (or area)	100,000 BTUs/hr.
Tested by	Arnold Greene Test Lab
Suggested retail price	$617.00
Brochure	Free
For nearest dealer call	616-745-4609
Mail order, if no dealer?	Yes

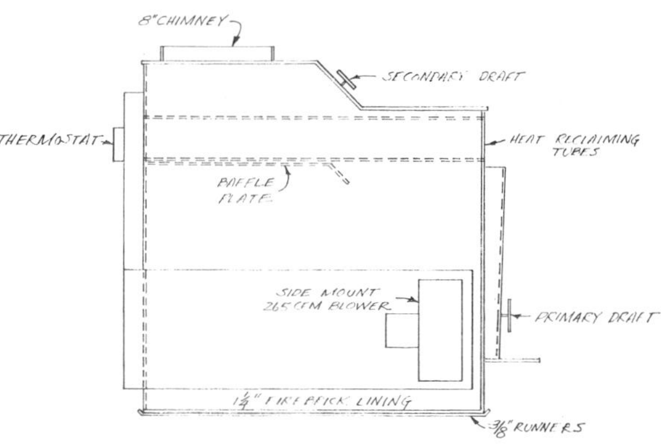

Manufacturer	Pheonix America Corp. P.O. Box 1144 (FF) Asheville, N.C. 28802
Model	4880
Function	Fireplace insert
Size (H, W, D)	24″, 32″, 22″
Weight	N/A
Colors	Black
Airtight?	Yes
Reduced clearance	N/A
Outside combustion air?	N/A
Glass? (type)	Yes
Cooking surface?	N/A
CONSTRUCTION *Material*	Hot rolled steel
Gauge or thickness	7 ga., 3/16″
Air blower? (output)	Optional 220 CFM
Flue size	5″ × 12″
Special features	Firebrick lined. Baffled. Gravity flow door. Double wall body. Takes up to 30″ logs.
Options and accessories	Blower.
Efficiency	N/A
Heat output (or area)	N/A
Tested by	Arnold Greene Test Lab
Suggested retail price	$688.00
Brochure	Free
For nearest dealer call	704-258-9265
Mail order, if no dealer?	Yes

Manufacturer	Precision Metal Products, Inc. Route 6 Box 79 D(F) Wilmington, N.C. 28405
Model	Hearth King Fireplace Insert
Function	Fireplace insert
Size (H, W, D)	3 sizes
Weight	300 lbs. and up
Colors	Black
Airtight?	Yes
Reduced clearance	N/A
Outside combustion air?	N/A
Glass? (type)	Optional, Vycor or Pyroceram
Cooking surface?	Yes
CONSTRUCTION *Material*	Hardened plate steel
Gauge or thickness	¼″, 7 ga., 11 ga.
Air blower? (output)	Yes, 465 CFM
Flue size	8″ (top)
Special features	Variable speed, floor-level blower. Removable door. Screen. Firebrick lined. Ash shovel.
Options and accessories	Optional glass door.
Efficiency	N/A
Heat output (or area)	150,000 BTUs/hr.
Tested by	Energy Systems Inc. (UL)
Suggested retail price	N/A
Brochure	Free
For nearest dealer call	919-763-6561
Mail order, if no dealer?	N/A

Manufacturer	Quaker Stove Co., Inc. 200 (FF) W. 5th St. Lansdale, PA 19446
Model	Moravian Fireplace Insert
Function	Fireplace insert (extended out)
Size (H, W, D)	24½″, 28¾″, 24″
Weight	540 lbs.
Colors	Red, blue, green
Airtight?	Yes
Reduced clearance	N/A
Outside combustion air?	N/A
Glass? (type)	Vycor
Cooking surface?	On extended model, 11″ × 7″
CONSTRUCTION *Material*	Plate steel, cast iron
Gauge or thickness	¼″, 3/16″
Air blower? (output)	Optional, 95 CFM
Flue size	5″ × 11″
Special features	Porcelain coated arch. Firebrick lined. Baffled. Double-wall body. Doors, front are cast iron.
Options and accessories	Flush fitting model available. Blower. Solid doors. Screen. Smaller size; custom sizes.
Efficiency	85% w/blower
Heat output (or area)	60,000 BTUs w/blower
Tested by	Underwriters Laboratories
Suggested retail price	$795.00
Brochure	Color, free
For nearest dealer call	215-362-2019
Mail order, if no dealer?	N/A

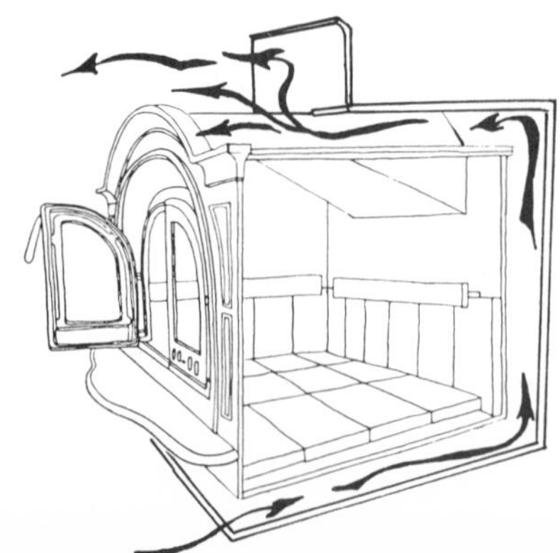

Manufacturer	Shayer Stove Inc. Dept. FF 3420 C St. N.E. #405 Auburn, WA 98002
Model	Country
Function	Fireplace insert
Size (H, W, D)	22″, 28″, 14″ (inserted half)
Weight	502 lbs./520 lbs.
Colors	Black
Airtight?	Yes
Reduced clearance	N/A
Outside combustion air?	N/A
Glass? (type)	N/A
Cooking surface?	Yes, 9″ × 28″
CONSTRUCTION *Material*	Plate steel
Gauge or thickness	¼″, 5/16″
Air blower? (output)	N/A
Flue size	8″
Special features	Double walled; aluminized inside of outer box. Firebrick lined. 5/16″ thick steel doors. Preheated drafts. Removable baffle.
Options and accessories	Brass or chrome trim. Black, brass, or chrome warming plates. Four flange sizes.
Efficiency	N/A
Heat output (or area)	13,000 cu. ft.
Tested by	N/A
Suggested retail price	$649.00
Brochure	Free
For nearest dealer call	206-854-2593
Mail order, if no dealer?	Yes

Manufacturer	Smokey Mountain Ent., Inc. P.O. Drawer 8789 (FF) Asheville, N.C. 28804
Model	Regular Buck Stove Insert
Function	Fireplace insert
Size (H, W, D)	24¾″, 37½″, 24″
Weight	415 lbs.
Colors	Black
Airtight?	Yes
Reduced clearance	N/A
Outside combustion air?	N/A
Glass? (type)	Optional
Cooking surface?	Yes
CONSTRUCTION *Material*	Boiler plate steel
Gauge or thickness	¼″, 3/16″
Air blower? (output)	Yes, 260-660 CFM
Flue size	N/A
Special features	Thermostatically controlled 3-speed blower. Air cooled door handles. Built-in damper. Screen. Draft control spark deflectors. Andirons.
Options and accessories	Optional glass door with Vycor glass.
Efficiency	N/A
Heat output (or area)	2,500 sq. ft.
Tested by	N/A
Suggested retail price	N/A
Brochure	Free
For nearest dealer call	704-255-8935
Mail order, if no dealer?	N/A

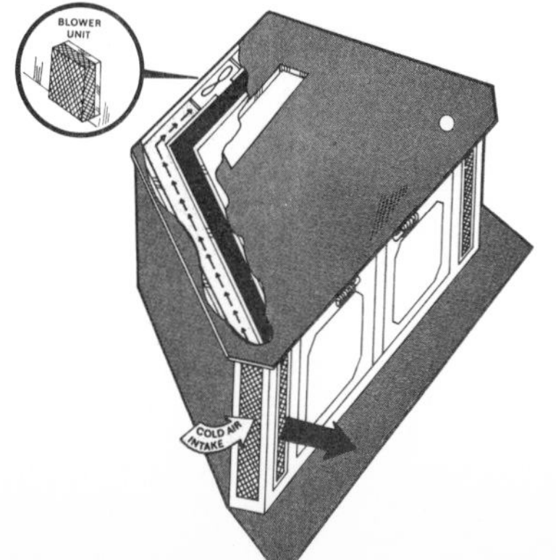

Manufacturer	Spalt Associates Corp. Dept. FF 275 Circuit St. Hanover, Mass. 02339
Model	Norseman #59
Function	Fireplace insert
Size (H, W, D)	25″, 28″, 14″
Weight	238 lbs./246 lbs.
Colors	Black
Airtight?	Yes
Reduced clearance	N/A
Outside combustion air?	N/A
Glass? (type)	Yes, isinglass
Cooking surface?	N/A
CONSTRUCTION *Material*	Steel
Gauge or thickness	3/16″
Air blower? (output)	Yes, 76 CFM
Flue size	10″
Special features	Double wall construction. Takes 19″ logs.
Options and accessories	Tile. Brass balls.
Efficiency	N/A
Heat output (or area)	5 to 6 rooms
Tested by	N/A
Suggested retail price	$518.00
Brochure	35¢
For nearest dealer call	617-871-3180
Mail order, if no dealer?	Yes

Manufacturer	Thermalite Corp. P.O. Box 658 (FF) Brentwood, TN 37027
Model	Hearth Aid II
Function	Glass fire screen (hot air)
Size (H, W, D)	N/A
Weight	N/A
Colors	Black w/brass; ant. gold
Airtight?	N/A
Reduced clearance	N/A
Outside combustion air?	N/A
Glass? (type)	Yes, tempered
Cooking surface?	N/A
CONSTRUCTION *Material*	Steel, stainless steel
Gauge or thickness	N/A
Air blower? (output)	Yes, 120 CFM
Flue size	N/A
Special features	Stainless steel heat exchange tube is 4 feet long, 5 inches in diameter. Varying speed thermostat controlled blower (UL listed).
Options and accessories	Unit complete.
Efficiency	N/A
Heat output (or area)	20,000 BTUs/hr.
Tested by	N/A
Suggested retail price	$270.00
Brochure	Color, free
For nearest dealer call	Write to above
Mail order, if no dealer?	N/A

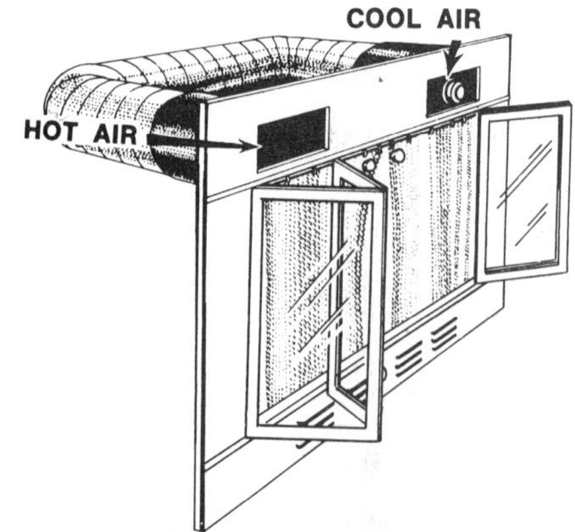

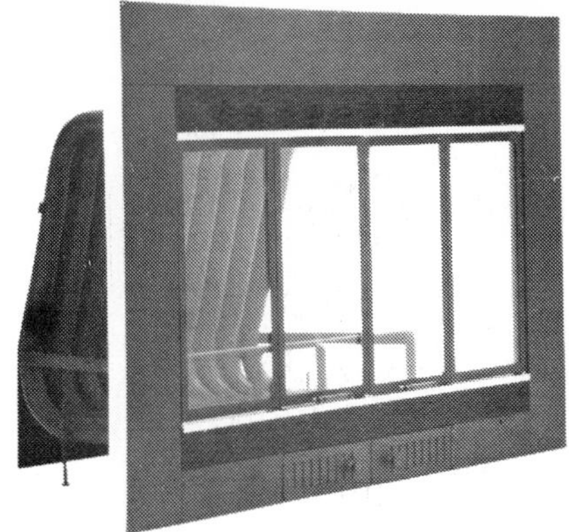

Manufacturer	Thermograte, Inc. P.O. Box 43566 (FF) St. Paul, MN 55164
Model	Fireplace Furnace
Function	Glass fire screen (hot air)
Size (H, W, D)	Sizes to fit most fireplaces
Weight	N/A
Colors	N/A
Airtight?	N/A
Reduced clearance	N/A
Outside combustion air?	N/A
Glass? (type)	Yes, tempered
Cooking surface?	N/A
CONSTRUCTION *Material*	Steel, stainless steel
Gauge or thickness	N/A
Air blower? (output)	Optional, 135 CFM
Flue size	N/A
Special features	# 304 stainless steal heat exchanger tube with thermal expansion seals. Wood/coal use. 5 year warranty against burnout. "Stay-Clean" doors. Thermoshield™ heat reflector.
Options and accessories	Screen. Blower.
Efficiency	N/A
Heat output (or area)	58,000 BTUs/hr. (with blower)
Tested by	Underwriters Laboratories
Suggested retail price	N/A
Brochure	Color, free
For nearest dealer call	612-636-7033
Mail order, if no dealer?	N/A

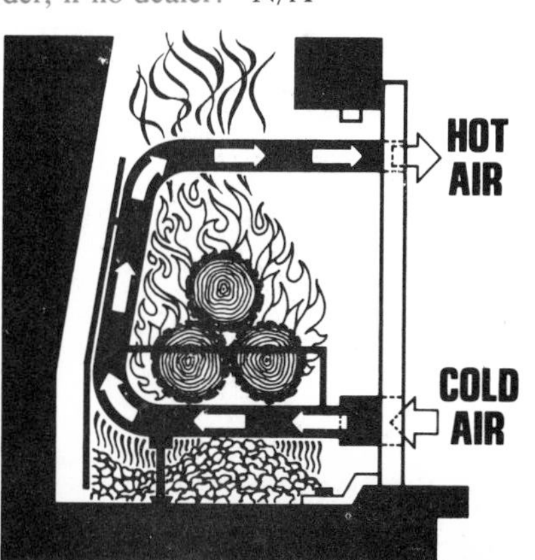

Manufacturer	Woodside Fireplaces P.O. Box 2249 (FF) Redwood City, CA 94064
Model	Warmth Machine
Function	Fireplace insert
Size (H, W, D)	2 sizes
Weight	100 lbs. (small unit)
Colors	Black
Airtight?	N/A
Reduced clearance	N/A
Outside combustion air?	N/A
Glass? (type)	Yes, tempered
Cooking surface?	N/A
CONSTRUCTION *Material*	Steel
Gauge or thickness	N/A
Air blower? (output)	Yes
Flue size	N/A
Special features	Double wall construction. Firebrick lined.
Options and accessories	Screen.
Efficiency	N/A
Heat output (or area)	N/A
Tested by	Underwriters Laboratories
Suggested retail price	$499.00 (sm.), $539.00 (lg.)
Brochure	Color, free
For nearest dealer call	415-368-2912
Mail order, if no dealer?	N/A

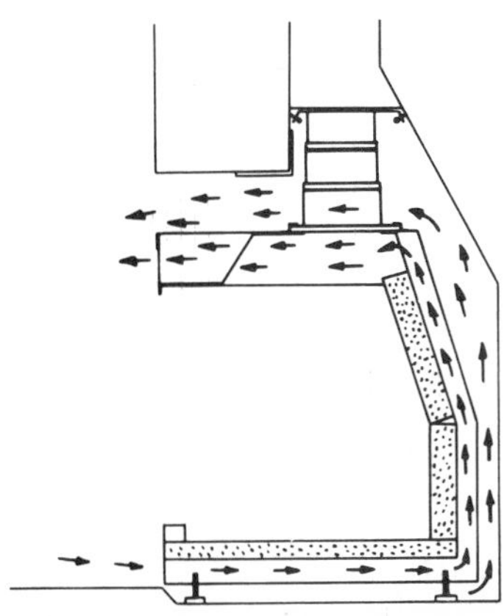

Manufacturer	Abundant Life Farm, Inc. P.O. Box 188 (FF) Lochmere, N.H. 03252
Model	Comforter
Function	Wood stove
Size (H, W, D)	29½", 25¾", 22½"
Weight	305 lbs.
Colors	Black
Airtight?	Yes
Reduced clearance	N/A
Outside combustion air?	N/A
Glass? (type)	Yes
Cooking surface?	Yes
CONSTRUCTION *Material*	Cast iron
Gauge or thickness	¼" and 5/16"
Air blower? (output)	N/A
Flue size	6" (rear)
Special features	Five year limited warranty. Baffled. Preheated combustion air. Takes 21" logs. Wood/coal use.
Options and accessories	Coal grate optional.
Efficiency	N/A
Heat output (or area)	70,000 BTUs/hr., 1,400 sq. ft.
Tested by	N/A
Suggested retail price	N/A
Brochure	Color, free
For nearest dealer call	603-528-1855
Mail order, if no dealer?	N/A

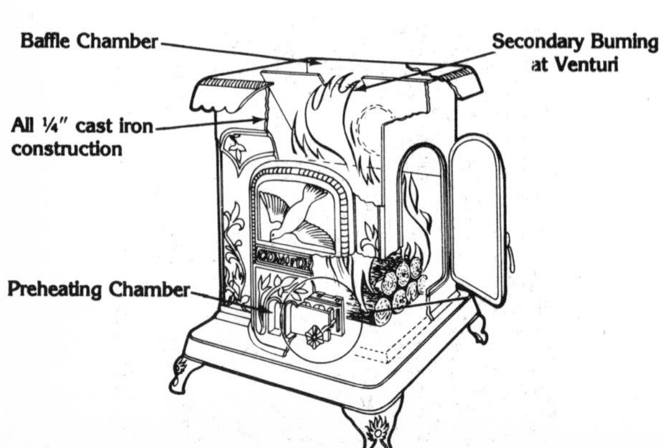

Manufacturer	All Nighter Stove Works 80 (FF) Commerce St. Glastonbury, CT 06033
Model	Big Moe
Function	Wood stove
Size (H, W, D)	31½", 23½", 41½"
Weight	524 lbs.
Colors	Available in most colors
Airtight?	Yes
Reduced clearance	N/A
Outside combustion air?	N/A
Glass? (type)	N/A
Cooking surface?	Yes
CONSTRUCTION *Material*	Sheet steel/cast iron door
Gauge or thickness	¼", 5/16"
Air blower? (output)	Yes (N/A)
Flue size	6"
Special features	Adjustable legs. Ash catcher pan. Firebrick lined. Lifetime and performance guarantees. Takes 28" logs. Wood/coal use.
Options and accessories	Domestic hot water jacket. Humidifier. Hot air plenum.
Efficiency	N/A
Heat output (or area)	30,000 to 75,000 BTUs/hr (3,000 sq. ft.)
Tested by	Underwriters Laboratories
Suggested retail price	N/A
Brochure	$1.00
For nearest dealer call	203-659-0344
Mail order, if no dealer?	N/A

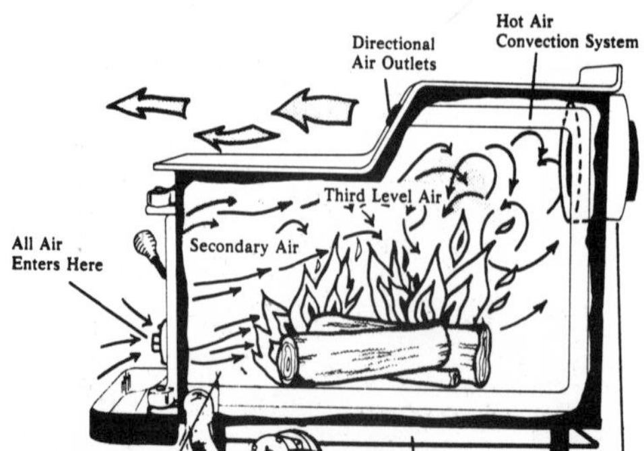

Manufacturer	All Nighter Stove Works 80 (FF) Commerce St. Glastonbury, CT 06033
Model	Giant Glo Moe
Function	Freestanding fireplace/stove
Size (H, W, D)	31″, 31″, 31″
Weight	470 lbs.
Colors	Most colors
Airtight?	Yes
Reduced clearance	N/A
Outside combustion air?	N/A
Glass? (type)	Yes, Vycor
Cooking surface?	Yes
CONSTRUCTION *Material*	Steel, cast iron
Gauge or thickness	¼″, 5/16″
Air blower? (output)	Yes
Flue size	8″
Special features	Adjustable legs. Ash catcher pan. Firebrick lined. Lifetime and performance guarantee.
Options and accessories	Domestic hot water jacket. Humidifier. Screen. Hot air plenum. Coal grate. Solid door.
Efficiency	N/A
Heat output (or area)	2,400 sq. ft.
Tested by	N/A
Suggested retail price	N/A
Brochure	$1.00
For nearest dealer call	203-659-0344
Mail order, if no dealer?	N/A

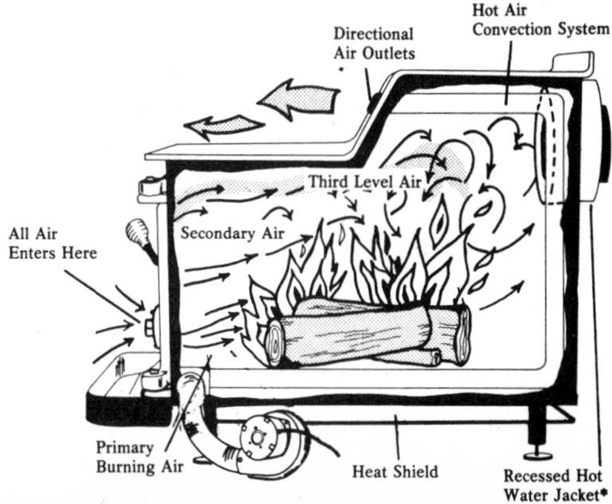

Manufacturer	American Home Heater Co. 50 Grimes Rd. P.O Box 10924 (FF) Eugene, OR 97440
Model	5-T
Function	Freestanding fireplace/stove
Size (H, W, D)	33″, 33″, 31″
Weight	430 lbs.
Colors	Most colors
Airtight?	Yes
Reduced clearance	N/A
Outside combustion air?	Optional
Glass? (type)	Yes, tempered, 10″ × 20″
Cooking surface?	Yes
CONSTRUCTION *Material*	Steel
Gauge or thickness	3/16″
Air blower? (output)	Optional
Flue size	8″ (top or rear)
Special features	Automatic draft control. Log stops. Firebrick lined. Steel screen may be inserted behind glass.
Options and accessories	Solid brass doors and stars. Outside combustion air kit. Porcelain enamel in most colors.
Efficiency	N/A
Heat output (or area)	N/A
Tested by	Northwest Laboratory
Suggested retail price	$695.00
Brochure	Color
For nearest dealer call	503-485-6245
Mail order, if no dealer?	Yes

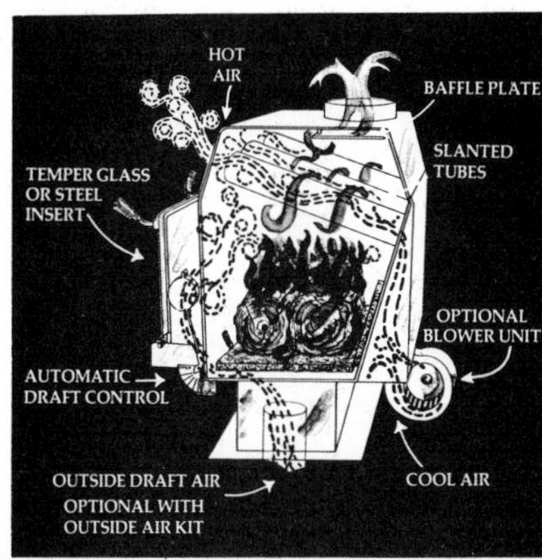

Manufacturer	Arizona Forest Supply P.O. Box 188 (FF) Flagstaff, AZ 86002
Model	HB-465
Function	Freestanding fireplace/stove
Size (H, W, D)	28″, 26″, 36″
Weight	400 lbs.
Colors	Flat black
Airtight?	Yes
Reduced clearance	Yes
Outside combustion air?	N/A
Glass? (type)	N/A
Cooking surface?	Yes
CONSTRUCTION *Material*	Hot rolled steel, cast iron
Gauge or thickness	¼″ & 5/16″
Air blower? (output)	Yes, 465 CFM
Flue size	8″
Special features	Cast iron doors. Damper. Firescreen. Thermostat. Firebrick lined. 5 yr. warranty on stove body. Wood/coal use.
Options and accessories	Unit complete.
Efficiency	66%
Heat output (or area)	2,400 sq. ft.
Tested by	N/A
Suggested retail price	$595.00
Brochure	Color, free
For nearest dealer call	602-774-0625
Mail order, if no dealer?	Yes

Burns directly on firebrick — no grate needed

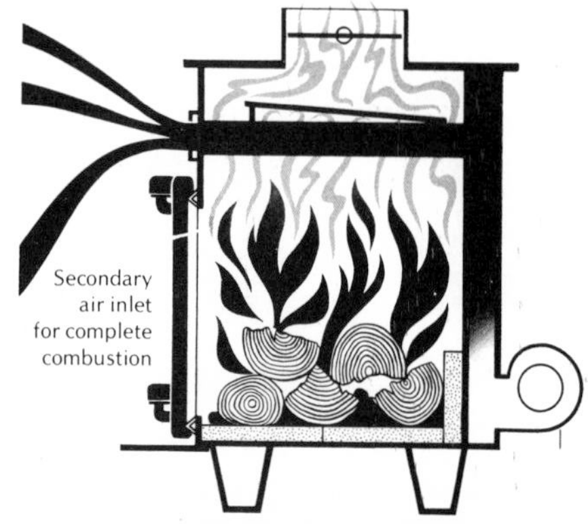

Manufacturer	Ashley Heater Company Dept. FF 1604 17th Ave., S.W. Sheffield, AL 35660
Model	Columbian 25-HFR
Function	Wood burning heater
Size (H, W, D)	34″, 20″, 30″
Weight	125 lbs. (shipping weight)
Colors	Blued steel
Airtight?	Yes
Reduced clearance	N/A
Outside combustion air?	N/A
Glass? (type)	N/A
Cooking surface?	Yes
CONSTRUCTION *Material*	Cold rolled steel, cast iron
Gauge or thickness	22 ga., 18 ga.
Air blower? (output)	Optional
Flue size	6″
Special features	Legs, top, flue collar, door frame, and door, all made of cast iron. Thermostat. Air shutter.
Options and accessories	Blower.
Efficiency	50%
Heat output (or area)	44,000 BTUs/hr., 4 to 5 rooms
Tested by	N/A
Suggested retail price	N/A
Brochure	Yes
For nearest dealer call	Write to above
Mail order, if no dealer?	N/A

Manufacturer	Ashley Heater Company Dept. FF 1604 17th Ave., S.W. Sheffield, AL 35660
Model	Deluxe C-60-E
Function	Wood stove
Size (H, W, D)	36″, 35¼″, 21¼″
Weight	260 lbs.
Colors	Brown with silver accents
Airtight?	Yes
Reduced clearance	N/A
Outside combustion air?	N/A
Glass? (type)	N/A
Cooking surface?	Yes, under hinged top
CONSTRUCTION *Material*	Steel, cast iron
Gauge or thickness	20 ga. (cabinet)
Air blower? (output)	Optional
Flue size	6″
Special features	Firebox liners, grate, feed door & frame, ash door & frame, flue collar are all cast iron. Unit stays cool to touch. Thermostat controlled burn.
Options and accessories	Blower with rheostat control. Draft equalizer.
Efficiency	50%
Heat output (or area)	55,000 BTUs/hr.
Tested by	Underwriters Laboratories
Suggested retail price	N/A
Brochure	6 page, color, 25¢
For nearest dealer call	Write to above
Mail order, if no dealer?	N/A

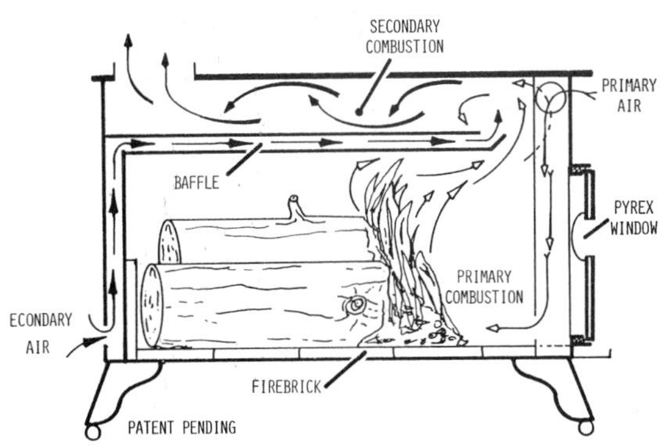

Manufacturer	Baffle Stove Co. P.O. Box 8731 (FF) Salt Lake City, UT 84108
Model	Cabin
Function	Wood stove
Size (H, W, D)	29″, 18″, 42″
Weight	600 lbs.
Colors	Black
Airtight?	Yes
Reduced clearance	N/A
Outside combustion air?	N/A
Glass? (type)	Pyrex, 5″ circular
Cooking surface?	Yes, 18″ × 42″
CONSTRUCTION *Material*	Plate steel
Gauge or thickness	¼″ and 5/16″
Air blower? (output)	N/A
Flue size	8″
Special features	Up-draft burn. Pre-heated primary and secondary air. Removable ash catcher. Adjustable legs.
Options and accessories	Nickel or brass trim. Different leg lengths.
Efficiency	N/A
Heat output (or area)	3.500 sq. ft.
Tested by	N/A
Suggested retail price	$820.00
Brochure	Free
For nearest dealer call	801-968-2411
Mail order, if no dealer?	Yes

Manufacturer	Baffle Stove Co. P.O. Box 8731 (FF) Salt Lake City, UT 84108
Model	Oven Cabin
Function	Wood stove
Size (H, W, D)	35″, 18″, 42″
Weight	650 lbs.
Colors	Black
Airtight?	Yes
Reduced clearance	N/A
Outside combustion air?	N/A
Glass? (type)	Pyrex (5″ circular)
Cooking surface?	Yes, 20″ × 20″
CONSTRUCTION *Material*	Plate steel
Gauge or thickness	¼″, 5/16″
Air blower? (output)	N/A
Flue size	8″ (top or back)
Special features	Up-draft burn. Oven has 750° thermometer. Pre-heated primary and secondary air. Removable ash pan. Adjustable legs. Nickel plated oven rack.
Options and accessories	Nickel or brass trim. Different leg lengths.
Efficiency	N/A
Heat output (or area)	4,000 sq. ft.
Tested by	N/A
Suggested retail price	$995.00
Brochure	Free
For nearest dealer call	801-968-2411
Mail order, if no dealer?	Yes

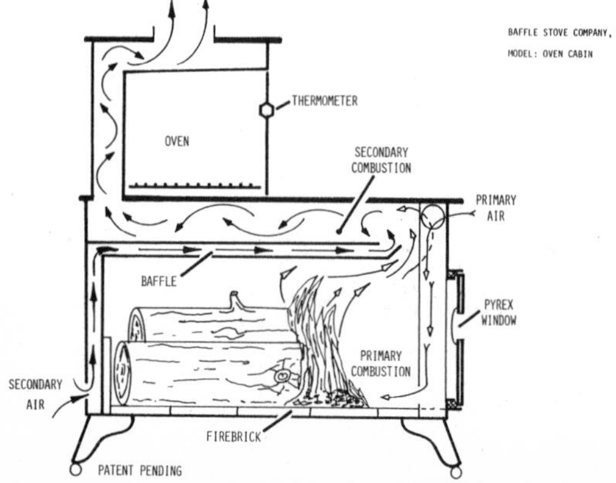

Manufacturer	Baffle Stove Co. P.O. Box 8731 (FF) Salt Lake City, UT 84108
Model	Upright Oven
Function	Wood stove with oven
Size (H, W, D)	39″, 20″, 25″
Weight	560 lbs.
Colors	Black
Airtight?	Yes
Reduced clearance	N/A
Outside combustion air?	N/A
Glass? (type)	Pyrex (5″ circular)
Cooking surface?	Yes
CONSTRUCTION *Material*	Plate steel
Gauge or thickness	¼″, 5/16″
Air blower? (output)	N/A
Flue size	8″ (top or back)
Special features	Fast warm-up oven. 5 to 8 hr. cooking on one loading. Preheated primary and secondary air. Removable ash pan. Adjustable legs. 750° thermometer. Up-draft burn.
Options and accessories	Nickel or brass trim. Different leg lengths.
Efficiency	N/A
Heat output (or area)	3,500 sq. ft.
Tested by	N/A
Suggested retail price	$845.00
Brochure	Free
For nearest dealer call	801-968-2411
Mail order, if no dealer?	Yes

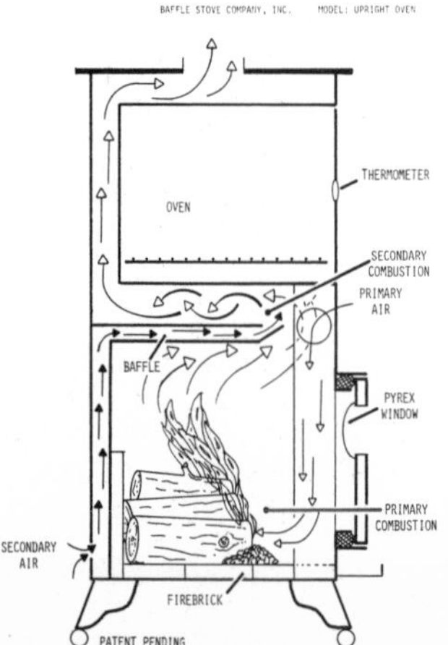

Manufacturer	Baffle Stove Co. P.O. Box 8731 (FF) Salt Lake City, UT 84108
Model	Fireplace - 32″
Function	Freestanding fireplace/stove
Size (H, W, D)	30″, 32″, 32″
Weight	650 lbs.
Colors	Black
Airtight?	Yes
Reduced clearance	Yes, 24″ from side and back
Outside combustion air?	N/A
Glass? (type)	Yes, Vycor, 12″ × 24″
Cooking surface?	Yes, (2), 14″ × 32″
CONSTRUCTION *Material*	Plate steel
Gauge or thickness	¼″, 5/16″
Air blower? (output)	N/A
Flue size	8″ (top or back)
Special features	Removable ash catcher. Adjustable door to maintain airtightness. Adjustable legs. Pre-heated primary and secondary air.
Options and accessories	Nickel or brass trim.
Efficiency	N/A
Heat output (or area)	3,500 sq. ft.
Tested by	N/A
Suggested retail price	$840.00
Brochure	Free
For nearest dealer call	801-968-2411 or 582-4274
Mail order, if no dealer?	Yes

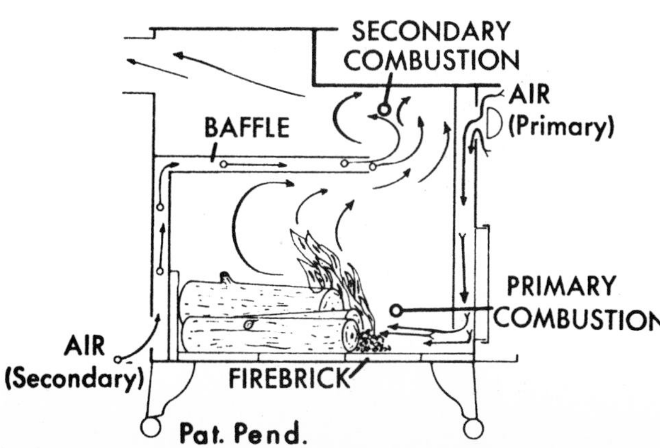

Manufacturer	Beaver Bill Stove Co. Dept. FF 5954 Brown Rd. Oxford, Ohio 45056
Model	80
Function	Wood stove
Size (H, W, D)	24″, 24″, 30″
Weight	310 lbs.
Colors	Black (colors, special order)
Airtight?	Yes
Reduced clearance	Yes
Outside combustion air?	N/A
Glass? (type)	Yes, Pyrex
Cooking surface?	Yes, 16″ × 10″
CONSTRUCTION *Material*	Steel plate, cast iron
Gauge or thickness	7 gauge
Air blower? (output)	Yes, 137 CFM
Flue size	8″
Special features	½″ thick black cast iron door. Firebrick lined. Grate. Burns wood/coal. Takes 27″ logs.
Options and accessories	Imported tile trim (shown). 14-piece set of brass trim (shown). Central air duct (top front mount).
Efficiency	N/A
Heat output (or area)	3,000 sq. ft.
Tested by	N/A
Suggested retail price	Base price $649.00
Brochure	Free
For nearest dealer call	513-523-4667
Mail order, if no dealer?	Yes

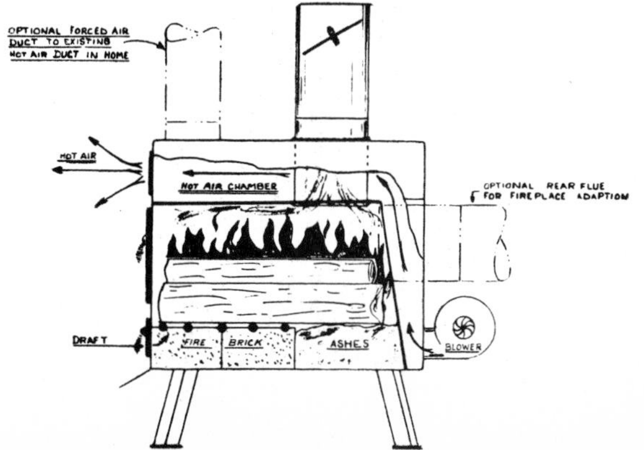

Manufacturer	Bow & Arrow Imports 14 (FF) Arrow St. Cambridge, Mass. 02138
Model	Le Petit Godin 3720
Function	Wood/coal stove
Size (H, W, D)	16″, 21″, 32″
Weight	121 lbs./133 lbs.
Colors	Br. gr., sand, black, blue
Airtight?	Yes
Reduced clearance	N/A
Outside combustion air?	N/A
Glass? (type)	Mica viewing window
Cooking surface?	Yes
CONSTRUCTION *Material*	Steel, cast iron
Gauge or thickness	19 gauge
Air blower? (output)	N/A
Flue size	6″ (rear)
Special features	French 1889 design. Pig iron cast parts. Takes 16″ logs (split), or nut coal, 1½″ to 2″ soft coal. Enamelled trim. Firebrick lined. Secondary air channel.
Options and accessories	Unit complete.
Efficiency	72% (coal)
Heat output (or area)	17,000 BTUs/hr.
Tested by	British Coal Board
Suggested retail price	$365 (East), $380 (West)
Brochure	Color, 35¢
For nearest dealer call	Write to above
Mail order, if no dealer?	N/A

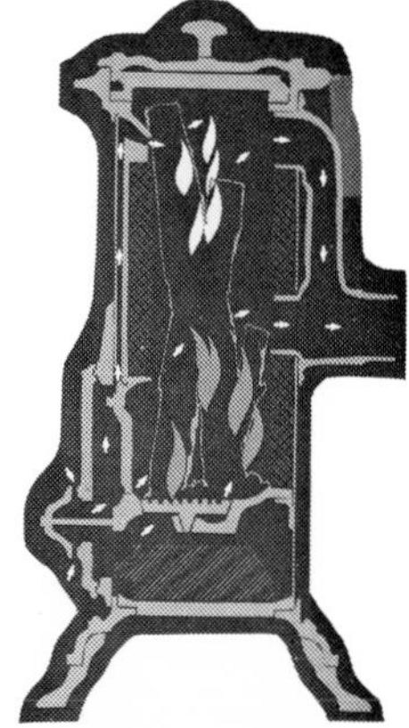

Manufacturer	Carmor Mfg. Ltd. Dept. FF 325 Hale St. London, Ontario, Canada
Model	1275
Function	Wood stove
Size (H, W, D)	28½″, 20″, 28¾″
Weight	235 lbs.
Colors	Black
Airtight?	Yes
Reduced clearance	N/A
Outside combustion air?	N/A
Glass? (type)	N/A
Cooking surface?	Yes
CONSTRUCTION *Material*	Steel
Gauge or thickness	1/8″
Air blower? (output)	N/A
Flue size	6″ (rear)
Special features	UNIMAX formed steel (pat. pending). Down draft (tube) air flow. Firebrick lined. 10 yr. warranty.
Options and accessories	Unit complete.
Efficiency	N/A
Heat output (or area)	55,000 BTUs/hr.
Tested by	N/A
Suggested retail price	$339.00
Brochure	Free
For nearest dealer call	519-453-8160
Mail order, if no dealer?	Yes

Manufacturer	Carmor Mfg. Ltd. Dept. FF 325 Hale St. London, Ontario, Canada
Model	1350
Function	Freestanding fireplace/stove
Size (H, W, D)	29″, 33″, 23″
Weight	265 lbs.
Colors	Black with brass trim
Airtight?	N/A
Reduced clearance	N/A
Outside combustion air?	N/A
Glass? (type)	Yes, Vycor
Cooking surface?	Yes
CONSTRUCTION *Material*	Steel
Gauge or thickness	1/8″
Air blower? (output)	N/A
Flue size	8″ (top)
Special features	UNIMAX formed steel (pat. pending). Downdraft (tube) air flow. Firebrick lined. Takes 26″ logs. 10 yr. warranty.
Options and accessories	Unit complete.
Efficiency	N/A
Heat output (or area)	40,000 BTUs/hr.; 1,800 sq. ft.
Tested by	N/A
Suggested retail price	$525.00
Brochure	Free
For nearest dealer call	519-453-8160
Mail order, if no dealer?	Yes

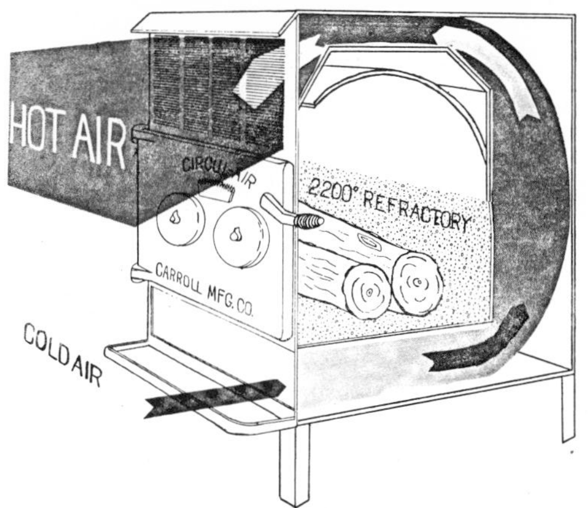

Manufacturer	Carrol Mfg. Co. Box 522 (FF) Eastwood Station Syracuse, N.Y. 13206
Model	Circul-air C-A3C
Function	Freestanding fireplace/stove
Size (H, W, D)	33″, 33″, 25″
Weight	578 lbs.
Colors	Maroon, blue, brown, gray, black
Airtight?	Yes
Reduced clearance	Yes, 12″ from rear wall
Outside combustion air?	N/A
Glass? (type)	N/A
Cooking surface?	N/A
CONSTRUCTION *Material*	Steel plate
Gauge or thickness	¼″
Air blower? (output)	Natural circulator
Flue size	8″
Special features	Cool to touch outside. Baffled. Firebrick lined. Adjustable legs. Silver or gold trim.
Options and accessories	Colors are optional.
Efficiency	N/A
Heat output (or area)	4,000 sq. ft.
Tested by	N/A
Suggested retail price	$695.00
Brochure	Free
For nearest dealer call	Write to above
Mail order, if no dealer?	N/A

Manufacturer	Cawley Stove Company, Inc. Dept. FF 27 N. Washington St. Boyertown, PA 19512
Model	Cawley/LeMay 400
Function	Wood stove
Size (H, W, D)	26-34″, 18″, 37″
Weight	300 lbs.
Colors	Black
Airtight?	Yes
Reduced clearance	N/A
Outside combustion air?	N/A
Glass? (type)	Sight window, Pyrex
Cooking surface?	Yes, 16″ × 22″
CONSTRUCTION *Material*	Cast iron
Gauge or thickness	3/16 and 5/16″
Air blower? (output)	N/A
Flue size	6″ (rear)
Special features	Adjustable firebox (size). Machined cook lids. Rotating, cast iron flue collar. Adjustable feet. Baffled.
Options and accessories	3 different leg lengths. (Larger size available)
Efficiency	63%
Heat output (or area)	900 sq. ft.
Tested by	Arnold Greene Test Lab.
Suggested retail price	$599.00
Brochure	32 page, $1.00
For nearest dealer call	215-367-2643
Mail order, if no dealer?	Yes

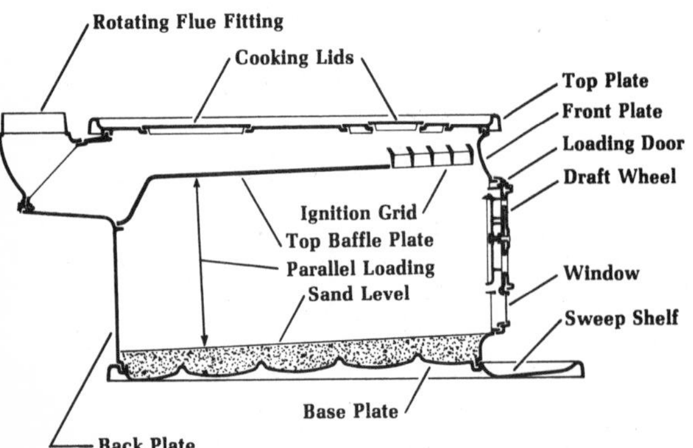

Manufacturer	C.E.M.I. Box 290 (FF) Ashland, Ohio 44805
Model	Independence
Function	Wood stove.
Size (H, W, D)	32″, 18½″, 35½″
Weight	420 lbs.
Colors	Black
Airtight?	Yes
Reduced clearance	N/A
Outside combustion air?	N/A
Glass? (type)	Optional (mica window)
Cooking surface?	Yes
CONSTRUCTION *Material*	Plate steel, cast iron
Gauge or thickness	¼″
Air blower? (output)	Optional, 210 CFM
Flue size	6″
Special features	Heat exchanger. Baffled. Cast iron door. Firebrick lined. 25 yr. limited warranty.
Options and accessories	Mica viewing window. Blower. (Smaller model available)
Efficiency	80%
Heat output (or area)	125,000 BTUs/hr., 3,000 sq. ft.
Tested by	CSA Laboratory
Suggested retail price	N/A
Brochure	Color, free
For nearest dealer call	419-289-2224
Mail order, if no dealer?	N/A

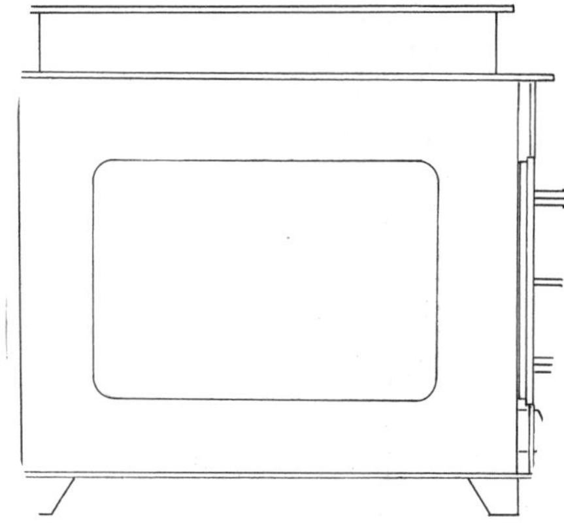

Manufacturer	Corning Stove Works P.O. Box 391 (FF) Corning, New York 14830
Model	Catcom 1
Function	Freestanding fireplace/stove
Size (H, W, D)	29″, 29″, 27″
Weight	420 lbs./480 lbs.
Colors	Blue, green, brown, black.
Airtight?	Yes
Reduced clearance	Yes
Outside combustion air?	Optional
Glass? (type)	Yes, Vycor, 18″ × 13″
Cooking surface?	Yes, 26″ × 21″
CONSTRUCTION *Material*	Hot rolled steel
Gauge or thickness	5/16″ and ¼″
Air blower? (output)	Optional, 260 CFM
Flue size	6″ (top or rear)
Special features	This stove is designed for retrofit of a catalytic converter module. Baffled. Firebrick lined. Takes 24″ logs. Side loading.
Options and accessories	Blower. Custom colors. (Note: Corning Stove Works is not affiliated with Corning Glass Works.)
Efficiency	60%; 85-90% with converter
Heat output (or area)	80,000 BTUs/hr. (at 60%)
Tested by	In progress
Suggested retail price	N/A
Brochure	Send s/a stamped envelope.
For nearest dealer call	Write to above.
Mail order, if no dealer?	Yes

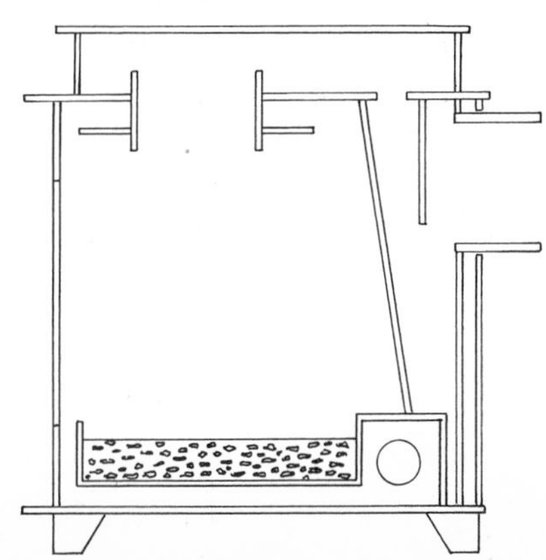

Manufacturer	DeVault Fab-Weld P.O. Box 98 (FF) DeVault, PA 19432
Model	Old Mill 50
Function	Freestanding fireplace/stove
Size (H, W, D)	22¼″, 25″, 28″
Weight	425 lbs.
Colors	Black
Airtight?	Yes
Reduced clearance	N/A
Outside combustion air?	N/A
Glass? (type)	N/A
Cooking surface?	Yes
CONSTRUCTION *Material*	Steel, cast iron
Gauge or thickness	¼″
Air blower? (output)	N/A
Flue size	8″ (top or rear)
Special features	Cast iron doors. 25 yr. limited warranty. Double baffle. Firebrick lined.
Options and accessories	Unit complete.
Efficiency	N/A
Heat output (or area)	2,500 sq. ft.
Tested by	N/A
Suggested retail price	$466.00
Brochure	Free
For nearest dealer call	215-647-5590
Mail order, if no dealer?	Yes

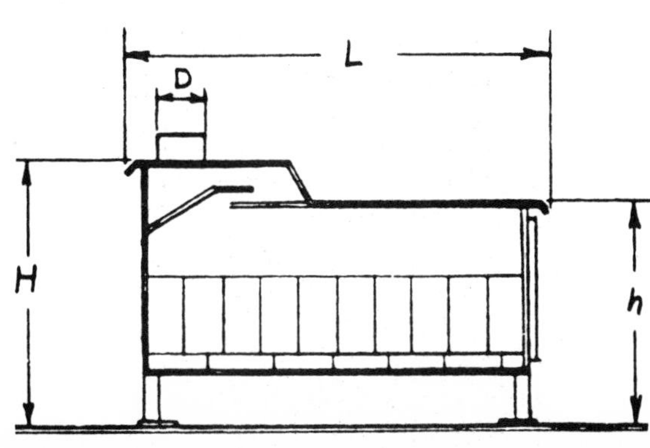

Manufacturer	D & L Distributors P.O. Box 2658 (FF) 22 South Columbia St. Wenatchee, WA 98801
Model	Spirit Woodstove
Function	Freestanding fireplace/stove
Size (H, W, D)	30½", 27½", 26"
Weight	380 lbs.
Colors	Black
Airtight?	Yes
Reduced clearance	Being tested
Outside combustion air?	N/A
Glass? (type)	N/A
Cooking surface?	Yes, 24" × 23"
CONSTRUCTION *Material*	Plate steel
Gauge or thickness	5/16", ¼", 3/16"
Air blower? (output)	Optional, 76 CFM
Flue size	8" (top)
Special features	Heat shield. Door removes and brass hood and screen attaches to front. Takes 18" logs. 15 yr. limited warranty.
Options and accessories	8 ceramic tiles to choose from. Bi-metal auto draft. Legs, or pedestal base.
Efficiency	N/A
Heat output (or area)	2,200 sq. ft.
Tested by	Warnock Hersey Int'l. Lab.
Suggested retail price	Under $600.00
Brochure	Free
For nearest dealer call	800-541-1619, in WA 509-662-3502
Mail order, if no dealer?	Yes

Manufacturer	Dulude Energy Systems, Inc. P.O. Box 205 (FF) 31 Mill St. Assonet, Mass. 02702
Model	Down Drafter
Function	Wood stove
Size (H, W, D)	29", 29", 22"
Weight	300 lbs.
Colors	Black
Airtight?	Yes
Reduced clearance	N/A
Outside combustion air?	N/A
Glass? (type)	N/A
Cooking surface?	Yes
CONSTRUCTION *Material*	Boiler plate steel
Gauge or thickness	¼"
Air blower? (output)	Optional, 76 CFM
Flue size	6" (rear only)
Special features	Top loading. Firebrick lined. Takes 22" logs. Down draft combustion system.
Options and accessories	Blower.
Efficiency	N/A
Heat output (or area)	60,000 BTUs/hr., 6 to 7 rooms
Tested by	Arnold Greene Test Lab
Suggested retail price	$305.00
Brochure	Free
For nearest dealer call	617-644-2278
Mail order, if no dealer?	Yes

Manufacturer	Dulude Energy Systems, Inc. P.O. Box 205 (FF) 31 Mill St. Assonet, Mass. 02702
Model	BT with Fan
Function	Wood stove
Size (H, W, D)	31″, 30″, 24″
Weight	415 lbs.
Colors	Black
Airtight?	Yes
Reduced clearance	N/A
Outside combustion air?	N/A
Glass? (type)	N/A
Cooking surface?	Yes
CONSTRUCTION *Material*	Boiler plate steel
Gauge or thickness	¼″
Air blower? (output)	Yes, 76 CFM
Flue size	8″ (top or rear)
Special features	Fire screen. Grate. Available with fireplace sealer plate attached (rear vent only). Takes 26″ logs. Cast iron doors.
Options and accessories	Coal grate
Efficiency	N/A
Heat output (or area)	55,000 BTUs/hr., 6 to 7 rooms
Tested by	Arnold Greene Test Lab
Suggested retail price	$460.00
Brochure	Free
For nearest dealer call	617-644-2278
Mail order, if no dealer?	Yes

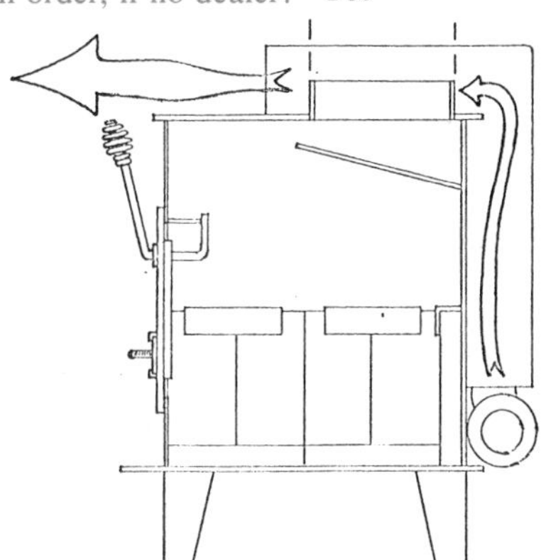

Manufacturer	Ember Box Fireplaces Dept. FF 1012 So. Agnew Oklahoma City, OK 73148
Model	Wigwam
Function	Freestanding fireplace
Size (H, W, D)	37″ H, 30″ dia.
Weight	180 lbs./200 lbs.
Colors	Black
Airtight?	N/A
Reduced clearance	Yes
Outside combustion air?	N/A
Glass? (type)	N/A
Cooking surface?	N/A
CONSTRUCTION *Material*	Steel
Gauge or thickness	16 ga. & 16 ga.
Air blower? (output)	N/A
Flue size	10″
Special features	Double wall construction. Includes flue to ceiling. Screen. 20 yr. warranty.
Options and accessories	Steel mask to cover opening (36″ dia. model available)
Efficiency	40% (with mask)
Heat output (or area)	N/A
Tested by	N/A
Suggested retail price	$589.00
Brochure	Color, free
For nearest dealer call	405-236-0404
Mail order, if no dealer?	Yes

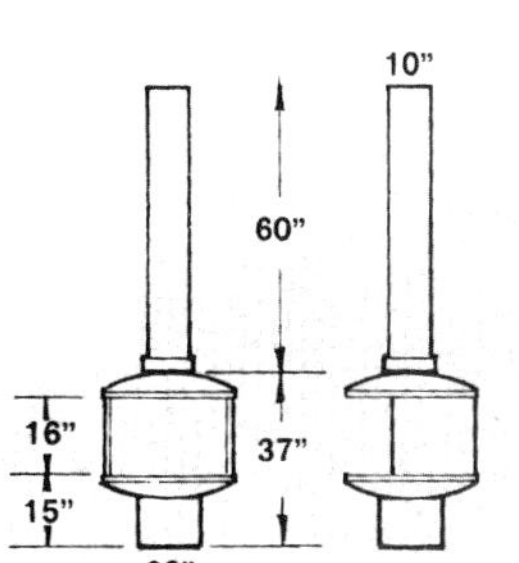

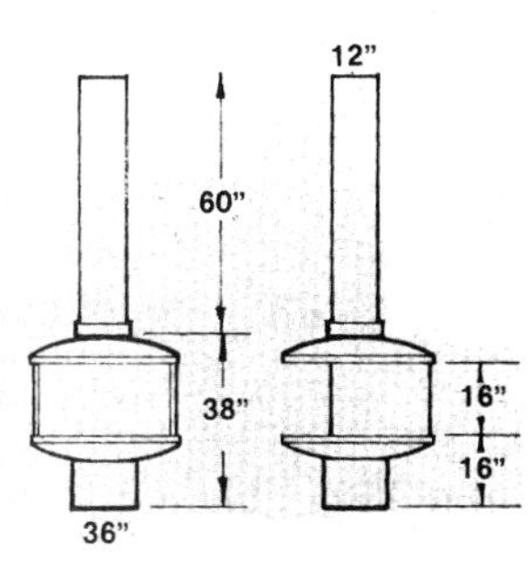

Manufacturer	ENAN, Inc. Dept. FF 961 Hamilton Hts. Rd. Corrallis, Montana 59828
Model	197816
Function	Wood stove
Size (H, W, D)	35″, 18″, 26″
Weight	249 lbs.
Colors	Black
Airtight?	Yes
Reduced clearance	Yes, 18″; 8″ with shield
Outside combustion air?	Yes
Glass? (type)	MacPherson BPS fireglass
Cooking surface?	Yes
CONSTRUCTION *Material*	Steel
Gauge or thickness	¼″ and 1/8″
Air blower? (output)	Optional, 256 CFM
Flue size	6″ (top)
Special features	Intake can mix outside and inside air for combustion and heated air. Primary and secondary air is preheated. Firebrick lined. Baffled.
Options and accessories	B-B-Que grill. Screen. Thermostat controls. Water heater. Heat shield for reduced clearance.
Efficiency	75%
Heat output (or area)	1,500 sq. ft.
Tested by	N/A
Suggested retail price	N/A
Brochure	Color, free
For nearest dealer call	406-961-4589
Mail order, if no dealer?	Yes

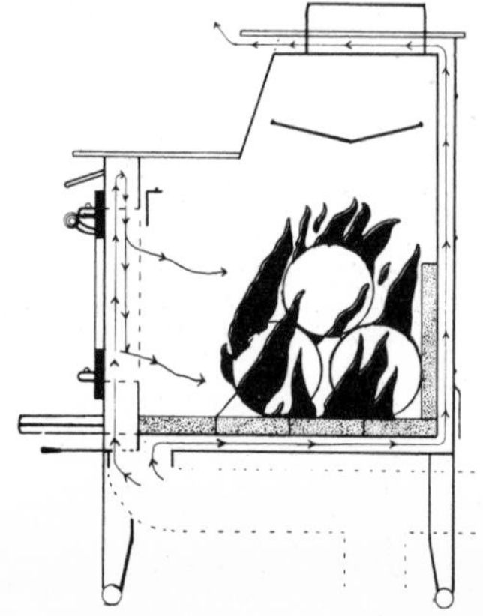

Manufacturer	ENAN, Inc. Dept. FF 961 Hamilton Hts. Rd. Corrallis, Montana 59828
Model	197818
Function	Freestanding fireplace/stove
Size (H, W, D)	34″, 27″, 27″
Weight	340 lbs.
Colors	Black
Airtight?	Yes
Reduced clearance	Yes, 18″; 8″ with shield
Outside combustion air?	Yes
Glass? (type)	MacPherson BPS fireglass
Cooking surface?	Yes
CONSTRUCTION *Material*	Steel
Gauge or thickness	¼″ and 1/8″
Air blower? (output)	Optional, 265 CFM
Flue size	8″ (top)
Special features	Intake can mix outside and inside air for combustion and heated air. Primary and secondary air is preheated. Firebrick line. Baffled.
Options and accessories	B-B-Que grill. Screen. Thermostat controls. Water heater. Heat shield for reduced clearance.
Efficiency	75%
Heat output (or area)	120.000 BTUs/hr.; 2,300 sq. ft.
Tested by	N/A
Suggested retail price	$649.00
Brochure	Color, free
For nearest dealer call	406-961-4589
Mail order, if no dealer?	Yes

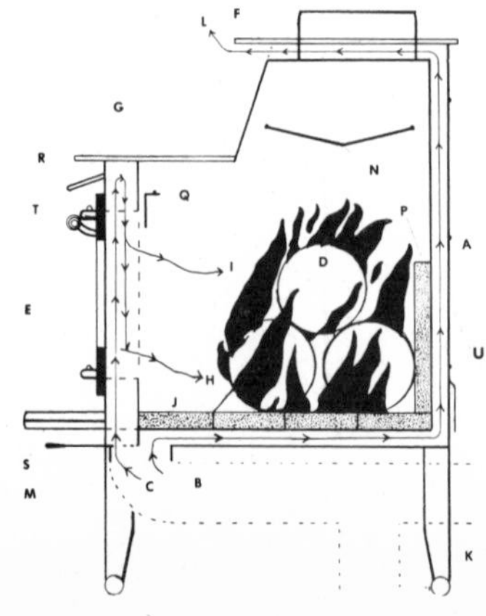

Manufacturer	Energy Harvesters Corp. Route 12, Box 19 (FF) Fitzwilliam, N.H. 03447
Model	Mt. Chocorua
Function	Wood stove
Size (H, W, D)	26¾", 18½", 34½"
Weight	220 lbs.
Colors	Black
Airtight?	Yes
Reduced clearance	N/A
Outside combustion air?	N/A
Glass? (type)	N/A
Cooking surface?	Yes, 8" × 17"
CONSTRUCTION *Material*	Class 30 grey cast iron
Gauge or thickness	¼"
Air blower? (output)	N/A
Flue size	5" (top or rear)
Special features	Removable hearth slate. Door stores on side when removed (shown). Primary and secondary draft. Guaranteed indefinitely.
Options and accessories	Screen. Two different side designs (Mt. Chocorua above).
Efficiency	55%
Heat output (or area)	55,000 BTUs/hr.
Tested by	ETLM
Suggested retail price	$448.00
Brochure	Free
For nearest dealer call	603-585-3300
Mail order, if no dealer?	Yes

Manufacturer	Feron Company Ltd. Dept. FF 45 Wright Ave. Dartmouth, N.S. B3B 1H1
Model	Moose
Function	Freestanding fireplace/stove
Size (H, W, D)	32", 28½", 38"
Weight	284 lbs.
Colors	Black
Airtight?	Yes
Reduced clearance	N/A
Outside combustion air?	N/A
Glass? (type)	N/A
Cooking surface?	N/A
CONSTRUCTION *Material*	Plate steel, cast iron
Gauge or thickness	¼"
Air blower? (output)	N/A
Flue size	8"
Special features	Moveable baffle for fast or slow burn. Cast iron door. Firebrick lining.
Options and accessories	Unit complete. (Three other models available.)
Efficiency	N/A
Heat output (or area)	N/A
Tested by	N/A
Suggested retail price	N/A
Brochure	Free
For nearest dealer call	902-463-2953
Mail order, if no dealer?	N/A

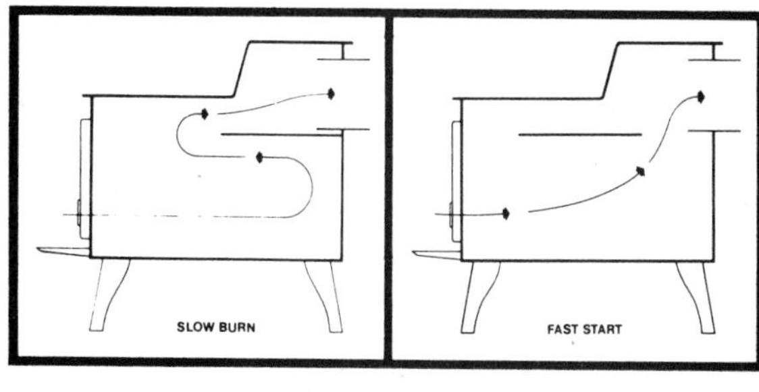

Manufacturer	Findlay Comfort Systems Dept. FF 60 Otonabee Dr. Kitchener, Ontario N2C 1L6
Model	Chatelaine
Function	Fireplace/cook stove
Size (H, W, D)	32″, 33″, 21″
Weight	325 lbs. (shipping weight)
Colors	Black
Airtight?	Yes
Reduced clearance	N/A
Outside combustion air?	N/A
Glass? (type)	Yes, Vycor
Cooking surface?	Yes
CONSTRUCTION *Material*	Steel, cast iron
Gauge or thickness	N/A
Air blower? (output)	N/A
Flue size	7″
Special features	Cast iron firebox. Baffled. Thermostatically controlled. Preheated secondary air. Takes 25″ logs. Slide out, full sized, ash pan.
Options and accessories	Unit complete.
Efficiency	N/A
Heat output (or area)	1,800 sq. ft.
Tested by	N/A
Suggested retail price	N/A
Brochure	Free
For nearest dealer call	Write to above
Mail order, if no dealer?	N/A

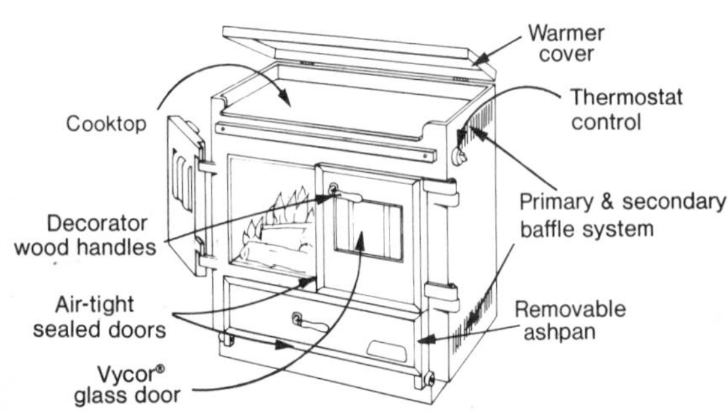

Manufacturer	Findlay Comfort Systems Dept. FF 60 Otonabee Dr. Kitchener, Ontario N2C 1L6
Model	Conestogo
Function	Wood stove
Size (H, W, D)	31½″, 25½″, 23½″
Weight	384 lbs.
Colors	Black
Airtight?	Yes
Reduced clearance	N/A
Outside combustion air?	N/A
Glass? (type)	N/A
Cooking surface?	Yes
CONSTRUCTION *Material*	Steel, cast iron
Gauge or thickness	N/A
Air blower? (output)	N/A
Flue size	8″
Special features	Conestoga wagon design is cast into doors. Baffled. Firebrick lined. Takes 20″ logs.
Options and accessories	Unit complete.
Efficiency	N/A
Heat output (or area)	1,800 sq. ft.
Tested by	N/A
Suggested retail price	N/A
Brochure	Free
For nearest dealer call	Write to above
Mail order, if no dealer?	N/A

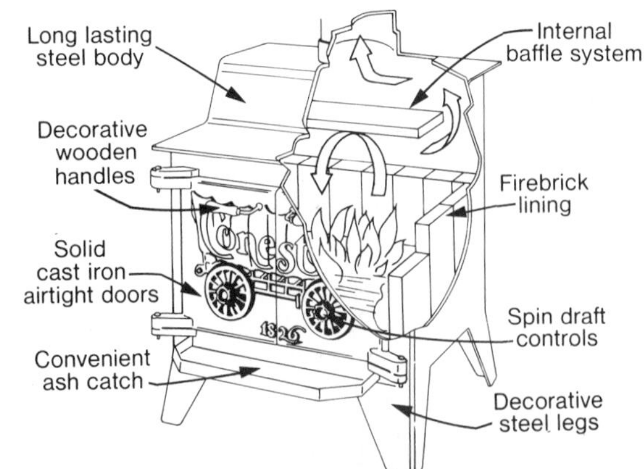

Manufacturer	Finest Stove Imports, Inc. P.O Box 1733 (FF) Silver Spring, MD 20902
Model	Koppe KH77
Function	Wood/coal stove
Size (H, W, D)	31″, 28″, 16″
Weight	313 lbs./425 lbs.
Colors	Green, brown
Airtight?	Yes
Reduced clearance	Yes, 8″ from rear
Outside combustion air?	N/A
Glass? (type)	N/A
Cooking surface?	Yes, 17″ × 9″
CONSTRUCTION *Material*	Ceramic, cast iron, steel
Gauge or thickness	Varies
Air blower? (output)	N/A
Flue size	6″ (with included adapter)
Special features	Fireclay lined. Ash pan. Grate with shaker. High-gloss tiles. Secondary air.
Options and accessories	Enamelled metal underlayment plate.
Efficiency	78% (coal)
Heat output (or area)	24,800 BTUs/hr.
Tested by	Deutsches Inst/Fur Normung
Suggested retail price	$747.00
Brochure	Color, send 60¢ in stamps
For nearest dealer call	301-946-4822
Mail order, if no dealer?	Yes

Manufacturer	Finest Stove Imports, Inc. P.O. Box 1733 (FF) Silver Spring, MD 20902
Model	Koppe 100/s
Function	Wood/coal stove
Size (H, W, D)	32″, 35″, 16″
Weight	452 lbs./630 lbs.
Colors	Beige, brown, green, white
Airtight?	Yes
Reduced clearance	Yes, 8″ from rear
Outside combustion air?	N/A
Glass? (type)	Yes, Tempax, 5″ × 7″
Cooking surface?	N/A
CONSTRUCTION *Material*	Ceramic, cast iron, steel
Gauge or thickness	Varies
Air blower? (output)	N/A
Flue size	6″ (with included adapter)
Special features	Fireclay lined. High-gloss tiles. Ash pan. Grate with shaker. Automatic draft.
Options and accessories	5 tile patterns. Enamelled metal underlayment plate.
Efficiency	78% (coal)
Heat output (or area)	22,000 BTUs/hr.
Tested by	Deutsches Inst/Fur Normung
Suggested retail price	$1,036.00
Brochure	Color, send 60¢ in stamps
For nearest dealer call	301-946-4822
Mail order, if no dealer?	Yes

Manufacturer	Finest Stove Imports, Inc. P.O. Box 1733 (FF) Silver Spring, MD 20902
Model	Koppe KK 125/s
Function	Wood/coal stove
Size (H, W, D)	33″, 35″, 15″
Weight	451 lbs./600 lbs.
Colors	Beige, green, brown
Airtight?	Yes
Reduced clearance	Yes, 8″ from rear
Outside combustion air?	N/A
Glass? (type)	Yes, Tempax, 5″ × 7″
Cooking surface?	N/A
CONSTRUCTION *Material*	Ceramic, cast iron, steel
Gauge or thickness	Varies
Air blower? (output)	N/A
Flue size	6″ (with included adapter)
Special features	Front door is hand-wrought iron. High-gloss tiles. Cast iron firebox, fireclay lined. Grate. Ash pan. Automatic draft.
Options and accessories	Enamelled metal underlayment plate.
Efficiency	78% (coal)
Heat output (or area)	22,400 BTUs/hr.
Tested by	Deutsches Inst/Fur Normung
Suggested retail price	$1,208.00
Brochure	Color, send 60¢ in stamps
For nearest dealer call	301-946-4822
Mail order, if no dealer?	Yes

Manufacturer	Finest Stove Imports, Inc. P.O. Box 1733 (FF) Silver Spring, MD 20902
Model	Koppe KK 400
Function	Wood/coal heater
Size (H, W, D)	36″, 36″, 20″
Weight	440 lbs./585 lbs.
Colors	Green, brown
Airtight?	Yes
Reduced clearance	Yes, 8″ from rear
Outside combustion air?	N/A
Glass? (type)	Yes, Tempax, 4″ × 12″
Cooking surface?	N/A
CONSTRUCTION *Material*	Ceramic, cast iron, steel
Gauge or thickness	N/A
Air blower? (output)	N/A
Flue size	6″ (with included adapter)
Special features	High gloss finish on tiles. Cast iron firebox, fireclay lined. Grate. Ash pan. Automatic draft.
Options and accessories	Enameled metal underlayment plate.
Efficiency	83%
Heat output (or area)	28,400 BTUs/hr. (coal)
Tested by	Deutsches Inst/Fur Normung
Suggested retail price	$1,078.00
Brochure	Color, send 60¢ in stamps
For nearest dealer call	301-946-4822
Mail order, if no dealer?	Yes

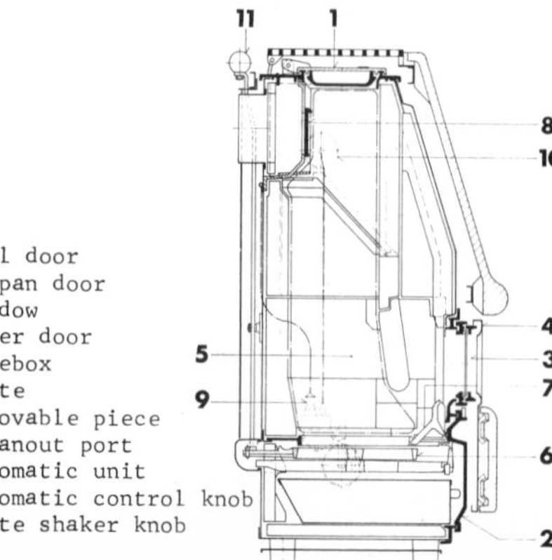

1 Fuel door
2 Ashpan door
3 Window
4 Outer door
5 Firebox
6 Grate
7 Removable piece
8 Cleanout port
9 Automatic unit
10 Automatic control knob
11 Grate shaker knob

Manufacturer	Finest Stove Imports, Inc. P.O. Box 1733 (FF) Silver Spring, Md. 20902
Model	Koppe KN 801
Function	Wood/coal heater
Size (H, W, D)	37″, 31″, 17″
Weight	484 lbs.
Colors	Beige, brown, green
Airtight?	Yes
Reduced clearance	Yes, 8″ from rear
Outside combustion air?	N/A
Glass? (type)	Yes, Tempax, 4″ × 12″
Cooking surface?	N/A
CONSTRUCTION *Material*	Ceramic, cast iron, steel
Gauge or thickness	N/A
Air blower? (output)	N/A
Flue size	6″ (with included adapter)
Special features	Front door is hand-wrought iron. High-gloss tile. Cast iron firebox, fireclay lined Grate. Ash pan. Automatic draft.
Options and accessories	Enameled metal underlayment plate.
Efficiency	83%
Heat output (or area)	28,400 BTUs/hr. (coal)
Tested by	Deutsches Inst/Fur Normung
Suggested retail price	$1,592.00
Brochure	Color, send 60¢ in stamps
For nearest dealer call	301-946-4822
Mail order, if no dealer?	Yes

Manufacturer	Finest Stove Imports, Inc. P.O. Box 1733 (FF) Silver Spring, MD 20902
Model	Koppe KN 850
Function	Wood/coal stove
Size (H, W, D)	45″, 31″, 17″
Weight	484 lbs.
Colors	Beige, brown, green
Airtight?	Yes
Reduced clearance	Yes, 8″ from rear
Outside combustion air?	N/A
Glass? (type)	N/A
Cooking surface?	Yes, 17″ × 9″
CONSTRUCTION *Material*	Ceramic, cast iron, steel
Gauge or thickness	Varies
Air blower? (output)	N/A
Flue size	6″ (with included adapter)
Special features	Fireclay lined. Ash pan. Grate with shaker.
Options and accessories	Enamelled metal underlayment plate
Efficiency	81% (coal)
Heat output (or area)	26,900 BTUs/hr.
Tested by	Deutsches Inst/Fur Normung
Suggested retail price	$1,834.00
Brochure	Color, send 60¢ in stamps
For nearest dealer call	301-946-4822
Mail order, if no dealer?	Yes

Manufacturer	Fire-View Products, Inc. P.O. Box 370 (FF) Rogue River, OR 97537
Model	270 Standard
Function	Freestanding fireplace/stove (MHA)
Size (H, W, D)	25″, 20″, 27″
Weight	210 lbs.
Colors	Black
Airtight?	N/A
Reduced clearance	Yes
Outside combustion air?	Available on model M-270
Glass? (type)	Yes, Tempered, 10″ × 20″
Cooking surface?	(2) 7″ in diameter
CONSTRUCTION *Material*	Hot rolled steel
Gauge or thickness	12 ga., 3/16″ & 10 ga.
Air blower? (output)	Optional, 140 CFM
Flue size	7″ (top or rear)
Special features	Model M-270 is ICBO and mobile home approved. Firebrick lined. Collapsable steel door behind glass. Takes 24″ logs.
Options and accessories	Blower. R. or L. loading door available on some models. (A furnace model is being developed).
Efficiency	N/A
Heat output (or area)	900 to 1,100 sq. ft.
Tested by	Northwest Laboratories
Suggested retail price	N/A
Brochure	Free
For nearest dealer call	503-582-3351
Mail order, if no dealer?	N/A

Manufacturer	Fisher Stoves Int'l., Inc. P.O. Box 10605 (FF) Eugene, Oregon 97440
Model	Goldilocks
Function	Freestanding fireplace/stove (MHA)
Size (H, W, D)	36″, 24″, 26″
Weight	420 lbs.
Colors	Black with nickel trim
Airtight?	Yes
Reduced clearance	Yes, 12″ from rear
Outside combustion air?	Yes
Glass? (type)	N/A
Cooking surface?	Yes
CONSTRUCTION *Material*	Steel, cast iron
Gauge or thickness	¼″, 5/16″
Air blower? (output)	N/A
Flue size	6″ (top)
Special features	Cast iron doors. Screen. Limited warranty. Firebrick lined. Takes 16″ logs.
Options and accessories	Unit complete. (Five other models available)
Efficiency	N/A
Heat output (or area)	1,250 sq. ft.
Tested by	Underwriters Laboratory
Suggested retail price	N/A
Brochure	Color, free
For nearest dealer call	Write to above
Mail order, if no dealer?	N/A

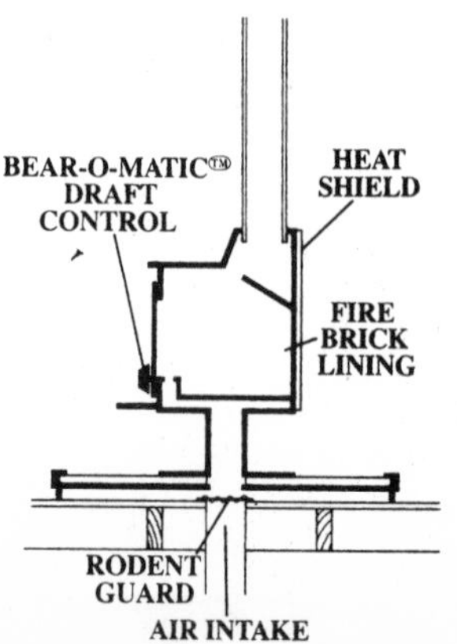

Manufacturer	Free Flow Stove Works Dept. FF South Strafford, VT 05070
Model	The Circulator
Function	Wood stove
Size (H, W, D)	33", 23", 32"
Weight	200 lbs./210 lbs.
Colors	Black
Airtight?	Yes
Reduced clearance	N/A
Outside combustion air?	N/A
Glass? (type)	N/A
Cooking surface?	N/A
CONSTRUCTION *Material*	Steel
Gauge or thickness	¼", 1/8", 14 ga.
Air blower? (output)	Natural circulator
Flue size	6"
Special features	The Circulator can put out 160 CFM of hot air with natural (passive) circulation. Baffled. All welded. 5 yr. limited warranty.
Options and accessories	Unit complete. (Three other sizes.)
Efficiency	56%
Heat output (or area)	60,000 BTUs/hr.
Tested by	E.T.L.M.
Suggested retail price	$550.00
Brochure	Free
For nearest dealer call	802-765-4022
Mail order, if no dealer?	Yes

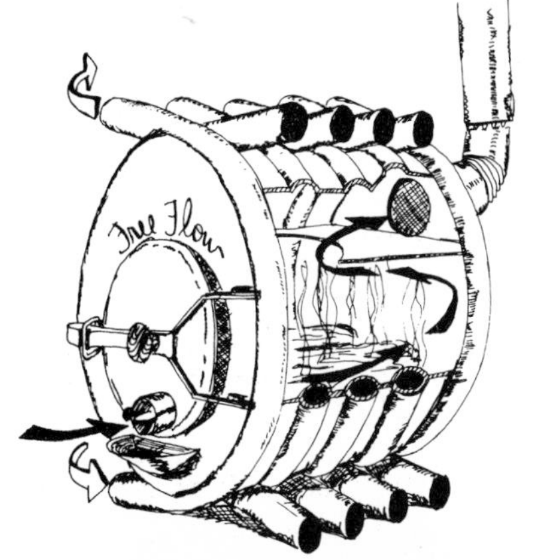

Manufacturer	Garrison Stove Works Box 412 (FF) Claremont, N.H. 03743; Box 42067 (FF) Portland, Oregon 97208
Model	Garrison One
Function	Wood stove
Size (H, W, D)	29½", 32", 21"
Weight	390 lbs.
Colors	Black
Airtight?	Yes
Reduced clearance	N/A
Outside combustion air?	N/A
Glass? (type)	N/A
Cooking surface?	Yes, 20" × 30"
CONSTRUCTION *Material*	Steel, cast iron
Gauge or thickness	¼", .375"
Air blower? (output)	N/A
Flue size	9" (top or rear)
Special features	Baffled. Screen. Removable brass key door handle for safety. Burn is from back to front. 20-year guarantee. Takes 24" logs.
Options and accessories	Soapstone griddle (Two small sizes available)
Efficiency	65%
Heat output (or area)	65,200 BTUs/hr.
Tested by	N/A
Suggested retail price	$498.00
Brochure	4 page, 50¢
For nearest dealer call	603-542-8761
Mail order, if no dealer?	N/A

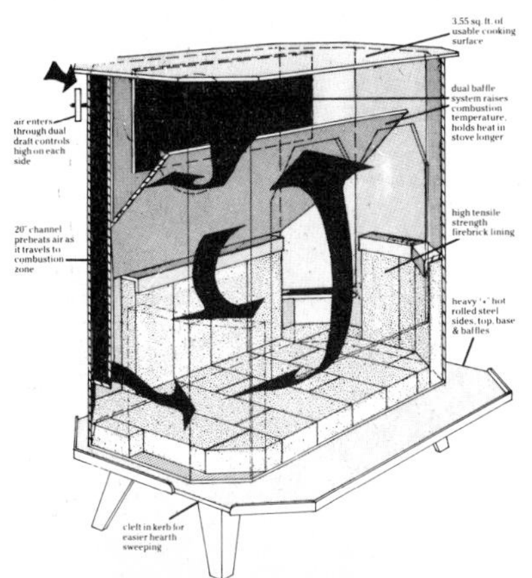

Manufacturer	Greenbriar Products, Inc. Box 473 (FF) Spring Green, Wisconsin 53588
Model	FP-44
Function	Freestanding fireplace/stove
Size (H, W, D)	33″, 45″, 23″
Weight	230 lbs./240 lbs.
Colors	Black
Airtight?	Yes
Reduced clearance	Optional (16″)
Outside combustion air?	Optional
Glass? (type)	Yes, Pyrex, 9″ × 26″
Cooking surface?	N/A
CONSTRUCTION *Material*	Steel
Gauge or thickness	14 gauge
Air blower? (output)	N/A
Flue size	8″
Special features	Continuously welded body. External seams are ground. Takes 40″ logs. Firebrick lined. Screen.
Options and accessories	Steel heat shield. Outside air kit. Hydronic heat exchanger. Solid steel door. Skirt. Grate. Thermostat.
Efficiency	70%
Heat output (or area)	100,00 BTUs/hr.
Tested by	N/A
Suggested retail price	$460.00 (base price)
Brochure	Free
For nearest dealer call	608-588-2923
Mail order, if no dealer?	Yes

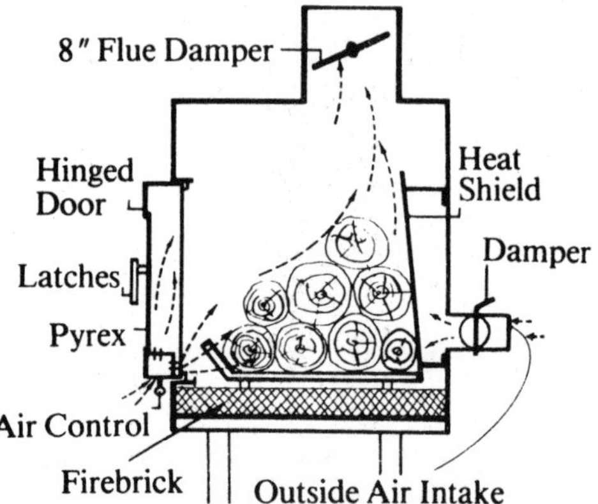

Manufacturer	Green Mountain Stoves Rt. #5 Box 107 (FF) Westminster Station Vermont 05159
Model	The Hour Glass
Function	Wood stove
Size (H, W, D)	38″, 16½″, 33″
Weight	260 lbs.
Colors	Blue, green, red, brown, black
Airtight?	Yes
Reduced clearance	N/A
Outside combustion air?	N/A
Glass? (type)	N/A
Cooking surface?	Yes
CONSTRUCTION *Material*	Hot rolled steel
Gauge or thickness	3/16″
Air blower? (output)	Optional
Flue size	6″
Special features	Preheated secondary combustion air enters through rear, second level. Takes up to 28″ logs.
Options and accessories	Furnace hood. Blower. (Smaller size available.)
Efficiency	65-70%
Heat output (or area)	60,000 BTUs/hr.
Tested by	Underwriters Laboratories
Suggested retail price	$425.00
Brochure	Free
For nearest dealer call	802-722-4117
Mail order, if no dealer?	Yes

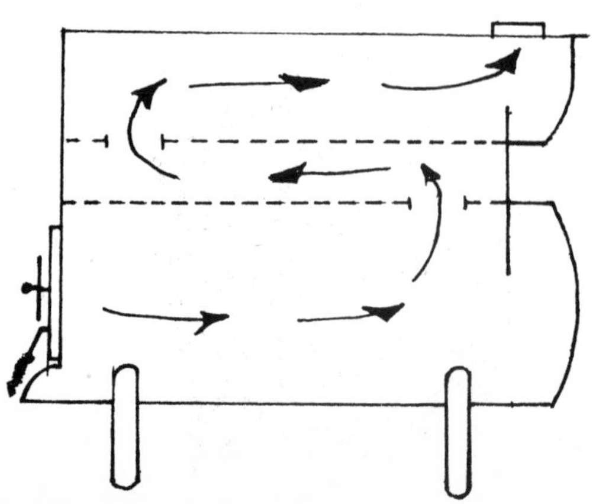

Manufacturer	Green Mountain Stoves RT #5 Box 107 (FF) Westminster Station Vermont 05159
Model	SEVCA Standard
Function	Wood stove
Size (H, W, D)	38″, 16″, 37″
Weight	225 lbs./250 lbs.
Colors	Blue, green, maroon, black
Airtight?	Yes
Reduced clearance	N/A
Outside combustion air?	N/A
Glass? (type)	N/A
Cooking surface?	Yes
CONSTRUCTION *Material*	Hot rolled steel
Gauge or thickness	3/16″, ¼″
Air blower? (output)	N/A
Flue size	6″
Special features	Rear air inlet for secondary combustion. Baffled. Takes 30″ logs.
Options and accessories	Hot water coil.
Efficiency	68%
Heat output (or area)	50,000 BTUs/hr.
Tested by	Arnold Greene Test Lab
Suggested retail price	$360.00
Brochure	Free
For nearest dealer call	802-722-4117
Mail order, if no dealer?	Yes

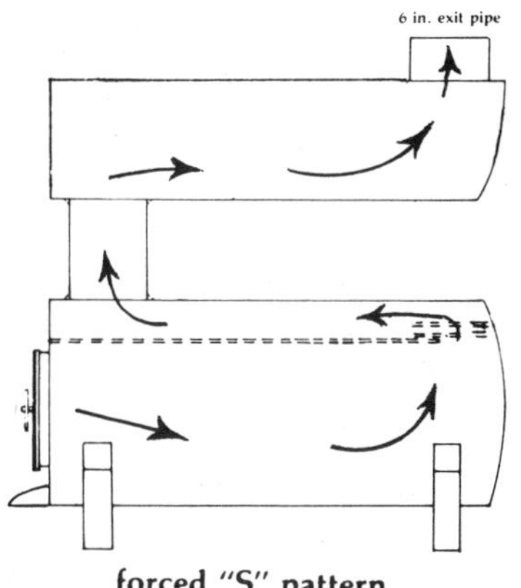

forced "S" pattern

Manufacturer	Green Mountain Stoves RT #5 Box 107 (FF) Westminster Station Vermont 05159
Model	Woodland III
Function	Wood stove
Size (H, W, D)	26″, 16½″, 35″
Weight	N/A
Colors	Black
Airtight?	Yes
Reduced clearance	N/A
Outside combustion air?	N/A
Glass? (type)	N/A
Cooking surface?	Yes
CONSTRUCTION *Material*	Hot rolled steel
Gauge or thickness	3/16″
Air blower? (output)	N/A
Flue size	6″
Special features	Baffled. Rear air inlet for secondary combustion. Takes 27″ logs.
Options and accessories	Unit complete.
Efficiency	N/A
Heat output (or area)	2 to 4 rooms
Tested by	N/A
Suggested retail price	N/A
Brochure	Free
For nearest dealer call	802-722-4117
Mail order, if no dealer?	Yes

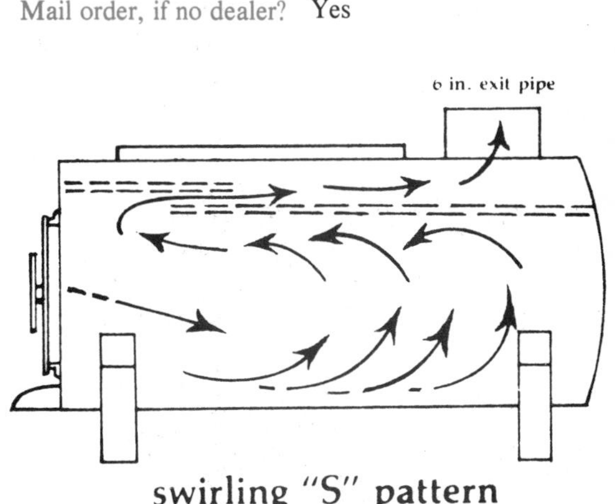

swirling "S" pattern

Manufacturer	Greyfriar's Imports, Ltd. Dept. FF 65 Broadway Greenlawn, NY 11740
Model	Esse "Dragon" Mark II
Function	Freestanding fireplace/stove
Size (H, W, D)	31″, 20½″, 22″
Weight	325 lbs.
Colors	Enamelled copper, blue, black
Airtight?	Yes
Reduced clearance	N/A
Outside combustion air?	N/A
Glass? (type)	Mica windows
Cooking surface?	Yes
CONSTRUCTION *Material*	Cast iron
Gauge or thickness	N/A
Air blower? (output)	N/A
Flue size	6″
Special features	Made in Scotland. cast iron damper. Baffled. Takes 21″ logs. Also has side load door.
Options and accessories	Coal conversion kit includes firebrick walls, grate, and ash bin. Screen.
Efficiency	70%
Heat output (or area)	10,000 cu. ft.
Tested by	British Coal Board
Suggested retail price	$1,095.00
Brochure	Free
For nearest dealer call	516-261-9672
Mail order, if no dealer?	N/A

Manufacturer	Grizzly Stoves/Derco Inc. P.O. Box 9 (FF) Blissfield, Michigan 49228
Model	Blazer
Function	Freestanding stove
Size (H, W, D)	31″, 28″, 28″
Weight	N/A
Colors	Black
Airtight?	Yes
Reduced clearance	N/A
Outside combustion air?	N/A
Glass? (type)	N/A
Cooking surface?	Yes
CONSTRUCTION *Material*	Plate steel
Gauge or thickness	¼″
Air blower? (output)	N/A
Flue size	8″ (top or rear)
Special features	Burns coal with coal grate. Baffled. Pre-heated combustion air. Firebrick lined. All welds ground smooth. 25 yr. limited warranty.
Options and accessories	Unit complete.
Efficiency	80%
Heat output (or area)	50,000 BTUs/hr.
Tested by	N/A
Suggested retail price	$495.00
Brochure	Color, free
For nearest dealer call	517-486-4337
Mail order, if no dealer?	Yes

Manufacturer	Grizzly Stoves/Derco Inc. P.O. Box 9 (FF) Blissfield, Michigan 49228
Model	Blazer Glass Door
Function	Freestanding fireplace/stove
Size (H, W, D)	31″, 27″, 28″
Weight	412 lbs./425 lbs.
Colors	Black
Airtight?	Yes
Reduced clearance	N/A
Outside combustion air?	N/A
Glass? (type)	Yes, Vycor
Cooking surface?	Yes
CONSTRUCTION *Material*	Plate steel
Gauge or thickness	¼″
Air blower? (output)	N/A
Flue size	8″ (top or rear)
Special features	Baffled. Preheated combustion air. Firebrick lined. Burns coal with coal grate. All welds ground smooth. 25 year limited warranty.
Options and accessories	Unit complete.
Efficiency	80%
Heat output (or area)	50,000 BTUs/hr.
Tested by	N/A
Suggested retail price	$563.00
Brochure	Color, free
For nearest dealer call	517-486-4337
Mail order, if no dealer?	Yes

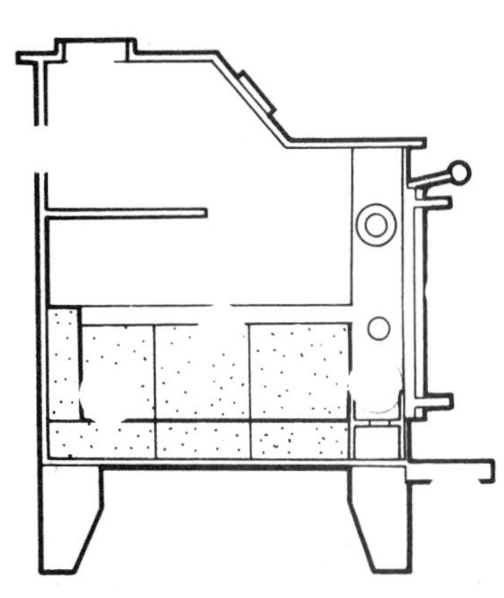

1. Top or back outlets available
2. Solid welds everywhere with grounded smooth edges.
3. Secondary combustion chamber
4. Door handle latch
5. Baffle plate
6. Air intake draft control knobs (2)
7. Primary combustion chamber
8. Airtight glass doors
9. The Unique Grizzly "Air-Channel" (Pat. Pend.)
10. Firebrick
11. Apron

Manufacturer	Harrowsmith Stove Co. Ltd. P.O. Box 40 (FF) Harrowsmith, Ontario Canada
Model	M 30
Function	Freestanding fireplace/stove
Size (H, W, D)	31½″, 30″, 26″
Weight	500 lbs.
Colors	Black
Airtight?	Yes
Reduced clearance	N/A
Outside combustion air?	N/A
Glass? (type)	Yes, Vycor
Cooking surface?	Yes
CONSTRUCTION *Material*	Plate steel
Gauge or thickness	5/16″, ¼″
Air blower? (output)	Optional, 76 to 465 CFM
Flue size	7″ (top or rear)
Special features	Double wall back and bottom. Baffled. Heat exchanger. Spark guard drafts. Firebrick lined. Lifetime guarantee.
Options and accessories	Blower. Gold or nickel trim.
Efficiency	80%
Heat output (or area)	2,200 sq. ft.
Tested by	N/A
Suggested retail price	Base price $648.00
Brochure	Color, free
For nearest dealer call	613-372-2434
Mail order, if no dealer?	N/A

Manufacturer	Hayes Equip. Corp P.O. Box 526 (FF) Unionville, Conn. 06085
Model	Better 'N' Ben's 501 F.S.
Function	Wood stove
Size (H, W, D)	31″, 19″, 30″
Weight	340 lbs.
Colors	Black
Airtight?	Yes
Reduced clearance	N/A
Outside combustion air?	N/A
Glass? (type)	Yes, Vycor
Cooking surface?	Yes
CONSTRUCTION *Material*	Plate Steel
Gauge or thickness	¼″
Air blower? (output)	N/A
Flue size	7″
Special features	Baffled. Firebrick lined. Safety screen behind glass.
Options and accessories	Broiler grill. Baking oven. Ash bucket.
Efficiency	60%
Heat output (or area)	49,000 BTUs/hr.
Tested by	Arnold Greene (BOCA) (ICBO)
Suggested retail price	$449.00
Brochure	Color, free.
For nearest dealer call	203-673-2557
Mail order, if no dealer?	N/A

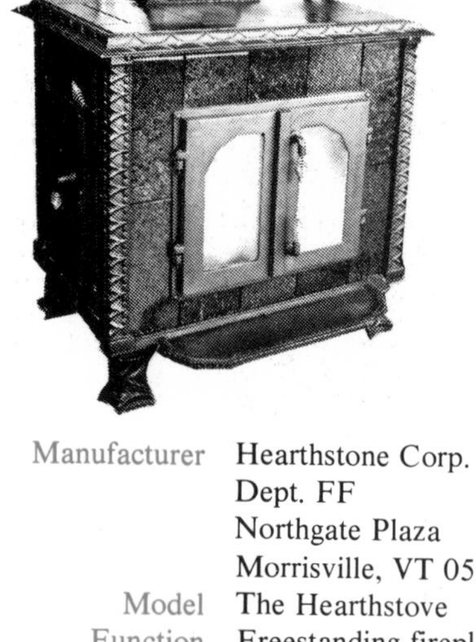

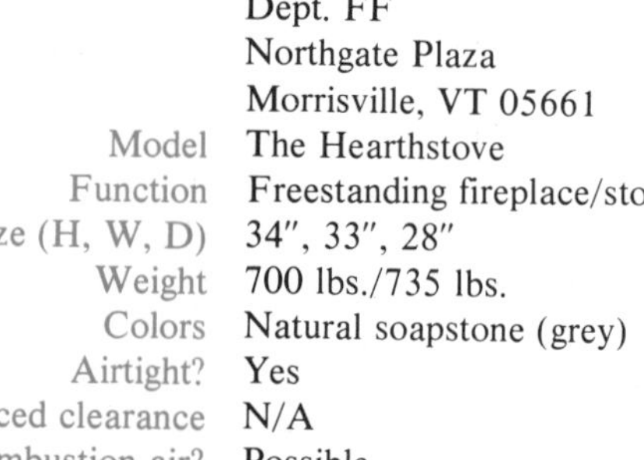

Manufacturer	Hearthstone Corp. Dept. FF Northgate Plaza Morrisville, VT 05661
Model	The Hearthstove
Function	Freestanding fireplace/stove
Size (H, W, D)	34″, 33″, 28″
Weight	700 lbs./735 lbs.
Colors	Natural soapstone (grey)
Airtight?	Yes
Reduced clearance	N/A
Outside combustion air?	Possible
Glass? (type)	Yes, Vycor
Cooking surface?	Yes, 22″ × 33″
CONSTRUCTION *Material*	Soapstone, cast iron
Gauge or thickness	1 & 3/16″ thick soapstone
Air blower? (output)	N/A
Flue size	8″
Special features	350 lbs. of 100% pig iron, plus 350 lbs. of hand polished soapstone. Thermostatically controlled draft. Baffled. 30 day money back guarantee Soapstone has 3,000° F TSR. Screen, 5 year ltd. warranty.
Options and accessories	Unit complete.
Efficiency	In process of testing
Heat output (or area)	In process of testing
Tested by	Arnold Greene Test Lab.
Suggested retail price	$849.00
Brochure	Color, 14 page, $2.00
For nearest dealer call	802-888-4586
Mail order, if no dealer?	Yes

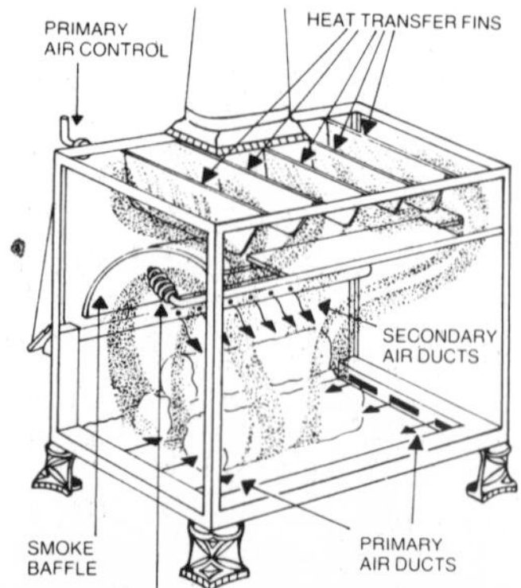

Manufacturer	Heat-N-Glo Dept. FF 1100 Riverwood Dr. Burnsville, MN 55337
Model	Classic
Function	Freestanding fireplace
Size (H, W, D)	34″ dia., 50″ H
Weight	145 lbs.
Colors	6 colors
Airtight?	N/A
Reduced clearance	Yes, 27″ from combustibles
Outside combustion air?	Optional
Glass? (type)	Yes, tempered
Cooking surface?	N/A
CONSTRUCTION *Material*	Steel
Gauge or thickness	12 gauge
Air blower? (output)	Yes, 200 CFM
Flue size	8″
Special features	Red, white, orange, almond, gold, black. Baffled. Can be suspended from ceiling.
Options and accessories	Full close, built-in damper. Outside combustion air kit.
Efficiency	N/A
Heat output (or area)	30,000 BTUs/hr.
Tested by	Twin City Testing (ICB0)
Suggested retail price	$599.00
Brochure	Color, free
For nearest dealer call	612-890-8367
Mail order, if no dealer?	Yes

Manufacturer	Heat-N-Glo Dept. FF 1100 Riverwood Rd. Burnsville, MN 55337
Model	Fantasy
Function	Freestanding fireplace
Size (H, W, D)	34″ dia., 50″ H.
Weight	170 lbs./180 lbs.
Colors	6 colors
Airtight?	Can be adapted
Reduced clearance	Yes, 27″ from combustibles
Outside combustion air?	Optional
Glass? (type)	Yes, tempered
Cooking surface?	N/A
CONSTRUCTION *Material*	Steel
Gauge or thickness	12 gauge
Air blower? (output)	Yes, 200 CFM
Flue size	8″ (top)
Special features	Red, white, black, gold, orange, coppertone. ½ of fireplace is glass. Baffled. Cone-shape fire bowl. Preheated combustion air.
Options and accessories	Outside combustion air kit. Full close, built-in damper.
Efficiency	N/A
Heat output (or area)	70,000 BTUs/hr.
Tested by	ICBO
Suggested retail price	$599.00
Brochure	Free
For nearest dealer call	612-890-8367
Mail order, if no dealer?	Yes

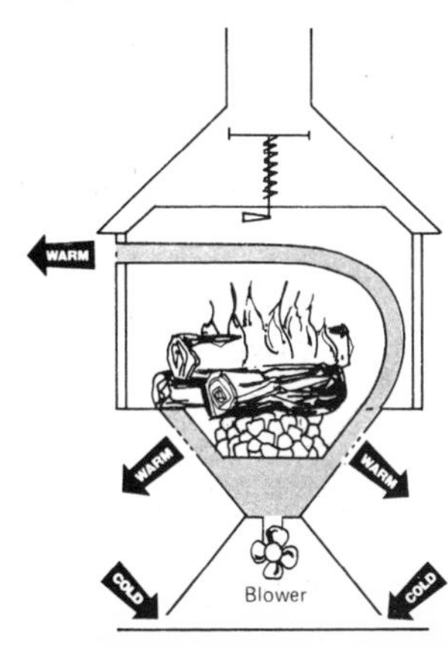

Manufacturer	Hinckley Foundry Dept FF 4 Mt. Pleasant St. Newmarket, N.H. 03857
Model	Hinckley Shaker
Function	Wood stove
Size (H, W, D)	29″, 17″, 12″
Weight	245 lbs.
Colors	Black
Airtight?	Yes
Reduced clearance	N/A
Outside combustion air?	N/A
Glass? (type)	N/A
Cooking surface?	Yes
CONSTRUCTION *Material*	Grey cast iron
Gauge or thickness	3/8″
Air blower? (output)	N/A
Flue size	6″ (top)
Special features	Original Shaker stove design. Each unit is sand casted, one piece body. Bottom and doors are also cast. Wrought iron legs. Baffled.
Options and accessories	Unit complete.
Efficiency	N/A
Heat output (or area)	N/A
Tested by	N/A
Suggested retail price	$395.00
Brochure	Free
For nearest dealer call	603-659-5836
Mail order, if no dealer?	Yes

Manufacturer	Humble Mfg. Co. Dept. FF 407 Mill St. Rushpond, MN 55971
Model	1624-H
Function	Wood stove
Size (H, W, D)	20″, 18″, 26½″
Weight	200 lbs.
Colors	Black
Airtight?	Yes
Reduced clearance	N/A
Outside combustion air?	N/A
Glass? (type)	N/A
Cooking surface?	Yes
CONSTRUCTION *Material*	Steel, cast iron
Gauge or thickness	10 gauge
Air blower? (output)	N/A
Flue size	6″ (top)
Special features	Firebrick lined. Baffled smoke chamber. Cast iron doors. Preheated combustion air. Thermostatic draft control.
Options and accessories	Unit complete.
Efficiency	55%
Heat output (or area)	3 to 4 rooms
Tested by	N/A
Suggested retail price	$225.00
Brochure	Free
For nearest dealer call	Write to above
Mail order, if no dealer?	N/A

Manufacturer	Humble Mfg. Co. Dept. FF 407 Mill St. Rushford, MN 55971
Model	1824 GTC
Function	Wood stove
Size (H, W, D)	31½", 17½", 28"
Weight	210 lbs (shipping weight)
Colors	Black
Airtight?	N/A
Reduced clearance	N/A
Outside combustion air?	N/A
Glass? (type)	N/A
Cooking surface?	Yes
CONSTRUCTION *Material*	Steel, cast iron
Gauge or thickness	14 ga., 3/8", 3/4"
Air blower? (output)	Optional, 265 CFM
Flue size	6" (top)
Special features	Can be used as add-on furnace. Cast iron top, grate, ash pan. Also has top loading door. Firebrick lined. Dual draft. Takes 22" logs
Options and accessories	Heat exchanger for use as furnace add-on. Blower.
Efficiency	55%
Heat output (or area)	3 to 4 rooms
Tested by	N/A
Suggested retail price	$269.00
Brochure	Free
For nearest dealer call	Write to above
Mail order, if no dealer?	N/A

Manufacturer	Hurricane Inc. Route 5, Box 71-A(F) Blackfoot, Idaho 83221
Model	HS-100
Function	Wood stove
Size (H, W, D)	25½", 18", 27"
Weight	250 lbs.
Colors	Five colors (see below)
Airtight?	Yes
Reduced clearance	Yes
Outside combustion air?	Optional
Glass? (type)	N/A
Cooking surface?	Yes
CONSTRUCTION *Material*	Steel plate, cast iron
Gauge or thickness	¼", 3/16"
Air blower? (output)	Yes, 160 CFM
Flue size	8"
Special features	Heat tube exchange system. Takes 18" logs. Double wall rear. Firebrick lined. Firebox is bent into shape. Cast iron doors. Screen.
Options and accessories	Domestic hot water coil. Colors: bk/gr/br/blu/maroon; same in metallic. Brass trim.
Efficiency	N/A
Heat output (or area)	1,200 sq. ft.
Tested by	N/A
Suggested retail price	N/A
Brochure	Color, free
For nearest dealer call	208-684-5111
Mail order, if no dealer?	Yes

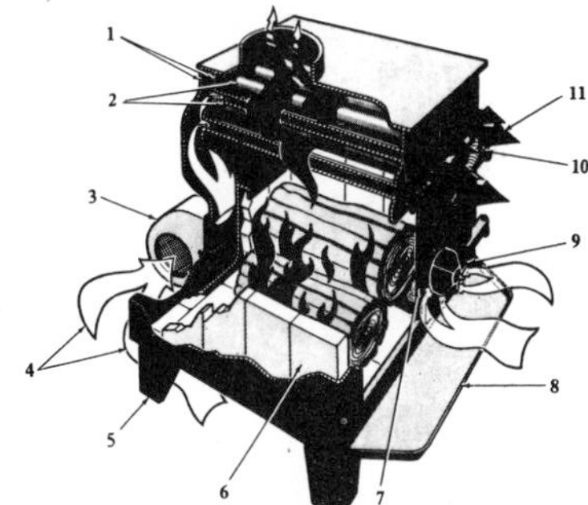

1. *Double-walled heat chamber.* **2.** *Heat tubes.* **3.** *Blower.* **4.** *Blower intake.* **5.** *Adjustable rear legs.* **6.** *2300° fire brick.* **7.** *Fiber-sealed doors.* **8.** *Quick clean ash pan.* **9.** *'Quick Spin' draft control caps.* **10.** *Wire spring grip door handles.* **11.** *Heat tube output.*

Manufacturer	Hurricane Inc. Route 5 Box 71-A(F) Blackfoot, Idaho 83221
Model	HS-300
Function	Freestanding fireplace/stove
Size (H, W, D)	27″, 29″, 25″
Weight	390 lbs.
Colors	Five colors (see below)
Airtight?	Yes
Reduced clearance	Yes, 12″ from rear wall
Outside combustion air?	Optional
Glass? (type)	N/A
Cooking surface?	Yes
CONSTRUCTION *Material*	Steel plate, cast iron
Gauge or thickness	¼″, 3/16″
Air blower? (output)	Yes, 160 CFM
Flue size	8″
Special features	Heat tube exchange system. Takes 21″ logs. Double wall rear. Firebrick lined. Firebox is bent into shape. Cast iron doors. Screen.
Options and accessories	Domestic hot water coil. Colors: gr/bk/br/bl/maroon; also same in metallic. Brass trim. (Larger model available)
Efficiency	N/A
Heat output (or area)	2,200 sq. ft.
Tested by	Underwriters Laboratories
Suggested retail price	N/A
Brochure	Color, free
For nearest dealer call	208-684-5111
Mail order, if no dealer?	Yes

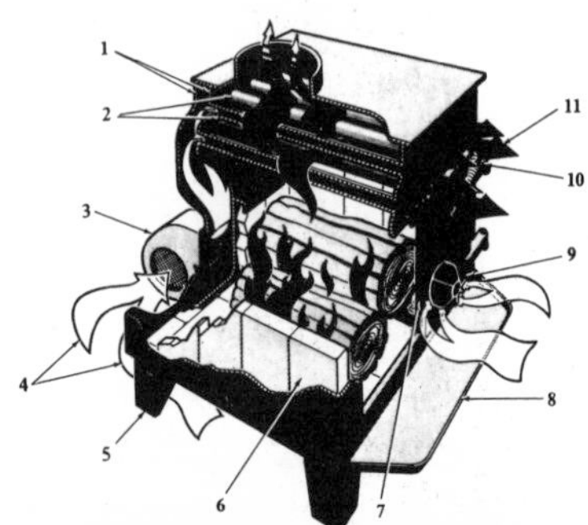

1. Double-walled heat chamber. 2. Heat tubes. 3. Blower. 4. Blower intake. 5. Adjustable rear legs. 6. 2300° fire brick. 7. Fiber-sealed doors. 8. Quick clean ash pan. 9. 'Quick Spin' draft control caps. 10. Wire spring grip door handles. 11. Heat tube output.

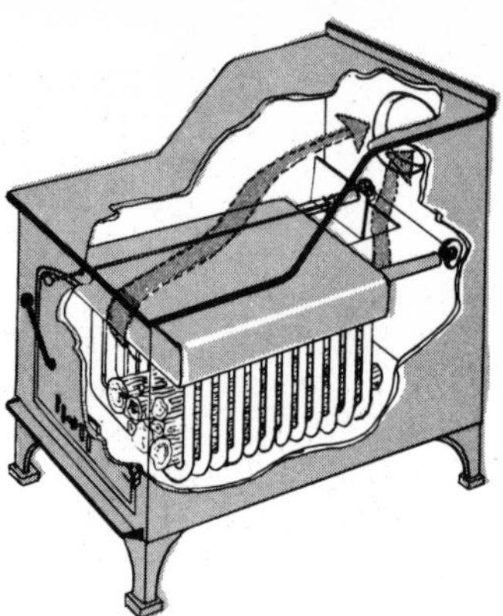

Manufacturer	Hydroheat Div./Ridgway Steel P.O. Box 382 (FF) Ridgway, PA 15853
Model	Hydroboiler
Function	Hydronic wood stove
Size (H, W, D)	38″, 21″, 35″
Weight	405 lbs.
Colors	Black
Airtight?	Yes
Reduced clearance	N/A
Outside combustion air?	N/A
Glass? (type)	N/A
Cooking surface?	Yes
CONSTRUCTION *Material*	Low carbon steel, cast iron
Gauge or thickness	¼″, 3/16″
Air blower? (output)	N/A
Flue size	8″ (rear)
Special features	Cast iron door, damper, and legs. 3/4″ schedule 40 steel water pipe. Holds 3½″ gals. Pressure relief valve.
Options and accessories	Heat exchange coil for hot air systems. Aquastat. Expansion tank. Stainless steel water pump.
Efficiency	85%
Heat output (or area)	50,000 BTUs/hr. hydronic; 16,000 radiant
Tested by	ETLM, ASME stamped
Suggested retail price	$845.00
Brochure	Free
For nearest dealer call	814-776-1323
Mail order, if no dealer?	Yes

HOT WATER SYSTEM

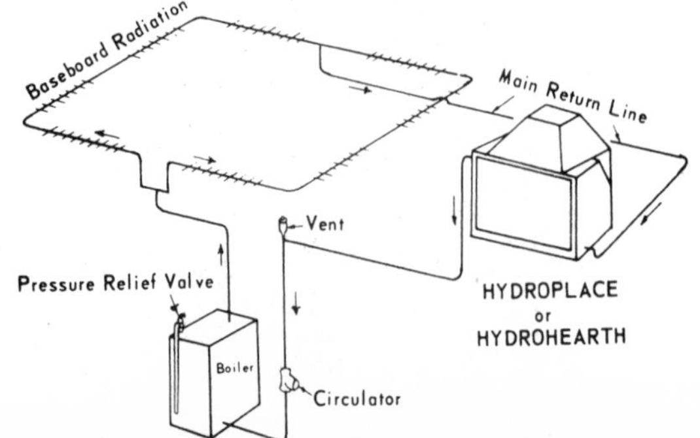

Manufacturer	Hydro-Temp RD #1 Box 14 (FF) Lewisberry, PA 17339
Model	Hydro-Heater Franklin
Function	Hydronic wood stove
Size (H, W, D)	28″, 36″, 19″
Weight	420 lbs./460 lbs.
Colors	Black
Airtight?	Yes
Reduced clearance	Yes, 6″ from back wall
Outside combustion air?	N/A
Glass? (type)	N/A
Cooking surface?	N/A
CONSTRUCTION *Material*	Boiler plate steel, cast iron
Gauge or thickness	8 ga., 11 ga.
Air blower? (output)	N/A
Flue size	8″
Special features	Preheated combustion air. Hot water control package included. Built-in draft. Cast iron doors, front, and top.
Options and accessories	Screen. Domestic hot water. Storage system. Hot air system available.
Efficiency	55%
Heat output (or area)	150,000 BTUs/hr.
Tested by	N/A
Suggested retail price	$895.00
Brochure	Free
For nearest dealer call	717-938-2673
Mail order, if no dealer?	Yes

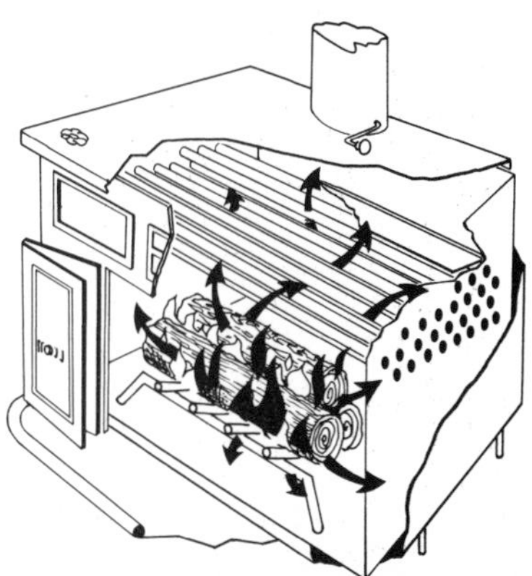

Manufacturer	The Inglewood Stove Co. Rt. 4 Dept. FF Woodstock, VT 05091
Model	Schooner
Function	Wood/coal stove
Size (H, W, D)	34½″, 16″, 22″
Weight	150 lbs.
Colors	Black
Airtight?	N/A
Reduced clearance	N/A
Outside combustion air?	N/A
Glass? (type)	N/A
Cooking surface?	Yes
CONSTRUCTION *Material*	Cast iron
Gauge or thickness	3/8″
Air blower? (output)	N/A
Flue size	Adapts to 5″
Special features	Primary use is coal, but can be fired with small bundles of wood or briquettes.
Options and accessories	Cooking top. Vertical extension rings to enlarge firebox. Screen.
Efficiency	77% (coal)
Heat output (or area)	60,000 BTUs/hr.
Tested by	N. Zealand Insurance Council
Suggested retail price	Base price $449.00
Brochure	Color, free
For nearest dealer call	802-457-3238
Mail order, if no dealer?	N/A

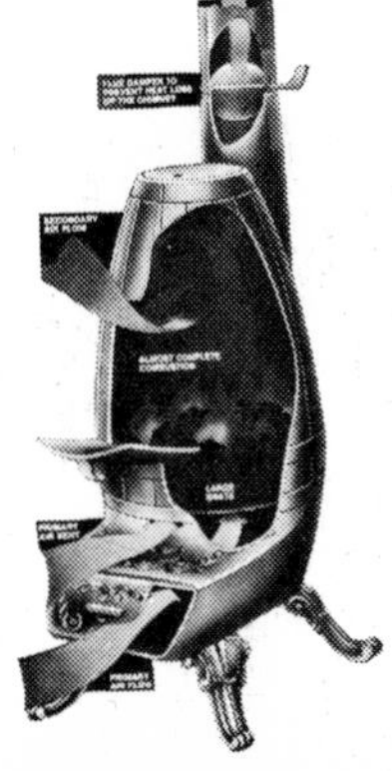

Manufacturer	Jackes-Evans Mfg. Co. Dept. FF 4427 Geraldine Ave. St. Louis, MO 63115
Model	Hearth Glo WFL-UL
Function	Freestanding fireplace/stove
Size (H, W, D)	36″, 35″, 24″
Weight	235 lbs.
Colors	Black with brass trim
Airtight?	Yes
Reduced clearance	N/A
Outside combustion air?	N/A
Glass? (type)	Vycor
Cooking surface?	N/A
CONSTRUCTION *Material*	Aluminized steel
Gauge or thickness	N/A
Air blower? (output)	Optional
Flue size	8″
Special features	Aluminized steel firebox. Firebrick lined. Baked enamel finish. Auto thermostat control. Large ashpan. Takes 24″ logs.
Options and accessories	Heat-diffusing hood. Floor heat blower (auto or manual). (Side loading, closed-in model shown.)
Efficiency	N/A
Heat output (or area)	N/A
Tested by	Underwriter's Laboratories
Suggested retail price	N/A
Brochure	Color, free
For nearest dealer call	314-385-4132
Mail order, if no dealer?	N/A

Manufacturer	Jackson Frontier Co. Dept. FF 4065 W. 11th Street Eugene, OR 97402
Model	Frontier MH-26-6
Function	Fireplace/wood stove (MHA)
Size (H, W, D)	27½″, 26″, 16½″
Weight	380 lbs.
Colors	Black
Airtight?	Yes
Reduced clearance	Yes, 6″ from rear
Outside combustion air?	Yes
Glass? (type)	Optional, alumina-silicate
Cooking surface?	Yes (2)
CONSTRUCTION *Material*	Plate steel
Gauge or thickness	1/4″
Air blower? (output)	N/A
Flue size	6″ (top)
Special features	Reduced clearance with patent pending shielded stovepipe assembly. Chrome-colored viewing screen. Flexible pipe for outside combustion air. 5/16″ thick doors.
Options and accessories	Chrome ball levelers for legs. Adjustable warming plates.
Efficiency	65%
Heat output (or area)	97,000 BTUs/hr; 1,000 sq. ft.
Tested by	McCormack Eng. (ICB0)
Suggested retail price	N/A
Brochure	Color, free
For nearest dealer call	503-484-2877
Mail order, if no dealer?	Yes

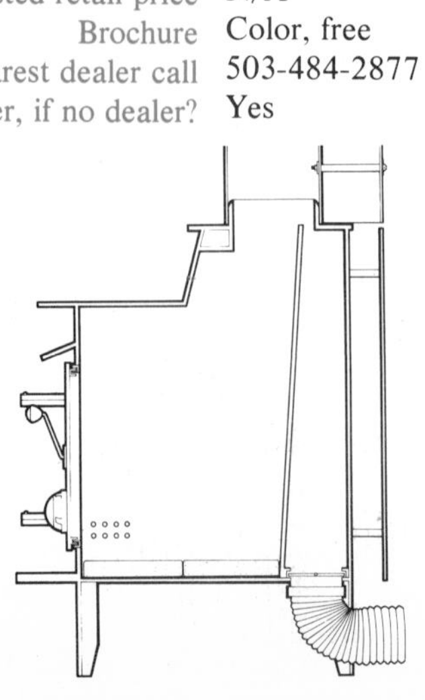

Manufacturer	Juca, Inc. P.O. Box 68 (FF) No. Judson, Ind. 46366
Model	B-3
Function	Freestanding fireplace/stove
Size (H, W, D)	53″, 33″, 31″
Weight	390 lbs./430 lbs.
Colors	Red, gold, orange, black
Airtight?	N/A
Reduced clearance	Yes, 17″ from rear
Outside combustion air?	N/A
Glass? (type)	Yes, tempered
Cooking surface?	N/A
CONSTRUCTION *Material*	Steel
Gauge or thickness	11 ga. to 14 ga.
Air blower? (output)	Yes, 465 CFM
Flue size	8″
Special features	7 tube heat exchange system. Cast firebrick bottom. Thermostat blower control. Grate. Dual draft. Takes 24″ logs.
Options and accessories	Larger blower 865 CFM. Belt-drive blowers from 1790 CFM up to 2,500 CFM. (Smaller model available.)
Efficiency	80%
Heat output (or area)	122,000 BTUs/hr.
Tested by	Arnold Greene Test Lab
Suggested retail price	$547.75
Brochure	Color, free
For nearest dealer call	219-393-5506
Mail order, if no dealer?	Yes

Manufacturer	Magellan Trading Co. Dept. FF 1315 King Street Alexandria, VA 22314
Model	Caldera
Function	Freestanding fireplace
Size (H, W, D)	42″, 26″, 26″
Weight	80 lbs.
Colors	Copper or iron
Airtight?	N/A
Reduced clearance	N/A
Outside combustion air?	N/A
Glass? (type)	N/A
Cooking surface?	N/A
CONSTRUCTION *Material*	Copper covered steel
Gauge or thickness	N/A
Air blower? (output)	N/A
Flue size	7″
Special features	Made in Chile. Hand hammered texture. Includes matching 8 foot chimney.
Options and accessories	Polished copper; scratched copper; (6 other models available.)
Efficiency	N/A
Heat output (or area)	40,000 BTUs/hr.
Tested by	N/A
Suggested retail price	$1,200.00
Brochure	Free
For nearest dealer call	703-549-2758
Mail order, if no dealer?	Yes

Manufacturer	Magellan Trading Co. Dept. FF 1315 King Street Alexandria, VA 22314
Model	Sevilla
Function	Freestanding fireplace
Size (H, W, D)	67″, 31½″, 26″
Weight	N/A
Colors	Copper or iron
Airtight?	N/A
Reduced clearance	N/A
Outside combustion air?	N/A
Glass? (type)	N/A
Cooking surface?	N/A
CONSTRUCTION *Material*	Copper covered steel
Gauge or thickness	N/A
Air blower? (output)	N/A
Flue size	7″ or 8″
Special features	Made in Chile. Includes matching 8 foot chimney.
Options and accessories	Polished copper; hand hammered copper; scratched copper (6 other models available.)
Efficiency	N/A
Heat output (or area)	50,000 BTUs/hr.
Tested by	N/A
Suggested retail price	$1,360.00
Brochure	Free
For nearest dealer call	703-549-2758
Mail order, if no dealer?	Yes

Manufacturer	Malm Fireplaces, Inc. Dept. FF 368 Yolanda Ave. Santa Rosa, CA 95404
Model	The Fire Count
Function	Freestanding fireplace. (MHA)
Size (H, W, D)	44″ H, 32″ W
Weight	N/A
Colors	Ten porcelain colors
Airtight?	N/A
Reduced clearance	Yes, 12″ from combustibles
Outside combustion air?	Yes
Glass? (type)	N/A
Cooking surface?	N/A
CONSTRUCTION *Material*	Sheet steel
Gauge or thickness	N/A
Air blower? (output)	N/A
Flue size	9″
Special features	Screen, plus steel sliding door. Includes chimney kit, storm collar, flashing, and rain cap. Brass trim on hood. Double wall & double hood construction. Refractory lined.
Options and accessories	Unit complete. (See other Malms for colors.)
Efficiency	N/A
Heat output (or area)	N/A
Tested by	RADCO listed for mobile homes
Suggested retail price	N/A
Brochure	Color, free
For nearest dealer call	707-546-8955
Mail order, if no dealer?	N/A

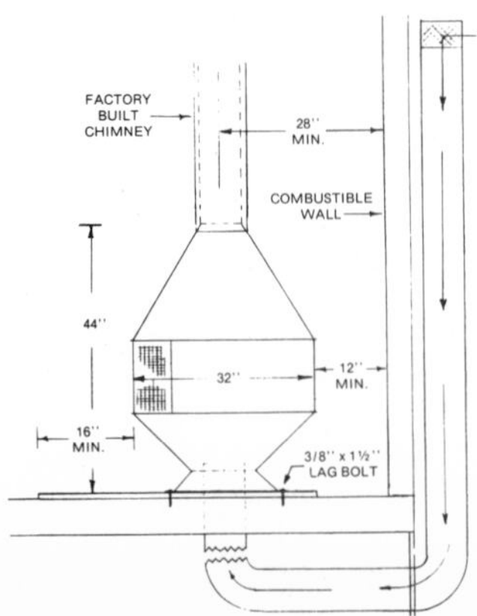

Manufacturer	Malm Fireplaces, Inc. Dept. FF 368 Yolanda Ave. Santa Rosa, CA 95404
Model	Fire Jester
Function	Corner fireplace
Size (H, W, D)	41″, 39″, 28″
Weight	N/A
Colors	Ten porcelain colors
Airtight?	N/A
Reduced clearance	Yes, 12″ from combustibles
Outside combustion air?	N/A
Glass? (type)	N/A
Cooking surface?	N/A
CONSTRUCTION *Material*	Sheet steel
Gauge or thickness	N/A
Air blower? (output)	N/A
Flue size	10″
Special features	With approved shields, can be installed within 6″ of corner walls. Colors: burnt orange, harvest gold, burnt gold, almond, white, rust, coppertone, burnt red, zinnea (lt. gr.), burnt green.
Options and accessories	Color matching chimney.
Efficiency	N/A
Heat output (or area)	N/A
Tested by	UL, ICBO
Suggested retail price	N/A
Brochure	Color, free
For nearest dealer call	707-546-8955
Mail order, if no dealer?	N/A

Manufacturer	Malm Fireplaces, Inc. Dept. FF 368 Yolanda Ave. Santa Rosa, CA 95404
Model	Imperial Carousel
Function	Freestanding fireplace
Size (H, W, D)	48″ H, 40″ dia.
Weight	N/A
Colors	Ten porcelain colors
Airtight?	N/A
Reduced clearance	No, must be 42″ from combustibles
Outside combustion air?	N/A
Glass? (type)	Yes
Cooking surface?	N/A
CONSTRUCTION *Material*	Sheet steel
Gauge or thickness	N/A
Air blower? (output)	N/A
Flue size	8″
Special features	Swirl flames. 360° glass area. Baffled. Swirl of air keeps glass clean. Colors: burnt orange, harvest gold, burnt gold, almond, white, rust, coppertone, burnt red, zinnea (lt. gr.), burnt green.
Options and accessories	Color matching chimney.
Efficiency	N/A
Heat output (or area)	N/A
Tested by	ICBO
Suggested retail price	N/A
Brochure	Color, free
For nearest dealer call	707-546-8955
Mail order, if no dealer?	N/A

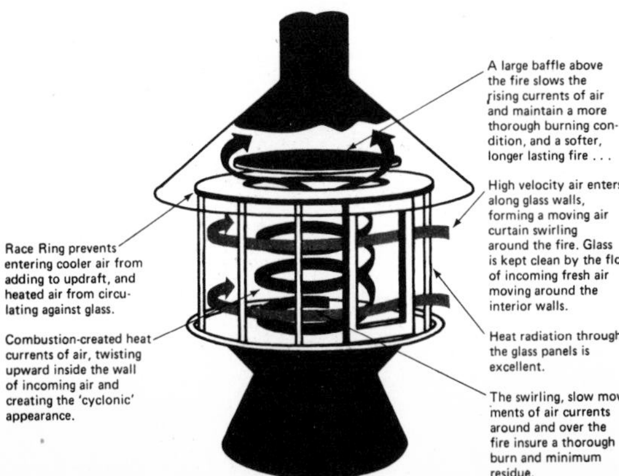

Manufacturer	Malm Fireplaces, Inc. Dept. FF 368 Yolanda Ave. Santa Rosa, CA 95404
Model	Plated Spin 'A' Fire
Function	Freestanding fireplace
Size (H, W, D)	35″ H, 32″ dia.
Weight	Varies
Colors	Copper (c), brass (b), nickel (n)
Airtight?	N/A
Reduced clearance	N/A
Outside combustion air?	N/A
Glass? (type)	Yes, tempered Pyrex
Cooking surface?	N/A
CONSTRUCTION *Material*	Copper; brass; or nickel
Gauge or thickness	N/A
Air blower? (output)	N/A
Flue size	8″
Special features	Includes plated flue to 8′ ceiling and plated ceiling collar. Refractory cement lined.
Options and accessories	Extra flue pipe. Trim collar for open beam installation.
Efficiency	N/A
Heat output (or area)	N/A
Tested by	ICBO
Suggested retail price	(c) $1,900.00; (b) $2,350.00; (n) $2,100.00
Brochure	Color, free
For nearest dealer call	707-546-8955
Mail order, if no dealer?	N/A

Manufacturer	Malm Fireplaces, Inc. Dept. FF 368 Yolanda Ave. Santa Rosa, CA 95404
Model	Royal Carousel
Function	Freestanding fireplace
Size (H, W, D)	70″ H, 32″ dia.
Weight	300 lbs.
Colors	Ten porcelain colors
Airtight?	N/A
Reduced clearance	No, must be 42″ from combustibles
Outside combustion air?	N/A
Glass? (type)	Yes
Cooking surface?	N/A
CONSTRUCTION *Material*	Sheet steel
Gauge or thickness	N/A
Air blower? (output)	N/A
Flue size	7″
Special features	360° glass area. Baffled. Swirled flames. Swirl of air keeps glass clean. Colors: burnt orange, harvest gold, burnt gold, almond, rust, white, coppertone, burnt red, zinnea (lt. gr.), burnt green.
Options and accessories	Color matching chimney.
Efficiency	N/A
Heat output (or area)	N/A
Tested by	ICBO
Suggested retail price	N/A
Brochure	Color, free
For nearest dealer call	707-546-8955
Mail order, if no dealer?	N/A

Manufacturer	Malm Fireplaces, Inc. Dept. FF 368 Yolanda Ave. Santa Rosa, CA 95404
Model	Spin 'A' Fire
Function	Freestanding fireplace (MHA)
Size (H, W, D)	35″ H, 32″ dia.
Weight	N/A
Colors	Ten porcelain colors
Airtight?	N/A
Reduced clearance	N/A
Outside combustion air?	Yes
Glass? (type)	Yes
Cooking surface?	N/A
CONSTRUCTION *Material*	Sheet steel
Gauge or thickness	N/A
Air blower? (output)	N/A
Flue size	8″
Special features	360° glass area. Interior screen protects glass. Colors: burnt orange, harvest gold, burnt gold, almond, white, rust, coppertone, burnt red, zinnea (lt. gr.), burnt green.
Options and accessories	Color matching chimney.
Efficiency	N/A
Heat output (or area)	N/A
Tested by	ICBO (RADCO)
Suggested retail price	N/A
Brochure	Color, free
For nearest dealer call	707-546-8955
Mail order, if no dealer?	N/A

Manufacturer	Mid American Stove Co. P.O. Box 35 (FF) Hanley Falls, MN 56245
Model	Mr. Heat
Function	Freestanding fireplace/stove
Size (H, W, D)	35″, 28″, 24″
Weight	260 lbs./270 lbs.
Colors	Metallic colors (see below)
Airtight?	Yes
Reduced clearance	Yes, with blower
Outside combustion air?	Optional
Glass? (type)	Vycor (3 windows)
Cooking surface?	Yes
CONSTRUCTION *Material*	Steel
Gauge or thickness	½″, 3/16″, 10 ga.
Air blower? (output)	Optional, 60 CFM
Flue size	7″ (top)
Special features	Colors: red, green, blue, brown, black. Burns wood/coal. Refractory inside base. Takes 18″ logs. Down draft.
Options and accessories	Blower. 2 rear Vycor windows (makes total of 5).
Efficiency	89% (combustion)
Heat output (or area)	55,000 BTUs/hr.
Tested by	Terra Lab. Engineers
Suggested retail price	$529.00
Brochure	Color, free
For nearest dealer call	507-768-3426
Mail order, if no dealer?	Yes

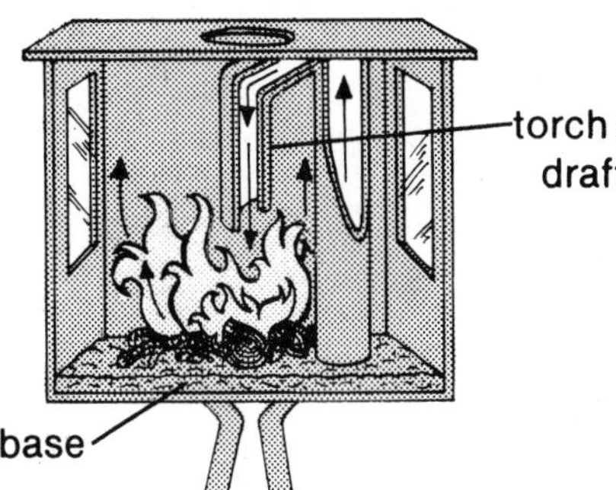

Manufacturer	National Stove Works, Inc. Dept FF Howe Caverns Road Cableskill, N.Y. 12043
Model	Showplace
Function	Freestanding fireplace/stove
Size (H, W, D)	28″, 36″, 24″
Weight	289 lbs.
Colors	Antique copper
Airtight?	Yes
Reduced clearance	Yes, 18″ from rear
Outside combustion air?	N/A
Glass? (type)	Yes, Vycor
Cooking surface?	N/A
CONSTRUCTION *Material*	Hot rolled steel
Gauge or thickness	3/16″
Air blower? (output)	Yes, 265 CFM
Flue size	8″ (top)
Special features	Double walled construction. Takes up to 28″ logs.
Options and accessories	Unit complete.
Efficiency	50% to 75%
Heat output (or area)	75,000 BTUs, 1,500 sq. ft.
Tested by	Arnold Greene Lab (UL)
Suggested retail price	$499.00
Brochure	Color, free
For nearest dealer call	518-296-8517
Mail order, if no dealer?	N/A

Manufacturer	National Stove Works, Inc. Dept. FF Howe Caverns Road Cableskill, N.Y. 12043
Model	Thermoplace
Function	Freestanding fireplace/stove
Size (H, W, D)	31″ H, 30″ W
Weight	240 lbs./250 lbs.
Colors	Maroon, blue, gr., br., bk.
Airtight?	Yes
Reduced clearance	N/A
Outside combustion air?	N/A
Glass? (type)	N/A
Cooking surface?	Yes
CONSTRUCTION *Material*	Steel plate
Gauge or thickness	N/A
Air blower? (output)	N/A
Flue size	8″
Special features	Baffled. Thermo-Control® thermostat. Grate. Screen. Takes up to 22″ logs.
Options and accessories	Unit complete.
Efficiency	75%
Heat output (or area)	65,000 BTUs, 1,200 sq. ft.
Tested by	ETLM
Suggested retail price	$399.00
Brochure	Free
For nearest dealer call	518-296-8517
Mail order, if no dealer?	N/A

Manufacturer	National Stove Works, Inc. Dept. FF Howe Caverns Road Cableskill, N.Y. 12043
Model	TM-2
Function	Wood stove
Size (H, W, D)	29½", 22", 36" (4 sizes)
Weight	210 lbs./220 lbs.
Colors	Blue, maroon, bk., gr., br.
Airtight?	Yes
Reduced clearance	N/A
Outside combustion air?	N/A
Glass? (type)	N/A
Cooking surface?	Yes, 22" × 30"
CONSTRUCTION *Material*	Hot rolled steel
Gauge or thickness	3/16", ¼"
Air blower? (output)	Optional, 265 CFM
Flue size	6"
Special features	Separate secondary chamber. Rear, secondary combustion airpipes. Firebrick lined. Auto thermostat.
Options and accessories	Domestic hot water coil. Fireplace plate (shown). Factory installed blower.
Efficiency	50% to 75%
Heat output (or area)	65,000 BTUs, 1,200 sq. ft.
Tested by	ETLM (UL listed hydronic use)
Suggested retail price	Base price $400.00
Brochure	Free
For nearest dealer call	518-296-8517
Mail order, if no dealer?	N/A

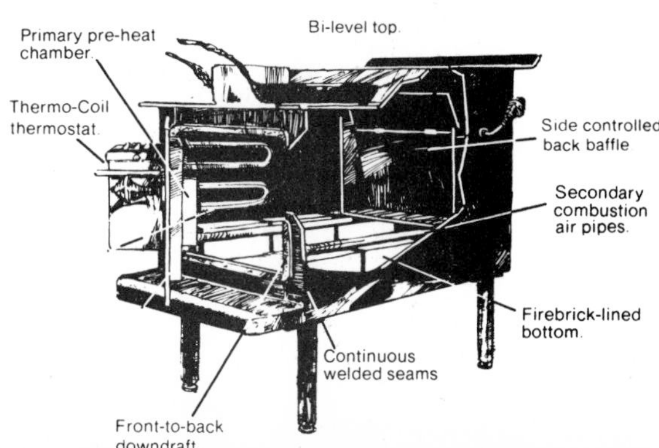

Manufacturer	National Stove Works, Inc. Dept. FF Howe Caverns Road Cableskill, N.Y. 12043
Model	500
Function	Wood stove / add-on furnace
Size (H, W, D)	33", 24", 30"
Weight	425 lbs./435 lbs.
Colors	Black
Airtight?	Yes
Reduced clearance	No, 48" from combustibles
Outside combustion air?	N/A
Glass? (type)	N/A
Cooking surface?	Yes, 24" × 36"
CONSTRUCTION *Material*	Hot rolled steel
Gauge or thickness	3/16", ¼"
Air blower? (output)	N/A
Flue size	8"
Special features	Separate secondary combustion chamber. Auto thermostat. Firebrick lined. Front controlled baffle.
Options and accessories	Hot air hood for plenum. Central hot water pipe. Domestic hot water pipe. (4 sizes available.)
Efficiency	50% to 75%
Heat output (or area)	135,000 BTUs, 3,000 sq. ft.
Tested by	ETLM (UL listed hydronic use)
Suggested retail price	Base price $700.00
Brochure	Free
For nearest dealer call	518-296-8517
Mail order, if no dealer?	N/A

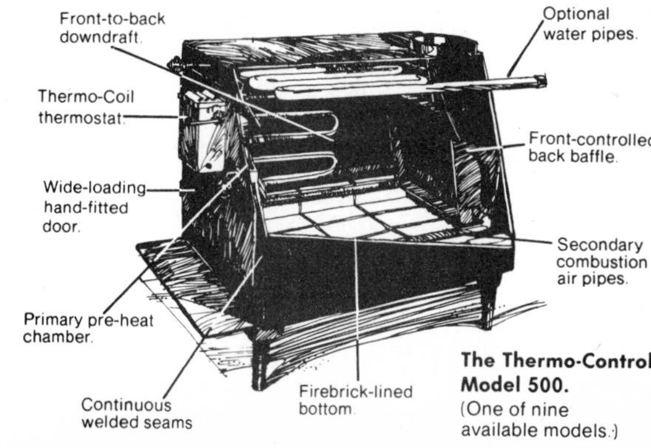

The Thermo-Control Model 500.
(One of nine available models.)

Manufacturer	New Hampshire Wood Stoves, Inc. Dept. FF Greenfield, Mass. 01301
Model	Home Warmer
Function	Wood stove
Size (H, W, D)	34″, 18″, 30″
Weight	347 lbs.
Colors	Black
Airtight?	Yes
Reduced clearance	N/A
Outside combustion air?	N/A
Glass? (type)	N/A
Cooking surface?	Yes
CONSTRUCTION *Material*	Steel
Gauge or thickness	3/8″ & 1/8″
Air blower? (output)	N/A
Flue size	6″
Special features	Triple-baffled heat exchanger. Thermostat control. Takes 29″ logs. Preheated combustion air. Lifetime guarantee.
Options and accessories	Unit complete. (Smaller size available.)
Efficiency	68%
Heat output (or area)	60,000 BTUs/hr.
Tested by	ETLM
Suggested retail price	$489.00
Brochure	8 page, free
For nearest dealer call	413-772-0328
Mail order, if no dealer?	Yes

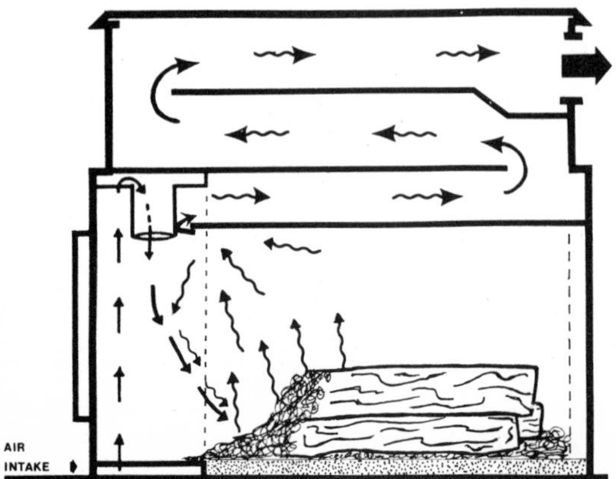

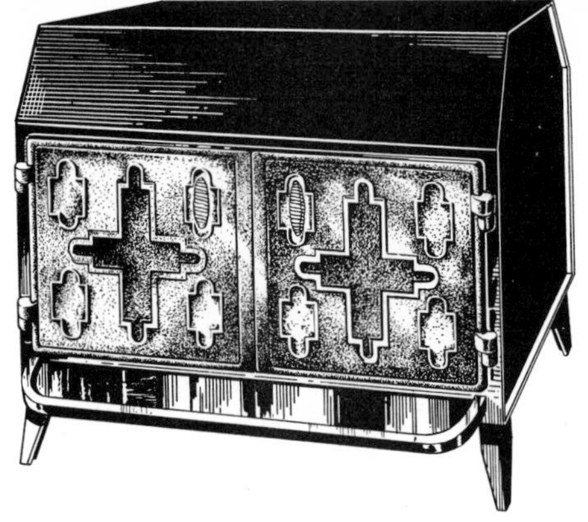

Manufacturer	New Hampshire Wood Stoves, Inc. Dept. FF Greenfield, Mass. 01301
Model	Home Warmer Fireplace III
Function	Freestanding fireplace/stove
Size (H, W, D)	28″, 22 3/8″, 16″
Weight	305 lbs.
Colors	Black
Airtight?	Yes
Reduced clearance	N/A
Outside combustion air?	N/A
Glass? (type)	N/A
Cooking surface?	Yes
CONSTRUCTION *Material*	Steel plate
Gauge or thickness	¼″
Air blower? (output)	N/A
Flue size	8″ (rear)
Special features	Thermostat controlled. Fire-brick lined. Pre-heated combustion air. Baffled. Down draft. Screen.
Options and accessories	Unit complete. (Larger model available.)
Efficiency	N/A
Heat output (or area)	36,000 BTUs/hr.
Tested by	N/A
Suggested retail price	$399.00
Brochure	Free
For nearest dealer call	413-772-0328
Mail order, if no dealer?	Yes

Manufacturer	Noble Steel Products Dept. FF 1688 Church st. Holbrock, N.Y. 11741
Model	Prince
Function	Freestanding fireplace/stove
Size (H, W, D)	36″, 30″, 26″
Weight	385 lbs.
Colors	Black
Airtight?	Yes
Reduced clearance	Yes, to 2″ (with shield)
Outside combustion air?	N/A
Glass? (type)	N/A
Cooking surface?	Yes
CONSTRUCTION *Material*	Boiler plate steel
Gauge or thickness	3/16″ & ¼″
Air blower? (output)	N/A
Flue size	8″ or 6″
Special features	Baffled. Preheated combustion air. Safety shut off system. Secondary air inlet pipe. Double wall door. Firebrick lined. Lifetime guarantee.
Options and accessories	Heat shield to reduce rear clearance to 2″. Screen. (2 sizes available)
Efficiency	N/A
Heat output (or area)	3,000 sq. ft.
Tested by	Arnold Greene Test Lab
Suggested retail price	$545.00
Brochure	$1.00
For nearest dealer call	516-737-0044
Mail order, if no dealer?	Yes

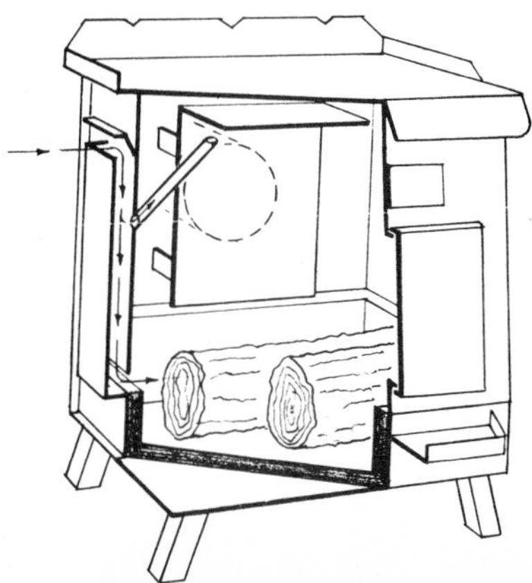

Manufacturer	Oliver Wood Stove Dept. FF 65 Yarnell St. Brentwood, NY 11717
Model	JBO 2616
Function	Freestanding fireplace/stove
Size (H, W, D)	24″, 16″, 26″
Weight	300 lbs.
Colors	Black
Airtight?	Yes
Reduced clearance	N/A
Outside combustion air?	N/A
Glass? (type)	N/A
Cooking surface?	Yes, 12″ × 28″, 5″ × 28″
CONSTRUCTION *Material*	Plate steel
Gauge or thickness	3/16″, ¼″
Air blower? (output)	N/A
Flue size	6″
Special features	Welded from the inside. Baffled. Firebrick lined. Takes 24″ logs. 20 yr. warranty.
Options and accessories	Bypass damper. Screen. Rear hot air exhaust blower. Hot water coil.
Efficiency	60%
Heat output (or area)	99,000 BTUs/hr., 1,500 sq. ft.
Tested by	N/A
Suggested retail price	$450.00
Brochure	Free
For nearest dealer call	516-231-4128
Mail order, if no dealer?	N/A

Manufacturer	Orleys, Mfg. Co. Dept. FF 6999 6th Street White City, OR 97501
Model	F 243 Rose Special
Function	Freestanding fireplace/stove
Size (H, W, D)	18″ to 30″, 24″, 16″
Weight	200 lbs.
Colors	Black, gold trim
Airtight?	Yes
Reduced clearance	N/A
Outside combustion air?	Yes
Glass? (type)	Yes, tempered
Cooking surface?	Yes (2)
CONSTRUCTION *Material*	Steel plate
Gauge or thickness	¼″
Air blower? (output)	N/A
Flue size	6″ (rear)
Special features	Round, tubular firebox. Double glass front. Dual draft. Baffled. Spark guards. Smoke guard. Ash tray. 3/8″ thick door.
Options and accessories	Plain, or 23 models of ornamentation.
Efficiency	N/A
Heat output (or area)	2,500 sq. ft.
Tested by	UL, ICBO
Suggested retail price	$690.00
Brochure	Color, free
For nearest dealer call	503-826-3233
Mail order, if no dealer?	N/A

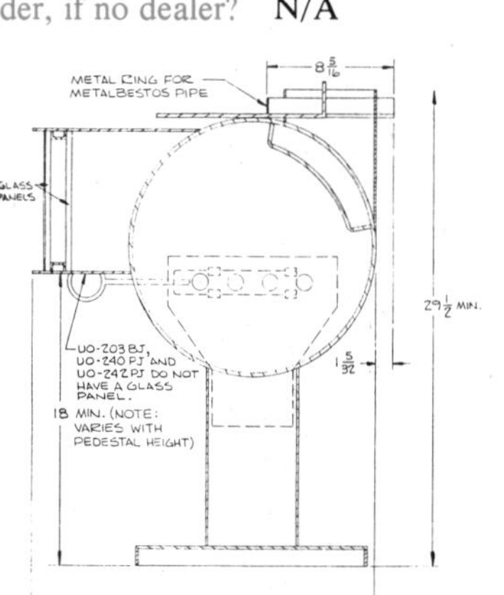

Manufacturer	Orleys Mfg. Co. Dept FF 6999 6th Street White City, OR 97501
Model	U 243 Wagon Wheel
Function	Freestanding fireplace/stove
Size (H, W, D)	31″, 24″, 16″
Weight	200 lbs.
Colors	Black, gold trim
Airtight?	Yes
Reduced clearance	N/A
Outside combustion air?	Yes
Glass? (type)	Yes, tempered
Cooking surface?	Yes (2)
CONSTRUCTION *Material*	Steel plate
Gauge or thickness	¼″, 3/8″
Air blower? (output)	N/A
Flue size	6″
Special features	Round, tubular firebox. Dual draft. Double glass front. Baffled. Spark guard. Smoke guard. Ash tray. 3/8″ thick door.
Options and accessories	Plain, or 23 models of ornamentation.
Efficiency	N/A
Heat output (or area)	2,500 sq. ft.
Tested by	UL, ICBO
Suggested retail price	$425.00 to $750.00
Brochure	Color, free
For nearest dealer call	503-826-3233
Mail order, if no dealer?	N/A

Manufacturer	Orleys Mfg. Co. Dept. FF 6999 6th Street White City, OR 97501
Model	Mobile Home Unit UO 243
Function	Freestanding fireplace/stove (MHA)
Size (H, W, D)	31″, 24″, 16″
Weight	200 lbs.
Colors	Black, gold trim
Airtight?	Yes
Reduced clearance	N/A
Outside combustion air?	Yes
Glass? (type)	Yes, tempered
Cooking surface?	Yes (2)
CONSTRUCTION *Material*	Steel plate
Gauge or thickness	¼″
Air blower? (output)	N/A
Flue size	6″
Special features	Round tubular firebox. Double glass front. Dual draft. Baffled. Ash tray. 3/8″ thick door. Smoke guard.
Options and accessories	Plain, or 23 models of ornamentation.
Efficiency	N/A
Heat output (or area)	2,500 sq. ft.
Tested by	UL, ICBO
Suggested retail price	$650.00
Brochure	Color, free
For nearest dealer call	503-826-3233
Mail order, if no dealer?	N/A

Manufacturer	Peacock Stove Works Rt. Box 2431 (FF) Baldwin, MI 49304
Model	Sundance
Function	Freestanding fireplace/stove
Size (H, W, D)	31″, 24″, 30″
Weight	384 lbs./400 lbs.
Colors	Black
Airtight?	Yes
Reduced clearance	N/A
Outside combustion air?	N/A
Glass? (type)	N/A
Cooking surface?	Yes
CONSTRUCTION *Material*	Plate steel
Gauge or thickness	7 gauge
Air blower? (output)	Yes, 265 CFM
Flue size	8″ (top or rear)
Special features	Secondary combustion air system. Thermostatically controlled blower. Heat exchange tubes. Screen. 25 year warranty. Firebrick lined.
Options and accessories	Unit complete.
Efficiency	88%
Heat output (or area)	100,000 BTUs/hr.
Tested by	Arnold Greene Test Lab
Suggested retail price	$585.00
Brochure	Free
For nearest dealer call	616-745-4609
Mail order, if no dealer?	Yes

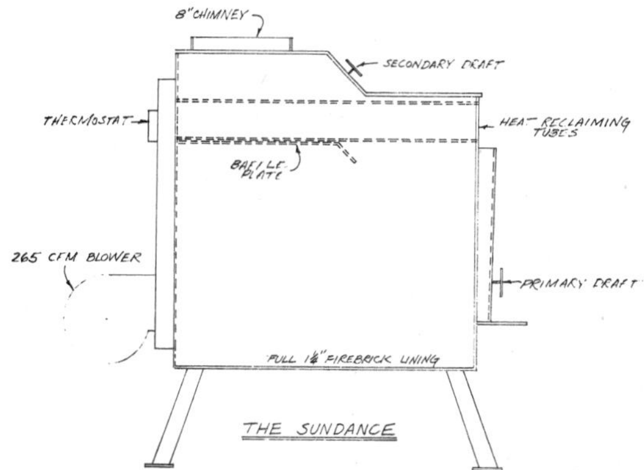

Manufacturer	The Pentagon Stove Works P.O. Box 32 F Tum Tum, WA 99034
Model	Pentagon 15
Function	Wood stove
Size (H, W, D)	27¾″ H, 27″ W
Weight	230 lbs.
Colors	Black, brown
Airtight?	Yes
Reduced clearance	Yes, 30″ from combustibles
Outside combustion air?	N/A
Glass? (type)	N/A
Cooking surface?	Yes
CONSTRUCTION *Material*	Steel plate, cast iron
Gauge or thickness	¼″
Air blower? (output)	N/A
Flue size	6″ (top or rear)
Special features	12 sided, has 18 sq. ft. of surface, 1/3 more than a comparable size box stove. Takes 18″ logs. Pre-heated combustion air. Cast iron door. Lifetime guarantee. Firebrick.
Options and accessories	Nickel plated scrolls and draft covers. Stove tools.
Efficiency	N/A
Heat output (or area)	1,200 sq. ft.
Tested by	N/A
Suggested retail price	$425.00
Brochure	Color, free
For nearest dealer call	509-276-6660
Mail order, if no dealer?	Yes

Manufacturer	The Pentagon Stove Works P.O. Box 32 F Tum Tum, WA 99034
Model	Pentagon 18
Function	Wood stove
Size (H, W, D)	31½″ H, 32″ W
Weight	330 lbs.
Colors	Black, brown
Airtight?	Yes
Reduced clearance	Yes, 30″ from combustibles
Outside combustion air?	N/A
Glass? (type)	N/A
Cooking surface?	Yes
CONSTRUCTION *Material*	Steel plate, cast iron
Gauge or thickness	¼″
Air blower? (output)	N/A
Flue size	8″ (top or back)
Special features	Has 22 sq. ft. surface, 1/3 more than a comparable size box. stove. Takes 24″ logs. Pre-heated combustion air. Cast iron door. Lifetime guarantee. Firebrick. 12 sided
Options and accessories	Nickel plated scrolls and draft covers.
Efficiency	N/A
Heat output (or area)	2,500 sq. ft.
Tested by	N/A
Suggested retail price	$485.00
Brochure	Color, free
For nearest dealer call	509-276-6660
Mail order, if no dealer?	Yes

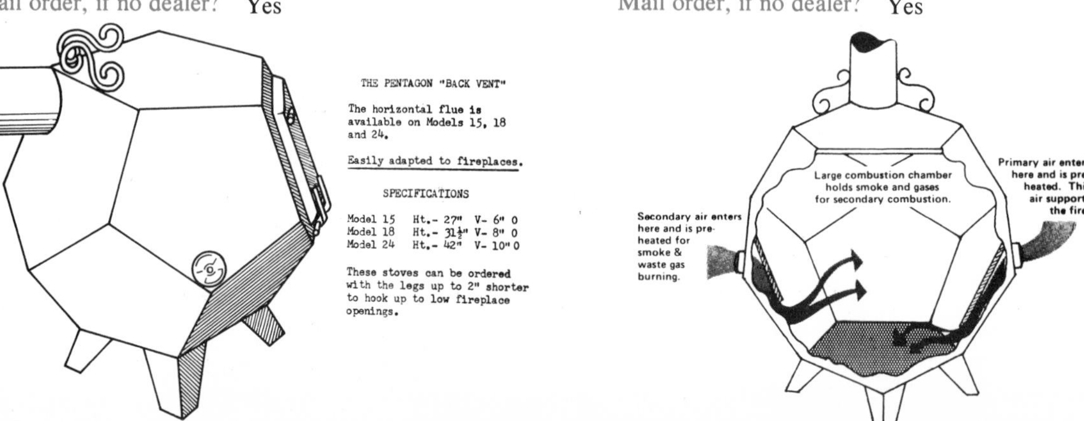

Manufacturer	Pine Barren Stove Co. Dept. FF RT 72 Chatsworth, N.J. 08109
Model	The Baron
Function	Wood stove
Size (H, W, D)	30″, 18″, 38″
Weight	468 lbs.
Colors	Black
Airtight?	Yes
Reduced clearance	N/A
Outside combustion air?	N/A
Glass? (type)	N/A
Cooking surface?	Yes, 15″ × 20″
CONSTRUCTION *Material*	Steel plate, cast iron
Gauge or thickness	¼″, 5/16″
Air blower? (output)	Optional, 265 CFM
Flue size	6″
Special features	Firebrick lined. Cast iron door. Five heat exchange tubes. Baffled. Preheated secondary combustion air. 5 yr. limited warranty.
Options and accessories	Domestic hot water. Blower unit
Efficiency	N/A
Heat output (or area)	24,000 cu. ft.
Tested by	ETLM
Suggested retail price	$473.95
Brochure	Free
For nearest dealer call	609-726-1550
Mail order, if no dealer?	N/A

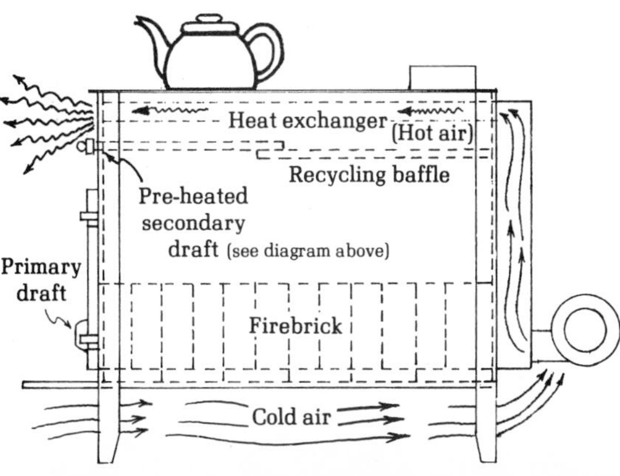

Manufacturer	Powrmatic of Canada Dept. FF 709 Leveille Terrebonne, Que., Canada
Model	Kresno PFS 78
Function	Freestanding fireplace/stove
Size (H, W, D)	32″, 28″, 15″
Weight	215 lbs./230 lbs.
Colors	Red, beige, charcoal
Airtight?	Yes
Reduced clearance	Yes, 28″ from rear
Outside combustion air?	N/A
Glass? (type)	Yes, Pyrex
Cooking surface?	Yes
CONSTRUCTION *Material*	Steel, cast iron
Gauge or thickness	N/A
Air blower? (output)	Optional
Flue size	8″
Special features	Enamel finish. Cast iron door. Takes 20″ logs. Hood raises to expose cast firebox top. Baffled.
Options and accessories	B-B-Que grill. Screen. Decorative cast iron front door. Decorative lower panel.
Efficiency	70%
Heat output (or area)	36,000 BTUs/hr.
Tested by	Underwriters Lab. of Canada
Suggested retail price	N/A
Brochure	Free
For nearest dealer call	514-471-6691
Mail order, if no dealer?	N/A

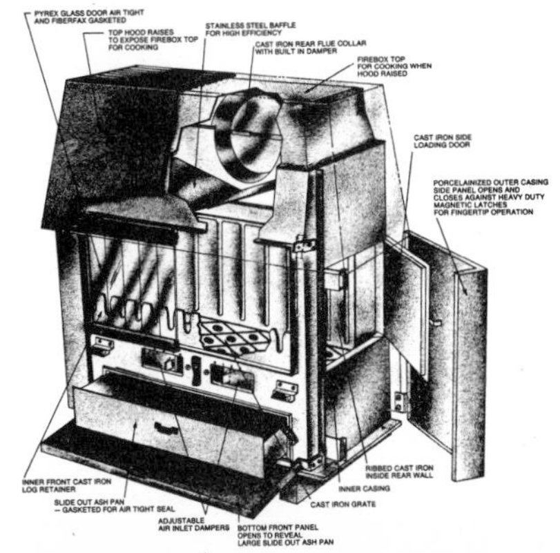

Manufacturer	Precision Metal Products, Inc. Route 6 Box 79 D (F) Wilmington, N.C. 28405
Model	Hearth King I
Function	Freestanding fireplace/stove
Size (H, W, D)	30″, 25½″, 33¾″
Weight	312 lbs.
Colors	Black
Airtight?	Yes
Reduced clearance	Yes
Outside combustion air?	N/A
Glass? (type)	Optional, Vycor or Pyroceram
Cooking surface?	Yes
CONSTRUCTION *Material*	Hardened plate steel
Gauge or thickness	¼″, 7 ga., 11 ga.
Air blower? (output)	Yes, 465 CFM
Flue size	8″ (top)
Special features	Thermostat. Floor level blower. Firebrick lined. Removable door. Screen. 5 yr. limited warranty. Wood/coal grate.
Options and accessories	Safety "cool to touch" side panels (red). Variable speed blower control. Central air duct. Optional glass door.
Efficiency	N/A
Heat output (or area)	150,000 BTUs/hr.
Tested by	Energy Systems Inc. (UL)
Suggested retail price	N/A
Brochure	Free
For nearest dealer call	919-763-6561
Mail order, if no dealer?	N/A

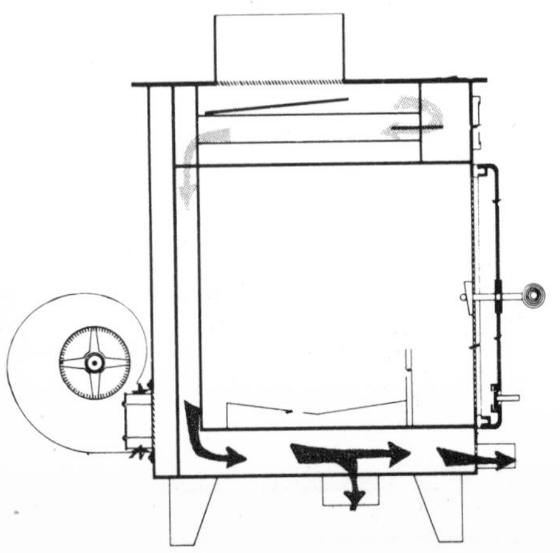

Manufacturer	Precision Metal Products, Inc. Route 6 Box 79 D (F) Wilmington, N.C. 28405
Model	Hearth King II
Function	Freestanding fireplace/stove
Size (H, W, D)	30″, 25½″, 33¾″
Weight	299 lbs.
Colors	Black
Airtight?	Yes
Reduced clearance	Yes
Outside combustion air?	N/A
Glass? (type)	Optional, Vycor or Pyroceram
Cooking surface?	Yes
CONSTRUCTION *Material*	Hardened plate steel
Gauge or thickness	¼″, 7 ga., 11 ga.
Air blower? (output)	Yes, 465 CFM
Flue size	8″ (top)
Special features	Thermostatically controlled blower. Firebrick lined. Removable door. Screen. Wood, coal. 5 yr. limited warranty.
Options and accessories	Safety "cool to touch" side panels (red). Variable speed blower. Optional glass door.
Efficiency	N/A
Heat output (or area)	100,000 BTUs/hr.
Tested by	N/A
Suggested retail price	N/A
Brochure	Free
For nearest dealer call	919-763-6561
Mail order, if no dealer?	N/A

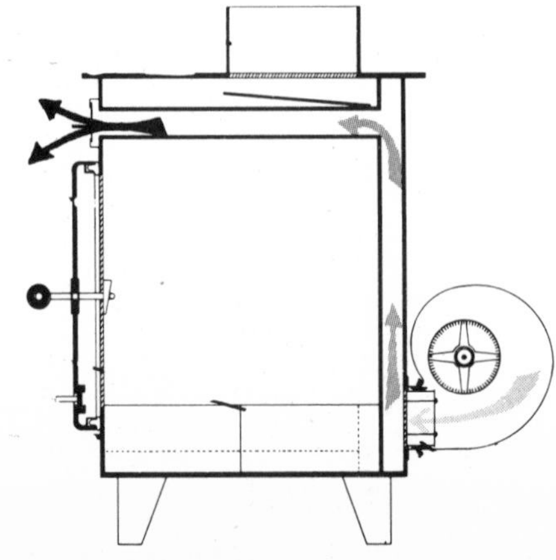

Manufacturer	Preston Dist./Imp. Dept. FF Whidden Street Lowell, MA 01852
Model	Chappee 8033
Function	Wood/coal stove
Size (H, W, D)	22¼″, 19¼″, 16¾″
Weight	224 lbs. (shipping weight)
Colors	Brown
Airtight?	N/A
Reduced clearance	N/A
Outside combustion air?	N/A
Glass? (type)	Yes
Cooking surface?	Yes
CONSTRUCTION *Material*	Cast iron
Gauge or thickness	N/A
Air blower? (output)	N/A
Flue size	4 15/16″ (adapts to 5″ or 6″)
Special features	Made in France. Burns wood, coal, briquets, or charcoal. Enamelled, cast iron body. Grate. Takes 13″ logs. Cooking surface under top.
Options and accessories	Cast iron base mat. (Smaller model available.)
Efficiency	N/A
Heat output (or area)	17,460 BTUs/hr. (coal)
Tested by	French Assoc./Home Heat Appliances
Suggested retail price	N/A
Brochure	Color, free
For nearest dealer call	617-458-6303
Mail order, if no dealer?	N/A

Manufacturer	Preway, Inc. Dept. FF 1430 Second St. N. Wisconsin Rapids, WI 54494
Model	Provider FB 24 F
Function	Freestanding fireplace (MHA)
Size (H, W, D)	N/A
Weight	252 lbs.
Colors	Red, black, mahogany
Airtight?	N/A
Reduced clearance	Yes
Outside combustion air?	Optional
Glass? (type)	Yes
Cooking surface?	N/A
CONSTRUCTION *Material*	Steel
Gauge or thickness	N/A
Air blower? (output)	Yes
Flue size	8″ (top)
Special features	Corner installation. Porcelain finishes. Positive seal damper. Manual and thermostat controlled fan. Matching chimney.
Options and accessories	Red or mahogany is optional. Air inlet kit. Duct adapter kit.
Efficiency	N/A
Heat output (or area)	N/A
Tested by	Underwriters Laboratories
Suggested retail price	Base price $813.00
Brochure	Color, free
For nearest dealer call	714-423-1100
Mail order, if no dealer?	N/A

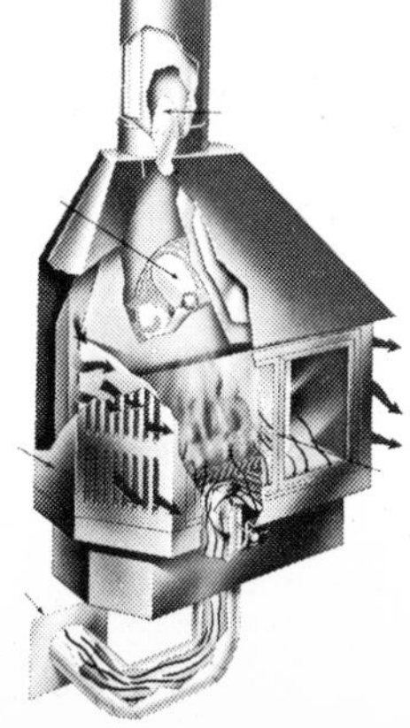

Manufacturer	Quaker Stove Co., Inc. Dept. FF 200 W. 5th St. Lansdale, PA 19446
Model	Moravian Parlor Stove
Function	Freestanding fireplace/stove
Size (H, W, D)	33½″, 29″, 21″
Weight	500 lbs.
Colors	Red, blue, green
Airtight?	Yes
Reduced clearance	N/A
Outside combustion air?	N/A
Glass? (type)	Vycor
Cooking surface?	Yes, 11″ × 21″ (w/rear flue)
CONSTRUCTION *Material*	Plate steel, cast iron
Gauge or thickness	5/16″, ¼″
Air blower? (output)	Optional
Flue size	8″ (top or rear)
Special features	Porcelain coated arch. Firebrick lined. Baffled. Doors, front, and legs are cast iron. Takes 25″ logs. Ash shelf. Lifetime limited guarantee.
Options and accessories	Smaller size available. Screen. Solid doors. Blower.
Efficiency	85%
Heat output (or area)	55,000 BTUs/hr.
Tested by	Underwriters Laboratories
Suggested retail price	$765.00
Brochure	Color, free
For nearest dealer call	215-362-2019
Mail order, if no dealer?	N/A

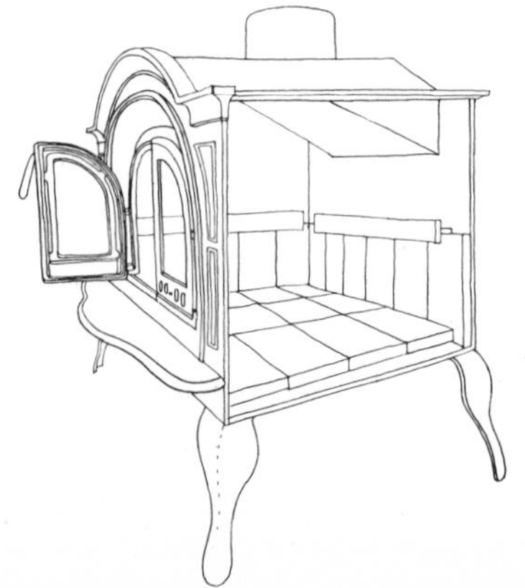

Manufacturer	Quaker Stove Co., Inc. Dept. FF 200 W. 5th St. Lansdale, PA 19446
Model	Quaker Buck II
Function	Wood stove
Size (H, W, D)	30″, 15″, 32″
Weight	530 lbs.
Colors	Black
Airtight?	Yes
Reduced clearance	N/A
Outside combustion air?	N/A
Glass? (type)	Vycor
Cooking surface?	Yes, 24″ × 17″
CONSTRUCTION *Material*	Plate steel, cast iron
Gauge or thickness	5/16″, ¼″
Air blower? (output)	N/A
Flue size	6″ (top or rear)
Special features	Firebrick lined. Front, doors, and legs are cast iron. Baffled. Preheated combustion air. Takes 28″ logs. Guarantee.
Options and accessories	Screen. Brass deer head. (Two smaller sizes available)
Efficiency	85%
Heat output (or area)	55,000 BTUs/hr.
Tested by	Gas and Mech. Lab. (BOCA)
Suggested retail price	$595.00
Brochure	Color, free
For nearest dealer call	215-362-2019
Mail order, if no dealer?	N/A

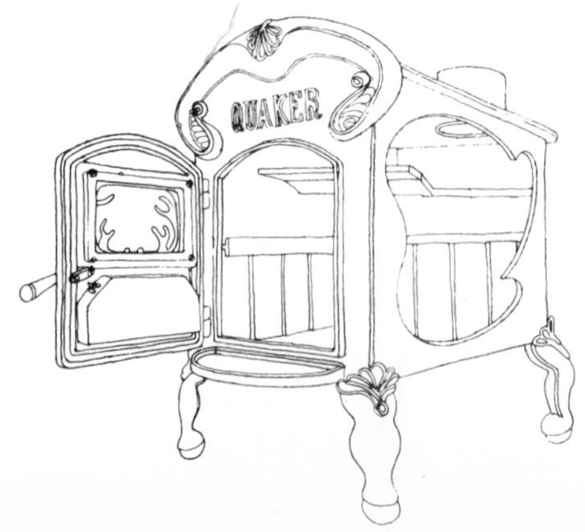

Manufacturer	Rais & Wittus Inc. Dept. FF Hack Green Road Pound Ridge, N.Y. 10576
Model	3
Function	Fireplace/stove
Size (H, W, D)	45″, 28″, 24″
Weight	386 lbs.
Colors	Black
Airtight?	N/A
Reduced clearance	N/A
Outside combustion air?	N/A
Glass? (type)	N/A
Cooking surface?	Yes, (2)
CONSTRUCTION *Material*	Wrought iron
Gauge or thickness	¼″
Air blower? (output)	N/A
Flue size	8″
Special features	Adjustable baffle. Double insulated doors. Primary and secondary air inlets. Grilling area.
Options and accessories	Screen. Grill back. Floor plate. (Smaller model available.)
Efficiency	70%
Heat output (or area)	50,000 BTUs/hr.
Tested by	N/A
Suggested retail price	$1,800.00
Brochure	Free
For nearest dealer call	914-764-5679
Mail order, if no dealer?	Yes

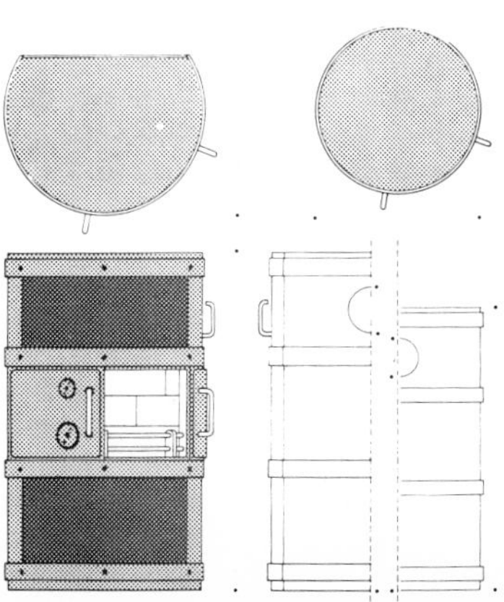

Manufacturer	Riteway Mfg. Co. P.O. Box 153 (FF) Harrisonburg, VA 22801
Model	Riteway 2000
Function	Woodstove
Size (H, W, D)	35½″, 20¾″, 34″
Weight	230 lbs.
Colors	Black
Airtight?	Yes
Reduced clearance	No, must be 38″ from combustibles
Outside combustion air?	N/A
Glass? (type)	N/A
Cooking surface?	N/A
CONSTRUCTION *Material*	Aluminized steel
Gauge or thickness	10 ga., 14 ga.
Air blower? (output)	N/A
Flue size	6″
Special features	Aluminized steel firebox and grate. Takes 24″ logs. Ash pan.
Options and accessories	Decorative cabinet. Hot water attachment. Hot air jacket. Domestic hot water coil. (Wood/coal model available)
Efficiency	N/A
Heat output (or area)	50,000 BTUs/hr.
Tested by	Underwriters Laboratories
Suggested retail price	N/A
Brochure	Free
For nearest dealer call	Write to above.
Mail order, if no dealer?	N/A

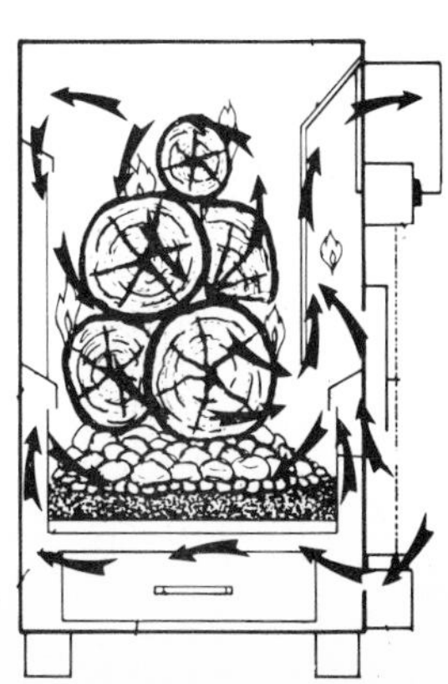

Manufacturer	Roslyn Metal Craft P.O. Box 53 (FF) Sea Cliff, N.Y. 11579
Model	Black Stove I
Function	Freestanding fireplace/stove
Size (H, W, D)	43″, 26″, 19″
Weight	325 lbs. (shipping weight)
Colors	Maroon, green, black, brown
Airtight?	Yes
Reduced clearance	Yes
Outside combustion air?	N/A
Glass? (type)	N/A
Cooking surface?	Yes (if rear vented)
CONSTRUCTION *Material*	Plate steel
Gauge or thickness	3/16″, ¼″
Air blower? (output)	N/A
Flue size	8″ (top or rear)
Special features	Removable door. Double wall interior. Firebrick lined. Double wall door. Takes 20″ logs. Baffled. 25 yr. warranty.
Options and accessories	Screen. Coal hopper grate.
Efficiency	60%
Heat output (or area)	10,000 cu. ft.
Tested by	N/A
Suggested retail price	$489.50
Brochure	Free
For nearest dealer call	516-671-7286
Mail order, if no dealer?	Yes

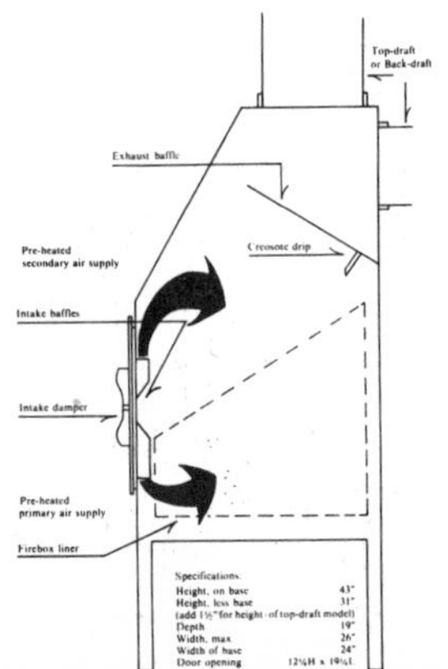

Manufacturer	Roslyn Metal Craft P.O. Box 53 (FF) Sea Cliff, N.Y. 11579
Model	Black Stove II
Function	Freestanding fireplace/stove
Size (H, W, D)	30¾″, 26″, 20½″
Weight	350 lbs. (shipping weight)
Colors	Maroon, green, black, brown
Airtight?	Yes
Reduced clearance	Yes
Outside combustion air?	N/A
Glass? (type)	N/A
Cooking surface?	Yes, 14½″ × 26″
CONSTRUCTION *Material*	Plate steel
Gauge or thickness	3/16″, ¼″, 5/16″
Air blower? (output)	N/A
Flue size	8″ (top or rear)
Special features	Removable door. Double wall interior. Firebrick lined. Double wall door. Takes 20″ logs. 25 yr. warranty. Baffled.
Options and accessories	Screen.Coal hopper grate.
Efficiency	60%
Heat output (or area)	8,000 cu. ft.
Tested by	N/A
Suggested retail price	$456.00
Brochure	Free
For nearest dealer call	516-671-7286
Mail order, if no dealer?	Yes

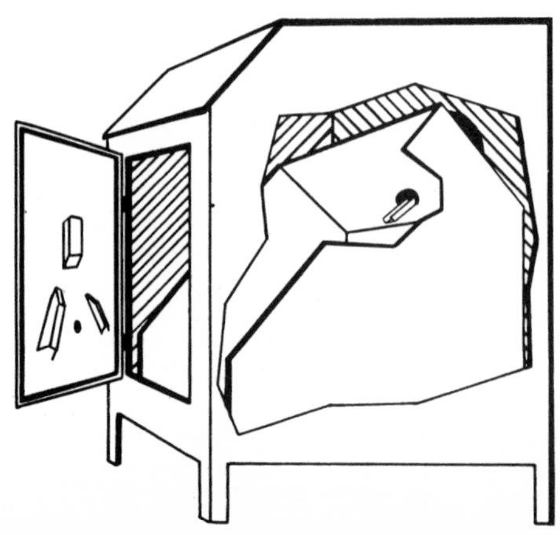

Manufacturer	Russo Wood Stove Mfg. Dept. FF Holbrook, Mass. 02343
Model	Glass View High Heat
Function	Freestanding fireplace/stove
Size (H, W, D)	27″, 30″, 22″
Weight	260 lbs.
Colors	Black
Airtight?	Yes
Reduced clearance	(On some models)
Outside combustion air?	N/A
Glass? (type)	Yes, 12″ × 24″
Cooking surface?	Yes, 30″ × 17″
CONSTRUCTION *Material*	Steel
Gauge or thickness	3/16″, 10 ga.
Air blower? (output)	Yes, 265 CFM
Flue size	6″ (top or rear)
Special features	Firebrick lined. Thermostatically controlled blower. Takes 25″ logs. 15 yr. warranty.
Options and accessories	Unit complete. (Other models available.)
Efficiency	N/A
Heat output (or area)	15,000 cu. ft.
Tested by	Arnold Greene Test Lab
Suggested retail price	$599.00
Brochure	Free
For nearest dealer call	617-767-2521
Mail order, if no dealer?	Yes

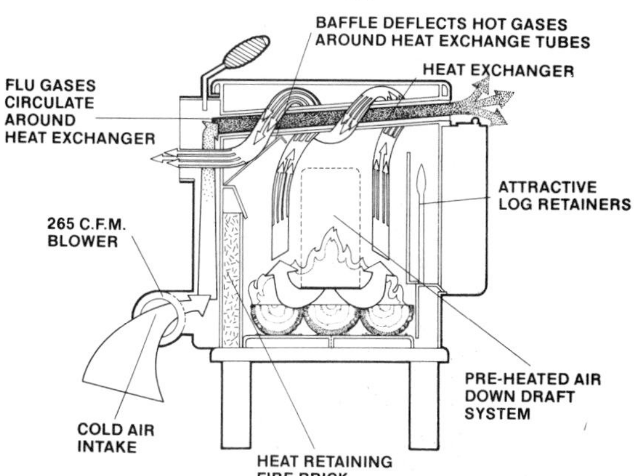

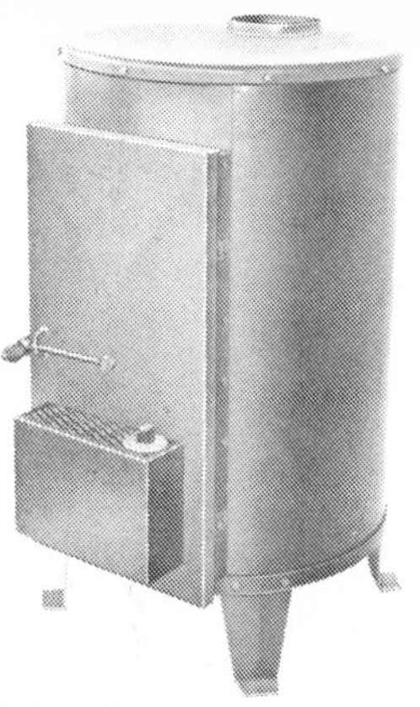

Manufacturer	Shenandoah Mfg. Co. P.O. Box 839 (FF) Harrisonburg, VA 22801
Model	R-65
Function	Wood/coal heater
Size (H, W, D)	36″ H, 21″ dia.
Weight	161 lbs.
Colors	Black
Airtight?	Yes
Reduced clearance	N/A
Outside combustion air?	N/A
Glass? (type)	N/A
Cooking surface?	N/A
CONSTRUCTION *Material*	Sheet steel, cast iron
Gauge or thickness	N/A
Air blower? (output)	N/A
Flue size	6″ (top)
Special features	Designed for small area. Takes 18″ logs (upright). Thermostat. Firebrick lined. Primary and secondary air inlet.
Options and accessories	Coal grate (3 other models available)
Efficiency	N/A
Heat output (or area)	1,000 sq. ft.
Tested by	ETLM
Suggested retail price	N/A
Brochure	Free
For nearest dealer call	703-434-3838
Mail order, if no dealer?	N/A

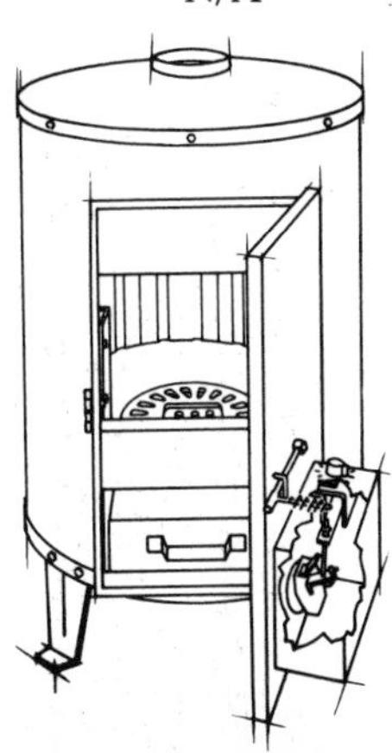

Manufacturer	Sierra Marketing, Inc. Box 346 (FF) Harrisonburg, VA 22801
Model	Classic 2000
Function	Freestanding fireplace/stove
Size (H, W, D)	25½″, 29¾″, 17¼″
Weight	350 lbs.
Colors	Blue, brown, green, black
Airtight?	Yes
Reduced clearance	N/A
Outside combustion air?	N/A
Glass? (type)	Vycor
Cooking surface?	Yes
CONSTRUCTION *Material*	Steel plate, cast iron
Gauge or thickness	5/16″, ¼″
Air blower? (output)	Optional
Flue size	6″ (rear)
Special features	Side loading, cast iron door. Baffled. Firebrick lined. Brass handle. Takes up to 27″ logs. 5 year warranty.
Options and accessories	Porcelain top for cooking. Fireplace cover kits. (Smaller model available.)
Efficiency	N/A
Heat output (or area)	2,000 sq. ft.
Tested by	Inquire from mfr.
Suggested retail price	$550.00
Brochure	Color, free
For nearest dealer call	Write to above
Mail order, if no dealer?	Yes

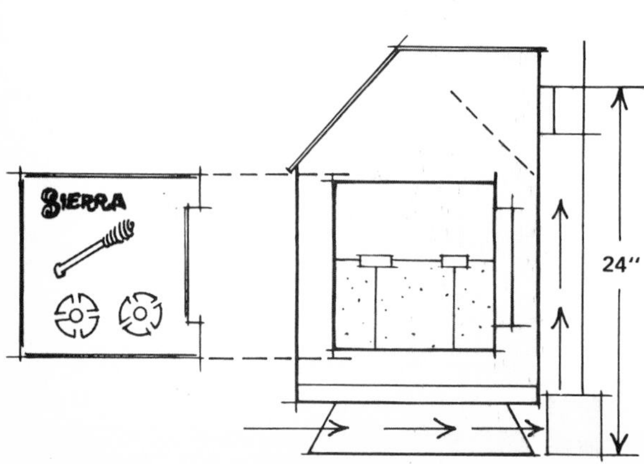

Manufacturer	Sierra Marketing, Inc. Box 346 (FF) Harrisonburg, VA. 22801
Model	Contemporary 1200
Function	Freestanding fireplace/stove
Size (H, W, D)	25″, 25″, 15¾″
Weight	330 lbs.
Colors	Blue, brown, green, black
Airtight?	Yes
Reduced clearance	N/A
Outside combustion air?	N/A
Glass? (type)	Vycor
Cooking surface?	Yes
CONSTRUCTION *Material*	Steel plate, cast iron
Gauge or thickness	5/16″, ¼″
Air blower? (output)	Optional
Flue size	6″ (any position available)
Special features	Cast iron doors. Baffled. Firebrick lined. Brass handles. 5 year warranty. Takes 22″ logs.
Options and accessories	Porcelain top cover for cooking. Fireplace cover kits. (Ceramic tile front model available.)
Efficiency	N/A
Heat output (or area)	1,500 sq. ft.
Tested by	Inquire from mfr.
Suggested retail price	$600.00
Brochure	Color, free
For nearest dealer call	Write to above
Mail order, if no dealer?	Yes

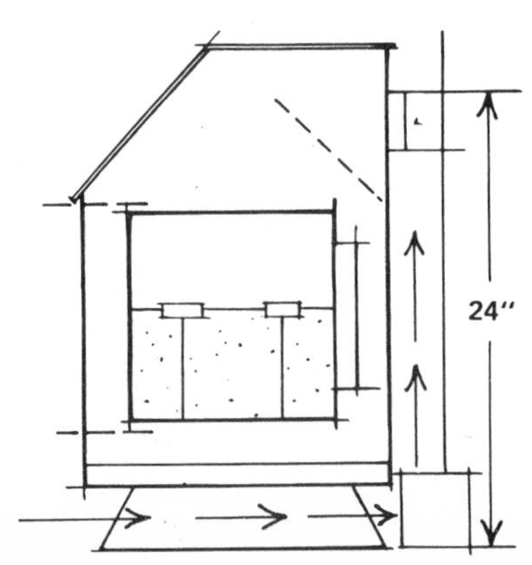

Manufacturer	Smokey Mountain Ent., Inc. P.O. Box 8789 (FF) Asheville, N.C. 28804
Model	Regular Buck Stove
Function	Freestanding fireplace/stove
Size (H, W, D)	25″, 35″, 20″
Weight	415 lbs.
Colors	Black
Airtight?	Yes
Reduced clearance	N/A
Outside combustion air?	N/A
Glass? (type)	Optional, Vycor
Cooking surface?	Yes
CONSTRUCTION *Material*	Steel
Gauge or thickness	N/A
Air blower? (output)	Yes, 260-660 CFM
Flue size	8″
Special features	Thermostatically controlled 3-speed blower. Grate. Hot air jacket is baffled.
Options and accessories	Glass doors. Screen.
Efficiency	60%
Heat output (or area)	2,500 sq. ft.
Tested by	Underwriters Laboratories
Suggested retail price	N/A
Brochure	Color, free
For nearest dealer call	704-255-8935
Mail order, if no dealer?	N/A

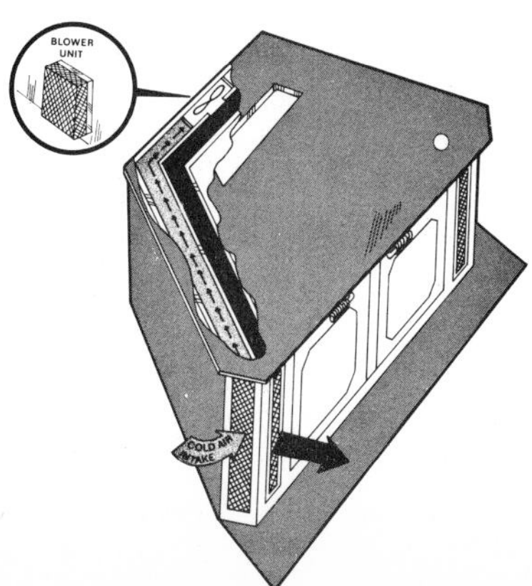

Manufacturer	Southport Stoves Dept. FF 959 Main Street Stratford, CT 06497
Model	Efel Kamina
Function	Freestanding fireplace/stove
Size (H, W, D)	32¼″, 28″, 15″
Weight	190 lbs.
Colors	Gr., br., red, bl., white, beige, grey
Airtight?	Yes
Reduced clearance	N/A
Outside combustion air?	N/A
Glass? (type)	Yes, Pyrex
Cooking surface?	Yes
CONSTRUCTION *Material*	Cast iron, steel
Gauge or thickness	N/A
Air blower? (output)	N/A
Flue size	8″ (rear)
Special features	Made in Belgium. Cast iron interior. Porcelain finish. Cook area under hood. Bar-B-Q. Stainless steel baffle plate. Front and side load. Ash pan.
Options and accessories	Screen. Log guard.
Efficiency	N/A
Heat output (or area)	55,000 BTUs/hr.
Tested by	Gas & Mech. Lab (ICBO) (BOCA) (SBCC)
Suggested retail price	N/A
Brochure	Free
For nearest dealer call	Write to above
Mail order, if no dealer?	N/A

Manufacturer	Southport Stoves Dept. FF 959 Main Street Stratford, CT 06497
Model	Morso 1 BO
Function	Wood stove
Size (H, W, D)	51″, 14½″, 30½″
Weight	320 lbs.
Colors	Black, grey
Airtight?	Yes
Reduced clearance	N/A
Outside combustion air?	N/A
Glass? (type)	N/A
Cooking surface?	Yes
CONSTRUCTION *Material*	Cast iron
Gauge or thickness	N/A
Air blower? (output)	N/A
Flue size	Adapts to 5″ (top)
Special features	Arch shaped heat exchanger.
Options and accessories	Available without arch heat exchanger. (Other sizes and models.)
Efficiency	N/A
Heat output (or area)	9,000 cu ft.
Tested by	ICBO (UL)
Suggested retail price	N/A
Brochure	Color, free
For nearest dealer call	Write to above
Mail order, if no dealer?	N/A

Manufacturer	Southport Stoves Dept. FF 959 Main Street Stratford, CT 06497
Model	Morso 1125
Function	Freestanding fireplace/stove
Size (H, W, D)	42″, 29½″, 23″
Weight	310 lbs.
Colors	Olive green, grey, black
Airtight?	N/A
Reduced clearance	N/A
Outside combustion air?	N/A
Glass? (type)	N/A
Cooking surface?	N/A
CONSTRUCTION *Material*	Cast iron
Gauge or thickness	N/A
Air blower? (output)	N/A
Flue size	8″ (top or rear)
Special features	Made in Denmark. Porcelain enamel finishes. Log stop. Firebrick lined.
Options and accessories	Screen.
Efficiency	N/A
Heat output (or area)	10,000 cu ft.
Tested by	ICBO (UL)
Suggested retail price	N/A
Brochure	Color, free
For nearest dealer call	Write to above
Mail order, if no dealer?	N/A

Manufacturer	Spalt Associates Corp. Dept. FF 275 Circuit St. Hanover, Mass. 02339
Model	Cohasset Boxwood Heater
Function	Wood stove
Size (H, W, D)	25½", 12", 32"
Weight	124 lbs., 132 lbs.
Colors	Black
Airtight?	N/A
Reduced clearance	N/A
Outside combustion air?	N/A
Glass? (type)	N/A
Cooking surface?	Yes
CONSTRUCTION *Material*	Cast iron
Gauge or thickness	Varies
Air blower? (output)	N/A
Flue size	6" (top)
Special features	Two 6" lids on a swing top. Sliding hearth plate for draft control. Takes up to 23" logs.
Options and accessories	Unit complete.
Efficiency	N/A
Heat output (or area)	3 to 4 rooms
Tested by	N/A
Suggested retail price	$92.50
Brochure	35¢
For nearest dealer call	617-871-3180
Mail order, if no dealer?	Yes

Manufacturer	Spalt Associates Corp. Dept. FF 275 Circuit St. Hanover, Mass. 02339
Model	Quincy Adams #190
Function	Wood stove
Size (H, W, D)	39¾", 22¾", 26"
Weight	223 lbs., 231 lbs.
Colors	Black
Airtight?	N/A
Reduced clearance	N/A
Outside combustion air?	N/A
Glass? (type)	Yes, isinglass
Cooking surface?	Yes
CONSTRUCTION *Material*	Cast iron
Gauge or thickness	Varies
Air blower? (output)	N/A
Flue size	6 " (rear)
Special features	Nickel plated trim. Front and side loading doors. Takes 21" logs.
Options and accessories	Unit complete.
Efficiency	N/A
Heat output (or area)	3 to 4 rooms
Tested by	N/A
Suggested retail price	$209.00
Brochure	35¢
For nearest dealer call	617-871-3180
Mail order, if no dealer?	Yes

Manufacturer	Spalt Associates Corp. Dept. FF 275 Circuit St. Hanover, Mass. 02339
Model	Viking #44
Function	Freestanding fireplace/stove
Size (H, W, D)	41″, 23½″, 21½″
Weight	314 lbs./322 lbs.
Colors	Black
Airtight?	Yes
Reduced clearance	N/A
Outside combustion air?	N/A
Glass? (type)	N/A
Cooking surface?	Yes
CONSTRUCTION *Material*	Cast iron
Gauge or thickness	Varies
Air blower? (output)	N/A
Flue size	7″ (rear)
Special features	Firebrick lined. Down draft. Built-in damper flue. Takes up to 20″ logs.
Options and accessories	Unit complete.
Efficiency	N/A
Heat output (or area)	4 to 5 rooms
Tested by	N/A
Suggested retail price	@38.00
Brochure	35¢
For nearest dealer call	617-871-3180
Mail order, if no dealer?	Yes

Manufacturer	Spalt Associates Corp. Dept. FF 275 Circuit St. Hanover, Mass. 02339
Model	Viking #63
Function	Wood stove
Size (H, W, D)	35½″, 15¼″, 34″
Weight	264 lbs.
Colors	Black
Airtight?	Yes
Reduced clearance	N/A
Outside combustion air?	N/A
Glass? (type)	N/A
Cooking surface?	Yes
CONSTRUCTION *Material*	Cast iron
Gauge or thickness	Varies
Air blower? (output)	N/A
Flue size	5″
Special features	Double cast lining on sidewalls and floor to extend life of stove. Bypass damper for lighting fires. Primary and secondary air controls. Takes up to 24″ logs.
Options and accessories	Unit complete.
Efficiency	N/A
Heat output (or area)	3 to 4 rooms
Tested by	N/A
Suggested retail price	$299.00
Brochure	35¢
For nearest dealer call	617-871-3180
Mail order, if no dealer?	Yes

Manufacturer	Stasa Machine Rt. #1, Box 101(FF) Berkey, Ohio 43504
Model	Cobra Conventional
Function	Freestanding fireplace/stove
Size (H, W, D)	35″, 30″, 28″
Weight	380 lbs./405 lbs.
Colors	Eleven different colors
Airtight?	Yes
Reduced clearance	N/A
Outside combustion air?	Optional
Glass? (type)	Tempered or Vycor
Cooking surface?	Yes
CONSTRUCTION *Material*	Hot rolled steel
Gauge or thickness	1/4″, 1/8″
Air blower? (output)	N/A
Flue size	8″ (top or rear)
Special features	Glass—(4) doors & windows. Baffled. Thermometer. Flue pipe to ceiling. Takes 28″ logs. Firebrick lined. Draft Controls.
Options and accessories	Colors: metallic blue, metallic green, tan (2), green (2), grey (2), aluminum, blue, black.
Efficiency	75%
Heat output (or area)	75,000 BTUs, 3,000 sq. ft.
Tested by	N/A
Suggested retail price	Base price $550.00
Brochure	Free
For nearest dealer call	419-829-5281
Mail order, if no dealer?	Yes

Manufacturer	Stasa Machine Rt. #1, Box 101(FF) Berkey, Ohio 43504
Model	Cobra Reclining
Function	Hanging fireplace
Size (H, W, D)	60″ H, 29″ hex dia.
Weight	250 lbs./275 lbs.
Colors	Eleven colors
Airtight?	Yes
Reduced clearance	N/A
Outside combustion air?	Option
Glass? (type)	Vycor
Cooking surface?	N/A
CONSTRUCTION *Material*	Hot rolled steel
Gauge or thickness	10 ga. & 16 ga.
Air blower? (output)	N/A
Flue size	8″
Special features	Glass—(2), (4), or (6) pieces. Baffled. Thermostat. Self-feeding, hearth cement grate. Takes 24″ logs.
Options and accessories	Base for wall mount. Colors: metallic blue, metallic green, tan (2), green (2), grey (2), aluminum, blue, black.
Efficiency	65%
Heat output (or area)	65,000 BTUs, 2,000 sq. ft.
Tested by	N/A
Suggested retail price	Base price, $675.00
Brochure	Free
For nearest dealer call	419-829-5281
Mail order, if no dealer?	Yes

Manufacturer	Sunshine Stove Works Dept. FF Brooks, Maine 04921
Model	Sunshine
Function	Wood stove
Size (H, W, D)	31″, 14″, 34″
Weight	280 lbs.
Colors	Black
Airtight?	Yes
Reduced clearance	N/A
Outside combustion air?	N/A
Glass? (type)	N/A
Cooking surface?	Yes
CONSTRUCTION *Material*	Steel, cast iron
Gauge or thickness	1/8″, ¼″
Air blower? (output)	N/A
Flue size	6″ (top)
Special features	Baffled. Firebrick lined. Front, sides, and back are bent from one continuous sheet of steel. Cast iron door and door frame. Takes 24″ logs.
Options and accessories	Unit complete.
Efficiency	N/A
Heat output (or area)	6,000 to 8,000 cu ft.
Tested by	ETLM (UL)
Suggested retail price	$325.00
Brochure	Free
For nearest dealer call	Write to above
Mail order, if no dealer?	N/A

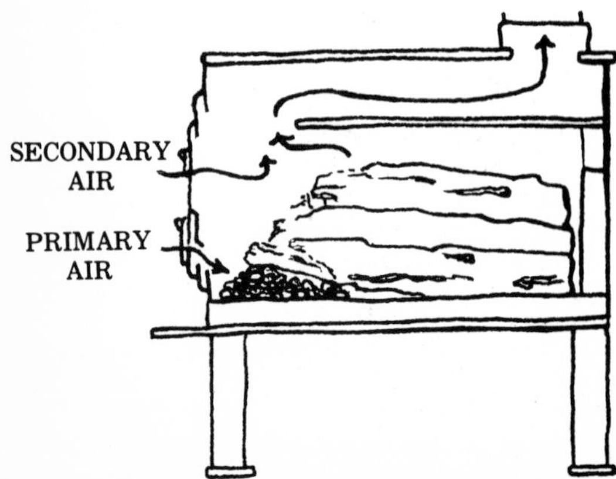

Manufacturer	Superior Stove Co., Inc. P.O. Box 218 (FF) 159 Mill Street Stoughton, MA 02072
Model	SS-2Sa
Function	Wood stove
Size (H, W, D)	26″, 28½″, 17¼″
Weight	240 lbs.
Colors	Black
Airtight?	Yes
Reduced clearance	N/A
Outside combustion air?	N/A
Glass? (type)	N/A
Cooking surface?	Yes, 15″ × 28″
CONSTRUCTION *Material*	Plate steel
Gauge or thickness	10 ga., 3/16″
Air blower? (output)	Optional, 40 CFM
Flue size	6″ (top or rear)
Special features	Wood and coal use. Firebrick lined. Baffled. Takes 23″ logs.
Options and accessories	Available without double wall, thermo-flow circulating system. Coal grate. Blower.
Efficiency	N/A
Heat output (or area)	45,000 BTUs/hr.
Tested by	Arnold Greene Lab (ICBO/BOCA/SBCC)
Suggested retail price	N/A
Brochure	Free
For nearest dealer call	617-344-9342
Mail order, if no dealer?	N/A

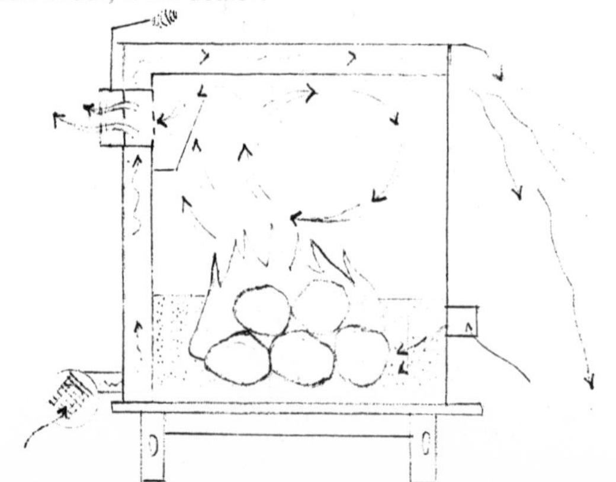

Manufacturer	Superior Stove Co., Inc. P.O. Box 218 (FF) 159 Mill Street Stoughton, MA 02072
Model	SS-2
Function	Freestanding fireplace/stove
Size (H, W, D)	26″, 28½″, 17¼″
Weight	265 lbs.
Colors	Black
Airtight?	Yes
Reduced clearance	N/A
Outside combustion air?	N/A
Glass? (type)	Yes, Vycor, 9″ × 13″
Cooking surface?	Yes, 15″ × 28″
CONSTRUCTION *Material*	Plate steel
Gauge or thickness	10 ga., 3/16″
Air blower? (output)	Optional, 40 CFM
Flue size	6″ (top or rear)
Special features	Wood/coal use. Firebrick lined. Takes 23″ logs. Baffled. Sliding steel doors separate glass from fire if desired.
Options and accessories	Screen substitute for glass. Coal grate. Blower. Safety rail.
Efficiency	N/A
Heat output (or area)	45,000 BTUs/hr.
Tested by	Arnold Greene Lab (ICBO/ BOCA/SBCC)
Suggested retail price	N/A
Brochure	Free
For nearest dealer call	617-344-9342
Mail order, if no dealer?	N/A

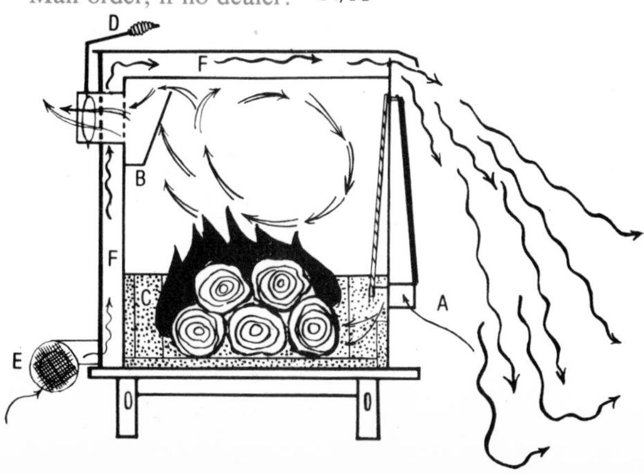

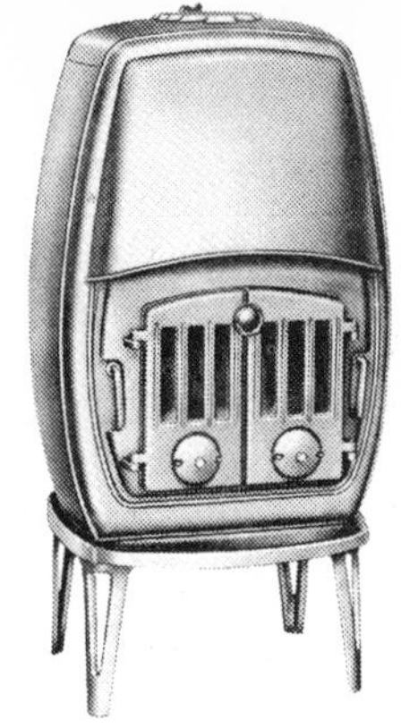

Manufacturer	Svenborg Co., Inc. P.O. Box 5 (FF) Hanover, N.H. 03775
Model	Lange 61 MF
Function	Freestanding fireplace/stove
Size (H, W, D)	38″, 20½″, 19″
Weight	265 lbs. (shipping weight)
Colors	Porcelain (see below)
Airtight?	Yes
Reduced clearance	N/A
Outside combustion air?	N/A
Glass? (type)	Yes, Vycor
Cooking surface?	Yes
CONSTRUCTION *Material*	Cast iron
Gauge or thickness	Varies
Air blower? (output)	N/A
Flue size	Adapts to 5″ or 6″
Special features	Made in Denmark. Entire door frame lifts off for fireplace use. Screen. Log guard. 5 yr. limited warranty.
Options and accessories	Porcelain, red, blue, black. Color matching stovepipe.
Efficiency	N/A
Heat output (or area)	6,000 cu ft.
Tested by	ETLM (UL)
Suggested retail price	Base price $652.00 (flat black)
Brochure	Color, free
For nearest dealer call	603-643-3771
Mail order, if no dealer?	N/A

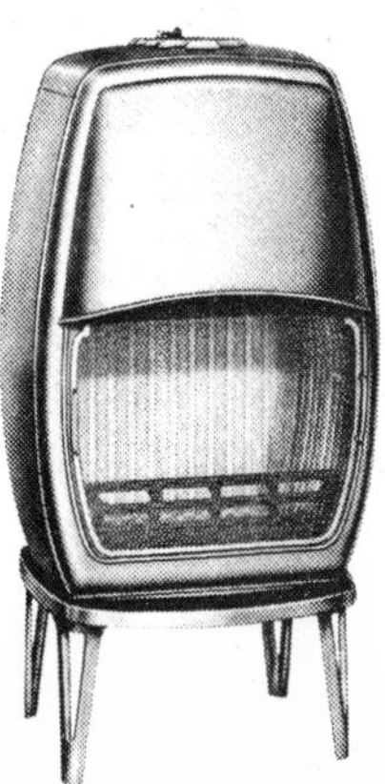

Manufacturer	Svendborg Co., Inc. P.O. Box 5 (FF) Hanover, N.H. 03755
Model	Lange 6203 BR
Function	Wood stove
Size (H, W, D)	33″, 13¼″, 30″
Weight	213 lbs. (shipping weight)
Colors	Porcelain (see below)
Airtight?	Yes
Reduced clearance	N/A
Outside combustion air?	N/A
Glass? (type)	N/A
Cooking surface?	Yes
CONSTRUCTION *Material*	Cast iron
Gauge or thickness	Varies
Air blower? (output)	N/A
Flue size	Adapts to 5″ or 6″
Special features	Made in Denmark. Takes up to 16″ logs. Baffled. 5 yr. limited warranty.
Options and accessories	Porcelain red, blue, green, black. Color matching stove-pipe. (Larger size available.)
Efficiency	N/A
Heat output (or area)	6,000 cu. ft.
Tested by	ETLM (UL)
Suggested retail price	Base price $580.00 (flat black)
Brochure	Color, free
For nearest dealer call	603-643-3771
Mail order, if no dealer?	N/A

Manufacturer	Svendborg Co., Inc. P.O. Box 5 (FF) Hanover, N.H. 03755
Model	Lange 6302 K
Function	Wood stove/oven
Size (H, W, D)	50½″, 16″, 34″
Weight	370 lbs. (shipping weight)
Colors	Porcelain (see below)
Airtight?	Yes
Reduced clearance	N/A
Outside combustion air?	N/A
Glass? (type)	N/A
Cooking surface?	Yes
CONSTRUCTION *Material*	Cast iron
Gauge or thickness	Varies
Air blower? (output)	N/A
Flue size	Adapts to 5″ or 6″
Special features	Made in Denmark. Takes 24″ logs. Baffled. Curved replaceable firebox liners. 5 yr. limited warranty.
Options and accessories	Porcelain red, blue, green, black. Color matching stove-pipe.
Efficiency	N/A
Heat output (or area)	10,000 cu. ft.
Tested by	ETLM (UL)
Suggested retail price	Base price $865.00 (flat black)
Brochure	Color, free
For nearest dealer call	603-643-3771
Mail order, if no dealer?	N/A

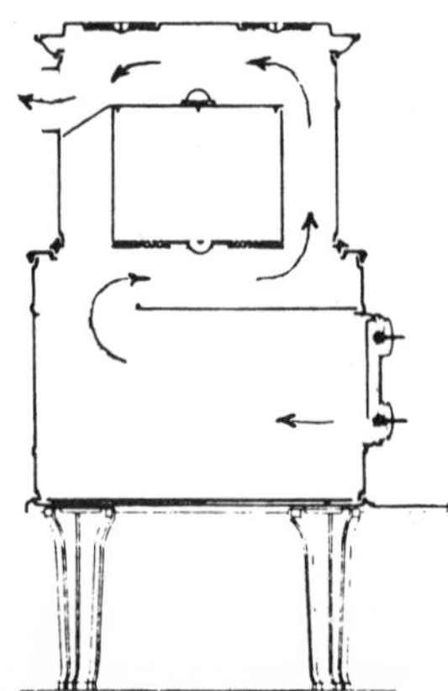

Manufacturer	Svendborg, Co., Inc. P.O. Box 5 (FF) Hanover, N.H. 03755
Model	Lange 6303 Arch
Function	Wood stove
Size (H, W, D)	37½", 16", 25"
Weight	220 lbs. (shipping weight)
Colors	Porcelain (see below)
Airtight?	Yes
Reduced clearance	N/A
Outside combustion air?	N/A
Glass? (type)	N/A
Cooking surface?	Yes
CONSTRUCTION *Material*	Cast iron
Gauge or thickness	Varies
Air blower? (output)	N/A
Flue size	Adapts to 5" or 6"
Special features	Made in Denmark. Curved replaceable firebox liners. Arch heat exchanger. 5 yr. limited warranty
Options and accessories	Porcelain red, blue, green, black. Color matching stovepipe.
Efficiency	N/A
Heat output (or area)	6,000 cu. ft.
Tested by	ETLM (UL)
Suggested retail price	Base price $485.00 (flat black)
Brochure	Color, free
For nearest dealer call	603-643-3771
Mail order, if no dealer?	N/A

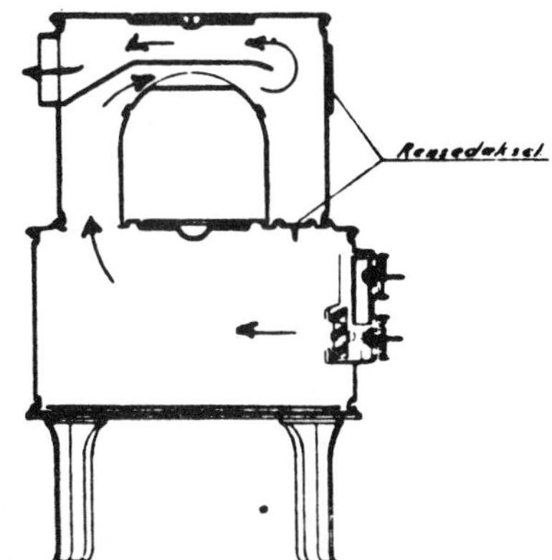

Manufacturer	Thelin-Thompson Co. P.O. Box 459 (FF) Kings Beach, CA 95719
Model	Thompson 2000
Function	Wood stove
Size (H, W, D)	45½" H, 21" W
Weight	265 lbs.
Colors	Black w/brass trim
Airtight?	Yes
Reduced clearance	N/A
Outside combustion air?	N/A
Glass? (type)	Mica
Cooking surface?	Yes
CONSTRUCTION *Material*	Steel, cast iron
Gauge or thickness	12 gauge
Air blower? (output)	N/A
Flue size	6"
Special features	Thermostat controlled combustion air. Legs, door, top are solid brass. Firecrete bottom. ¼" cast iron interior. 5 yr. limited warranty.
Options and accessories	Unit complete
Efficiency	N/A
Heat output (or area)	1,700 sq. ft.
Tested by	N/A
Suggested retail price	$995.00 to $1129.00
Brochure	Color, free
For nearest dealer call	916-546-4852
Mail order, if no dealer?	Yes

Manufacturer	Therm-Kon Products Dept. FF 207 E. Mill Rd. Galesville, WI 54630
Model	MMI-Aunt Sarah
Function	Freestanding fireplace/stove
Size (H, W, D)	34″, 30″, 28″
Weight	402 lbs./420 lbs.
Colors	Black (colors optional)
Airtight?	Yes
Reduced clearance	N/A
Outside combustion air?	N/A
Glass? (type)	Yes, tempered Pyrex
Cooking surface?	Yes
CONSTRUCTION *Material*	Steel or stainless steel
Gauge or thickness	10 gauge
Air blower? (output)	Optional, 260 CFM
Flue size	8″
Special features	4 heat exchange tubes. Cast iron doors. Door vents keep glass clean.Thermostat controlled. Firebrick lined.
Options and accessories	Solid stainless steel body. Ceramic center pieces. Blower. Rail on top.
Efficiency	50%
Heat output (or area)	40,000; 60,000 w/blower
Tested by	N/A
Suggested retail price	Base price $640.00
Brochure	Color, free
For nearest dealer call	608-582-2276
Mail order, if no dealer?	Yes

Manufacturer	Thermograte, Inc. P.O. Box 43566 (FF) St. Paul, MN 55164
Model	Fireplace/Stove
Function	Freestanding fireplace/stove
Size (H, W, D)	33″ H, 38″ W
Weight	N/A
Colors	Burnt red, black
Airtight?	N/A
Reduced clearance	Yes
Outside combustion air?	N/A
Glass? (type)	Yes, tempered
Cooking surface?	N/A
CONSTRUCTION *Material*	Steel, stainless steel
Gauge or thickness	12 gauge
Air blower? (output)	Optional, 135 CFM
Flue size	N/A
Special features	Corner installation. Triple wall construction. Stainless steel tubes with thermal expansion seals. 5 yr. warranty against burnout. Ash pan.
Options and accessories	Blower. Screen.
Efficiency	63%
Heat output (or area)	55,400 BTUs/hr.
Tested by	Underwriters Laboratories
Suggested retail price	N/A
Brochure	Color, free
For nearest dealer call	612-636-7033
Mail order, if no dealer?	N/A

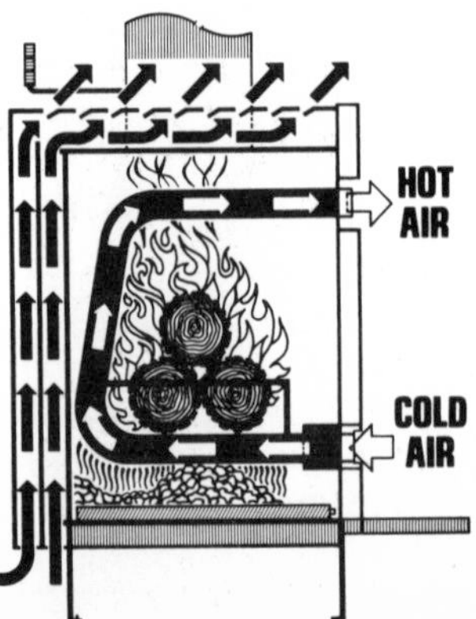

Manufacturer	Timberline Productions P.O. Box 4307 (FF) Boise, Idaho 83704
Model	Timberline TDF M/H
Function	Freestanding fireplace/stove (MHA)
Size (H, W, D)	33¼″, 23″, 24¾″
Weight	447 lbs.
Colors	Black
Airtight?	Yes
Reduced clearance	N/A
Outside combustion air?	Yes
Glass? (type)	N/A
Cooking surface?	Yes
CONSTRUCTION *Material*	Plate steel, cast iron
Gauge or thickness	¼″
Air blower? (output)	N/A
Flue size	6″
Special features	Baffled. Firebrick lined. Cast iron doors. Dual draft. Sliding grate.
Options and accessories	Nickel trim.
Efficiency	N/A
Heat output (or area)	1,400 sq. ft.
Tested by	Northwest Laboratories
Suggested retail price	N/A
Brochure	Free
For nearest dealer call	Write to above
Mail order, if no dealer?	N/A

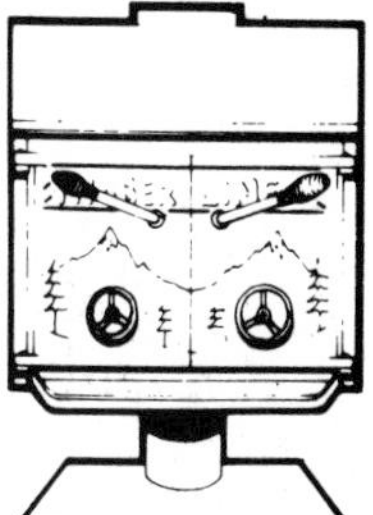

Manufacturer	Timberline Productions P.O Box 4307 (FF) Boise, Idaho 83704
Model	Timberline T-SF
Function	Freestanding fireplace/stove
Size (H, W, D)	26″ W, 26″ D
Weight	480 lbs.
Colors	Black
Airtight?	Yes
Reduced clearance	N/A
Outside combustion air?	N/A
Glass? (type)	N/A
Cooking surface?	Yes
CONSTRUCTION *Material*	Plate steel, cast iron
Gauge or thickness	¼″
Air blower? (output)	N/A
Flue size	8″ (top or rear)
Special features	Baffled. Dual draft. Cast iron door. Takes 20″ logs. Firebrick lined.
Options and accessories	Nickel trim. (Larger model available)
Efficiency	N/A
Heat output (or area)	1,600 sq. ft.
Tested by	Northwest Laboratories
Suggested retail price	N/A
Brochure	Free
For nearest dealer call	Write to above
Mail order, if no dealer?	N/A

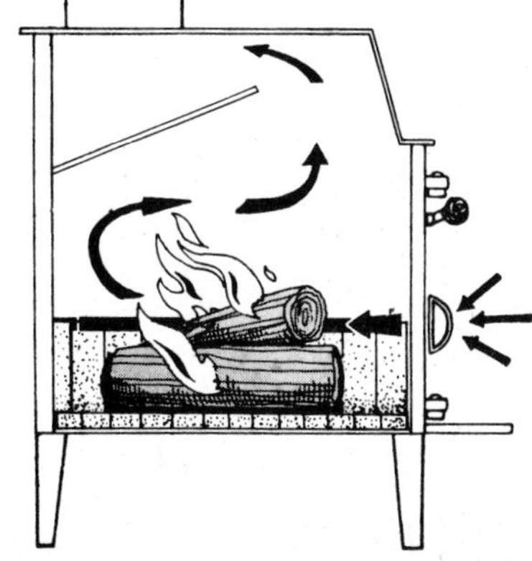

Manufacturer	Torrid Mfg. Co., Inc. Dept. FF 1248 Poplar Pl. So. Seattle, WA 98144
Model	Caribe
Function	Freestanding fireplace
Size (H, W, D)	72¾", 38", 26½"
Weight	450 lbs./525 lbs.
Colors	Red, green, black
Airtight?	N/A
Reduced clearance	Yes, 1" from rear wall
Outside combustion air?	N/A
Glass? (type)	N/A
Cooking surface?	N/A
CONSTRUCTION *Material*	Steel
Gauge or thickness	5/16", 12 ga.
Air blower? (output)	Yes, 210 CFM
Flue size	10" (top)
Special features	Built in thermostatically controlled heat exchanger. Screen.
Options and accessories	Unit complete.
Efficiency	N/A
Heat output (or area)	19,000 BTUs/hr.
Tested by	ICBO
Suggested retail price	$833.70
Brochure	Free
For nearest dealer call	206-324-2754
Mail order, if no dealer?	Yes

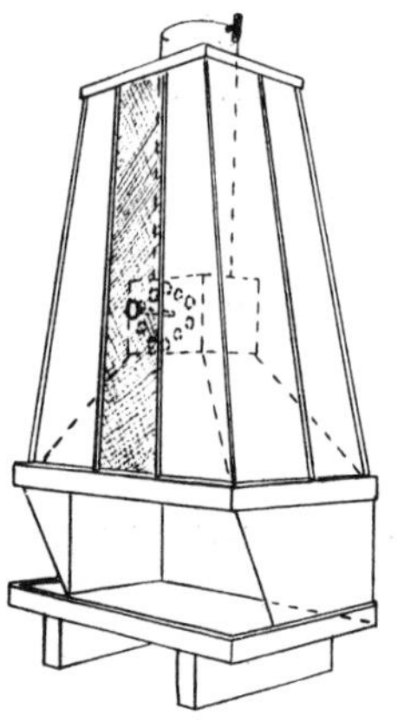

Manufacturer	Torrid Mfg. Co., Inc. Dept. FF 1248 Poplar Pl. So. Seattle, WA 98144
Model	Triumph
Function	Freestanding fireplace/stove
Size (H, W, D)	29", 32", 25"
Weight	465 lbs. (shipping weight)
Colors	Black
Airtight?	N/A
Reduced clearance	Yes, 18" from rear
Outside combustion air?	N/A
Glass? (type)	Mica
Cooking surface?	Yes
CONSTRUCTION *Material*	Steel plate
Gauge or thickness	5/16"
Air blower? (output)	N/A
Flue size	8" (top)
Special features	Burns wood or coal. Firebrick lined. Two baffles. Screen. One year guarantee.
Options and accessories	Water tank. Rear heat shield.
Efficiency	N/A
Heat output (or area)	N/A
Tested by	N/A
Suggested retail price	$529.40
Brochure	Free
For nearest dealer call	206-324-2754
Mail order, if no dealer?	Yes

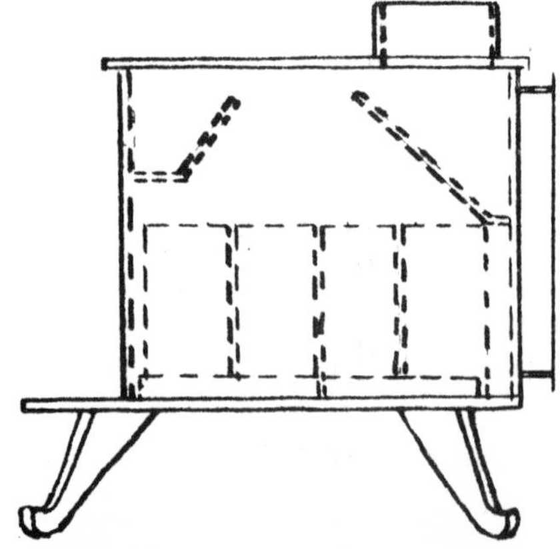

Manufacturer	Transmetal Inc. Dept. FF 117 East Fir St. Mt. Vernon, Wash. 98273
Model	GEOMID Bulldog
Function	Freestanding fireplace/stove
Size (H, W, D)	23″, 18″, 24″
Weight	270 lbs.
Colors	Blue, rust, green, black
Airtight?	Yes
Reduced clearance	Yes, 24″ from rear
Outside combustion air?	N/A
Glass? (type)	Optional, tempered
Cooking surface?	Yes
CONSTRUCTION *Material*	Steel plate
Gauge or thickness	¼″
Air blower? (output)	N/A
Flue size	6″
Special features	Baffled. Preheated combustion air. Adjustable legs. Takes 19″ logs. Firebrick lined. Lifetime guarantee.
Options and accessories	Handmade brass artwork on solid door. Leg length. (Five sizes available.)
Efficiency	60% to 70%
Heat output (or area)	800 sq. ft.
Tested by	N/A
Suggested retail price	$375.00
Brochure	Free
For nearest dealer call	206-424-5695
Mail order, if no dealer?	Yes

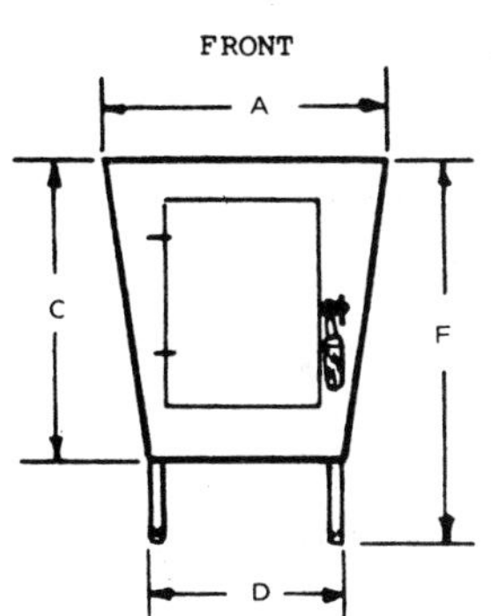

Manufacturer	Transmetal Inc. Dept. FF 117 East Fir St. Mt. Vernon, WA 98273
Model	GEOMID Sasquatch
Function	Freestanding fireplace/stove
Size (H, W, D)	26″, 21″, 32½″
Weight	415 lbs.
Colors	Blue, rust, green, black
Airtight?	Yes
Reduced clearance	Yes, 24″ from rear
Outside combustion air?	N/A
Glass? (type)	Optional, tempered
Cooking surface?	Yes
CONSTRUCTION *Material*	Steel plate
Gauge or thickness	¼″
Air blower? (output)	N/A
Flue size	6″ (top, rear or side)
Special features	Preheated combustion air. Baffled. Adjustable legs. Takes 27″ logs. Firebrick lined. Lifetime guarantee.
Options and accessories	Hand made brass art work (shown). Glass door. Leg length. (Fireplace insert model available.)
Efficiency	70%
Heat output (or area)	2,000 sq. ft.
Tested by	N/A
Suggested retail price	Base price $545.00
Brochure	Free
For nearest dealer call	206-424-5695
Mail order, if no dealer?	Yes

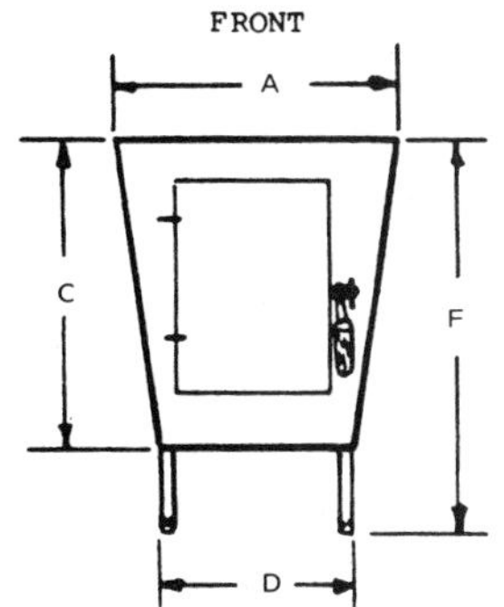

Manufacturer	Upland Stove Co., Inc. P.O. Box 87 (FF) Greene, N.Y. 13778
Model	Upland 27
Function	Wood stove
Size (H, W, D)	27". 12½", 21¾"
Weight	150 lbs.
Colors	Blue, black, green, brown
Airtight?	Yes
Reduced clearance	N/A
Outside combustion air?	N/A
Glass? (type)	N/A
Cooking surface?	Yes
CONSTRUCTION *Material*	Cast iron
Gauge or thickness	¼"
Air blower? (output)	N/A
Flue size	6" (top or rear)
Special features	Ash catcher. Takes 20" logs.
Options and accessories	Unit complete.
Efficiency	65%
Heat output (or area)	33,000 BTUs/hr., 5,875 cu. ft.
Tested by	ETLM
Suggested retail price	N/A
Brochure	Free
For nearest dealer call	607-656-4156
Mail order, if no dealer?	N/A

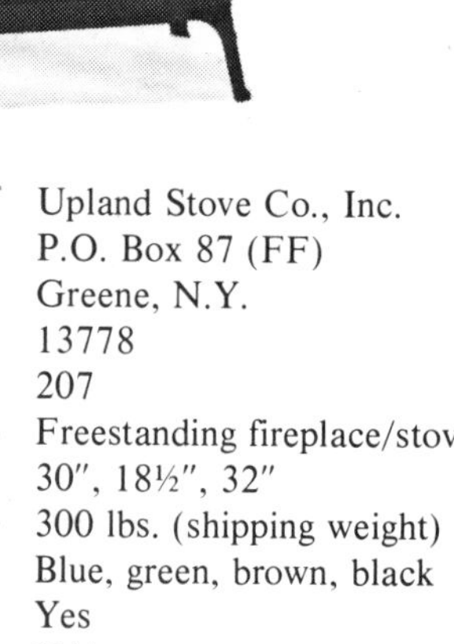

Manufacturer	Upland Stove Co., Inc. P.O. Box 87 (FF) Greene, N.Y. 13778
Model	207
Function	Freestanding fireplace/stove
Size (H, W, D)	30", 18½", 32"
Weight	300 lbs. (shipping weight)
Colors	Blue, green, brown, black
Airtight?	Yes
Reduced clearance	N/A
Outside combustion air?	N/A
Glass? (type)	N/A
Cooking surface?	Yes
CONSTRUCTION *Material*	Cast iron
Gauge or thickness	¼"
Air blower? (output)	N/A
Flue size	7" (top or rear)
Special features	Screen. Slide baffle. 28" stove hoe. Takes 26" logs. Front and side load.
Options and accessories	Unit complete.
Efficiency	60%
Heat output (or area)	50,000 BTUs/hr., 10,000 cu. ft.
Tested by	ETLM
Suggested retail price	N/A
Brochure	Free
For nearest dealer call	607-656-4156
Mail order, if no dealer?	N/A

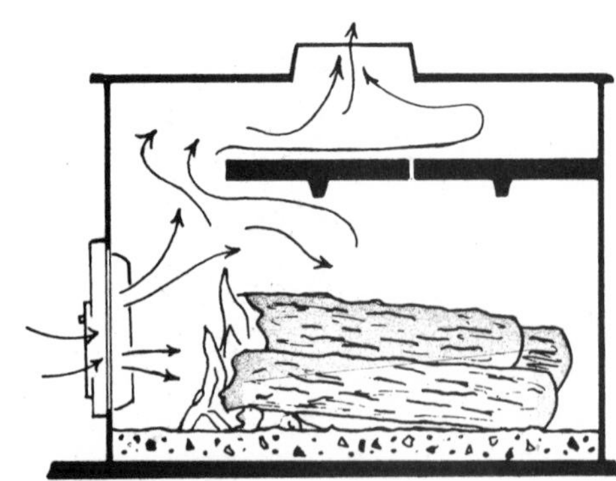

Manufacturer	Valco Corp. Dept. FF 215 Johnson Rd. Michigan City, Ind. 46360
Model	Mark I
Function	Wood stove
Size (H, W, D)	35″, 14″, 26″
Weight	210 lbs./225 lbs.
Colors	Green or black
Airtight?	Yes
Reduced clearance	Yes, 24″ from rear
Outside combustion air?	N/A
Glass? (type)	N/A
Cooking surface?	Yes
CONSTRUCTION *Material*	Boiler plate steel, cast iron
Gauge or thickness	¼″, 3/16″
Air blower? (output)	N/A
Flue size	5″
Special features	Cast iron door. Bypass damper (see Mark IV). Guarantee. Wood/coal use. Baffled. Preheated air.
Options and accessories	Unit complete.
Efficiency	83%
Heat output (or area)	75,000 BTUs/hr.
Tested by	Inquire from Mfr.
Suggested retail price	$391.00
Brochure	Free
For nearest dealer call	219-872-5082
Mail order, if no dealer?	Yes

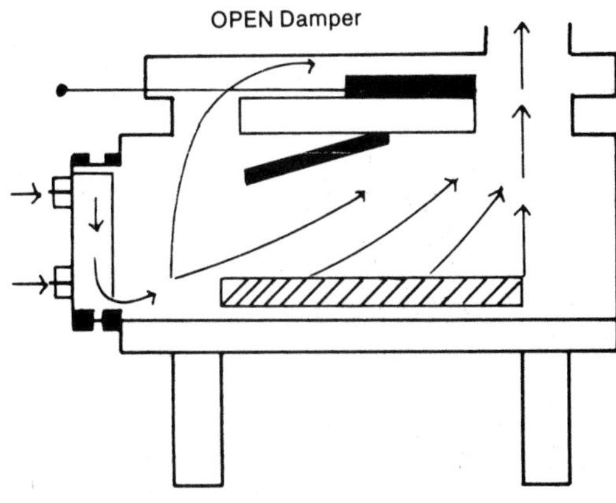

Manufacturer	Valco Corp. Dept. FF 215 Johnson Rd. Michigan City, Ind. 46360
Model	Mark II
Function	Wood stove
Size (H, W, D)	22″, 14″, 24″
Weight	185 lbs./195 lbs.
Colors	Black
Airtight?	Yes
Reduced clearance	N/A
Outside combustion air?	N/A
Glass? (type)	Optional, Vycor
Cooking surface?	Yes
CONSTRUCTION *Material*	Boiler plate steel, cast iron
Gauge or thickness	3/16″
Air blower? (output)	N/A
Flue size	5″
Special features	Cast iron door. Baffled and bypass damper in one unit. Preheated combustion air. Fireplace cover included.
Options and accessories	Side mount with Vycor glass.
Efficiency	78%
Heat output (or area)	55,000 BTUs/hr.
Tested by	Inquire from Mfr.
Suggested retail price	$315.00
Brochure	Free
For nearest dealer call	219-872-5082
Mail order, if no dealer?	Yes

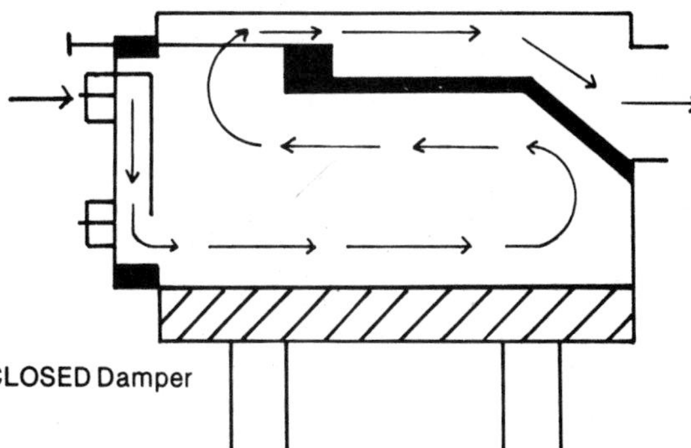

Manufacturer	Valco Corp. Dept. FF 215 Johnson Rd Michigan City, Ind. 46360
Model	Mark III
Function	Freestanding fireplace/stove
Size (H, W, D)	42″, 30″, 19″
Weight	350 lbs.
Colors	Green or black
Airtight?	Yes
Reduced clearance	Yes, 24″ from rear
Outside combustion air?	N/A
Glass? (type)	Yes, Vycor
Cooking surface?	Yes
CONSTRUCTION *Material*	Boiler plate steel, cast iron
Gauge or thickness	3/16″
Air blower? (output)	N/A
Flue size	5″ (top or rear)
Special features	Cast iron door. Firebrick lined. Log stop. Baffle and bypass damper same as used in Mark I.
Options and accessories	Unit complete. (Smaller model available.)
Efficiency	80%
Heat output (or area)	65,000 BTUs/hr.
Tested by	Inquire from mfr.
Suggested retail price	$614.00
Brochure	Free
For nearest dealer call	219-872-5082
Mail order, if no dealer?	Yes

Manufacturer	Valco Corp. Dept. FF 215 Johnson Rd. Michigan City, Ind. 46360
Model	Mark IV
Function	Wood stove
Size (H, W, D)	35″, 17″, 26″
Weight	240 lbs./250 lbs.
Colors	Green or Black
Airtight?	Yes
Reduced clearance	Yes, 24″ from rear
Outside combustion air?	N/A
Glass? (type)	N/A
Cooking surface?	Yes
CONSTRUCTION *Material*	Boiler plate steel, cast iron
Gauge or thickness	3/16″, ¼″
Air blower? (output)	N/A
Flue size	5″
Special features	Cast iron door. Bypass damper (see Mark I). Guarantee. Wood/coal use. Baffled. Preheated air.
Options and accessories	Unit complete.
Efficiency	83%
Heat output (or area)	80,000 BTUs/hr.
Tested by	Inquire from mfr.
Suggested retail price	$511.00
Brochure	Free
For nearest dealer call	219-872-5082
Mail order, if no dealer?	Yes

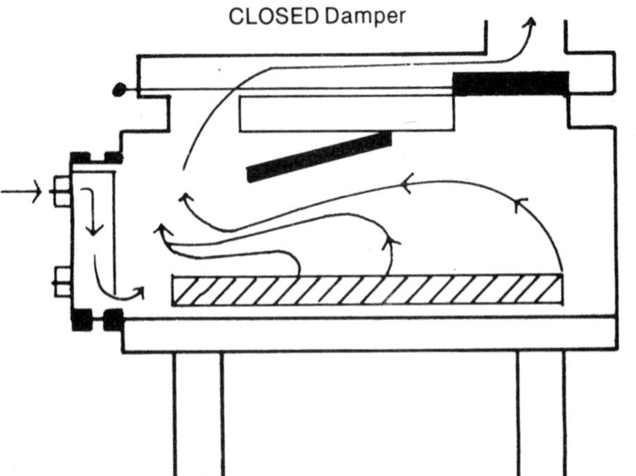

Manufacturer	Vermont Castings, Inc. Dept. FF Prince Street Randolph, VT 05060
Model	Defiant
Function	Freestanding fireplace/stove
Size (H, W, D)	32½", 36", 22½"
Weight	350 lbs./370 lbs.
Colors	Black
Airtight?	Yes
Reduced clearance	Optional, see below
Outside combustion air?	N/A
Glass? (type)	N/A
Cooking surface?	Yes
CONSTRUCTION *Material*	Cast iron
Gauge or thickness	¼"
Air blower? (output)	N/A
Flue size	8" (top or rear)
Special features	Front or side load. Thermostat controlled. Baffled. Screen. Preheated combustion air. Griddle. 30 day money back guarantee. 3 year ltd. warranty.
Options and accessories	Rear, bottom and stovepipe heat shields.
Efficiency	65%
Heat output (or area)	55,000 BTUs/hr.
Tested by	(BOCA) (SBCC)
Suggested retail price	$575.00
Brochure	Color, $1.00
For nearest dealer call	802-728-3111
Mail order, if no dealer?	Yes 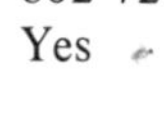

Manufacturer	Vermont Castings, Inc. Dept. FF Prince Street Randolph, VT 05060
Model	Vigilant
Function	Freestanding fireplace/stove
Size (H, W, D)	30½", 29¾", 27
Weight	265 lbs., 310 lbs.
Colors	Black
Airtight?	Yes
Reduced clearance	Optional, see below
Outside combustion air?	N/A
Glass? (type)	N/A
Cooking surface?	Yes
CONSTRUCTION *Material*	Cast iron
Gauge or thickness	¼"
Air blower? (output)	N/A
Flue size	8" (top or rear)
Special features	Top and front load. Thermostat controlled Baffled. Screen. Preheated combustion air. Griddle. 30 day money back guarantee. 3 year limited warranty.
Options and accessories	Rear, bottom and stovepipe heat shields.
Efficiency	65%
Heat output (or area)	47,000 BTUs/hr.
Tested by	(BOCA) (SBCC)
Suggested retail price	$470.00
Brochure	Color, $1.00
For nearest dealer call	802-728-3111
Mail order, if no dealer?	Yes

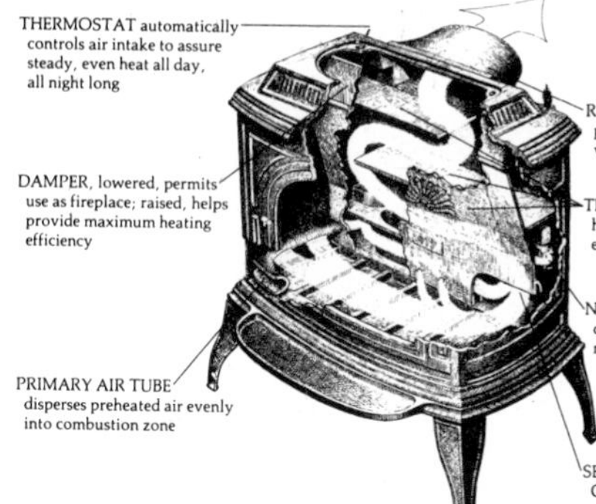

Manufacturer	Vermont Castings, Inc. Dept. FF Prince Street Randolph, VT 05060
Model	Resolute
Function	Freestanding fireplace/stove
Size (H, W, D)	26″, 17¼″, 26¼″
Weight	195 lbs.
Colors	Black
Airtight?	Yes
Reduced clearance	Optional, see below
Outside combustion air?	N/A
Glass? (type)	N/A
Cooking surface?	Yes
CONSTRUCTION *Material*	Cast iron
Gauge or thickness	⅛″, ¼″
Air blower? (output)	N/A
Flue size	6″ top or rear
Special features	Low profile. Removable door. Screen. Smokeless top loading. Thermostat. Bypass damper. Baffled. Pre-heated air. Polished griddle. Takes 16″ logs.
Options and accessories	Rear, bottom, and stove-pipe shields. Short legs.
Efficiency	65%
Heat output (or area)	35,000 BTUs/hr, 5–7,000 cu. ft
Tested by	In progress–Arnold Greene
Suggested retail price	$410.00
Brochure	Color, $1.00
For nearest dealer call	802-728-3111
Mail order, if no dealer?	Yes

Manufacturer	Vermont Iron Stove Works Dept. FF The Bobbin Mill Warren, Vermont 05674
Model	Elm
Function	Wood stove
Size (H, W, D)	25½″, 23″, 38″
Weight	280 lbs./300 lbs.
Colors	Black
Airtight?	Yes
Reduced clearance	N/A
Outside combustion air?	N/A
Glass? (type)	2 layer, Vycor & Pyrex
Cooking surface?	Yes
CONSTRUCTION *Material*	Cast iron and steel
Gauge or thickness	¼″
Air blower? (output)	N/A
Flue size	6″ (top or rear)
Special features	Nickel trim. Firebrick lined. Maple wood handles. Takes up to 24″ logs. 45° rotating, cast iron flue elbow.
Options and accessories	Tool set. (2 sizes available)
Efficiency	N/A
Heat output (or area)	40,000 BTUs/hr.
Tested by	N/A
Suggested retail price	$450.00
Brochure	Free
For nearest dealer call	802-496-2617
Mail order, if no dealer?	Yes

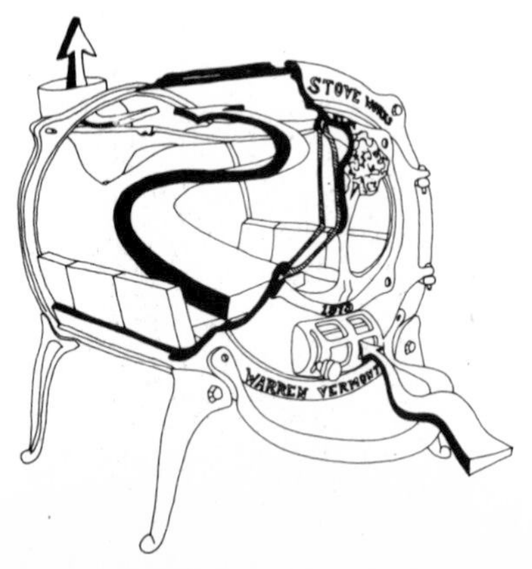

Manufacturer	Vermont Woodstove Co. P.O. Box 1016 (FF) Bennington, VT 05201
Model	Vermont Down Drafter DDIA
Function	Wood stove
Size (H, W, D)	33″, 26″, 35″
Weight	500 lbs./520 lbs.
Colors	Black
Airtight?	Yes
Reduced clearance	N/A
Outside combustion air?	Optional
Glass? (type)	N/A
Cooking surface?	Yes
CONSTRUCTION *Material*	Steel, cast iron
Gauge or thickness	¼″, 11 ga.
Air blower? (output)	Yes, 265 CFM
Flue size	8″ (rear)
Special features	Double wall construction. Cast iron lined firebox. Rear combustion air inlet.
Options and accessories	Domestic hot water coil. Central hot air manifold ducts (connect to front screen mesh slots). (Smaller model available.)
Efficiency	60%
Heat output (or area)	60,000 BTUs/hr.
Tested by	N/A
Suggested retail price	$749.00
Brochure	6 page, 50¢
For nearest dealer call	802-442-8197
Mail order, if no dealer?	Yes

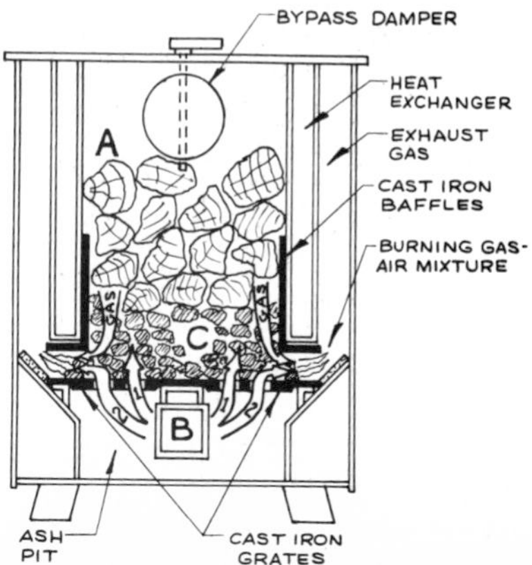

Manufacturer	Willow Creek Co. Dept. FF 2225 N. Chestnut Colorado Springs, CO 80907
Model	Willow Creek Hexagon
Function	Freestanding fireplace/stove
Size (H, W, D)	34″, 26″, 20″
Weight	300 lbs.
Colors	Black
Airtight?	Yes
Reduced clearance	N/A
Outside combustion air?	N/A
Glass? (type)	N/A
Cooking surface?	Yes
CONSTRUCTION *Material*	Diamond plate steel, cast iron
Gauge or thickness	3/16″
Air blower? (output)	N/A
Flue size	8″ (any location)
Special features	Cast iron door. With NFPA approved reduced clearance, it will fit into right angle corners. Takes 24″ logs. Firebrick lined. 7 yr. guarantee. Uses wood, coal.
Options and accessories	Smooth steel. Custom sizes.
Efficiency	N/A
Heat output (or area)	1,800 sq. ft.
Tested by	N/A
Suggested retail price	$390.00
Brochure	Free
For nearest dealer call	303-634-0446
Mail order, if no dealer?	Yes

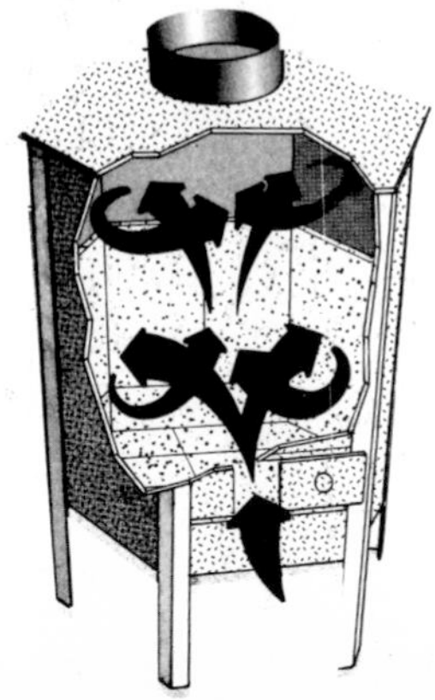

Manufacturer	Woodland Stoves of America P.O. Box 462 (FF) Waterloo, Iowa 50704
Model	Woodland W-12
Function	Wood stove
Size (H, W, D)	19″, 12½″, 19½″
Weight	114 lbs.
Colors	Black
Airtight?	Yes
Reduced clearance	N/A
Outside combustion air?	N/A
Glass? (type)	N/A
Cooking surface?	Yes, (2)
CONSTRUCTION *Material*	Steel plate
Gauge or thickness	¼″, 3/16″
Air blower? (output)	N/A
Flue size	4″ or 6″
Special features	Firebrick lined. Inward extended flue with stainless steel lining.
Options and accessories	Nickel plated trim. Cast iron aluminum murals. (Two larger sizes available.)
Efficiency	N/A
Heat output (or area)	800 sq. ft.
Tested by	Northwest Laboratories
Suggested retail price	N/A
Brochure	Color, free
For nearest dealer call	319-234-5567
Mail order, if no dealer?	Yes

Manufacturer	Woodland Stoves of America P.O. Box 462 (FF) Waterloo, Iowa 50704
Model	Woodland WF-15
Function	Freestanding fireplace/stove
Size (H, W, D)	23″, 23″, 26″
Weight	300 lbs.
Colors	Black
Airtight?	Yes
Reduced clearance	N/A
Outside combustion air?	N/A
Glass? (type)	Option, Vycor
Cooking surface?	Yes (2)
CONSTRUCTION *Material*	Plate steel
Gauge or thickness	¼″, 5/16″
Air blower? (output)	N/A
Flue size	6″ (top or rear)
Special features	Firebrick lined. Screen. Inward extended flue with stainless steel lining.
Options and accessories	Nickel plated trim. Cast aluminum murals. (Larger size available.)
Efficiency	N/A
Heat output (or area)	1,500 sq. ft.
Tested by	Northwest Laboratories (ICBO)
Suggested retail price	N/A
Brochure	Color, free
For nearest dealer call	319-234-5567
Mail order, if no dealer?	Yes

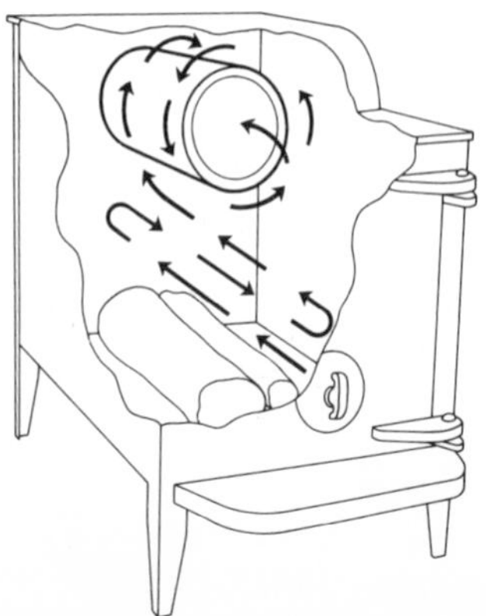

Manufacturer	Woodland Stoves of America P.O. Box 462 (FF) Waterloo, Iowa 50704
Model	Woodland F-20 6
Function	Freestanding fireplace/stove
Size (H, W, D)	28″, 26″, 33″
Weight	436 lbs.
Colors	Black
Airtight?	Yes
Reduced clearance	N/A
Outside combustion air?	N/A
Glass? (type)	Yes, Vycor
Cooking surface?	Yes (2)
CONSTRUCTION *Material*	Plate steel
Gauge or thickness	¼″, 5/16″
Air blower? (output)	N/A
Flue size	8″ (top or rear)
Special features	Firebrick lined. Inward extended flue with stainless steel lining.
Options and accessories	Nickel plated trim. Cast aluminum murals. (Smaller size available.)
Efficiency	N/A
Heat output (or area)	2,000 sq. ft.
Tested by	Northwest Laboratories
Suggested retail price	N/A
Brochure	Color, free
For nearest dealer call	319-234-5567
Mail order, if no dealer?	Yes

Manufacturer	Woodsman West, Inc. Dept. FF 2382 So. Redwood, Rd. Salt Lake City, UT 84119
Model	Woodsman 18
Function	Wood stove
Size (H, W, D)	28″, 18″, 28″
Weight	275 lbs.
Colors	Black
Airtight?	Yes
Reduced clearance	N/A
Outside combustion air?	N/A
Glass? (type)	N/A
Cooking surface?	Yes (2)
CONSTRUCTION *Material*	Steel plate, cast iron
Gauge or thickness	5/16″, ¼″
Air blower? (output)	N/A
Flue size	6″ (top or rear)
Special features	Firebrick lined. Cast iron doors. Damper. Wood/coal use. Takes 22″ logs. 7 yr. guarantee.
Options and accessories	Nickel trim.
Efficiency	N/A
Heat output (or area)	1,200 sq. ft.
Tested by	Terralab (ICBO)
Suggested retail price	N/A
Brochure	Free
For nearest dealer call	801-972-8590
Mail order, if no dealer?	Yes

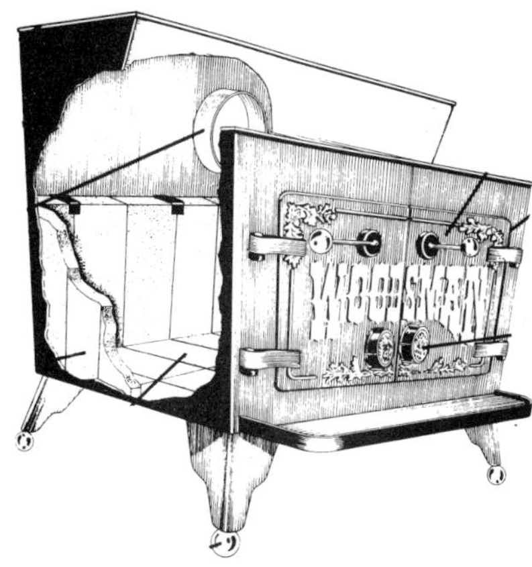

Manufacturer	Woodsman West, Inc. Dept. FF 2382 So. Redwood Rd. Salt Lake City, UT 84119
Model	Woodsman 30
Function	Freestanding fireplace/stove
Size (H, W, D)	31″, 30″, 26″
Weight	415 lbs.
Colors	Black
Airtight?	Yes
Reduced clearance	N/A
Outside combustion air?	N/A
Glass? (type)	N/A
Cooking surface?	Yes (2)
CONSTRUCTION *Material*	Steel plate, cast iron
Gauge or thickness	5/16″, ¼″
Air blower? (output)	N/A
Flue size	8″ (top or rear)
Special features	Firebrick lined. Screen. Cast iron doors. Takes 21″ logs. Damper. Wood/coal use. 7 yr. guarantee.
Options and accessories	Nickel trim.
Efficiency	N/A
Heat output (or area)	2,000 sq. ft.
Tested by	Terralab (ICBO)
Suggested retail price	N/A
Brochure	Free
For nearest dealer call	801-972-8590
Mail order, if no dealer?	Yes

Manufacturer	Woodstock Soapstone Co., Inc. Box 223 (FF) Woodstock, VT 05901
Model	Soapstone Stove
Function	Wood stove
Size (H, W, D)	28″, 26″, 19″
Weight	432 lbs.
Colors	Silver grey stone w/ bk. trim
Airtight?	N/A
Reduced clearance	N/A
Outside combustion air?	N/A
Glass? (type)	N/A
Cooking surface?	Yes
CONSTRUCTION *Material*	Soapstone, cast iron
Gauge or thickness	1 ¼″
Air blower? (output)	N/A
Flue size	5″
Special features	Frame is cast from original 1860 N. England soapstone stove. Each set of stones is matched for color and grain, and hand polished. Bottom is solid cast with firebrick. Top or side load. Money back guarantee.
Options and accessories	Unit complete
Efficiency	N/A
Heat output (or area)	45,000 BTUs/hr.
Tested by	N/A
Suggested retail price	$760.00
Brochure	$1.00
For nearest dealer call	802-672-5133
Mail order, if no dealer?	Yes

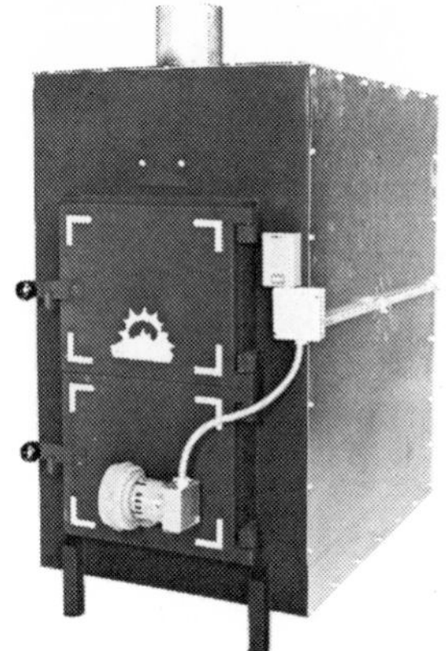

Manufacturer	Alternate Energy Sources Dept. FF 752 Duvall St. Salina, Kansas 67401
Model	85
Function	Hot air furnace
Size (H, W, D)	52″, 29″, 67″
Weight	615 lbs.
Colors	Black
Airtight?	Yes
Reduced clearance	Yes, 18″ from combustibles
Outside combustion air?	N/A
Glass? (type)	N/A
Cooking surface?	N/A
CONSTRUCTION *Material*	Steel and cast iron
Gauge or thickness	1/8″ and 12 ga.
Air blower? (output)	Yes, 1,460 CFM, ¼ hp blower
Flue size	8″
Special features	Firebrick lined. Log holder. Remote thermostat. Takes 36″ logs. 2 machined, cast iron feed doors; opening is 15″ × 27″
Options and accessories	1/3 or ½ hp. blowers. Filter. Assembly. Domestic hot water heating.
Efficiency	63%
Heat output (or area)	100,000 BTUs/hr.
Tested by	ICBO
Suggested retail price	$1,175.00
Brochure	Yes
For nearest dealer call	913-825-8218
Mail order, if no dealer?	Yes

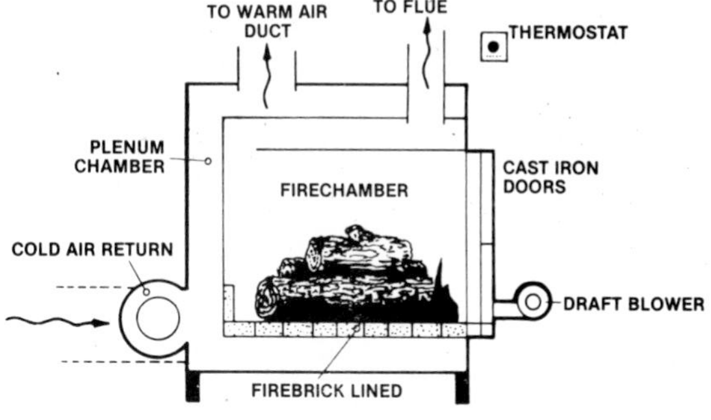

Manufacturer	American Energy Systems Dept. FF 1111 21st Ave. North Wisconsin Rapids, WI 54494
Model	EM-I and EM-II
Function	Add-on or primary hot air furnace
Size (H, W, D)	25″ & 30″, 20″, 20″ & 24″
Weight	185 lbs., 231 lbs.
Colors	Gold
Airtight?	Yes
Reduced clearance	N/A
Outside combustion air?	N/A
Glass? (type)	N/A
Cooking surface?	N/A
CONSTRUCTION *Material*	Al./steel, steel, cast iron
Gauge or thickness	14 ga. firebox, 7 and 10 ga. body
Air blower? (output)	Yes, 256 CFM
Flue size	6″
Special features	8″ duct hot air plenum. Baffled heat exchanger. Double wall door. Slide out ash pan. 14 ga. aluminized steel firebox. 7 ga. steel bottom, 10 ga. front, back. Cast iron grates.
Options and accessories	Unit complete.
Efficiency	N/A
Heat output (or area)	N/A
Tested by	N/A
Suggested retail price	N/A
Brochure	Yes, free
For nearest dealer call	715-421-4990
Mail order, if no dealer?	N/A

Manufacturer	Ashley Heater Company Dept. FF 1604 17th Ave., S.W. Sheffield, Ala. 35660
Model	F78-80
Function	Hot air furnace
Size (H, W, D)	37″, 48″, 21 1/8″
Weight	321 lbs.
Colors	Mahagony enamel
Airtight?	Yes
Reduced clearance	N/A
Outside combustion air?	N/A
Glass? (type)	N/A
Cooking surface?	N/A
CONSTRUCTION *Material*	Steel, cast iron
Gauge or thickness	20 ga. (cabinet)
Air blower? (output)	Yes, 700 CFM (250 CFM, if add-on)
Flue size	6″
Special features	Firebox liners, feed door, & frame, ash door & frame, grate, flue collar are all cast iron. Insulated cabinet. Protected motor. Thermostatic blower.
Options and accessories	Gravity damper. Floor blower. (wood/coal model available)
Efficiency	65%
Heat output (or area)	75,000 to 78,000 BTUs/hr.
Tested by	Underwriters Laboratories
Suggested retail price	N/A
Brochure	2 page, 2 color, 25¢
For nearest dealer call	write to above
Mail order, if no dealer?	N/A

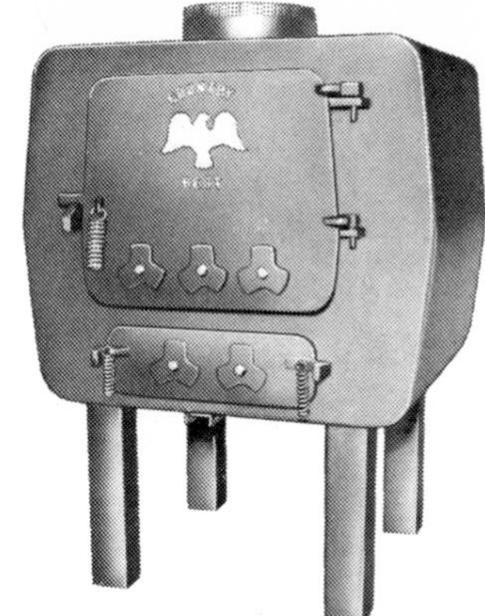

Manufacturer	Country Best Dept. FF 5700 Walnut St. Richmond, Illinois 60071
Model	Warm Air Add-On
Function	Add-on hot air furnace
Size (H, W, D)	33″, 24″, 33″
Weight	330/350 lbs.
Colors	Black
Airtight?	N/A
Reduced clearance	N/A
Outside combustion air?	N/A
Glass? (type)	N/A
Cooking surface?	Yes
CONSTRUCTION *Material*	Cast iron
Gauge or thickness	N/A
Air blower? (output)	Yes, 265 CFM
Flue size	6″
Special features	Can be used as primary or add-on furnace. Thermostat. Double walled heat exchanger. 10 year warranty. Cast iron grate. 8″ plenum collar. Takes 20″ logs.
Options and accessories	Unit complete.
Efficiency	70%
Heat output (or area)	35,000 BTUs/hr. 2,200 sq. ft.
Tested by	N/A
Suggested retail price	$655.00
Brochure	Free
For nearest dealer call	815-678-2811
Mail order, if no dealer?	Yes

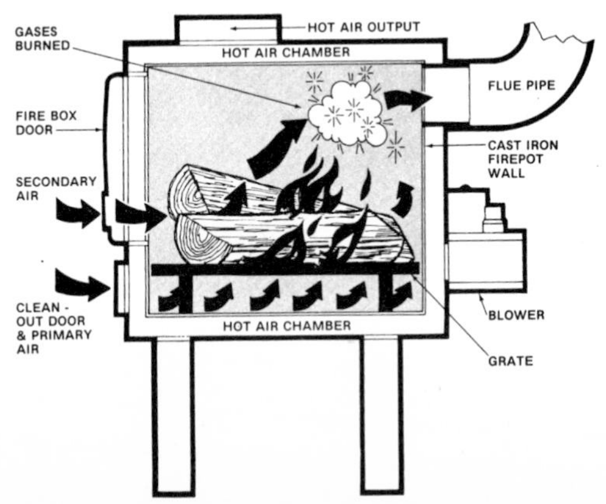

Manufacturer	DAKA Corp. RR #3 Box 63 (FF) Pine City, MN 55063
Model	Mark IV
Function	Add-on hot air furnace
Size (H, W, D)	37″, 19″, 32″
Weight	240 lbs.
Colors	Black
Airtight?	Yes
Reduced clearance	Yes, 18″ from combustibles
Outside combustion air?	N/A
Glass? (type)	N/A
Cooking surface?	N/A
CONSTRUCTION *Material*	Steel
Gauge or thickness	12 ga., 14 ga.
Air blower? (output)	Yes, 265 CFM
Flue size	6″ (top)
Special features	Cast iron grate. Ash pan. Automatic draft. Rheostat controlled fan. 6″ hot air outlet.
Options and accessories	Unit complete.
Efficiency	50%
Heat output (or area)	70,000 BTUs/hr.
Tested by	N/A
Suggested retail price	$510.00
Brochure	Free
For nearest dealer call	312-629-6737
Mail order, if no dealer?	Yes

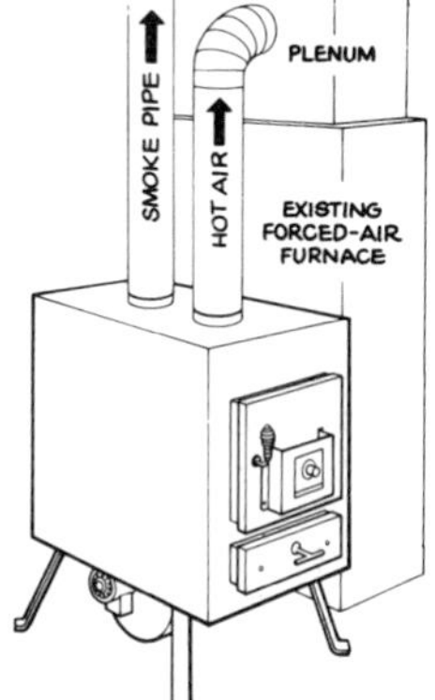

Manufacturer	DAKA Corp. RR #3 Box 63 (FF) Pine City, MN 55063
Model	Mark V
Function	Add-on hot air furnace
Size (H, W, D)	48″, 24″, 30″
Weight	380 lbs.
Colors	Black
Airtight?	Yes
Reduced clearance	N/A
Outside combustion air?	N/A
Glass? (type)	N/A
Cooking surface?	N/A
CONSTRUCTION *Material*	Steel
Gauge or thickness	3/16″, 22 ga.
Air blower? (output)	Yes, 465 CFM
Flue size	6″
Special features	Cast iron grate. Draft blower. Remote thermostat. Firebrick lined. Ash pan. Smoke bypass damper. Fan limit control.
Options and accessories	Unit complete.
Efficiency	N/A
Heat output (or area)	100,000 BTUs/hr.
Tested by	N/A
Suggested retail price	$910.00
Brochure	Free
For nearest dealer call	312-629-6737
Mail order, if no dealer?	Yes

Manufacturer	Dulude Energy Systems, Inc. P.O. Box 205 (FF) 31 Mill St. Assonet, Mass. 02072
Model	Warm air add-on
Function	Add-on hot air furnace
Size (H, W, D)	32″, 22″, 32″
Weight	440 lbs.
Colors	Black
Airtight?	Yes
Reduced clearance	N/A
Outside combustion air?	N/A
Glass? (type)	N/A
Cooking surface?	N/A
CONSTRUCTION *Material*	Boiler plate steel
Gauge or thickness	¼″, 1/8″
Air blower? (output)	Optional, 250 CFM
Flue size	7″ (rear only)
Special features	Firebrick lined. Takes 26″ logs. Plenums are 8″ × 12″
Options and accessories	Blower. coal grate. 2 plenum connections 8″ × 12″ each.
Efficiency	N/A
Heat output (or area)	70,000 BTUs/hr. (6-9 rooms)
Tested by	N/A
Suggested retail price	$562.00
Brochure	Free
For nearest dealer call	617-644-2278
Mail order, if no dealer?	Yes

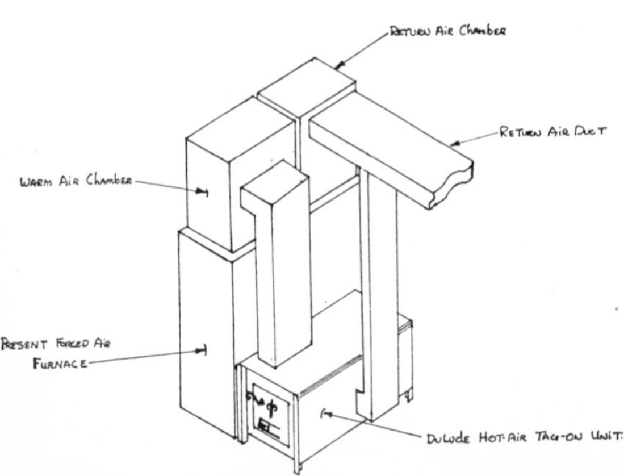

Manufacturer	Dulude Energy Systems, Inc. P.O. Box 205 (FF) 31 Mill St. Assonet, Mass. 02702
Model	Hot Water Add-On
Function	Add-on hot water furnace
Size (H, W, D)	38″, 20″, 30″
Weight	440 lbs.
Colors	Black
Airtight?	Yes
Reduced clearance	N/A
Outside combustion air?	N/A
Glass? (type)	N/A
Cooking surface?	Yes
CONSTRUCTION *Material*	Boiler plate steel
Gauge or thickness	¼″, 1/8″
Air blower? (output)	N/A
Flue size	7″ (top or rear)
Special features	Heat exchanger is seamless, industrial grade steel pipe with yield (strength) of 30,000 lbs./sq. inch. Holds 8 gals. Takes 26″ logs.
Options and accessories	Unit complete.
Efficiency	N/A
Heat output (or area)	65,000 BTUs/hr.
Tested by	N/A
Suggested retail price	$562.00
Brochure	Free
For nearest dealer call	617-644-2278
Mail order, if no dealer?	Yes

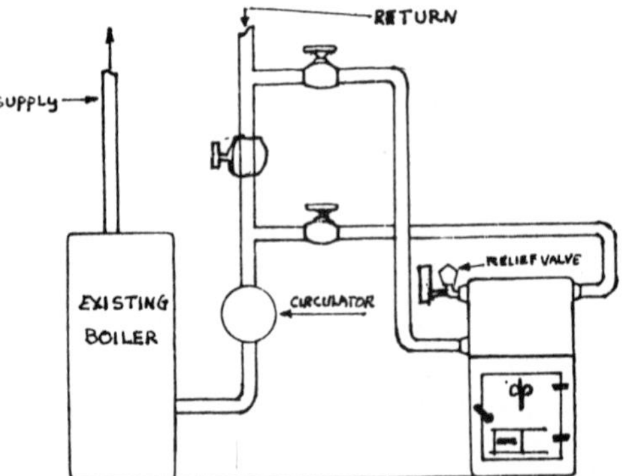

DULUDE HOT WATER TAG ON UNIT.

Manufacturer	Enheat Ltd. Fawcett Div. Dept. FF Sackville, New Brunswick Canada E0A 3C0
Model	WF 200
Function	Hot air furnace
Size (H, W, D)	45", 28", 42"
Weight	460 lbs.
Colors	Green enamel
Airtight?	Yes
Reduced clearance	N/A
Outside combustion air?	N/A
Glass? (type)	N/A
Cooking surface?	N/A
CONSTRUCTION *Material*	Plate steel
Gauge or thickness	1/8"
Air blower? (output)	Option, 1200 CFM
Flue size	7" (rear)
Special features	Thermostat controlled. Fan control. Hi-limit control. Motorized damper. Firebox is 22" dia X 36" long. Takes up to 30" wood.
Options and accessories	12" blower. 1/3 HP motor.
Efficiency	N/A
Heat output (or area)	120,000 BTUs/hr.
Tested by	ETL (USA), CSA (Canada)
Suggested retail price	$599/$825 (w/blower)
Brochure	Free
For nearest dealer call	506-536-1520
Mail order, if no dealer?	N/A

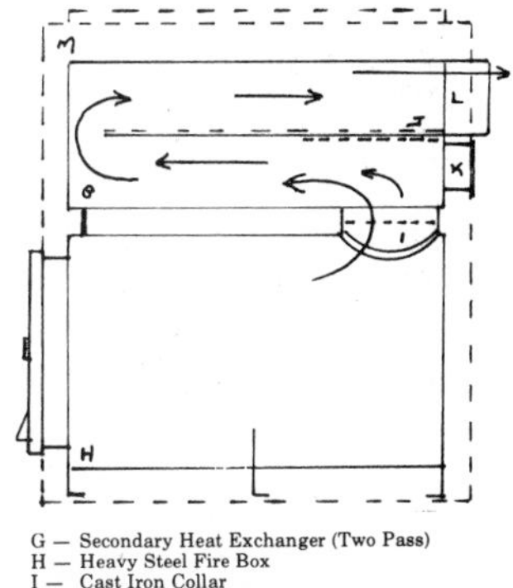

G — Secondary Heat Exchanger (Two Pass)
H — Heavy Steel Fire Box
I — Cast Iron Collar
J — Steel Baffle
K — Cleanout
L — 7" Smoke Pipe
M — Baked Enamel Casing

Manufacturer	Enheat, Ltd. Fawcett Div. Dept. FF Sackville, New Brunswick Canada E0A 2C0
Model	W B 140
Function	Hot water furnace
Size (H, W, D)	26", 24", 28"
Weight	325 lbs.
Colors	Almond
Airtight?	Yes
Reduced clearance	Yes
Outside combustion air?	N/A
Glass? (type)	N/A
Cooking surface?	N/A
CONSTRUCTION *Material*	Plate steel
Gauge or thickness	3/16"
Air blower? (output)	N/A
Flue size	7"
Special features	Use separately or as add-on furnace. Safety valve. Damper motor and chain. Triple aquastat. Combo pressure and temp gauge. Meets ASME boiler codes. Insulated. 10 yr. limited warranty.
Options and accessories	Unit complete
Efficiency	N/A
Heat output (or area)	140,000 BTUs/hr.
Tested by	In progress
Suggested retail price	$1,095.00
Brochure	Free
For nearest dealer call	506-536-1520
Mail order, if no dealer?	N/A

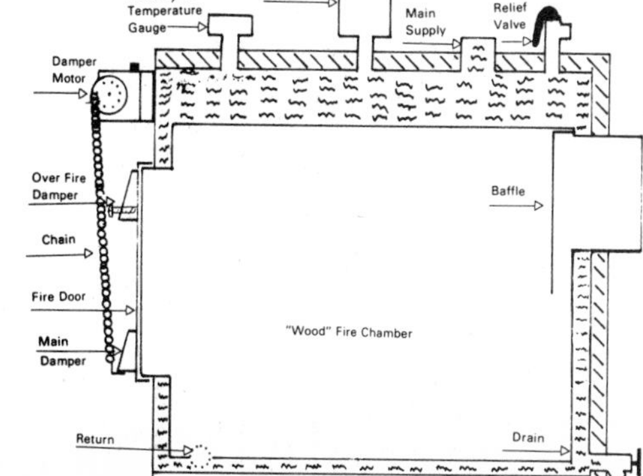

Manufacturer	Glenwood Stoves Dept. FF RD #1 Glenwood Dr. Ephrate, Penna. 17522
Model	850 BP
Function	Hot air furnace
Size (H, W, D)	45 3/4″, 28¼″, 50 7/8″
Weight	712 lbs.
Colors	N/A
Airtight?	Yes
Reduced clearance	N/A
Outside combustion air?	N/A
Glass? (type)	N/A
Cooking surface?	N/A
CONSTRUCTION *Material*	Hot rolled steel
Gauge or thickness	¼″
Air blower? (output)	Optional
Flue size	8″
Special features	Electronic draft control. Firebrick lined. Baffled. Bypass damper. Takes 32″ logs.
Options and accessories	Blower. Domestic hot water coil.
Efficiency	N/A
Heat output (or area)	165,000 BTUs/hr.
Tested by	N/A
Suggested retail price	N/A
Brochure	Free
For nearest dealer call	717-733-9644
Mail order, if no dealer?	Yes

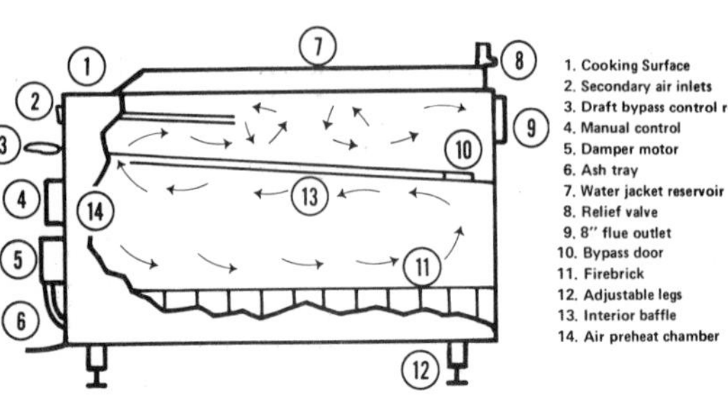

Manufacturer	Glenwood Stoves Dept. Ff RD #1 Glenwood Dr. Ephrata, Penna. 17522
Model	1250
Function	Hot water furnace
Size (H, W, D)	42″, 26″, 38″
Weight	825 lbs.
Colors	Black
Airtight?	Yes
Reduced clearance	Yes
Outside combustion air?	N/A
Glass? (type)	N/A
Cooking surface?	Yes
CONSTRUCTION *Material*	Hot rolled steel
Gauge or thickness	¼″
Air blower? (output)	N/A
Flue size	8″
Special features	Primary or add-in unit. Baffled. Safety valve. Temp/press. gauge. Electronic draft control. Firebrick lined. Takes 32″ logs.
Options and accessories	Dual-feed systems. Domestic hot water. (Industrial models available.)
Efficiency	65%
Heat output (or area)	200,00 BTUs/hr.
Tested by	N/A
Suggested retail price	$1,095.00
Brochure	Free
For nearest dealer call	717-733-9644
Mail order, if no dealer?	Yes

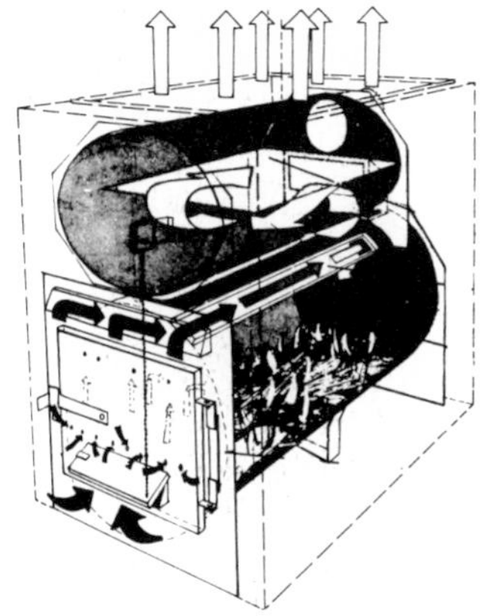

Manufacturer	Kerr Controls Ltd. P.O. Box 1500 FF Truro, N.S. Canada, B2N 5V2
Model	Scotsman
Function	Hot air furnace
Size (H, W, D)	44½″, 29″, 39″
Weight	392 lbs. (shipping weight)
Colors	Green enamel
Airtight?	Yes
Reduced clearance	N/A
Outside combustion air?	N/A
Glass? (type)	N/A
Cooking surface?	N/A
CONSTRUCTION *Material*	Plate steel
Gauge or thickness	1/8″, 14 gauge
Air blower? (output)	N/A
Flue size	7″ (rear)
Special features	Can operate as a natural flow, hot air circulator, or as an add-on. Pre-heated combustion air. Auto/control. 1″ thick door. 1/8″ firebox.
Options and accessories	Unit complete.
Efficiency	N/A
Heat output (or area)	140,000 BTUs/hr.
Tested by	ETLM and AIRI
Suggested retail price	$595.00
Brochure	Free
For nearest dealer call	902-895-9281
Mail order, if no dealer?	Yes

Manufacturer	Kerr Controls Ltd. P.O. Box 1500 (FF) Truro, N.S. Canada B2N 5V2
Model	Titan
Function	Hot water furnace
Size (H, W, D)	43½″, 26½″, 35½″
Weight	675 lbs. (shipping weight)
Colors	Green enamel
Airtight?	Yes
Reduced clearance	N/A
Outside combustion air?	N/A
Glass? (type)	N/A
Cooking surface?	N/A
CONSTRUCTION *Material*	Plate steel
Gauge or thickness	¼″
Air blower? (output)	N/A
Flue size	7″ top
Special features	1″ thick plate steel door. Firebrick lined. Firebox and heat exchanger with ¼″ plate steel. 20 heat exchange tubes. Conforms to ASME boiler codes. Fully automatic. Safety system blows steam over fire should boiler overheat.
Options and accessories	Unit complete.
Efficiency	N/A
Heat output (or area)	140,000 BTUs/hr.
Tested by	ETLM and AIRI
Suggested retail price	$1,047.00
Brochure	Free
For nearest dealer call	902-895-9281
Mail order, if no dealer?	Yes

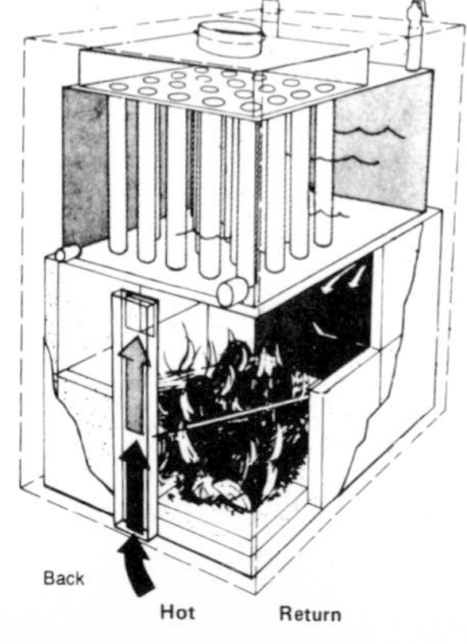

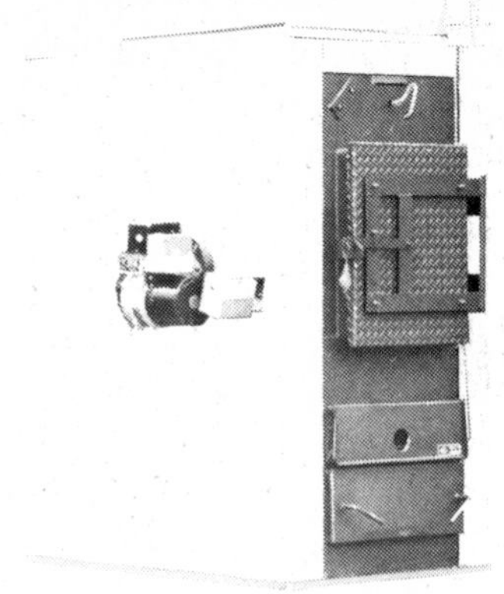

Manufacturer	Marathon Heater Co. Dept. FF 16 Crawford St. Cortland, NY 13045
Model	Lo-Profile WOF16
Function	Hot air furnace
Size (H, W, D)	52″, 32″, 33″
Weight	700 lbs. (shipping wt.)
Colors	N/A
Airtight?	Yes
Reduced clearance	N/A
Outside combustion air?	N/A
Glass? (type)	N/A
Cooking surface?	N/A
CONSTRUCTION *Material*	Steel
Gauge or thickness	1/8″, 3/16″
Air blower? (output)	Optional, 600 CFM
Flue size	7″
Special features	Double wall body. Forced air *or* gravity operation.
Options and accessories	Blower. (Other models available)
Efficiency	N/A
Heat output (or area)	80,000 BTUs/hr.
Tested by	N/A
Suggested retail price	N/A
Brochure	Free
For nearest dealer call	607-756-8246
Mail order, if no dealer?	N/A

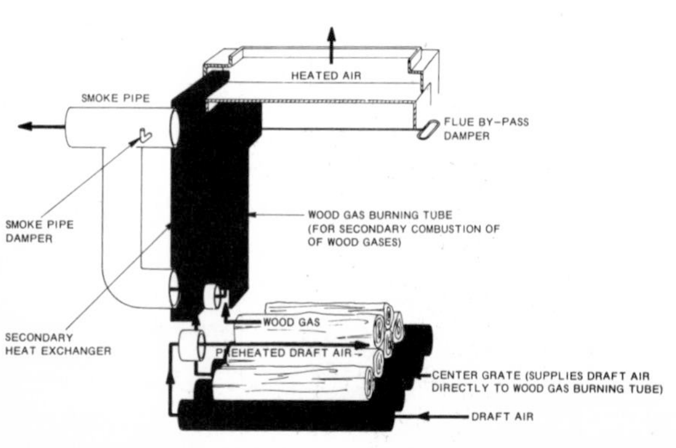

Manufacturer	Marathon Heater Co. Dept. FF 16 Crawford St. Cortland, NY 13045
Model	AOB 24
Function	Add-on hot water furnace
Size (H, W, D)	N/A
Weight	485 lbs.
Colors	Red jacket
Airtight?	Yes
Reduced clearance	N/A
Outside combustion air?	N/A
Glass? (type)	N/A
Cooking surface?	N/A
CONSTRUCTION *Material*	Boiler plate steel
Gauge or thickness	¼″
Air blower? (output)	N/A
Flue size	6″
Special features	Round firebox. Cast iron tube grate. Safety system extinguishes fire if overheated. 5 yr. limited warranty.
Options and accessories	Circulating pump. Aquastat. (Other models available)
Efficiency	N/A
Heat output (or area)	80,000 BTUs/hr.
Tested by	N/A
Suggested retail price	$1455.00
Brochure	Free
For nearest dealer call	607-756-8246
Mail order, if no dealer?	N/A

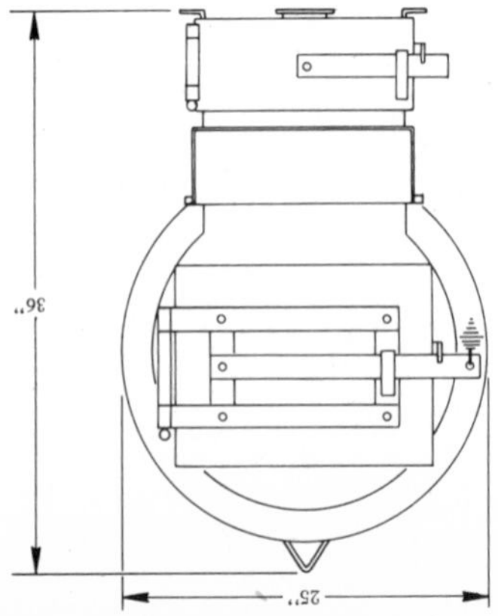

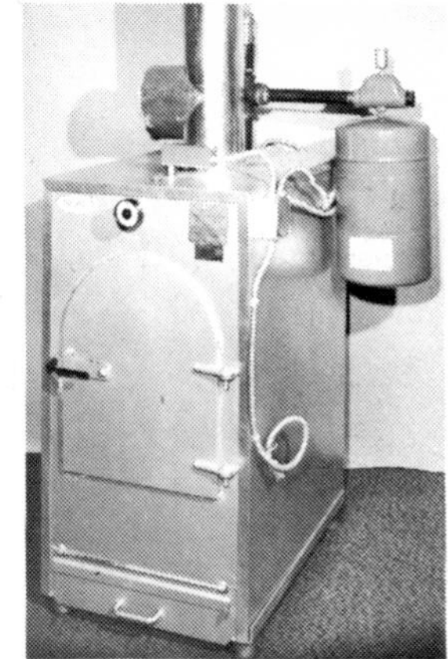

Manufacturer	Melvin Mfg. Corp. (MEMCO) P.O. Box 38 D (F) Jay, Maine 04239
Model	MW 100
Function	Hot water furnace
Size (H, W, D)	48", 22", 32"
Weight	600 lbs.
Colors	N/A
Airtight?	N/A
Reduced clearance	N/A
Outside combustion air?	N/A
Glass? (type)	N/A
Cooking surface?	N/A
CONSTRUCTION *Material*	Plate steel
Gauge or thickness	¼"
Air blower? (output)	N/A
Flue size	7"
Special features	Hydronic baffle. Insulated. Thermostat controls. Ash pan. 5 yr. limited warranty
Options and accessories	Domestic hot water coil puts out 5 GPM.
Efficiency	N/A
Heat output (or area)	120,000 BTUs/hr.
Tested by	ETLM
Suggested retail price	N/A
Brochure	Free
For nearest dealer call	207-645-4732
Mail order, if no dealer?	N/A

Manufacturer	Multi-Fuel Energy Systems Dept. FF 2185 N. Sherman Dr. Indianapolis, IN 46208
Model	MF-75
Function	Add-on hot air furnace
Size (H, W, D)	30", 20", 33"
Weight	340 lbs.
Colors	Black
Airtight?	Yes
Reduced clearance	N/A
Outside combustion air?	Yes, 3" inlet
Glass? (type)	N/A
Cooking surface?	N/A
CONSTRUCTION *Material*	Carbon steel, cast iron
Gauge or thickness	3/16"
Air blower? (output)	Yes, 320 CFM
Flue size	6"
Special features	Can use independently. Cast iron grate. Copper lined heat exchanger. Wood, coal, or any solid fuel. Pre-heated air beneath fire & pressurized firebox, 54 CFM.
Options and accessories	Emergency power system (12 v.). Wall thermostat kit.
Efficiency	65% to 70%
Heat output (or area)	60,000 BTUs/hr.
Tested by	Energy Systems (UL, ICBO, BOCA)
Suggested retail price	$849.00
Brochure	Free
For nearest dealer call	317-542-0691
Mail order, if no dealer?	Yes

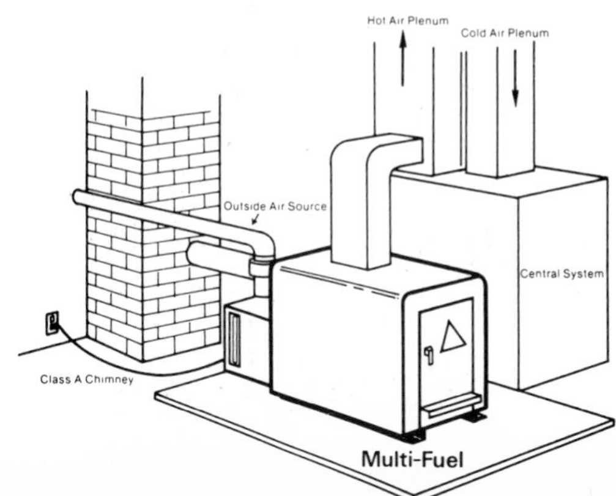

Manufacturer	Oneida Heater Co., Inc. P.O. Box 148 (FF) Oneida, N.Y. 13421
Model	AWGO
Function	Dual fuel hot air furnace
Size (H, W, D)	six sizes
Weight	N/A
Colors	N/A
Airtight?	Yes
Reduced clearance	N/A
Outside combustion air?	N/A
Glass? (type)	N/A
Cooking surface?	N/A
CONSTRUCTION *Material*	Steel, cast iron
Gauge or thickness	N/A
Air blower? (output)	Yes, 800 CFM up to 1,600 CFM
Flue size	7", 8"
Special features	Wood/oil use. Tubular heat exchanger. Takes 22" logs.
Options and accessories	Unit complete (Wood only models available)
Efficiency	N/A
Heat output (or area)	80,000 BTUs up to 160,00 BTUs/hr.
Tested by	N/A
Suggested retail price	N/A
Brochure	Free
For nearest dealer call	315-363-5500
Mail order, if no dealer?	N/A

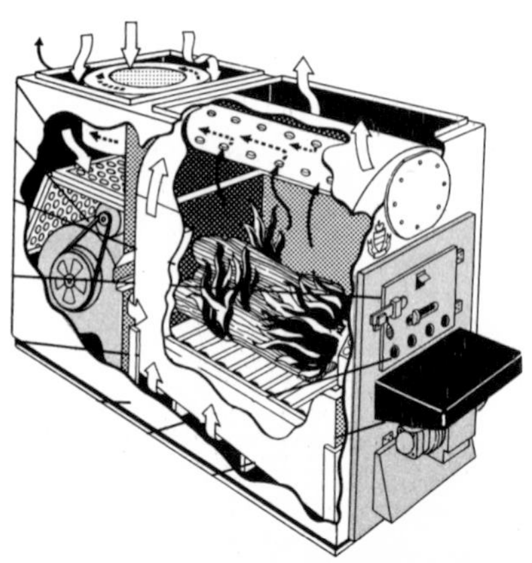

Manufacturer	Passat U.S.A., Inc. Dept. FF One North Road E. Kingston, N.H. 03827
Model	HO-20
Function	Hot water furnace
Size (H, W, D)	55", 29", 47"
Weight	442 lbs.
Colors	N/A
Airtight?	Yes
Reduced clearance	N/A
Outside combustion air?	N/A
Glass? (type)	N/A
Cooking surface?	N/A
CONSTRUCTION *Material*	Cor-Ten steel
Gauge or thickness	N/A
Air blower? (output)	N/A
Flue size	N/A
Special features	Made in Denmark. Galvanized steel hood. Insulated.
Options and accessories	Cast iron grate. Steel chimney. Damper. Oil burner attachment.
Efficiency	N/A
Heat output (or area)	72,000 BTUs/hr.
Tested by	N/A
Suggested retail price	N/A
Brochure	Free
For nearest dealer call	603-642-8553
Mail order, if no dealer?	N/A

Manufacturer	Peacock Stove Works Rt. 2 Box 2431 (FF) Baldwin, MI 49304
Model	Sunmate
Function	Add-on hot air furnace
Size (H, W, D)	31", 24", 30"
Weight	N/A
Colors	Black
Airtight?	Yes
Reduced clearance	N/A
Outside combustion air?	N/A
Glass? (type)	N/A
Cooking surface?	Yes
CONSTRUCTION *Material*	Plate steel
Gauge or thickness	7 gauge
Air blower? (output)	Yes, 265 CFM
Flue size	8" (top)
Special features	Secondary combustion air system. Firebrick lined. 25 year warranty.
Options and accessories	Unit complete.
Efficiency	88%
Heat output (or area)	100,000 BTUs/hr.
Tested by	Arnold Greene Test Lab
Suggested retail price	$715.00
Brochure	Free
For nearest dealer call	616-745-4609
Mail order, if no dealer?	Yes

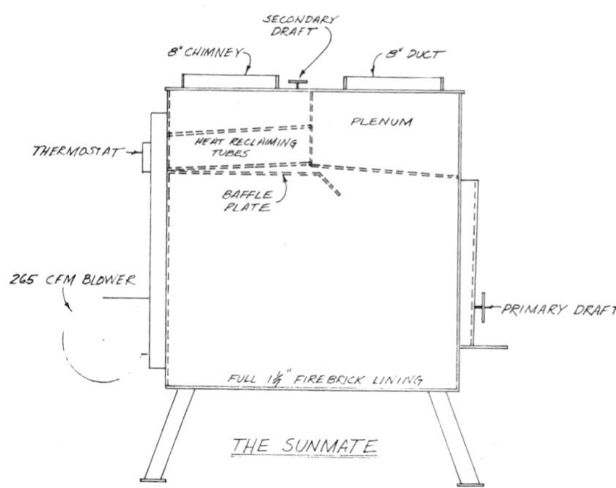

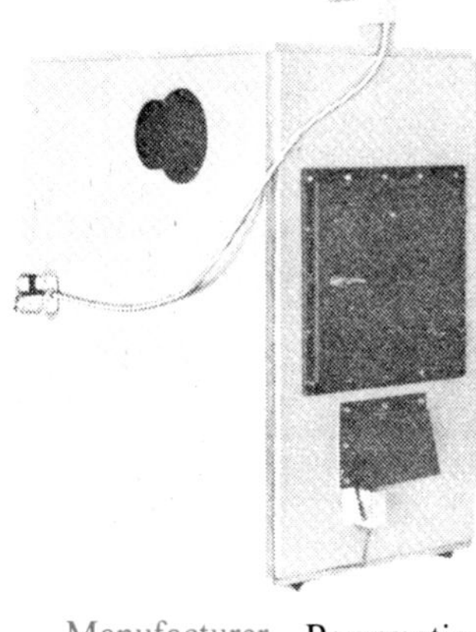

Manufacturer	Powrmatic, Inc. Dept. FF 2906 Balto Blvd. Finksburg, MD 21048
Model	SFW-150
Function	Add-on hot air furnace
Size (H, W, D)	55", 51", 31"
Weight	745 lbs.
Colors	Blue
Airtight?	Yes
Reduced clearance	N/A
Outside combustion air?	N/A
Glass? (type)	N/A
Cooking surface?	N/A
CONSTRUCTION *Material*	Mild steel
Gauge or thickness	11 ga., 14 ga., 18 ga.
Air blower? (output)	Yes, 1,700 CFM
Flue size	7"
Special features	1/3 HP blower motor. Air filters. Will burn without electricity. Thermostat control. Takes 23" logs.
Options and accessories	Larger, ½ HP blower motor.
Efficiency	N/A
Heat output (or area)	150,000 BTUs/hr.
Tested by	N/A
Suggested retail price	$900.00
Brochure	Free
For nearest dealer call	301-833-9100
Mail order, if no dealer?	N/A

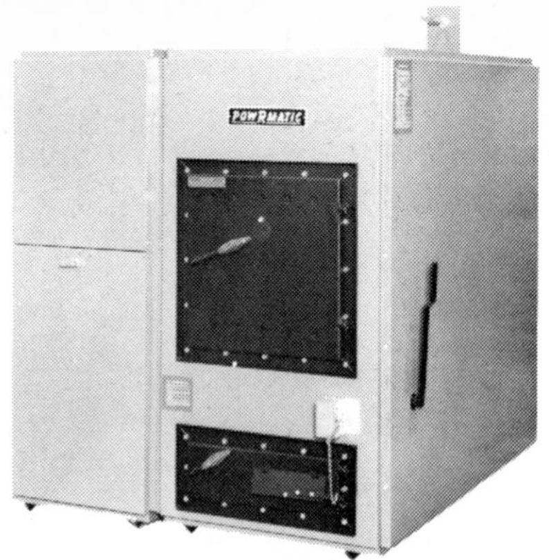

Manufacturer	Powrmatic, Inc. Dept. FF 2906 Balto Blvd. Finksburg, MD 21048
Model	OWc & GWC
Function	Hot air furnace
Size (H, W, D)	54″, 51″, 48″
Weight	1,000 lbs.
Colors	Blue
Airtight?	Yes
Reduced clearance	N/A
Outside combustion air?	N/A
Glass? (type)	N/A
Cooking surface?	N/A
CONSTRUCTION *Material*	Mild steel, cast iron
Gauge or thickness	11 ga., 14 ga., 18 ga.
Air blower? (output)	Yes, 1,900 CFM
Flue size	8″
Special features	Cast iron grates. Ash pan cleanout. Burns oil, wood, coal, or gas, wood, coal. Burns wood or coal without electricity.
Options and accessories	Unit complete.
Efficiency	N/A
Heat output (or area)	110,000 to 170,000 BTUs/hr.
Tested by	N/A
Suggested retail price	$1,800.00
Brochure	Free
For nearest dealer call	301-833-9100
Mail order, if no dealer?	N/A

Manufacturer	Therm-Kon Products Dept. FF 207 E. Mill Rd. Galesville, WI 54630
Model	TK 102 Convert-A-Furnace
Function	Add-on hot air furnace
Size (H, W, D)	44″, 21″, 33″
Weight	280 lbs., 310 lbs.
Colors	Grey
Airtight?	Yes
Reduced clearance	N/A
Outside combustion air?	N/A
Glass? (type)	N/A
Cooking surface?	N/A
CONSTRUCTION *Material*	Cast iron, steel
Gauge or thickness	16 ga., 12 ga.
Air blower? (output)	Optional, 500 CFM
Flue size	6″
Special features	Cast iron door, door frame, and grate. Firebox is cast iron lined. Thermostatically controlled blower.
Options and accessories	Blower. (Wood/coal model available.)
Efficiency	50%
Heat output (or area)	40,000 BTUs/hr.
Tested by	N/A
Suggested retail price	$670.00
Brochure	Free
For nearest dealer call	608-582-2276
Mail order, if no dealer?	Yes

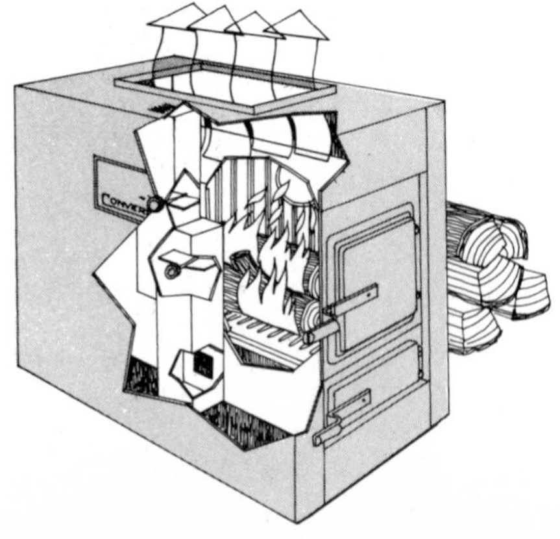

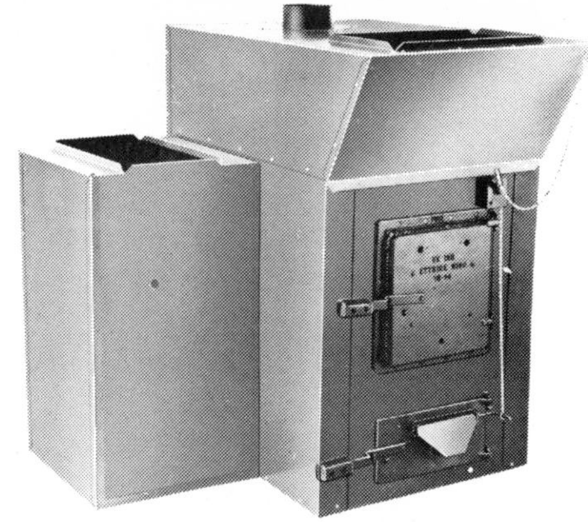

Manufacturer	Therm-Kon Products Dept. FF 207 E. Mill Rd. Galesville, WI 54630
Model	29 MMU Maxi-Miser
Function	Hot air furnace
Size (H, W, D)	46″, 29″, 43″
Weight	575 lbs., 609 lbs.
Colors	Grey
Airtight?	Yes
Reduced clearance	Yes, 4″ from rear wall
Outside combustion air?	N/A
Glass? (type)	N/A
Cooking surface?	N/A
CONSTRUCTION *Material*	Cast iron, steel
Gauge or thickness	12 ga.
Air blower? (output)	Yes
Flue size	N/A
Special features	Double walled cast iron firebox. Cast iron door. Thermostatic damper. Firebrick. (2) heat exchange tubes. 1/3 HP blower motor. Plenum outlet is 12″ × 20″. Takes 27″ logs.
Options and accessories	Unit complete.
Efficiency	50%
Heat output (or area)	120,000 BTUs/hr.
Tested by	Underwriters Laboratories
Suggested retail price	$1,160.00
Brochure	Free
For nearest dealer call	608-582-2276
Mail order, if no dealer?	Yes

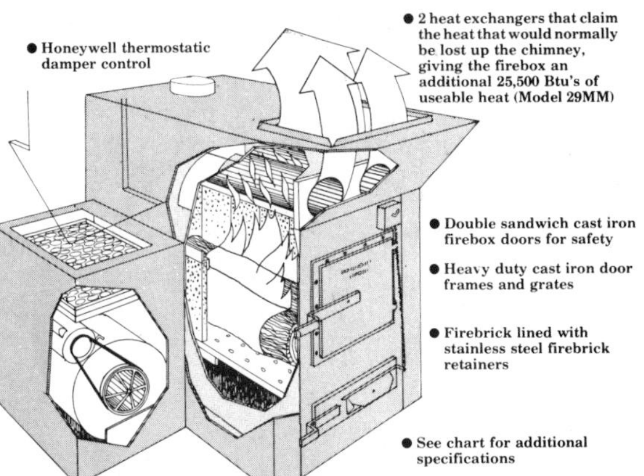

Manufacturer	Triton Corporation Dept. FF 723 Highway W Allenton, WI 53002
Model	Naturalair 3800
Function	Add-on hot air furnace
Size (H, W, D)	42″, 22″, 36″
Weight	477 lbs.
Colors	Black
Airtight?	Yes
Reduced clearance	N/A
Outside combustion air?	Optional
Glass? (type)	N/A
Cooking surface?	N/A
CONSTRUCTION *Material*	Steel, cast iron
Gauge or thickness	1/8″, 3/16″
Air blower? (output)	Yes, 465 CFM
Flue size	6″
Special features	Double wall body. Firebrick rear. Takes 27″ logs. 5 yr. limited warranty.
Options and accessories	Humidifier. Automatic outlet damper.
Efficiency	70%
Heat output (or area)	96,000 BTUs/hr.
Tested by	N/A
Suggested retail price	$549.00
Brochure	Free
For nearest dealer call	414-629-5276
Mail order, if no dealer?	N/A

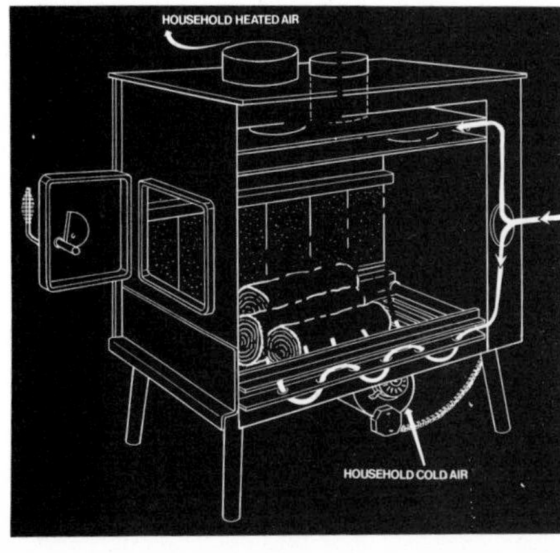

Manufacturer	Valco Corp. Dept. FF 215 Johnson Rd. Michigan City, Ind 46360
Model	Mark V
Function	Add-on hot air furnace
Size (H, W, D)	47″, 23″, 34″
Weight	385 lbs.
Colors	Black
Airtight?	Yes
Reduced clearance	N/A
Outside combustion air?	N/A
Glass? (type)	N/A
Cooking surface?	N/A
CONSTRUCTION *Material*	Boiler plate steel, cast iron
Gauge or thickness	3/16″
Air blower? (output)	Yes, 530 CFM
Flue size	6″
Special features	Air filter. Double wall construction. Thermostat control. 8″ plenum duct. Firebrick lined. Cast door and grate.
Options and accessories	Optional 265 CFM blower.
Efficiency	N/A
Heat output (or area)	140,000 BTUs/hr.
Tested by	Inquire from mfr.
Suggested retail price	$617.00
Brochure	6 page, free
For nearest dealer call	219-872-5082
Mail order, if no dealer?	Yes

Manufacturer	Yukon Industries Dept. FF 65 Airport Blvd. McGregor, MN
Model	Klondike
Function	Dual fuel hot air furnace
Size (H, W, D)	N/A
Weight	720 lbs.
Colors	N/A
Airtight?	Yes
Reduced clearance	N/A
Outside combustion air?	N/A
Glass? (type)	N/A
Cooking surface?	N/A
CONSTRUCTION *Material*	Steel, cast iron
Gauge or thickness	N/A
Air blower? (output)	Yes, 800 to 1400 CFM
Flue size	8″ (left, rear, right)
Special features	Burns wood or oil. Grates are cast iron. Firebrick lined. Two heat exchangers.
Options and accessories	Unit complete (Other models available)
Efficiency	N/A
Heat output (or area)	N/A
Tested by	ETLM
Suggested retail price	N/A
Brochure	Free
For nearest dealer call	218-768-4444
Mail order, if no dealer?	N/A

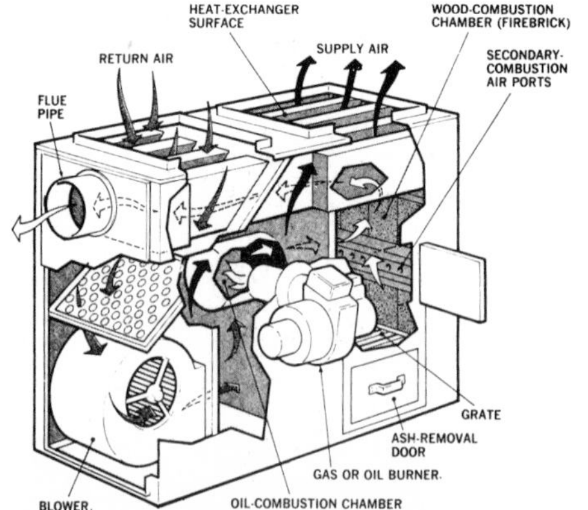

Manufacturer	Aqua Heater Corp. Box 815 (FF) Clark, Colorado 80428
Model	Aqua Heater
Function	Hot water heater
Size (H, W, D)	3 sizes
Weight	27 lbs., 55 lbs., 68 lbs.
Colors	Green, brown, avocado
Airtight?	Yes
Reduced clearance	N/A
Outside combustion air?	N/A
Glass? (type)	N/A
Cooking surface?	N/A
CONSTRUCTION *Material*	Galvanized steel
Gauge or thickness	14 ga.
Air blower? (output)	N/A
Flue size	4″
Special features	Can be used for domestic hot water heating; for a solar backup system; or for a hot tub. The small unit is designed to be portable.
Options and accessories	Chimney adapter for 6″. Dura-vent Chimney.
Efficiency	N/A
Heat output (or area)	N/A
Tested by	N/A
Suggested retail price	\$139.00, \$159.00, \$189.00
Brochure	Free
For nearest dealer call	303-879-3908
Mail order, if no dealer?	Yes

Manufacturer	Bruce Mfg. Inc. Nippa Sauna Heater Dept. FF Bruce Crossing, MI 49912
Model	WB-18
Function	Sauna (wood-fired)
Size (H, W, D)	18″, 22″, 18″
Weight	165 lbs.
Colors	Black
Airtight?	N/A
Reduced clearance	N/A
Outside combustion air?	Yes
Glass? (type)	N/A
Cooking surface?	N/A
CONSTRUCTION *Material*	Steel, cast iron
Gauge or thickness	3/16″
Air blower? (output)	N/A
Flue size	6″ (top)
Special features	Cast iron grate and ash pan. Holds 150 lbs. of rocks. Burns wood, coal, coke. (Manufactured since 1930.)
Options and accessories	Water jacket. Water tank. 6″, 8″, or 12″ extensions for outside mounting. Custom sizes available.
Efficiency	N/A
Heat output (or area)	8′ × 10′ room
Tested by	N/A
Suggested retail price	\$339.00
Brochure	Free
For nearest dealer call	906-827-3906
Mail order, if no dealer?	Yes

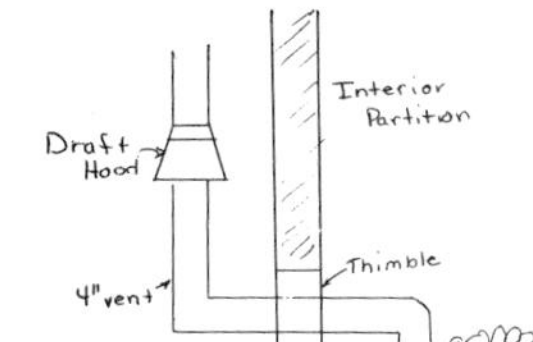

Typical Sauna Heater Installation

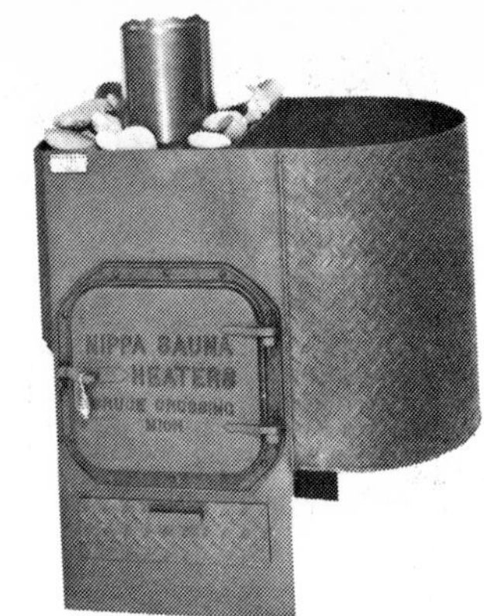

Manufacturer	Bruce Mfg. Inc Nippa Sauna Heater Dept. FF Bruce Crossing, MI 49912
Model	WC-22
Function	Sauna (wood-fired)
Size (H, W, D)	22″, 26″, 28″
Weight	190 lbs.
Colors	Black
Airtight?	N/A
Reduced clearance	N/A
Outside combustion air?	Yes
Glass? (type)	N/A
Cooking surface?	N/A
CONSTRUCTION *Material*	Steel, cast iron
Gauge or thickness	3/16″
Air blower? (output)	N/A
Flue size	6″ (top)
Special features	Direct heated water tank. Cast iron grate and ash pan. Holds 125 lbs. of rock. Burns wood, coal, coke.
Options and accessories	Custom sizes. 6″, 8″, or 12″ extensions to mount outside of sauna.
Efficiency	N/A
Heat output (or area)	20′ × 20′ room
Tested by	N/A
Suggested retail price	$359.00
Brochure	Color, free
For nearest dealer call	906-827-3906
Mail order, if no dealer?	Yes

Manufacturer	Solar Sauna Box 466 (FF) Hollis, N.H. 03049
Model	AITO
Function	Sauna (wood-fired)
Size (H, W, D)	7 sizes
Weight	7 weights
Colors	Blue
Airtight?	N/A
Reduced clearance	N/A
Outside combustion air?	N/A
Glass? (type)	N/A
Cooking surface?	N/A
CONSTRUCTION *Material*	Steel, cast iron, firebrick
Gauge or thickness	N/A
Air blower? (output)	N/A
Flue size	Varies
Special features	Made in Finland. Cast iron flue damper.
Options and accessories	Water jacket. Water tank. (Sauna design: 16 pages, $5)
Efficiency	N/A
Heat output (or area)	N/A
Tested by	N/A
Suggested retail price	N/A
Brochure	Color, $1.00
For nearest dealer call	603-465-7811
Mail order, if no dealer?	Yes

Manufacturer	Solar Sauna Box 466 (FF) Hollis, N.H. 03049
Model	KOTA
Function	Sauna (wood-fired)
Size (H, W, D)	800 mm. H, 500 mm. W
Weight	120 kg.
Colors	Aluminized or stainless steel
Airtight?	N/A
Reduced clearance	N/A
Outside combustion air?	N/A
Glass? (type)	N/A
Cooking surface?	N/A
CONSTRUCTION *Material*	Cast iron, steel plate
Gauge or thickness	Varies
Air blower? (output)	N/A
Flue size	150 mm.
Special features	Made in Finland. Flue collar rotates. Stainless steel double wall outer mantle. Takes 30 kg. of stones. Easily dismantled.
Options and accessories	Water tank. (Sauna design: 16 pages., $5)
Efficiency	N/A
Heat output (or area)	N/A
Tested by	N/A
Suggested retail price	N/A
Brochure	Color, $1.00
For nearest dealer call	603-465-7811
Mail order, if no dealer?	Yes

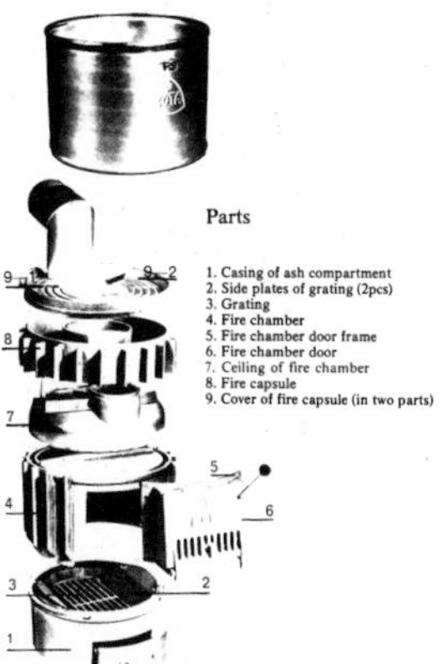

Manufacturer	Elmira Stove Works Dept. FF 22 Church St. Elmira, Ontario, Canada
Model	Queen
Function	Kitchen range
Size (H, W, D)	34½″, 24″, 45″
Weight	335 lbs.
Colors	Black with nickel trim
Airtight?	N/A
Reduced clearance	N/A
Outside combustion air?	N/A
Glass? (type)	N/A
Cooking surface?	Top 24″ × 24″
CONSTRUCTION *Material*	Cast iron
Gauge or thickness	N/A
Air blower? (output)	N/A
Flue size	
Special features	Oven is 21″ × 12″ × 12½″. Height to cooking surface is 20″. Fuel may be added through a side fuel door.
Options and accessories	Unit complete. (Three modern wood-fired cook stoves are available from Elmira.)
Efficiency	N/A
Heat output (or area)	N/A
Tested by	N/A
Suggested retail price	$569.00
Brochure	Free
For nearest dealer call	519-669-5103
Mail order, if no dealer?	N/A

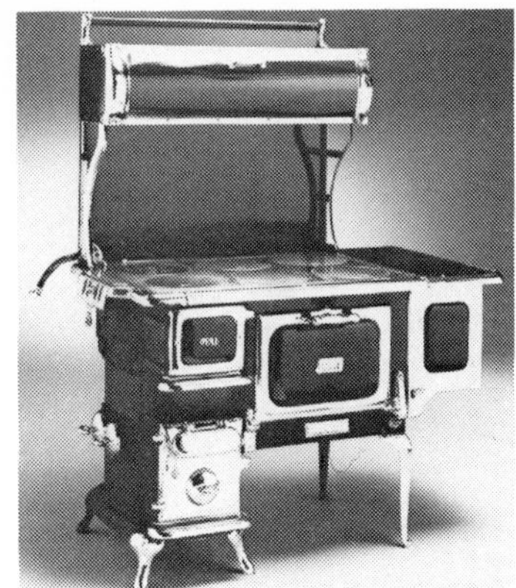

Manufacturer	Elmira Stove works Dept. FF 22 Church St. Elmira, Ontario, Canada
Model	Findlay Oval 9919-2
Function	Kitchen range
Size (H, W, D)	62″, 50″, 30″
Weight	525 lbs.
Colors	Gold, white, black-porcelain
Airtight?	Yes
Reduced clearance	Yes
Outside combustion air?	N/A
Glass? (type)	N/A
Cooking surface?	Yes, 25″ × 34″
CONSTRUCTION *Material*	Cast iron and steel
Gauge or thickness	½″ and 19 ga.
Air blower? (output)	N/A
Flue size	7″
Special features	½″ thick cast iron firebox, with firebrick lining. Warming closets. Hi/lo grate. Porcelain oven interior. Top is hand polished. Nickel trim.
Options and accessories	Copper, silver-soldered hot water reservoir (Model 9919-3).
Efficiency	65%
Heat output (or area)	50,000 BTUs/hr.; 1,500 sq. ft.
Tested by	N/A
Suggested retail price	$1,695.00
Brochure	Color, free
For nearest dealer call	519-669-5103
Mail order, if no dealer?	N/A

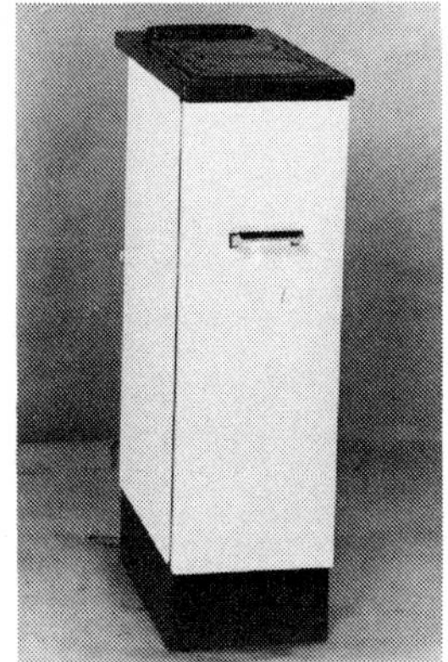

Manufacturer	Enheat Ltd. Fawcett Div. Dept. FF Sackville, New Brunswick Canada E0A 3C0
Model	Annex
Function	Wood/coal range
Size (H, W, D)	36″, 13″, 25″
Weight	135 lbs.
Colors	White
Airtight?	N/A
Reduced clearance	Yes
Outside combustion air?	N/A
Glass? (type)	N/A
Cooking surface?	Yes
CONSTRUCTION *Material*	Steel, cast iron
Gauge or thickness	N/A
Air blower? (output)	N/A
Flue size	6″
Special features	Porcelain white finish. Polished top. Includes dual grate (one is a wood overlay grate).
Options and accessories	Unit complete.
Efficiency	N/A
Heat output (or area)	N/A
Tested by	N/A
Suggested retail price	$289.00
Brochure	Free
For nearest dealer call	506-536-1520
Mail order, if no dealer?	N/A

Manufacturer	Enheat Ltd. Fawcett Div. Dept. FF Sackville, New Brunswick Canada E0A 3C0
Model	Little Dandy
Function	Cook stove
Size (H, W, D)	31″, 30¼″, 23″
Weight	140 lbs./150 lbs.
Colors	Steel blue
Airtight?	N/A
Reduced clearance	N/A
Outside combustion air?	N/A
Glass? (type)	N/A
Cooking surface?	Yes, 30¼″ × 21¾″
CONSTRUCTION *Material*	Steel, cast iron
Gauge or thickness	N/A
Air blower? (output)	N/A
Flue size	6″ (rear)
Special features	Made of oiled, blue polished steel. Cast iron firebox, key plates, and covers. Insulated. 100° to 600° Thermometer.
Options and accessories	Coal grate. Waterfront. Hang-on reservoir. Retort oil burner.
Efficiency	N/A
Heat output (or area)	N/A
Tested by	N/A
Suggested retail price	$339.00
Brochure	Free
For nearest dealer call	506-536-1520
Mail order, if no dealer?	N/A

Manufacturer	Enheat LTD. Fawcett Div. Dept. FF Sackville, New Brunswick Canada E0A 3C0
Model	110-6L
Function	Kitchen range
Size (H, W, D)	32″, 32″, 28″
Weight	380 lbs.
Colors	Gold or white-enameled
Airtight?	N/A
Reduced clearance	N/A
Outside combustion air?	N/A
Glass? (type)	Yes, Permaview
Cooking surface?	Yes, 29½″ × 18″
CONSTRUCTION *Material*	Steel and cast iron
Gauge or thickness	N/A
Air blower? (output)	N/A
Flue size	7″
Special features	Cast iron firebox. Multi-fuel range. Oil, coal, wood. Oven is 17″ × 20″ × 11 5/8″. Duplex grate firebox.
Options and accessories	High closet. High shelf. Retort oil burner. (3 other models available)
Efficiency	N/A
Heat output (or area)	N/A
Tested by	N/A
Suggested retail price	$599.00
Brochure	Free
For nearest dealer call	506-536-1520
Mail order, if no dealer?	N/A

Manufacturer	The Kroupa Stove Dept. FF Grand Etang, Nova Scotia Canada, B0E 1L0
Model	Kroupa stove
Function	Multi-function range
Size (H, W, D)	46", 20", 40"
Weight	N/A
Colors	Custom colors
Airtight?	Yes
Reduced clearance	N/A
Outside combustion air?	N/A
Glass? (type)	Vycor, and Pyrex
Cooking surface?	Two—20" × 20" (ea)
CONSTRUCTION *Material*	Plate steel, cast iron
Gauge or thickness	5/16", 1/4"
Air blower? (output)	N/A
Flue size	8" (right side)
Special features	Cooking, baking, fireplace. Cast iron doors (frame for glass). Vycor firebox door. Pyrex oven doors (2). Rear load door. Firebrick lined. Stainless steel firebox door plate. Cook grate.
Options and accessories	Optional hot water coil
Efficiency	N/A
Heat output (or area)	50,000 BTUs/hr.
Tested by	N/A
Suggested retail price	$970.00
Brochure	Color, free
For nearest dealer call	902-224-2849
Mail order, if no dealer?	Yes

Manufacturer	Pioneer Lamp & Stove Dept. FF 75 Yesler Seattle, Wash. 98104
Model	Pacific Princess
Function	Kitchen range
Size (H, W, D)	N/A
Weight	350 lbs., 375 lbs.
Colors	Black, with white porcelain trim
Airtight?	N/A
Reduced clearance	N/A
Outside combustion air?	N/A
Glass? (type)	N/A
Cooking surface?	Yes, 30" × 24"
CONSTRUCTION *Material*	Cast iron
Gauge or thickness	N/A
Air blower? (output)	N/A
Flue size	7"
Special features	Polished griddle with grease run-off. Trivets and trim are nickel plated. Uses wood, coal. Stainless steel water reservoir. Thermometer. Blue door art. Broiling hatch.
Options and accessories	Write to manufacturer.
Efficiency	N/A
Heat output (or area)	N/A
Tested by	N/A
Suggested retail price	Base price, $985.00
Brochure	Free
For nearest dealer call	206-624-8035
Mail order, if no dealer?	Yes

Manufacturer	Svendborg Co., Inc. P.O. Box 5 (FF) Hanover, N.H. 03755
Model	Lange 911 W
Function	Kitchen range
Size (H, W, D)	33¼", 36¼" 24"
Weight	375 lbs. (shipping weight)
Colors	Porcelain (see below)
Airtight?	Yes
Reduced clearance	N/A
Outside combustion air?	N/A
Glass? (type)	N/A
Cooking surface?	Yes
CONSTRUCTION *Material*	Cast iron
Gauge or thickness	Varies
Air blower? (output)	N/A
Flue size	Adapts to 5" or 6"
Special features	Made in Denmark. Two grates, one for quick "summer fires". Top or rear flue. Fire-brick lined. 5 yr. limited warranty.
Options and accessories	Porcelain red or black. Color matching stovepipe.
Efficiency	N/A
Heat output (or area)	5,000 cu. ft.
Tested by	ETLM (UL)
Suggested retail price	Base price $885.00 (flat black)
Brochure	Color, free
For nearest dealer call	603-643-3771
Mail order, if no dealer?	N/A

Manufacturer	Tirolia of America Dept. FF 169 Dunning Rd. Middletown, N.Y. 10940
Model	Tirol 7 HT
Function	Kitchen range
Size (H, W, D)	35", 35½", 24"
Weight	560 lbs.
Colors	White, harvest gold
Airtight?	N/A
Reduced clearance	Yes, 7" from rear wall
Outside combustion air?	N/A
Glass? (type)	N/A
Cooking surface?	Yes
CONSTRUCTION *Material*	Steel, cast iron
Gauge or thickness	N/A
Air blower? (output)	N/A
Flue size	6" (rear or side)
Special features	Domestic hot water jacket. Enamel finish. Burns wood/coal. Fireclay lined firebox.
Options and accessories	Available without hot water jacket—or with larger jacket.
Heat output (or area)	12,000 (radiant), 31,000 (water)
Tested by	N/A
Suggested retail price	N/A
Brochure	Color, free
For nearest dealer call	Write to above
Mail order, if no dealer?	N/A

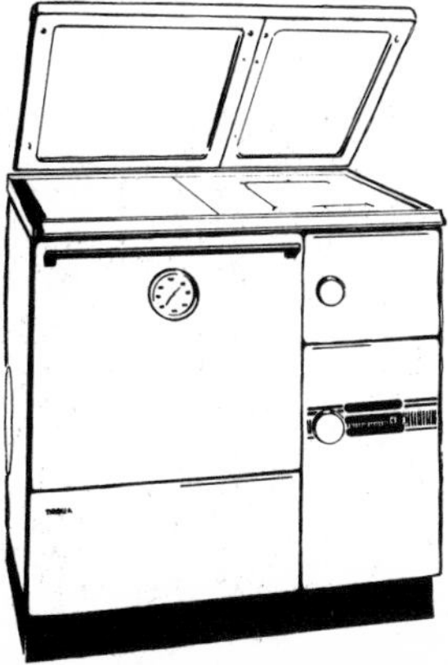

Manufacturer	Arcadia Sheds Dept. FF 82 Arcadia Road Westwood, MA 20290
Model	Wood Shed Complex Plan
Function	Plans to build a 3 section wood shed
Size	Holds 3½ cords.
Weight	N/A
Colors	N/A
Special features	2 page, simple instructions. (Other models available.)
Suggested retail price	$1.70
Brochure	Free
For nearest dealer call	617-762-8778
Mail order, if no dealer?	Yes

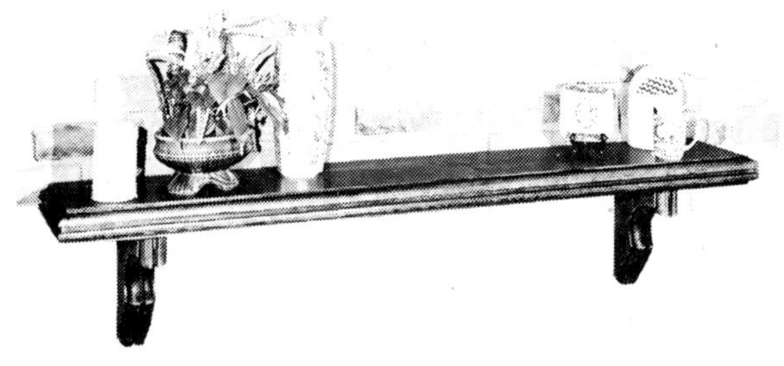

Manufacturer	Barclay Industries, Inc. Dept. FF 65 Industrial Rd. Lodi, NJ 07644
Model	Wood Mantles
Function	Mantles for built-in fireplaces.
Size	4′, 5′, 6′
Weight	N/A
Colors	Natural, brown grey
Special features	Can be installed on brick fire-place front.
Suggested retail price	N/A
Brochure	Free
For nearest dealer call	201-473-2100
Mail order, if no dealer?	N/A

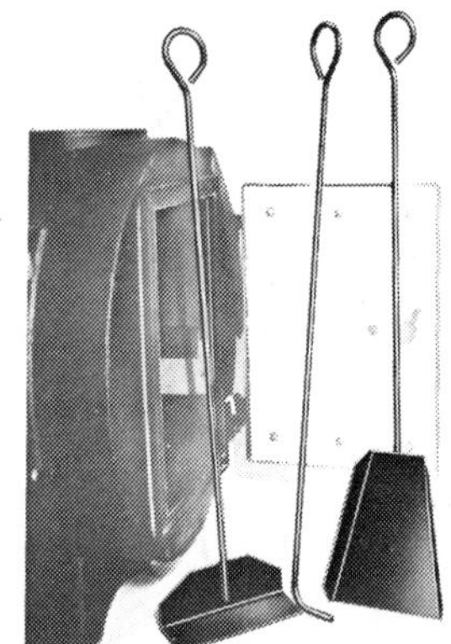

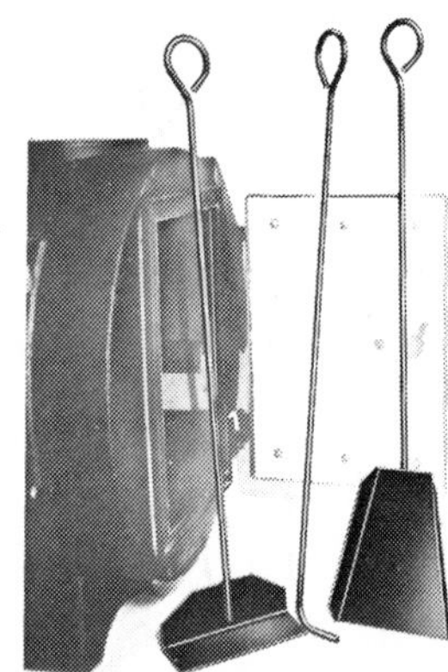

Manufacturer	Auto Hoe Inc. P.O. Box W121R9 (F) De Pere, WI 54115
Model	Fireplace Tools
Function	Poker, scoop and hoe
Size	30″
Weight	N/A
Colors	Black
Special features	16 ga. steel with 3/8″ dia. handles
Suggested retail price	$14.95
Brochure	Free
For nearest dealer call	Write to above
Mail order, if no dealer?	Yes

Manufacturer	Belvent Limited P.O. Box 190 (FF) 235 Belfield Road Rexdale, Ontario Canada M9W 5L1
Model	BEL-A Chimney
Function	Class A chimney. ULC listed. Double-wall mineral insulated.
Size	Any
Weight	N/A
Colors	N/A
Special features	Can provide professional engineering assistance.
Suggested retail price	N/A
Brochure	Free
For nearest dealer call	416-249-8444
Mail order, if no dealer?	N/A

Manufacturer	Black Magic Chimney Sweeps P.O. Box 977 (FF) Stowe, VT 05672
Model	N/A
Function	Professional chimney sweep equipment. Training seminars.
Size	N/A
Weight	N/A
Colors	N/A
Special features	Also can help locate local chimney sweeps. Do-it-yourself kits.
Suggested retail price	N/A
Brochure	Yes
For nearest dealer call	802-253-4867
Mail order, if no dealer?	N/A

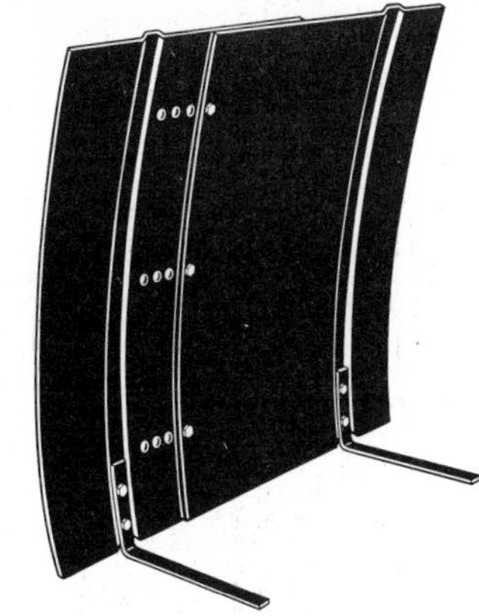

Manufacturer	Bryce-Branton Dept. FF 690 Southern Ave. Muskegon, MI 49441
Model	Fireplace Heat Reflector
Function	Reflects heat; also can help cure smoking fireplaces.
Size	28″ H, 28″ to 40″ W
Weight	N/A
Colors	Black
Special features	Rolled-rib reinforced 22 ga. steel.
Suggested retail price	$29.95 (plus $3 shipping, $4 in West)
Brochure	Free
For nearest dealer call	Write to above
Mail order, if no dealer?	Yes

Manufacturer	Broad-Axe Beam Co. RD 2, Box 181-E (F) Brattleboro, VT 05301
Model	Hand-Hewn Mantles
Function	Hand cut (with broad-axe) beams for mantles and structural supports.
Size	To order
Weight	N/A
Colors	Stained or waxed
Special features	Can be shipped anywhere.
Suggested retail price	$4.00 per linear foot
Brochure	$1.00
For nearest dealer call	802-257-0064
Mail order, if no dealer?	Yes

Manufacturer	Canterbury Enterprises P.O. Box 2870 (FF) 567 San Nicolas Dr. Newport Beach, CA 92660
Model	Blue Flame Log Lighter
Function	Gas lighter for damp wood.
Size	2 sizes
Weight	N/A
Colors	N/A
Special features	A.G.A and C.G.A approved
Suggested retail price	N/A
Brochure	Free
For nearest dealer call	714-640-5330
Mail order, if no dealer?	Yes

Manufacturer	Carolina Narrow Fabric Co. P.O. Box 1400 (FF) Winston-Salem, NC 27102
Model	BLAZEBAN
Function	Fireproof hearth rugs.
Size	2′ × 4′
Weight	N/A
Colors	Gold, gr., br., autumn gold
Special features	Used by Navy, Coast Guard, FAA. Custom sizes available.
Suggested retail price	$34.95
Brochure	Color, free
For nearest dealer call	919-724-3638
Mail order, if no dealer?	Yes

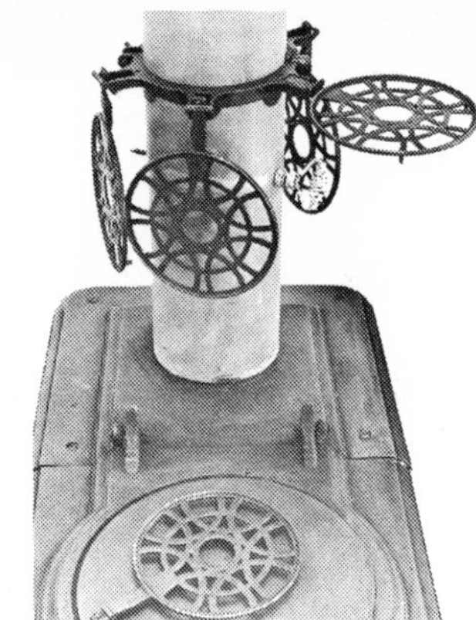

Manufacturer	Chelsea Stove Access. Inc. P.O. Box 203 (FF) Chelsea, VT 05038
Model	Trivetree
Function	Warming rack for stove pipe.
Size	6″ or 8″
Weight	N/A
Colors	Black
Special features	Cast iron.
Suggested retail price	$30.00; $36.00
Brochure	Free
For nearest dealer call	802-685-7746
Mail order, if no dealer?	Yes

Manufacturer	Century Fireplace Furnishings, Inc. P.O. Box 248 (FF) 71 S. Turnpike Rd. Wallingford, CT 06492
Model	Fireplace Screens
Function	Fine mesh spark guards.
Size	Sizes to fit most fireplaces.
Weight	Varies
Colors	Black w/brass trim
Special features	Arch, flat top, or brass frame folding screens available.
Suggested retail price	Varies
Brochure	Free
For nearest dealer call	203-265-1686
Mail order, if no dealer?	Yes

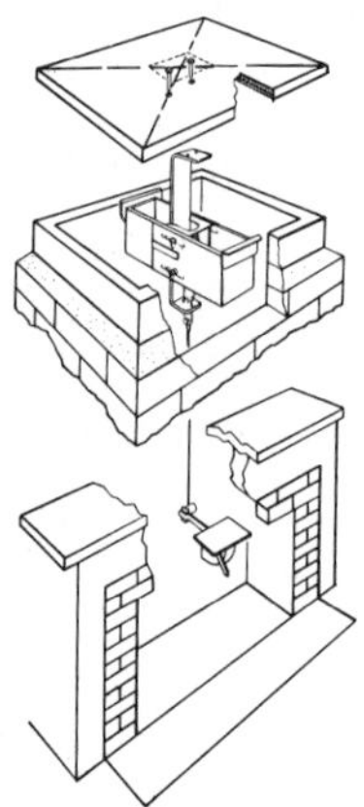

Manufacturer	Chim-a-Lator Co. Dept. FF 8824 Wentworth Ave. S. Minneapolis, MN 55420
Model	Chim-a-lator
Function	Insulated chimney cap
Size	12 sizes
Weight	Varies from 10 to 24 lbs.
Colors	N/A
Special features	When shut, chimney becomes airtight. Models for masonry or metal flues.
Suggested retail price	$96.00 and up
Brochure	Free
For nearest dealer call	612-884-7274
Mail order, if no dealer?	Yes

Manufacturer	Christen, Inc. Dept. FF 59 Branch St. St. Louis, MO 63147
Model	57-460-0
Function	Log lighter for damp wood.
Size	11½″ L, 3½″ W, 1½″ H
Weight	5 lbs.
Colors	Black
Special features	Cast iron. Uses charcoal lighter fluid.
Suggested retail price	$14.98
Brochure	Yes
For nearest dealer call	314-241-7033
Mail order, if no dealer?	Yes

Manufacturer	Cleanweld Turner Dept. FF 821 Park Ave. Sycamore, Ill. 60178
Model	93-001
Function	Log lighter (portable), for use with propane cylinders.
Size	16″, 8″, 8″
Weight	7 lbs.
Colors	Black w/brass trim
Special features	Underwriters Laboratories listed.
Suggested retail price	$39.95; $19.95 (case)
Brochure	Yes
For nearest dealer call	800-435-6957
Mail order, if no dealer?	N/A

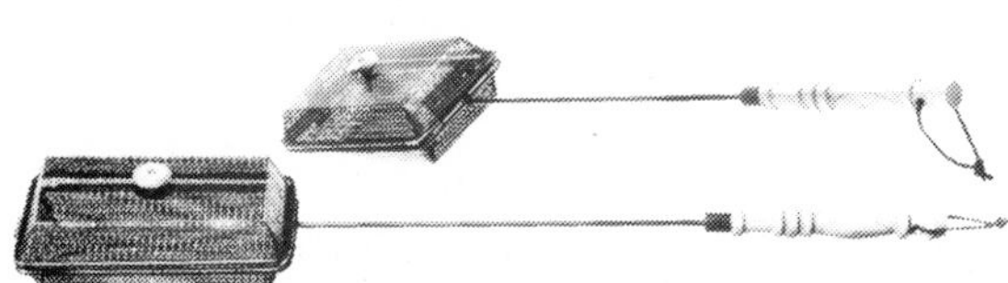

Manufacturer	Christen, Inc. Dept. FF 59 Branch St. St. Louis, MO 63147
Model	57-476-0
Function	Popcorn popper
Size	36″ long
Weight	1¼ lbs.
Colors	Black w/maple handle
Special features	Aluminum pan
Suggested retail price	$12.98
Brochure	Free
For nearest dealer call	314-241-7033
Mail order, if no dealer?	Yes

Manufacturer	Condar Company P.O. Box 264 (FF) Garrettville, OH 44231
Model	Chimfin Radiators
Function	Five alloy spring-loaded bands attach to stovepipe to radiate heat.
Size	4″ to 10″
Weight	N/A
Colors	Black
Special features	(Because they radiate heat, they must be 24″ from wall.)
Suggested retail price	$9.95
Brochure	Free
For nearest dealer call	216-569-7325
Mail order, if no dealer?	Yes

Manufacturer	Country Floors, Inc. Dept. FF 300 East 61st St. N.Y., NY 10021
Model	Ceramic Tiles
Function	For fireplace facing or reduced clearance shield.
Size	Any
Weight	N/A
Colors	All varieties
Special features	Imported from Mexico, Italy, Spain, Israel, France, Portugal, Holland.
Suggested retail price	N/A
Brochure	Write to above
For nearest dealer call	212-758-7414
Mail order, if no dealer?	N/A

Manufacturer	Dura-Vent Corporation Dept. FF 2525 El Camino Real Redwood City, CA 94064
Model	Dura-Vent Chimneys
Function	Class A Chimney. UL listed. Triple-wall air insulated.
Size	Any
Weight	N/A
Colors	N/A
Special features	Can provide professional engineering assistance.
Suggested retail price	N/A
Brochure	Free
For nearest dealer call	415-368-2912
Mail order, if no dealer?	N/A

Manufacturer	The Dampney Company Dept. FF 85 Paris St. Everett, Mass. 02149
Model	Thurmalox 270 Series
Function	High temp. wood stove paint, withstands 1200 F.
Size	13 oz. can
Weight	13 oz.
Colors	Blue, maroon, brown, green, black
Special features	Metallic: charcoal, green, brown, blue, maroon
Suggested retail price	N/A
Brochure	Free (#270)
For nearest dealer call	617-389-2805
Mail order, if no dealer?	N/A

Manufacturer	Fire Genie, Inc. Rt. 3, Box 184A(F) Batesville, Arkansas 72501
Model	5 A
Function	Air inducer for outside combustion air.
Size	3″H, 8″W, 10″D
Weight	7½ lbs.
Colors	Black
Special features	1/8″ thick steel tubes. Replaces ash dump door.
Suggested retail price	$29.95
Brochure	Free
For nearest dealer call	501-793-6422
Mail order, if no dealer?	Yes

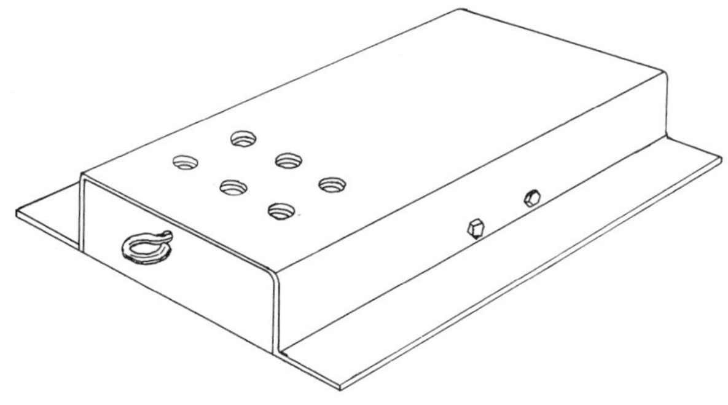

Manufacturer	F&W Econoheat, Inc. Route 2 Box 485 (FF) #7 Andrea Drive Bruce Industrial Park Belgrade, MT 59714
Model	Mity Mizer
Function	Replaces ash dump door, supplies outside combustion air.
Size	2″ × 6″ × 14″
Weight	8 lbs.
Colors	N/A
Special features	12 ga. steel
Suggested retail price	$39.95
Brochure	Free
For nearest dealer call	406-388-4911
Mail order, if no dealer?	Yes

Manufacturer	Great Amer. Ash Remover P.O. Box 5525 (FF) Incline Village, Nevada 89450
Model	Fireplace Model
Function	Ash catcher for fireplaces and large wood stoves.
Size	Small and large
Weight	N/A
Colors	Black or silver
Special features	Smaller size for small stoves available.
Suggested retail price	N/A
Brochure	Free
For nearest dealer call	702-831-4037
Mail order, if no dealer?	Yes

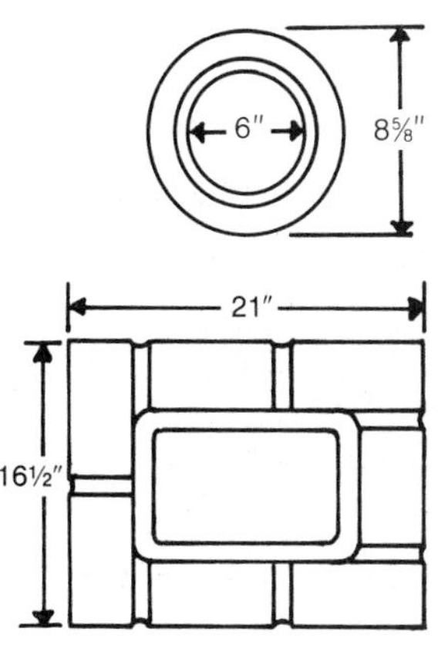

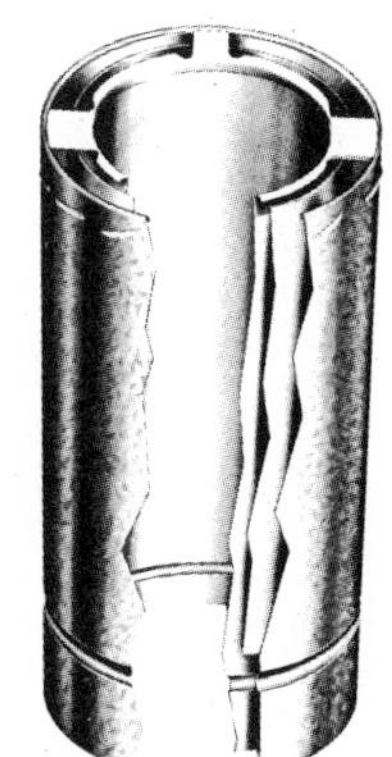

Manufacturer	General Products Co., Inc. P.O. Box 887 (FF) Fredericksburg, VA 22401
Model	Air-jet Chimney
Function	Class A chimneys. UL listed. Triple-wall air insulated.
Size	Any
Weight	N/A
Colors	N/A
Special features	Can provide professional engineering assistance.
Suggested retail price	N/A
Brochure	Free
For nearest dealer call	703-371-5700
Mail order, if no dealer?	N/A

Manufacturer	Greeley Iron Works Box 184 (FF) Rowland Road Greeley, PA 18425
Model	Handy Mate Log Lifter
Function	Lifts logs for bucking. Can lift 20″ logs.
Size	48″ long
Weight	N/A
Colors	N/A
Special features	All steel, jig welded. Optional spring loaded hook.
Suggested retail price	$34.95; $39.95 (spring model)
Brochure	Free
For nearest dealer call	717-685-7455
Mail order, if no dealer?	Yes

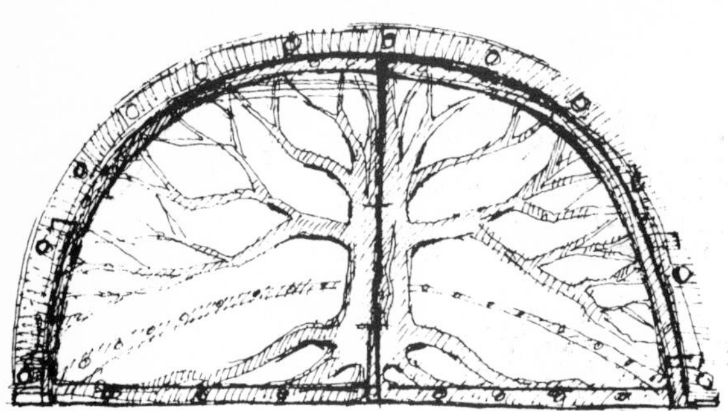

Manufacturer	Mr. Robert Hanson, Blacksmith R.D. #3 Box 185 (FF) Felton, PA 17322
Model	Hand Forged Accessories
Function	Complete line of handmade fireplace accessories and household items.
Size	N/A
Weight	N/A
Colors	Wrought iron, copper
Special features	Glass or screen doors.
Suggested retail price	Custom order
Brochure	Free ($2.00 for iron work catalogue)
For nearest dealer call	717-993-6594
Mail order, if no dealer?	Yes

Manufacturer	Heat-N-Glo Fireplaces Dept. FF 1100 Riverwood Dr. Burnsville, MN 55337
Model	The Grate Heater
Function	Fireplace grate with hot air blower built-in.
Size	3 sizes
Weight	N/A
Colors	N/A
Special features	100 CFM, UL approved blower. 12 ga. Warranted.
Suggested retail price	$219.00
Brochure	Free
For nearest dealer call	612-890-8367
Mail order, if no dealer?	N/A

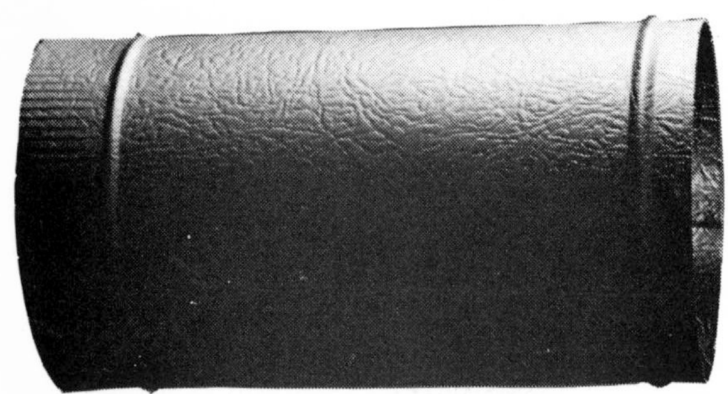

Manufacturer	Heat-Fab Inc. Dept. FF 38 Haywood St. Greenfield, Mass 01301
Model	Leather Grain Stovepipe
Function	Textured stovepipe, 22 ga.
Size	5″, 6″, 175 mm, 7″, 8″
Weight	N/A
Colors	Special order
Special features	Spot-welded seam, beaded for furnace cement.
Suggested retail price	N/A
Brochure	Free
For nearest dealer call	413-774-2356
Mail order, if no dealer?	Yes

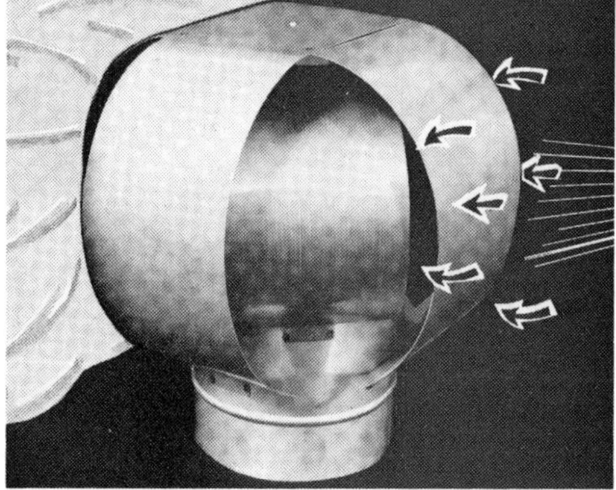

Manufacturer	Improved Consumer Products Dept. FF 100 Towne Street Attleboro Falls, MA 02763
Model	Vacu-Stack
Function	Chimney cap; helps vent out smoke when the wind is blowing.
Size	6″ thru 10″
Weight	N/A
Colors	N/A
Special features	Stainless steel. Adapters available for square chimneys.
Suggested retail price	$49.95 to $99.95
Brochure	Free
For nearest dealer call	617-695-7000
Mail order, if no dealer?	Yes

Manufacturer Mr. Steve Kayne, Blacksmith
Dept. FF
17 Harmon Place
Smithtown, N.Y. 11787
Model Hand Forged Accessories
Function Complete line of handmade fireplace accessories and household items.
Size N/A
Weight N/A
Colors Wrought iron, brass, bronze
Special features Fireplace items; colonial hardware
Suggested retail price $250.00 up (doors)
Brochure $2.50 (3 booklets)
For nearest dealer call 516-724-3669
Mail order, if no dealer? Yes

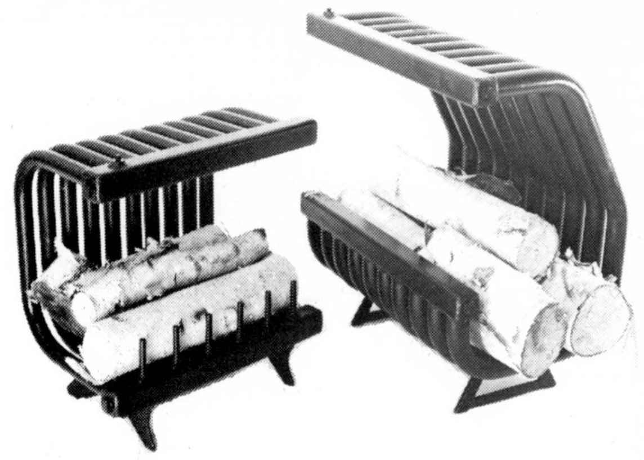

Manufacturer LaFont Corporation
Dept. FF
1319 Town St.
Prentice, WI 54556
Model ST3-10, ST2-10
Function Fireplace hydronic unit to supplement solar or hot water heat.
Size 2 sizes
Weight N/A
Colors N/A
Special features (Should be installed by licensed plumber)
Suggested retail price N/A
Brochure Free
For nearest dealer call 715-428-2881
Mail order, if no dealer? N/A

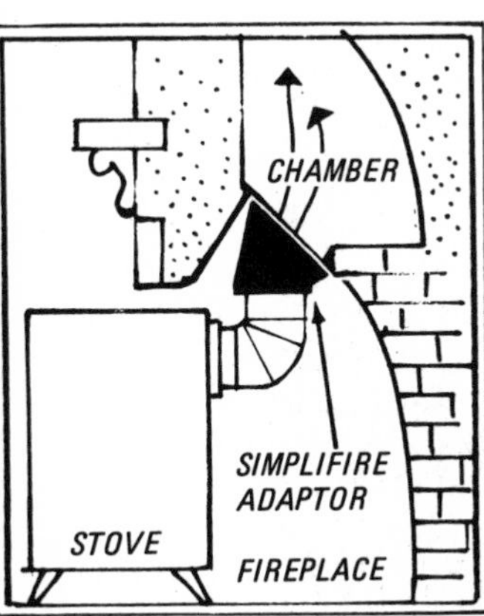

Manufacturer Kent Products, Inc.
P.O. Box 281 (FF)
Kent, CT
06757
Model Simplifire Adaptor
Function Damper replacement for wood stove hookup to fireplace.
Size 27¾″ × 5¾″ or 33¾″ × 6″
Weight 25 lbs.
Colors N/A
Special features 3/16″ cast iron 8″ flue opening.
Suggested retail price $69.00; $72.00
Brochure Free
For nearest dealer call 203-927-3781
Mail order, if no dealer? Yes

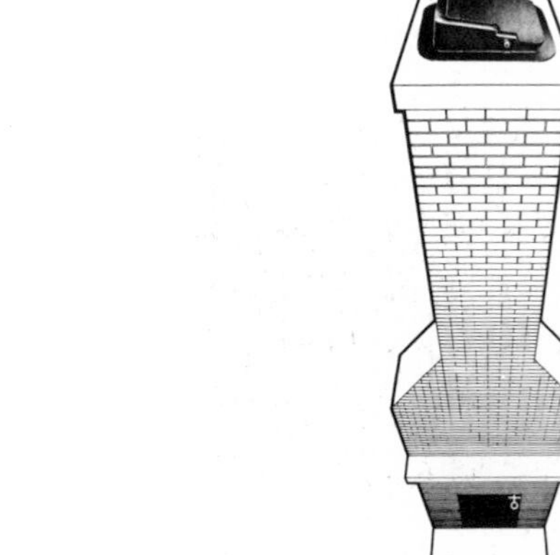

Manufacturer Lyemance International
P.O. Box 6651 (FF)
141 N. Sherrin Ave.
Louisville, KY 40206
Model Fireplace Damper
Function Chimney top damper. Firebox control. Cast aluminum. Stainless steel cable.
Size 9″ × 13″, 13″ × 13″, 13″ × 18″
Weight N/A
Colors N/A
Special features Note: for fireplaces only, not for inserts.
Suggested retail price $49.95 to $62.50
Brochure Free
For nearest dealer call 502-896-2441
Mail order, if no dealer? Yes

Manufacturer	Malm Fireplaces Inc. Dept. FF 368 Yolanda Ave. Santa Rosa, CA 95404
Model	Astro-Hearth
Function	Lightweight, fireproof hearths, wall panel, and surrounds (fireplace facing).
Size	4 sizes and shapes
Weight	1/3 the weight of masonry
Colors	White or used brick
Special features	Cast from concrete with steel reinforcement.
Suggested retail price	N/A
Brochure	Color, free
For nearest dealer call	707-546-8955
Mail order, if no dealer?	N/A

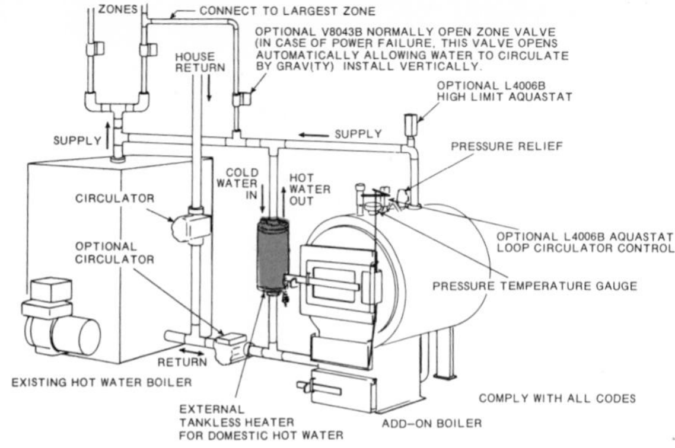

Manufacturer	Marathon Heater Co., Inc. Dept. FF 16 Crawford Street Cortland, N.Y. 13045
Model	External Tankless Heater
Function	Domestic hot water heater.
Size	N/A
Weight	N/A
Colors	N/A
Special features	Can be added to any boiler system.
Suggested retail price	$146.00
Brochure	Free
For nearest dealer call	607-756-8246
Mail order, if no dealer?	N/A

Manufacturer	The Mantle Gallery Dept. FF 1485 Berger Drive San Jose, CA 95112
Model	Period Mantles
Function	Hand made, clear pine mantles. Any period.
Size	24 sizes and styles
Weight	N/A
Colors	Primer white
Special features	Custom sizes and finishes available.
Suggested retail price	$600.00 (model shown)
Brochure	Color, free
For nearest dealer call	402-292-4715
Mail order, if no dealer?	Yes

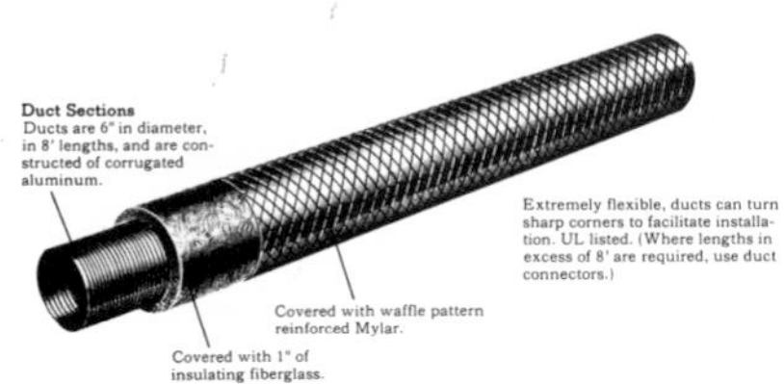

Manufacturer	Martin Industries Building Products Div. P.O. Box 128 (FF) Florence, Ala. 35630
Model	Duct Sections
Function	Hot air ducting.
Size	8′ × 6″
Weight	N/A
Colors	N/A
Special features	UL listed. Flexible. Mylar covered, 1″ fiberglass.
Suggested retail price	N/A
Brochure	Free
For nearest dealer call	Write to above.
Mail order, if no dealer?	N/A

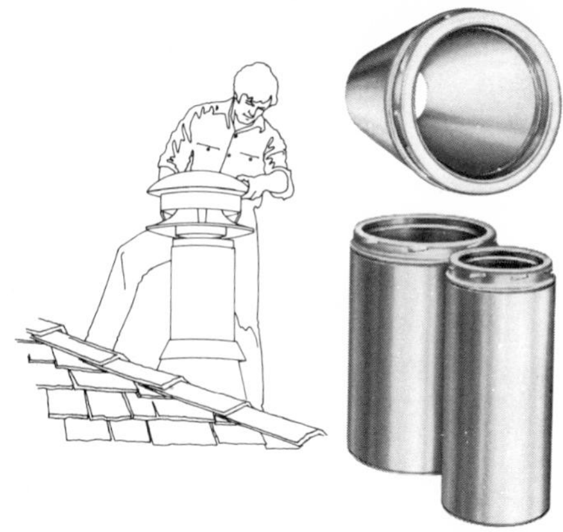

Manufacturer Metalbestos Systems
P.O. Box 372 (FF)
Nampa, Idaho
83651
Model Metalbestos Chimneys
Function Class A chimneys. UL listed. Double-wall mineral listed.
Size Any
Weight N/A
Colors N/A
Special features Can provide professional engineering assistance.
Suggested retail price N/A
Brochure Free
For nearest dealer call 208-467-7411
Mail order, if no dealer? N/A

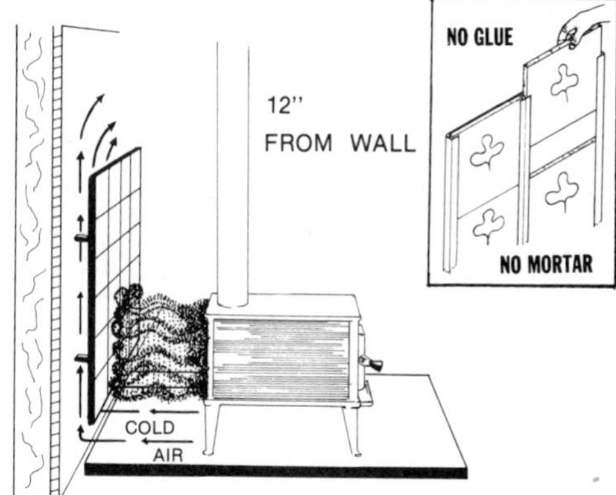

Manufacturer Norwegian Wood Stoves
Box 219 (FF), Clarkson P.O.
Mississauga, Ontario
Canada, L5J 3Y1
Model Fire Shield Frames
Function Reduces wall clearance from 36″ to 12″; designed for back wall and floor.
Size For 8″ × 8″ or 4″ × 8″ tiles
Weight N/A
Colors N/A
Special features Frames for ceramic floor tiles.
Suggested retail price N/A
Brochure Free
For nearest dealer call 800-268-5355
Mail order, if no dealer? N/A

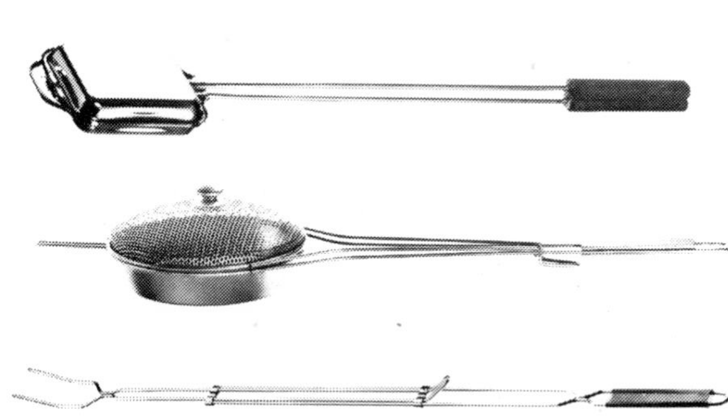

Manufacturer Muza Metal Products
Dept. FF
606 E. Murdock Ave.
Oshkosh, WI 54901
Model Cooking Utensils
Function Long forks, sandwich cookers, popcorn poppers.
Size N/A
Weight N/A
Colors N/A
Special features (There is a handling charge on small orders)
Suggested retail price N/A
Brochure Free
For nearest dealer call 414-235-4963
Mail order, if no dealer? Yes

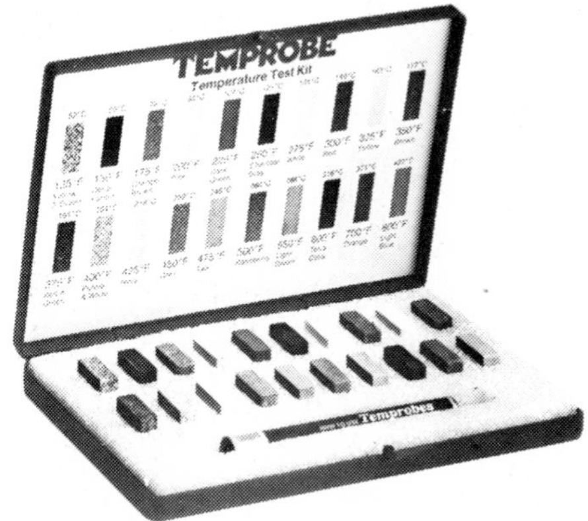

Manufacturer Omega Engineering Inc.
P.O. Box 4047 (FF)
Stamford, CT
06907
Model Temprobe
Function Measures surface temperatures from 125° F to 800° F.
Size N/A
Weight N/A
Colors N/A
Special features Simple to use, crayons melt at indicated temperature.
Suggested retail price $10.00
Brochure Free (bulletin #775)
For nearest dealer call 203-359-1660
Mail order, if no dealer? N/A

Manufacturer Pan-L-Cast Corp.
Dept. FF
8076 River Road, N.E.
Salem, OR 97303
Model Pan-L-Cast
Function Lightweight brick casting. Can replace 3/8" thick asbestos millboard.
Size 6 shapes (sq.; round; corner)
Weight 1/3 weight of brick
Colors Used brick
Special features Complies with Uniform Building Code 3701(1)
Suggested retail price Varies
Brochure Color, free
For nearest dealer call 503-393-0185
Mail order, if no dealer? Yes

Manufacturer Robert H. Peterson Co.
Dept. FF
2835 Sierra Grande St.
Pasadena, CA 91107
Model Hallmark Brass Collection
Function Solid brass accessories. (Andirons shown)
Size N/A
Weight N/A
Colors Brass
Special features Tool sets. Fireplace fenders. Andirons. Screens.
Suggested retail price N/A
Brochure Color
For nearest dealer call 213-793-3118
Mail order, if no dealer? N/A

Manufacturer PASALCO
Dept. FF
400 Demarest Ave.
Closter, N.J. 07624
Model Brown coal FIRE-BRICKS
Function Compressed brown coal briquettes. 8,000 BTU/lb.
Size N/A
Weight 18 lb. or 55 lb.
Colors N/A
Special features Made in W. Germany. Portable. Non-polluting.
Suggested retail price $3.59
Brochure Free
For nearest dealer call 201-768-2133
Mail order, if no dealer? N/A

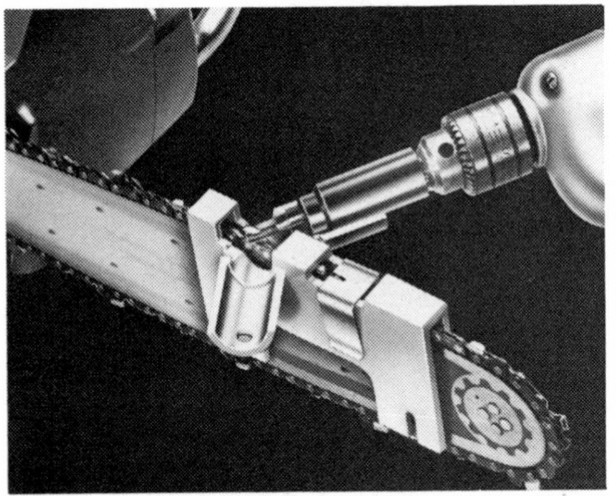

Manufacturer Pro Sharp Corp.
P.O. Box 11378 (FF)
Newington, CT 06111
Model Pro Sharp
Function Chain saw sharpener for use with a portable household drill.
Size N/A
Weight N/A
Colors N/A
Special features (You must order grind wheels that match your saw tooth size)
Suggested retail price N/A
Brochure Free
For nearest dealer call 203-247-9117
Mail order, if no dealer? Yes

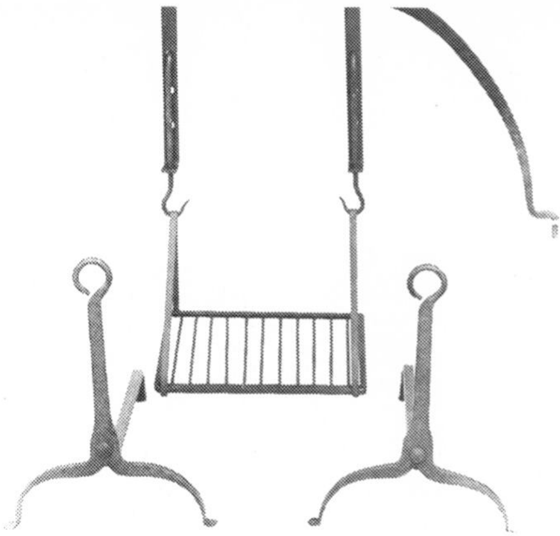

Manufacturer Mr. A. Russell, Blacksmith
P.O. Box 373 (FF)
Waitsfield, VT
05673
Model Hand Forged Accessories
Function Handmade fireplace and household accessories.
Size N/A
Weight N/A
Colors Wrought iron
Special features Cooking cranes. Andirons & tool sets.
Suggested retail price $70.00 (crane)
Brochure $1.00
For nearest dealer call 802-496-2401
Mail order, if no dealer? Yes

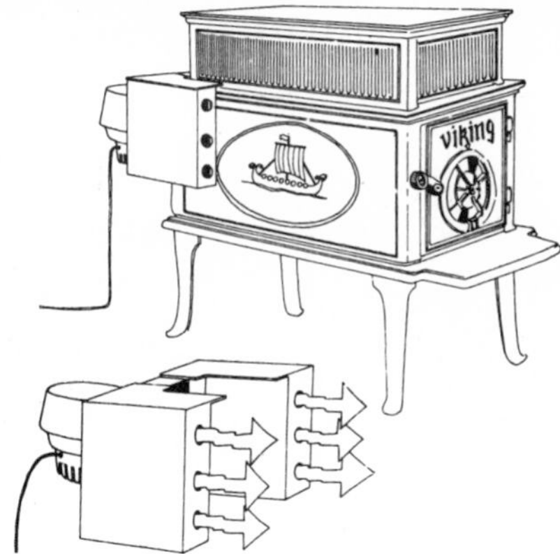

Manufacturer Spalt Associates Corp.
Dept. FF
275 Circuit St.
Hanover, MA
02339
Model Viking Xtra Heat
Function Add-on blower for any wood stove.
Size 5 models
Weight 13 lbs. to 17 lbs.
Colors Black
Special features UL listed motor.
Suggested retail price $76.95 to $89.95
Brochure 4 page, 35¢
For nearest dealer call 617-871-3180
Mail order, if no dealer? Yes

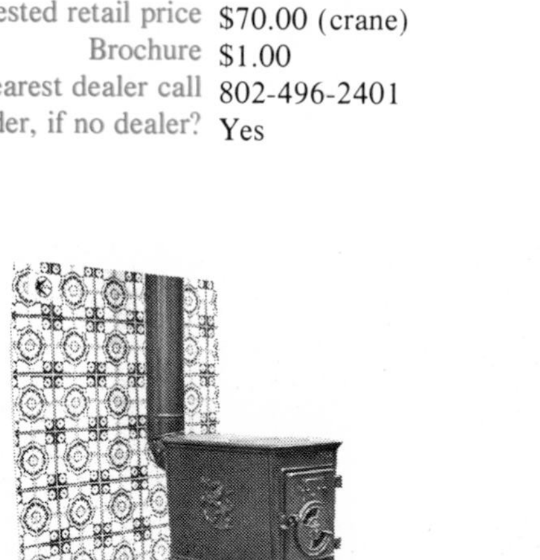

Manufacturer Schaefer Construction
P.O. Box 649 (FF)
Ellsworth, Maine
04605
Model Katrina Wall Mats
Function Place directly on wall to reduce clearance by half.
Size 31″ × 31″ or 36″ × 48″
Weight 50 lbs., 75 lbs.
Colors 10 mosaic tile patterns
Special features ETLM tested. 1½″ thick with built-in air space.
Suggested retail price $75.00 to $120.00
Brochure Color, free
For nearest dealer call 207-667-9205
Mail order, if no dealer? Yes

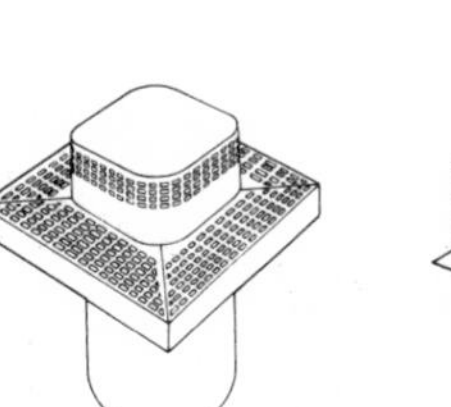

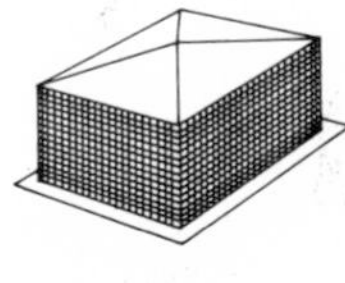

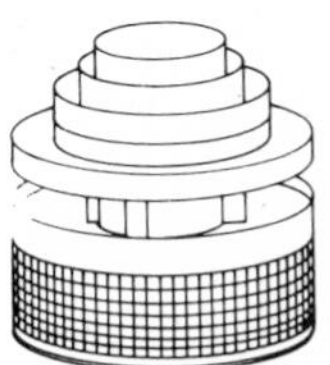

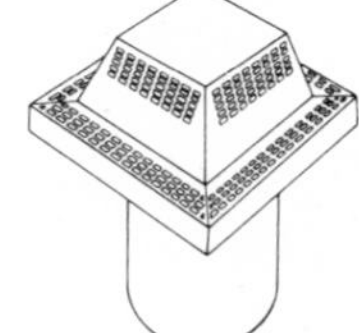

Manufacturer Superior Fireplace Co.
Dept. FF
4325 Artesia Ave.
Fullerton, CA 92633
Model Chimney Terminators
Function Rain caps and spark guards in one unit.
Size Any size
Weight N/A
Colors N/A
Special features Fits masonry and/or metal chimneys.
Suggested retail price $37.00 to $100.00
Brochure Free
For nearest dealer call 714-521-7302
Mail order, if no dealer? N/A

Manufacturer	Superior Fireplace Co. Dept. FF 4325 Artesia Ave. Fullerton, CA 92633
Model	Outside Air Kit
Function	Supplies outside combustion air.
Size	30 3/8″, 4 1/8″, 10 1/8″
Weight	N/A
Colors	N/A
Special features	Fits any masonry fireplace.
Suggested retail price	$60.00
Brochure	Free
For nearest dealer call	714-521-7302
Mail order, if no dealer?	N/A

Manufacturer	Tempil Division Big Three Industries Dept. FF Hamilton Blvd. So. Plainfield, N.J. 07080
Model	Pyromark Wood Stove Paint
Function	Do-it-yourself paint, withstands 1200° F.
Size	13 oz. can
Weight	1 lbs.
Colors	Blue, brown, black
Special features	Metallic: green, rust, and brown.
Suggested retail price	$6.95
Brochure	Free
For nearest dealer call	201-757-8300
Mail order, if no dealer?	Yes

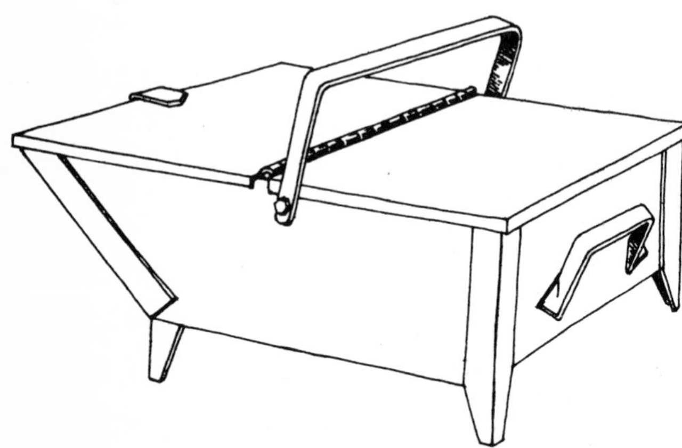

Manufacturer	Mr. Pete Taggett, Blacksmith P.O. Box 15 (FF) Mt. Holly, VT 05758
Model	Ash Away
Function	Ash box.
Size	9″H, 12½″W, 22¼″L
Weight	13 lbs.
Colors	Black
Special features	Also: fireplace screen doors, cooking utensils, grills.
Suggested retail price	$39.95
Brochure	Yes
For nearest dealer call	Write to above
Mail order, if no dealer?	Yes

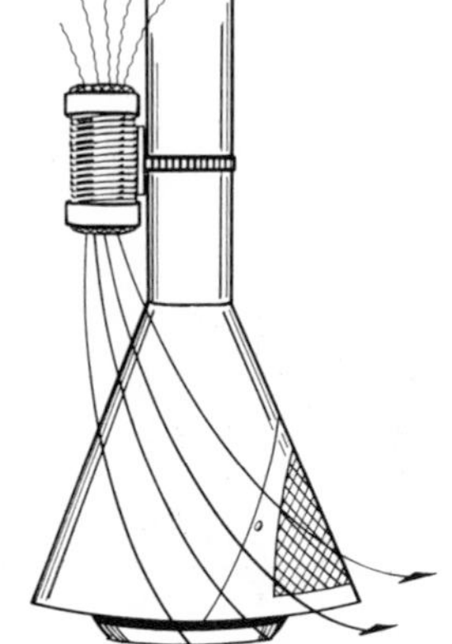

Manufacturer	Thermalite Corp. P.O. Box 658 (FF) Brentwood, TN 37027
Model	Piggyback
Function	Electrically powered heat circulator
Size	N/A
Weight	N/A
Colors	Stainless steel
Special features	Thermostat controlled. 10 yr. guarantee.
Suggested retail price	N/A
Brochure	Free
For nearest dealer call	Write to above
Mail order, if no dealer?	Yes

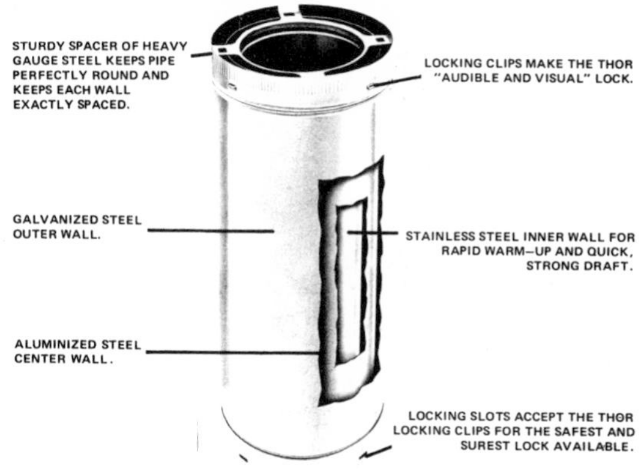

Manufacturer	Thor Metal Products Co., Inc. P.O. Box 218 (FF) Eastwood Station Syracuse, NY 13206
Model	Thor Chimneys
Function	Class A chimneys. UL listed. Triple-wall air insulated.
Size	Any
Weight	N/A
Colors	N/A
Special features	Can provide professional engineering assistance.
Suggested retail price	N/A
Brochure	Free
For nearest dealer call	315-454-3215
Mail order, if no dealer?	N/A

Manufacturer	Traction, Inc. Dept. FF North Troy, VT 05859
Model	Quadractor
Function	Wood harvest in mud or snow. Plows fields and snow. 4 wheel drive. Zero turning radius.
Size	63″ W, 7′ L
Weight	540 lbs.
Colors	Red
Special features	Tested by Vermont Dept. of Forests. Can move 4,000 lbs.
Suggested retail price	$3,400.00
Brochure	Color, free
For nearest dealer call	802-988-4411
Mail order, if no dealer?	N/A

Manufacturer	Tjernlund Products Dept. FF 1620 Terrace Drive St. Paul, MN 55113
Model	CT (8) (10) (12)
Function	Draft inducer to stop a fireplace from smoking.
Size	3 sizes
Weight	38 lbs. to 75 lbs.
Colors	Black
Special features	Varying speed motor. Permanently lubricated.
Suggested retail price	N/A
Brochure	Color, free
For nearest dealer call	612-636-7500
Mail order, if no dealer?	N/A

Manufacturer	Traditional Tiles Intl. P.O. Box 103 (FF) Ellicott City, MD 21043
Model	Deft Blue Tiles
Function	Fireplace facing. 75 different patterns.
Size	4¼″ × 4¼″ or 6″ × 6″
Weight	N/A
Colors	Blue, sepia brown
Special features	100% hand painted in Holland.
Suggested retail price	N/A
Brochure	$1.00
For nearest dealer call	301-624-4083
Mail order, if no dealer?	Yes

Manufacturer	Valley Products & Designs Rt. 418 P.O. Box 396 (FF) Milford, PA 18337
Model	Persist-Alert
Function	Chimney fire alarm.
Size	N/A
Weight	N/A
Colors	N/A
Special features	Sensing wires included. Master and remote alarm. 30 day money back guarantee.
Suggested retail price	$49.95 (master) $25.00 (remote)
Brochure	Free
For nearest dealer call	717-296-8009
Mail order, if no dealer?	Yes

Manufacturer	Warm Up Stove Co. P.O. Box 51 (FF) Helmsburg, Ind. 47435
Model	Stainless Steel Lining
Function	For relining old chimneys.
Size	30″ long, 6″ or 8″ diameter
Weight	3 lbs. per section
Colors	Stainless steel
Special features	Straight sections, elbows, cleanout tees. 28 gauge.
Suggested retail price	$14.00 & $20.00 per section
Brochure	Free
For nearest dealer call	812-988-7876
Mail order, if no dealer?	Yes

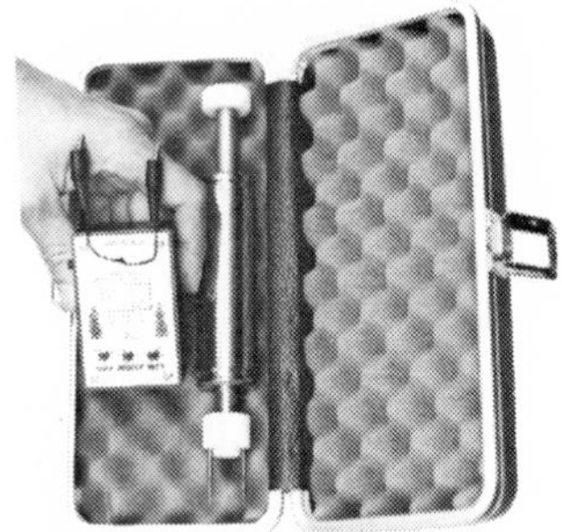

Manufacturer	Valley Products & Designs Rt. 418 P.O. Box 396 (FF) Milford, PA 18337
Model	Triton 3
Function	Wood fuel moisture gauge. 3 settings of 25% up. Uses common nails.
Size	N/A
Weight	N/A
Colors	N/A
Special features	30 day money back guarantee. (Probe in tree is extra.)
Suggested retail price	$59.95
Brochure	Free
For nearest dealer call	717-296-8009
Mail order, if no dealer?	Yes

Appendix

Corning Glass Works

Corning Glass Works began in 1851 when Amory Houghton purchased interest in and became the director of the Bay State Glass Company, in Cambridge, Massachusetts. He began experimenting with the addition of earth metals to the oxides of silica, calcium and sodium (which yields common window and bottle glass called soda-lime glass). In 1875, Corning Glass Works was established in Corning, New York; four years later the company was making hand-blown bulbs for Thomas Edison's electric lamps. By 1915, Pyrex® brand glass was introduced as a heat-resistant glass for the railroads, and for the new automobile kerosine headlamps which prevented rain and snow from cracking the hot lenses. Steuben® crystal was introduced in 1933; and by 1939, Vycor® was on its way.

Today, Corning Glass Works is the leader in the field of specialty glass. They invented and manufacture Pyrex®, Pyroceram™, Vycor®. In all, they produce over 750 different types of glass and glass-ceramics.

In modern glass, the basic mixture of silica, calcium and sodium is still used. This mixture accounts for 90% of the tonnage of all glass produced. It is also the most commonly used glass for firescreen applications. That is the choice of the manufacturers of wood heat appliances because of cost. However, though this type of glass—*soda-lime glass*—is tempered before use, it is not necessarily safe for all fireplace and wood stove designs. It is acceptable *only* if used at an operating temperature of under 400° F. Red-hot burning logs 1400° F, and therefore considerable care must be exercised if your wood heat unit or fireplace glass door is made of basic, tempered soda-lime glass. Remember to keep burning logs away from the glass; and do not splash water or snow on hot glass doors or windows. Even Pyrex® and tempered Pyrex® should be treated with care. They have a greater resistance to breakage from temperature change, but they too can break if abused. Amber colored Pyroceram™ glass is good to 1200° F, and exhibits qualities suitable for use in close proximity to flame. But the safest of all is Vycor® brand glass, which can be used in contact with flame and can withstand an instant temperature change from 1650° down to 0° F without breakage. If you have children that frequently play in the vicinity of your wood stove or fireplace, Vycor is the best insurance against the possibility of fractured glass.

The following is a chart of the physical properties and serviceability of Corning's wood stove and fireplace glasses:

PHYSICAL PROPERTIES

¼" Thick Materials	°F Normal Service	°F Extreme Service	°F Max. Thermal Shock	°F Max Thermal Gradient	In/In/°F Coefficient of Thermal Expansion	PSI Design Tensile
VYCOR® 96% Silica Code 7913	1652	2192	1800	396	4.2×10^{-7}	1000
PYROCERAM® Transparent Glass-Ceramic Code 9618	1202	1382	1400	450	3.3×10^{-7}	1500
Tempered PYREX® Borosilicate Code 7740	500	554	580	194	18×10^{-7}	2000
PYREX® Borosilicate Code 7740	446	914	270	97	18×10^{-7}	1000
Soda-Lime Tempered Code 0080	428	482	366	88	52×10^{-7}	3000
Soda-Lime Code 0080	230	860	122	29	52×10^{-7}	1000

Normal Service-No breakage from excessive thermal shock is assumed. Nonabused glass should last indefinitely.

Extreme Limit-The glass will be very vulnerable to thermal shock and physical degradation. Recommendations in this range are based on mechanical stability considerations only. Tests should be made before adopting final designs. These data approximate only.

Thermal Shock-The physical shock glass undergoes when evenly heated to the above listed temperature, then plunged into water at 50° F without breakage. This data approximate only and varies with thickness.

Temperature Gradient-The difference in temperature between the two surfaces that will cause 1000 psi tensile stress on the cooler surface.

Coefficient of Thermal Expansion-The relative increase in size of a material when heated.

Tensile Strength-The resistance of a material to breakage under the stress of pulling or stretching.

Design Tensile Strength-The anticipated tensile load that a material can withstand over an indefinite period of time.

REFERENCE: *Properties of Glasses and Glass-Ceramics.* Corning Publication-PGGC-8/73-5M-HP

Vycor® and Pyroceram™ brand glasses are the most stable and the safest glasses where high heat use and close proximity to the fire is necessary.

Pyrex®, tempered Pyrex™, and tempered soda-lime glass (commonly called "tempered glass") are acceptable for fire screens or windows provided they do not get too hot. If your wood stove or freestanding fireplace has this type of glass, do not fill the unit full of newspaper, kindling, or allow flame to come in contact with the glass. If fireplace doors become so hot that you cannot touch them to open them, then the glass is in danger of breaking.

When examining a wood heat unit for quality, pay particular attention to the way that the glass is mounted. Glass should never be in contact with metal at any point, surface, side, top or bottom. The following Corning diagrams illustrate some acceptable methods for mounting glass that is subjected to extreme heat. Note that a certain amount of movement of the glass within the frame is desirable and will minimize spontaneous failure.

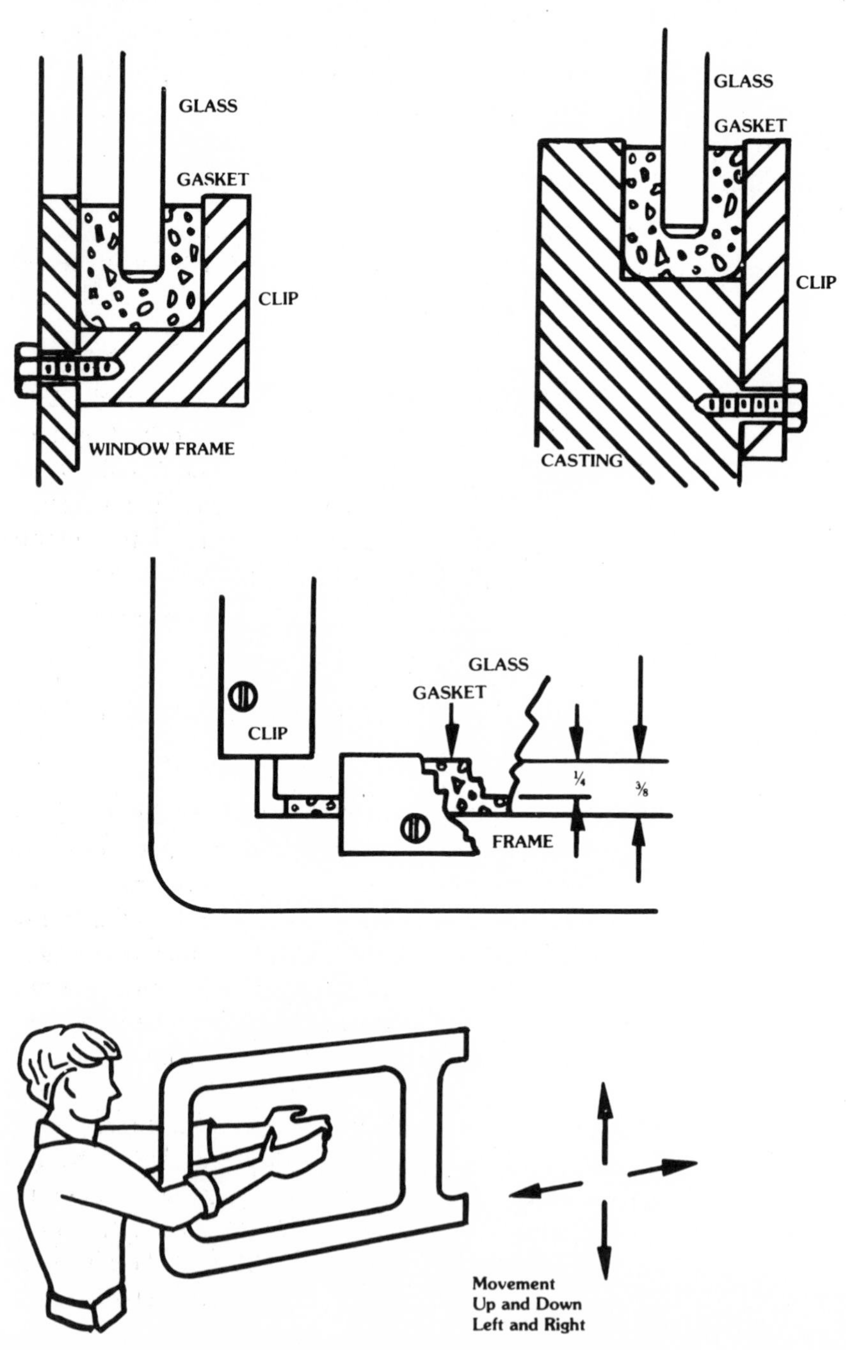

Cleaning of dirty glass is easily accomplished with common oven cleaner. (Never use scouring powder because it contains abrasives and can scratch the surface.) Remove all oven cleaner residue before lighting a fire or it could stain the glass.

The purchase of a wood heat unit that has quality glass will return many dividends, among them safety, and twenty five percent greater heat transfer (through the window) than metal. Though quality Corning glass costs more than common soda-lime glass, the safety of your home and family should be reason enough to demand the best glass available.

New Developments in Woodstove Design: A Catalytic Convertor?

For years, the down-drafter has been regarded as a very efficient design, because, by drawing the flue gases down through the red hot coals, more of the combustible gases generated in the primary combustion chamber are ignited before they are exhausted up the chimney.

By adding baffles and heat exchanges to a woodstove or furnace, as much as ninety percent of the heat generated can be transferred to the surrounding environment. On low fire with the damper closed, the heat transfer efficiency of most woodstoves is approximately eighty-five percent. On high fire this figure may drop to approximately sixty percent. Some manufacturers cite this figure in their literature as being their product's efficiency rating. This is just one factor, however, in the overall efficiency rating of a woodburning device.

The second factor is the combustion efficiency (see also page 87): how much of the available fuel is actually converted into heat. This is the point where most woodburning devices fall short.

So much energy is available in wood-gas that the Econ Company, located in Alexander City, Alabama, has developed a wood-fueled automobile. The Ecar is a mid-size station wagon attached to a trailered wood-gas generator. The wood-gas generator is a device somewhat similar to a sophisticated woodstove that is designed to partially burn a solid fuel, reducing it to a gaseous state. The wood-gas leaves the generator through a piping system that adds the proper mixture of air and the fuel to the engine. The Ecar completed a coast-to-coast trip using about a cord of wood, at a penny a mile.

Most woodstoves produce a considerable amount of crude wood-gas. This is especially true on low fire, when the fire is being controlled by oxygen starvation and the fire box is running cool. These gases are able to escape before being burned because they are not adequately mixed with available oxygen and they are not permitted to reach their ignition temperature of 1000°–1500°. In addition, wood-gas has a slow flame velocity which enables those gases that do pass through high temperature sections of the fire to be whisked away by the much faster moving flow of gases up the flue before they can be completely burned. Because of this, the secondary air systems used on most woodstove designs are only partially effective.

Commercial woodburning power generation plants and furnaces sometimes employ an after burner and a secondary combustion chamber to salvage the wasted wood-gas. These systems generally are very large and complex in the instrumentation required. The overall design does lend itself to residential application especially for space heaters, which is the function of most woodstoves.

A number of firms are addressing the problem of poor combustion efficiency. Radical new designs are expected to appear on the market late in 1980 and 1981.

One such configuration will use a highly insulated primary fire box and smoke chamber that allows the fire to operate at much higher temperatures, enabling more of the volatiles to be burned. Several "down-drafter type" designs using this concept burn so hot that ceramic grates and outlet ducts are required to withstand the continuous red hot operation. After the gases leave the high temperature smoke chamber they are then passed through a heat exchanger.

Automobile manufacturers have had to resort to the use of catalytic convertors to reduce the emission of unburned hydrocarbons. Unfortunately, the catalytic convertor increases the price of the automobile by approximately $400, reduces efficiency, and poses some safety hazards due to its high temperature operation and location under the chassis.

But catalytic convertors are used on other appliances that do not have these drawbacks. Self-cleaning ranges use a catalytic coating on the inside of the oven to enhance the decomposition of grease and splatter. A small catalytic convertor is used in the oven vent to reduce smoke that would otherwise enter the house.

It is anticipated that this or a similar technology will soon be applied to the woodburning devices industry (see also pages 56, 88). There is considerable support by the Environmental Protection Agency and The National Fire Protection Agency, because a catalytic device would presumably minimize pollution while reducing creosote buildup.

Institutional Resources

Alliance to Save Energy

The ASE is a non-profit organization dedicated to the wise use of energy. It publishes a monthly newsletter on such subjects as: government policy; fairs and expositions; current solar energy trends and developments; and book reviews. They also provide the following services: Maintenance of an energy library; assistance in forming local alliance groups; addresses of energy organizations and institutes; help in locating films and speakers; legislative review; and the co-sponsorship of the World Energy Engineering Congress.
Individual dues, $15.

Alliance to Save Energy
1925 K Street, N.W. Suite 507
Washington D.C. 20006
202-857-0666

American Forestry Association

The American Forestry Association is a national citizens conservation organization—independent and nonpolitical—for the advancement of wise management and use of forests and other natural resources. Membership is open to all individuals. Woodlot owners, backyard gardeners, and woodstove owners enjoy the colorful monthly magazine. The magazine features articles on forests and the outdoors and includes many regular columns such as Washington Lookout, Woodlot World, and Reading About Resources. Other membership benefits include the famous Trail Riders of the Wilderness camping program, book discounts, regional meetings and retreats, membership information service, reprints, matches, binders and other sale items, international forestry tours and full voting rights at the annual meeting.

Individual dues, $15.
The American Forestry Association
1319 18th St., NW.
Washington, D.C. 20036.

American Tree Farm System

If you are interested in becoming a commercial tree farmer, the American Tree Farm System, under the direction of the American Forest Institute, has a complete information package that is free to anyone interested.

American Tree Farm System
1619 Massachusetts Ave. N.W.
Washington D.C. 20036

Association of Energy Engineers

The Association of Energy Engineers, The Alliance to Save Energy, and the U.S. Department of Energy are co-sponsors of the annual World Energy Engineering Congress which features a conference and exposition on energy conservation, solar energy engineering, wind power, and new energy sources.

4025 Pleasantdale Road, Suite 340
Atlanta, Georgia 30340

Auburn University's Woodburning Laboratory

The woodburning laboratory has 16 different publications designed to assist manufacturers and engineers in the field of wood heat. For more information, write to:

Dr. Timothy T. Maxwell
Mechanical Engineering Dept.
Auburn University
Auburn, Alabama 36830
205-826-4574

Fireplace Institute

The Fireplace Institute is a non-profit, professional organization dedicated to serving the fireplace and wood energy industry. It maintains the Fireplace Institute test center at Auburn University, a branch office in Washington, D.C., and provides regular press releases to newspapers, radio stations, and television stations across the U.S. It has been so successful over the past few years that there has been a dues reduction for new members in 1980. For more information, please write to:

Fireplace Institute
Membership Office
111 East Wacker Drive
Chicago, Illinois 60601
312-644-6610

Lightning Protection Institute

The Lightning Protection Institute is a non-profit organization that serves the lightning protection industry. Though public concern about lightning has diminished over the years, the "Underrated Killer" is still taking human lives and destroying property. The institute has prepared a free booklet titled "Lightning Protection For Home, Farm, And Family." It is also an approved institute for training and licensing lightning rod installation specialists. For more information, please write to:

The Lightning Protection Institute
Harvard, Illinois 60033
815-943-7211

National Center for Appropriate Technology

The NCAT addresses the need for small-scale technologies as solutions to the problems of rapidly rising costs of energy, the increasing shortages of non-renewable energy resources, and the continuing problem of devising ways in which individuals and communities can become self-reliant and self-sufficient. The NCAT is funded by the U.S. Community Services Administration The primary mission of NCAT is the development and application of technologies appropriate to the needs of low-income communities. For more information, please write to:

National Center For Appropriate Technology
P.O. Box 3838
Butte, Montana 59701
406-723-5474

National Chimney Sweep Guild

The guild has members in forty states. The prime objective is the training and recognition of qualified chimney sweeps. For more information, please write to:

Chimney Sweep Guild
P.O. Box 1314
Nashua, N.H. 03060
207-772-2821

National Fire Protection Association

The NFPA is the most recognized authority on fire prevention in the United States. It publishes several bulletins designed for the homeowner as well as professional fire code inspectors. The bulletin "Using Coal and Wood Stoves Safely" is available for $5 by writing to:

National Fire Protection Association
470 Atlantic Ave.
Boston, MA 02210

National Wildlife Federation

The NWF is a non-profit organization dedicated "to create and encourage an awareness among the people of this nation of the need for the wise use and proper management of those resources of the earth upon which the lives and welfare of men depend; the soils, the waters, the forests, the minerals, the plant life, the air, and the wildlife."

Membership includes a subscription to *National Wildlife* magazine. Membership is $8. They also publish the *Conservation Directory*, a comprehensive list of environmental organizations, agencies, and offices in the U.S. For more information, please write to:

National Wildlife Federation
1412 Sixteenth St., N.W.
Washington, D.C. 20036
202-797-6800

U.S. Department of Energy

The USDE publishes two bulletins that are free to every taxpayer in the United States. They are the "Energy Insider", and "Weekly Announcements." The contain some of the most up-to-date writing on energy, books and publications from the U.S. government, news about grants for wood energy and solar energy research, and the facts and figures on how and where your tax money is being spent. Simply write and ask to receive "Energy Insider" and "Weekly Announcements:"

Office of Public Affairs
U.S. Dept. of Energy
Washington, D.C. 20585
202-252-5568

Consumer comment on energy policy should be addressed to:

Office of the Assistant Secretary
for Policy and Evaluation
U.S. Dept. of Energy
Washington, D.C. 20585

Wood Energy Institute

The prime objectives of the institute are government and public relations. The institute also sponsors an annual trade show. The Wood Energy Institute has undergone a change in structure; it is now being managed by a professional management company in Washington, D.C. For more information, please write to:

Wood Energy Institute
1101 Connecticut Ave.
Suite 700
Washington, D.C. 20036
202-857-1100

World Watch Institute

The World Watch Institute, a think tank of twelve researchers, analyzes many of the problems of our complex world. They have a well-deserved, international reputation for credibility. They have published over twenty seven papers and books and that may change your thinking on the future of the human race. Of particular interest is *The Other Energy Crisis: Firewood*, which describes the energy crisis in the third world. For this and a list of others, send $2 to:

World Watch Institute,
1776 Massachusetts Ave., N.W.
Washington, D.C. 20036

Glossary

AIRI Atlantic Industrial Research Institute

Aluminized steel Steel that is plated with aluminum on one side to reflect heat.

ASME American Society of Mechanical Engineers.

ASTM American Society for Testing Materials.

Borosilicate glass The generic name for Pyrex™ and Tempax™.

BOCA Building Officials and Code Administrators International.

Canopy — All the crowns of the trees in a forest.
Chimney — A chimney is usually referred to as an insulated flue.
Chimney, Class A — One that is legally listed for solid fuel—wood and coal.
Coal grate — A cast iron, fine-mesh grate.
Commerical forests — Any forest, industrial or private, that can furnish salable trees.
Connector pipe — Commonly called stovepipe.
Creosote — A chemical compound that is liquid when distilled from wood, crystalline when cooled. (To prevent liquid creosote from dripping out of stovepipe seams, place each successive joint inside the last one.)
Crop tree — Trees that are salable for lumber or veneer, commonly called "saw timber."
Crown — The branches and leaves of a tree.
Crown lean — The lopsided growth of a tree.
CSA — Canadian Standards Association
Cull — To cut and thin woodlots. An inferior tree or an inappropriate species of tree in a woodlot.
ETLM — Eastern Testing Laboratory of Maine
Firebrick — Specially-made brick for use next to a fire; common brick is not firebrick.
Fireclay — Specially-made clay products that withstand high heat, like chimney flue tile.
Flue — Any pipe-like tubing that vents hot gasses from a firebox; most commonly, the lining of a chimney.
Galvanized steel — Zinc-plated steel.
Girdling — Cutting a band around a tree to remove a ring of bark, causing the tree to die.
Hydronic — Water heating or cooling.
ICBO — International Congress of Building Code Officials
Isinglass — A transparent organic gelatin.
MHA — Mobile-home-approved according to Federal Housing and Urban Development regulations, which require the use of outside combustion air.
NFPA — National Fire Protection Association
"On the stump" — A timberman's term for a standing tree.
Plenum — Housing about a firebox that collects hot air to be blown into air ducts.
Reduced Clearance — Installation of a wood heat unit closer than NFPA minimum clearances for unprotected combustible walls, provided approved fire protection is applied.
"Release" cutting — Thinning a woodlot to allow crop trees to expand their crowns and grow faster.
Residue wood energy — The excess wood that naturally falls to the ground and decays.
SBCC — Southern Building Code Congress International.
Shotts Glass Co. — High-temperature glass made in Germany: Tempax™ borosilicate and Rubex™.
Stovepipe — Single-wall pipe that connects a wood heat unit to a chimney.
TSI — Timberstand improvement.
TSR — Thermal shock resistance: the ability of glass to withstand breakage from heat or sudden temperature change.
ULC — Underwriters Laboratory of Canada.
Unified Chimney System — A continuous flue, without open areas or breaks, from the flue collar to the top of the chimney, with all joints sealed airtight.
Zero clearance — Installation of a unit with built-in heat shield, touching walls and floors.

Subject Index

Indexes to Buying Guide

BY FUNCTION

MODELS AND MANUFACTURERS